IN SEARC
ZO

Elizabeth Kerr-Waller

Published by
KERR-WALLER
SURBITON SURREY

British Library Cataloguing-in-Publication Data.
A catalogue record for this book is available from the British Library.

ISBN 0 9538030 0 7
Printed in Great Britain by
Arthur H. Stockwell Ltd.
Elms Court Ilfracombe
Devon

For Kerry,
my lifelong travelling companion

Acknowledgements

With acknowledgement for the valuable advice and assistance I received in compiling this book from my friends Maria and Adam Czermak and Morwen Jenkins.

Contents

List of Illustrations

Preface

DREAMS AND PRACTICALITIES

It took us three months to travel to India, but in our thoughts we had been journeying towards the East for almost twenty years. "One day we shall go there," we promised each other, "when we have fewer responsibilities, more money, more time," and so it went on and the years slipped by. Then, in April 1973, we took stock of our position and decided that the moment had come to make our dreams a reality. The following year I would be sixty and due to retire from the Headship of an Inner London Comprehensive School and my husband Kerry, an electronics engineer, was going to be made redundant at sixty-one years of age. The time had come for us to make a move.

The Orient, especially India, held for us both an irresistible fascination. We were eager to learn at first-hand about its religion and customs, its towns and villages, ancient sites and temples and above all, its colourful and varied people. Kerry's roots were there, for he was a Parsee born and educated in India. When he was twenty years old he travelled to England to complete his engineering training, so he was very keen to see his brother and sisters and their families in Bombay again. He wanted to show me his old haunts and to pick up the threads of his past. As for me, a native of these often bleak and chilly shores, I longed for the steady warmth and brilliant light of the tropics and I dreamt of golden sunsets, against the backdrop of the Indian Ocean and the Himalayas. But it was not just a woolly-minded romanticism that drew us towards the Indian sub-continent; there was a great deal of specific information, which we hoped to glean from our journey. From the standpoint of education I wanted to know more about the background of these wan, fragile looking children from Pakistan and India (via Kenya and Uganda), who since the sixties, had been seen in increasing numbers in London classrooms. We were therefore very happy to accept an invitation from the Pakistani

Government to visit schools, colleges and universities in their country to see for ourselves what progress had been made. As an engineer, Kerry was interested in technical education and in the economic development of the countries on our route. His close involvement with politics in this country made him keen to find out what was stirring in the East and Middle East.

Looking back on our experiences during our fifteen months of travelling, we can truthfully say, that not only did we fulfil all our original objectives, but we had, as bonuses, many unusual encounters and adventures quite beyond our expectations. One of these extra pleasures was the fellowship of other travellers and the friendship we formed with them. Other pleasurable surprises were the discovery of the remote province of Ladakh in Kashmir, which has only recently been opened to tourists and our first encounter with the art of the Hittites in Northern Turkey. When we are asked if we had any regrets, there is only one that we felt was worth mentioning. On our visit to Dharmsala we had hoped to have an interview with the Dalai Lama, a meeting which, unfortunately we were not able to arrange. On the other hand, we had the good fortune of making the acquaintance of many influential Indians, including ministers of state, senators, judges, religious leaders and the most outstanding of all, the Chief Minister of Kashmir, the remarkable Sheikh Abdullah. From these individuals we gathered a great deal of valuable information about life in present-day India.

It took us more than twelve busy months to prepare for our trip, as there were so many factors to be considered. First of all, we had to decide when to set out on our 7,000-mile journey overland to India and Nepal. We had to keep in mind that most of India suffers from monsoon rains from late May until early September, and is at its best and coolest between October and the end of March. As both of us had commitments until August, we decided to leave England in September hoping to reach India by the end of November. This would enable us to travel to the South of India and North to Nepal by March. Then we would spend the fiery monsoon months in the heights of Kashmir. But "the best laid schemes of mice and men gang aft aglee". Leaving out the mice at the moment, we shall return to them later, our plans went awry by one month due to an unexpected delay in Bombay resulting in an uncomfortable dash over the Gangetic Plain at the height of India's summer. If we were to do the trip again, we would leave this country in July or August in order to enjoy a longer spell in India during its winter months.

As we intended to travel overland, the choice of a suitable vehicle was of paramount importance. Originally we had intended to travel in a Land Rover, towing a caravan but when motor homes came on the market we realised that they were the most suitable vehicles for our purpose. We were very glad that we abandoned our original scheme when we heard the tales of travellers who had set out for India towing a caravan. All of them had decided to jettison their troublesome appendage by the time they reached Iran. For many years we had been regular visitors to the Caravan Exhibition at Earls Court and we knew what was available in auto homes. There were the splendid Winnebagos from America with their sturdy Dodge engines, the last word in travelling luxury; the comfortable, roomy Mercedes motor homes, and the cheaper British versions built on Comer, Bedford, Ford and Toyota chassis. As the stoutly built Winnebagos with their air-conditioning units and their Mercedes counterparts were beyond our means, we finally settled on a nineteen-foot motor home on a Ford Transit chassis, built by a local firm at half the cost of the foreign models.

We were really proud of our splendid motor home. It was gleaming white with a rail on top around the storage area that housed initially tyres and later in Iran, cans of petrol. The access to this part was by a ladder at the rear of the vehicle that proved an irresistible attraction for the nimble youngsters we encountered on our travels. Because of the weight of the vehicle we were advised to have two tyres in the front and four at the rear. As the tyres were to be our Achilles heel, it would have been more prudent to have had eight tyres instead of six. What made the caravan especially attractive was the large window at the rear of the vehicle. I will never forget one memorable occasion on board a ferry crossing the Ganges, when we steadily ate our porridge watched by dozens of bemused passengers, their noses pressed on the glass window.

To suit our requirements, we had a number of modifications made on the interior of the van, including the addition of two extra cupboards to hold all our gear. Besides the usual caravan fittings: stove, sink, refrigerator, etc., we had a shower compartment with a fold-up hand basin, a chemical toilet and a dinette which converted into a double bed. Above the driving compartment was a single bed which, curtained off, served as a guest room on numerous occasions during our journey. To make our little home look cheerful and snug, we chose gay orange cushions and curtains. Of course there were a number of snags that we had not anticipated. When the fluid for our potty ran out in India, we regretted that we had not installed a flushing type of toilet. Our indispensable water filter became clogged up after six months and we had to wait weeks for a replacement from England. The floor carpet defied all our efforts to keep it clean, being covered with dust in the Iranian desert and thick with mud when it poured in Kashmir. In the end we purchased a roll of lino in Srinagar and cut out most of the housework. The two

15lb Calor gas containers we carried were quite inadequate for our cooking needs in India where we had to wait for weeks to have our cylinders refilled. However, as we were able to get electricity most of the time and had brought our own cable with us, we purchased a small electric cooker, an immersion heater and a fan in Delhi.

We tested our motor home on British roads for five months before we set out on our long journey, adjusting it to fit our future needs. Extra water and petrol tanks were installed as we and the car were bound to be thirsty. Thus we carried thirty-nine gallons of water and thirty gallons of petrol; every drop of water was filtered through a cartridge type filter. To cool the engine in the heat of the tropics we put an additional fan in the bonnet and it justified itself on the 14,000-foot passes we had to climb. As for our own comfort, we reckoned optimistically that we could manage without an air-conditioning unit — an error of judgement — for which we paid for later in exhaustion and sweat. We had been dissuaded from purchasing an air-conditioning unit because of the extra cost and weight involved, as we would also have required a motor generator. However, if we had invested in a unit that is powered by the engine, it would have been of immense benefit as we would have been able to travel with the windows closed, thus excluding most of the dust. In spite of this omission and the havoc which rough roads wrought on our suspension and fittings, not to mention the tyres which were our greatest source of worry, our motor home was a snug and happy abode for the two of us for fifteen months. In fact, our relationship with our vehicle was so close that together we made a threesome and its success and tribulations were also ours. We congratulated it when it manfully negotiated the shifting sands of the desert in Iran, felt its humiliation at being pulled behind a bulldozer up the Zozo-Lá Pass in Kashmir, and nursed it gently as it limped home from Yugoslavia after a burst tyre.

The next problem to be solved was what to do with our house during our long absence. If we left it empty, would we, on our return, find it damaged by the elements or occupied by an army of squatters? We settled for tenants rather than squatters, as we needed the income to help to finance our trip. By the time every cupboard, shelf and drawer had been cleared of their contents, the accumulation of years, and stored away in the attic under the eaves, we might just as well have moved house. At least we had a home to come back to, or would we? What if our tenants refused to move out on our return? Legal contracts do not seem to be as binding as they used to be. We had therefore some nagging doubts as we transferred our stores and our allegiance from the house to the van. As it happened, we were more fortunate than most people who rent their houses during an absence abroad. As for our garden, it managed to survive the summer drought of 1975 and the football games of our tenants' children.

Campers of many years' experience we had some knowledge of what we were likely to require in stores and kit. Our food stock, tins of meat, fish and fruit, marmalade and dry stores, lasted us for almost three months, supplemented with fresh fruit, vegetables, eggs and bread. In Iran, we found plenty of cheese imported from Bulgaria; delicious but expensive. In India, we made our own from yoghurt. In Turkey and Iran, where bread was unpalatable, we made do with rusks, those in Iran being a very acceptable substitute. Had we realized how difficult it was to obtain meat in India, we would have filled all available storage space with tins of meat or packets of dried meat, and omitted such goods as dried vegetables, fruit, tea, custard powder and spices. Marmite was one of our best stand-bys, but we didn't take enough of it and we should have taken more packets of sweets, matches and cigarettes to dispense as small gifts to the many kind people we met. As far as our cooking utensils were concerned, we should have had the foresight to take a pressure cooker with us to make such meat as was available tasty and palatable.

Blankets and warm clothes were packed away in plastic bags, as they would not be required until our return journey. They took up a good deal of our precious space but we were thankful for the comfort they gave us when we travelled back to Europe through ice and snow. Kerry's old woollen dressing gown only came into its own the following November in Northern Turkey when I wore it to keep out the cold in Bogasköy, the ancient capital of the Hittites. For most of our trip, the only bedding we needed was nylon sheets and Terylene sleeping bags. We did not need all our blankets until we arrived back in Austria where we encountered a twenty-five degree frost that froze our engine oil to the consistency of honey. As for light clothes, we took with us the bare minimum, knowing that we would be able to purchase suitable garments on our way. Thus, in Pakistan, I bought sandals, cotton suits (full bottomed and bright with embroidery) in India, saris, blouses and batik skirts. At the same time, Kerry bought lightweight suits, denim trousers and cotton shirts. Later, in Kashmir, we had our winter wardrobe made to measure by an expert tailor whose father had been trained in Saville Row. We gave a good deal of thought to our medical kit and prepared for most eventualities. As it happened, we needed very few remedies apart from aspirins, vitamin tablets, sting relief and healing ointments. When we were planning our route we benefited from other people's experience and especially from that of the overland tour operators. We sneaked in to some of their promotion talks in order to discover the best route to follow and the places worth visiting between this country and Nepal. We studied travel brochures from every type of agency, including those that cater for tourists with special interests, such as flowers, historical sites, pony trekking and mountain climbing. Good, detailed maps were difficult to obtain, but with the help of the AA route guides, we found our way through Europe and Asia without any difficulty. We would not, however, have derived nearly as much enjoyment and knowledge from our journey had we not been accompanied by Fodor's admirable guidebooks on Turkey, Islamic Asia and India. These gave us the background of the countries we visited, their history and customs and we consulted them at every stage of our journey. At a nod from Fodor, we would leave our planned route and make a detour to see a rock carving, a royal tomb or Hindu temple.

As D-day, the 1st September, 1974, approached there was still a great deal to be done. Gas, electrical and telephone services had to be transferred to the new tenants. Arrangements had to be made for the payment of rates, insurance policies, etc., friends and acquaintances informed of our imminent departure. We had to make a number of visits to the doctor for inoculations against cholera, polio, smallpox and typhoid. We had heard of the danger of contracting hepatitis in India and Nepal but as there was no suitable long-term vaccine we decided to carry our own stock with us in our refrigerator. This would have been an excellent scheme had we not run out of Calor gas and consequently of refrigeration in Istanbul. Faced with the prospect of losing our precious hepatitis vaccine, we called in a doctor to administer the dose. We shall never forget the astonishment on his face when he saw our camping vehicle, equipped like a hospital theatre with sterilised syringes and vaccine. I think he must have been stung with envy, as his jabs were extremely vicious. Our vaccination problems were far from over, however, as we discovered when we reached Afghanistan, but more of that anon.

Our money problems were more difficult to solve than medical ones. For months before we left we had studied the *Financial Times* to decide which was the most stable international currency. In the end, we took with us a considerable sum of money in German marks, in preference to dollars and we had no cause to regret that decision. However, the bulk of our money was in sterling traveller's cheques and we lost a considerable amount when the pound floated downwards. With better advice we would have relied upon money drafts which are accepted by most large foreign banks and would not have entailed the loss of interest on the large sum we had to withdraw. We also discovered that there were banks in the main towns of Iran, India and Pakistan that were happy to cash cheques accompanied by a banker's card from British banks. Nevertheless, in spite of the devaluation of the pound and the rise in the price of petrol we were still solvent when we returned to Dover, with sufficient money to pay the custom dues on the many articles we had purchased abroad.

In concluding this preface, we would like to thank our friends who proved to us by their letters, that "out of sight is not out of mind" with a special word of gratitude to Don Simpson for his invaluable assistance with our paperwork in our absence.

Alexander Nevski Basilica — Sofia

Chapter One

TOWARDS THE BOSPHORUS

It was late in the evening of the 3rd September when we reached our first camp site in the woods at St Niklaas near Antwerp. There was an end-of-season look about the place, with its pathways strewn with fallen leaves and empty caravans looming through a dank mist. These depressing signs of approaching winter, however, only served to heighten our feelings of joy and elation, for we were leaving the chill and the turmoil of Europe behind us for the sunshine and peace of the East.

Three days later, after a speedy journey through the familiar landscapes of Germany and Austria, we were travelling much more slowly along Yugoslavia's mini-motorway, the Autoput. It was fifteen years since we had last passed this way and little in the countryside seemed to have changed. Skinny cows and goats were nibbling the grass on the verges, supervised by wizened old men and women. Children were chasing black geese over the stubble and rounding up unruly piglets, which were heading towards the motorway. The Autoput, slicing its way through the maize fields, was just as we remembered it; narrow and uneven with its edges littered with the recent wrecks and ancient skeletons of cars and trucks. Turkish workers, returning from Germany with their second-hand cars piled high with Western loot, weaved in and out of the stream of traffic, tempting providence at every bend of the road.

Belgrade, with its large clusters of new houses, skyscrapers and factories, looked more prosperous than formerly. People were better dressed and there were more goods for sale. At Nis, where we spent the night in a parking lot in the middle of the town, the car refused to start as we had left the refrigerator connected to the battery instead of to the gas cylinder. Unfortunately, as it was a public holiday, all the garages were closed and our requests for help were ignored by Yugoslavian motorists and bystanders. "Capitalists will get no help from me," shouted one angry young man. However, two young Germans came to our assistance and we pushed the van up and down the square until it started.

Over the frontier in Bulgaria, although the landscape was bleak, the well-tilled fields, trim villages and sturdy peasant folk made a good first impression. The officials at the tourist kiosk on the outskirts of Sofia welcomed us in excellent English and showered us with glossy travel brochures and pamphlets about Bulgaria. This was a very promising start. We set off towards the camp site, to which we had been directed, about five miles south of the town. Alas, the camp gates were shut and the site deserted. A waiter in a restaurant nearby informed us that the camp always closed at the end of August, so we trundled back to the centre of Sofia through beflagged streets and squares decorated with enormous portraits of Bulgarian and Russian leaders. Everywhere we looked we saw red — in the flags, banners, posters and street decorations. It was, as we discovered, the thirtieth anniversary of the foundation of the Bulgarian Republic and the country was on holiday to celebrate the event. Peasants and townsfolk in their Sunday best, who had come in their thousands to hear speeches and watch the military parade, were dispersing from the Central Square in an orderly, quiet fashion. There was no shouting, cheering, or jostling and pushing such as we are accustomed to see in Britain on occasions like these. Even the children were silent and restrained as they made their way past the neat flowerbeds in the town centre. As we watched the scene from a distance, we felt as if we were witnessing a pageant of a bygone age when children were dutiful and did not gorge themselves with ice creams and candy in the streets.

We drove up and down in the gathering darkness, trying to find somewhere to spend the night, without success, until we reached the vast square, which surrounds the Alexander Nevski Church. It was completely empty, so we parked there. Our white van looked so conspicuous that we expected at any moment to be asked to move on. Fortunately, even the policemen seemed to be on holiday. As all shops and restaurants in the town centre were closed we wandered as far as the new railway station in search of bread and fruit. But there was nothing for sale in this imposing edifice which few trains seemed to patronize. Footsore, we boarded a tramcar without purchasing tickets from a kiosk, which is the custom. Seeing our dilemma, a kind passenger quickly handed us two and refused to take any money in return. Incidentally, these tickets cost about 1p each and were valid for any distance in the town.

The tram deposited us at the Municipal Turkish Bath, which apart from the railway station, was the only place not closed during the holiday. "Look," said Kerry, pointing to the grim-looking building, "these are the Public Baths and they are actually open. What about having a clean-up?" As we had our last warm bath several days before in Munich, the opportunity was too good to miss. In a few moments we were inside Sofia's Municipal Turkish Baths, facing formidable matrons in uniform who led us to separate areas, as there was no mixed bathing. There, in huge, dented iron baths we had a good soaping and scrub down in steaming mineral water for a mere 15p; soap and towel included. There was also a swimming pool where you could sit for hours in one of the little niches, letting the beneficent water soak into every pore. Some bathers had brought reading material with them, whilst others lay prone and still on the buoyant surface of the water. There were other pools, tepid and cold where you could take a dip to cool down or to prepare for the return to the chilly, tiled cubicle.

That night we were the sole occupants of the Alexander Nevski Square, under the glare of hundreds of floodlights which lit up the façade and domes of the great Greek Orthodox Church. Just before midnight there was a knock on the caravan door and we feared that our time in the square had come to an end. Then a voice called out in very stilted English, "Can we see your house, please?" Kerry opened the door to find four friendly youngsters, students of Economics at Sofia's University, who wanted to see inside our motor home and converse with us in English. "No one in Bulgaria," they said, "would dare to stay overnight in a vehicle parked on the street, let alone in the most important square in the town." Our luck held and apart from the intermittent loud pealing of bells from the Basilica, our sleep was undisturbed.

The next morning we spent several hours trying to get our gas cylinders refilled. An elderly woman, speaking fluent French came to our assistance and travelled with us all over town in search of International Camping Gaz. She had been born in Istanbul and had worked in France for several years before marrying a Bulgarian, now deceased. A sad, pathetic figure, she longed to return to Turkey but could not obtain a visa, as relations between Turkey and Bulgaria are far from cordial. The gas station was a dilapidated church, around which bulldozers were churning up the remains of a cemetery. Unfortunately, the fittings in our cylinders did not match those used in Bulgaria and our friend assured us that we would find what we wanted in Istanbul, which we hoped to reach within a few days. First however, we wanted to see a little more of Bulgaria, so we headed towards Varna on the Black Sea. Our route took us through rich, agricultural land, past orchards full of apples, pears and plums and vineyards where the grape harvest was just beginning. We were astonished, however, to find that very few of these fruits were on sale in the village shops where we queued for butter, milk and bread. Foreigners we met told us that almost all Bulgaria's produce goes to the USSR, although some finds its way to lucrative markets in Iran.

We were very disappointed with Varna and the Black Sea. Perhaps because it was late in the season, there were few people on the beaches, which were poorly maintained, with a scattering of down-at-heel cafés and shabby hotels. The weather was overcast and the sea looked black and forbidding. "No wonder," said Kerry, "it is called the Black Sea." What we had not expected, however, was to be approached constantly and rather furtively by scores of strangers wanting foreign currency and willing to pay handsomely for it. Not all of them were Bulgarians, some of them were Polish and they all said they wanted to travel abroad. They seemed quite desperate and would not take "no" for an answer. Tired of the hassle and bleak sea outlook, we set off the next day for Turkey, after a very unpleasant encounter at the frontier.

When we entered Bulgaria from Yugoslavia we had to purchase, with German marks, enough Bulgarian currency (levas) to pay for all our needs during our stay in the country. We miscalculated the number of days and therefore, the number of levas we needed. So it was quite a large sum of money, which we wished to return at the frontier, as Bulgarian currency can only be used in Bulgaria. When I went to the exchange kiosk and presented my paper and my store of levas, the woman attendant pointed to my form and said, "You have written on this form, so it is invalid and you can't have any money." I had foolishly recorded the number of gallons of petrol we had purchased on the back of the form. I was completely taken aback. The woman shut the window and disappeared so I returned disconsolately to the motor home. When I told Kerry what had happened, he leapt out of the motor home snatching his stout walking stick, which he kept behind his seat. This mild mannered, non-bellicose husband of mine was suddenly transformed. Battering on the kiosk door with his stick, he thundered, "I want to see the supervisor, come out of there, I can see you skulking behind that woman." There was an ominous silence. Then the window opened slightly, and a stream of Deutsche marks fell onto the ledge. Kerry returned triumphant and I felt very proud of him. This was a side of his character with which, even after twenty-eight years of marriage, I was not acquainted. On many occasions during our journey, I had reason to admire his ability to cope with stressful situations in a commanding way.

On the long, slow climb up to Istanbul, we were battered by wind and rain; the caravan shuddered and we were almost toppled by the tremendous force of the gale. As the sun began to dip below the horizon and we mounted the last incline, the mosques rose gradually, etched in black against the evening sky. When we reached the confines of the city we were swept forward by a relentless stream of traffic towards a horizon of minarets and domes, silhouetted in the setting sun. How thankful we were to slip out of the maelstrom when we saw the flashing neon sign of the BP Mocamp not far from the centre of the town.

The mocamp with its trees, lawns and fountains was a veritable oasis, a very pleasant haven for campers. With electricity on tap for cooking and light, hot showers, a store and a restaurant, this camp compared very favourably with the best we had seen in Europe. After the cool, dull and often rainy days we had experienced on our journey, it was wonderful to hang out washing and toast oneself in the sun. The site was full of tents and caravans of travellers from all over the Western world, and for the first time on our journey we sampled some of the main joys of overland travel, namely unusual encounters and the swapping of tales and information. On the camp sites of Turkey and Iran, the modern equivalents of the ancient caravanserais which plied the silk route to the East, foregather to relate their adventures, warn of hazards ahead and display the wares they have purchased. A wiry Englishman, looking very spry at seventy-five had just arrived from Britain on a moped with his seventy-three-year-old girlfriend. In spite of the fact that they had been robbed of all their money in Yugoslavia and had been involved in an accident in Bulgaria, they were determined to press on and reach India. We made friends with an Iranian doctor returning to Germany in a Volkswagen van. His wife, who was German and also a doctor, told us how her father-in-law in Mashhad had ordered her to wear a veil and to behave with decorum like his other daughters-in-law. Strangely enough, in spite of this experience she was very keen to live permanently in Iran. When we parted, they left us a valuable store of medicine to combat the ills of the tropics, their maps and a large bag of pistachio nuts.

A teenage Italian boy, who was not interested in exploring Istanbul with his parents, discovered that Kerry played chess and he used to appear with his chess board whenever boredom overcame him — sometimes before we had breakfasted. Clifford and Sheila Lee were constant visitors to our caravan. They were proud to call themselves English gypsies, and we marvelled at the fact that Clifford was able to converse with people of many races in his own gypsy tongue. It appears that many words and phrases in Romany are common to Eastern and Western languages. The Lees, travelling in a Land Rover, were regular visitors to Turkey and were a mine of information on Turkish customs and food and the sights of Istanbul.

It would be difficult to find two great cities situated so close to each other, which are as different in character and appearance as Sofia and Istanbul. Although they are less than 300 miles from each other as the crow flies, they are worlds apart. In the streets of Sofia there is an atmosphere of almost martial discipline, with order and restrained behaviour. The public buildings have a solid Western look about them and lack visual appeal; here are queues in the shops where there are few goods for sale; here are no signs of either poverty or riches and people are decently, if dowdily, attired. When your reach Istanbul, however, you are immediately aware that you have left the West with its semblance of order far behind and have entered the mysterious world of the East, with its contrasts of beauty and ugliness, wealth and squalor.

One never tires of strolling through the streets of Istanbul which, with its hundreds of mosques and breathtaking seascapes, must be one of the world's most beautiful cities. The centre of the old town — Eminonu — near the covered bazaar, is a veritable beehive of activity. Porters bent double under piles of mattresses, baskets of fruit and vegetables or sacks of garbage push their way through the crowds. With wide smiles and flattering remarks the street vendors try to tempt the passers-by to purchase their salted melon seeds, roasted chestnuts, doughnuts and semmit cakes. As you pass along the street, scruffy-looking individuals with antiquated instruments offer to take your blood pressure, count your heartbeats or measure your weight. Squatting on the pavement, diminutive shoe-blacks point at your feet and then at the tins of polish which lie in gilded containers. Surely nowhere in the world are there such magnificent containers for such humble contents and it is worthwhile spending a few Turkish lira just to have a closer look. Men walk hand in hand with men and appear to have much more in common with their own sex than with their womenfolk. It is the Muslim tradition, which keeps women very much in the background and prevents them even from attending prayers in the mosques. What these Muslim men and women think of our brazen Western hussies who kiss and cuddle their boyfriends in public one can only conjecture.

After the lean days we spent in Yugoslavia and Bulgaria it was a delight to find plenty of food for sale. The street stalls and barrows were piled high with luscious white and black grapes, green and yellow melons, gigantic pumpkins, quinces, black figs, peaches and apples. We bought some large quinces, which cooked slowly with sugar, made a delicious sweet. There was plenty of fresh fish for sale at a reasonable price. When we ordered fish in the restaurants, however, we found that it cost four times as much. Patisseries had a mouth-watering display of cakes and pastries and bakers' shops offered an amazing variety of bread and rolls.

The covered bazaar in Istanbul is rivalled in size and diversity only by its counterpart in Isfahan in Iran. Like Aladdin's Cave, its treasures unfold as you penetrate further into its great vaulted chambers. Everywhere there are outstretched hands beckoning and insistent voices calling, "Sir, Madam, just step in and have a look." There is a wide selection of carpets and rugs, hand and machine woven, cheap but well-made slippers and shoes, and magnificent coats and jackets in fine soft leather. The jewellery shops are unrivalled in the East and West. Wealthy Iranians and Pakistanis come here to buy their jewellery and especially the gold rings and necklaces which form part of the Muslim woman's wedding dowry. We made a note of the prices of gold and silver settings of rings in order to compare them with those further East and on our return journey we brought back semi-precious stones to be set in gold in Istanbul. The leather coats were so beautifully made that, had we not been heading for warmer climates, I would have been tempted to buy one. Fifteen months later, however, having seen what Afghanistan, India and Nepal had to offer, I purchased a leather coat in the bazaar at Istanbul.

Whatever the hour, it always seems to be tea time in Istanbul. Bare-footed urchins race up and down the streets carrying brass trays laden with tiny tumblers of tea for the traders and shoppers. Tea is used by the shopkeeper as in inducement to the customer to buy his goods. If his client can't make up his mind, he will find a glass of tea at his elbow to sip whilst the contents of the shop are brought for scrutiny. One of our favourite occupations in Istanbul was to order tea in a street café and to sit and watch the world go by. What a motley crowd: there can be few cities where the vicissitudes of history have left such a mark on the features of its inhabitants as they have done in Istanbul. There is the typical Turkish face, narrow with hollow cheeks and dusky skin, inherited from the Seljuks who overran the country in the eleventh century. Others with fair skins and rounded features may be descendants of the Greek and Roman invaders who held sway in Asia Minor before the Turks arrived, or they could perhaps claim ancestry from the Crusaders who passed through Constantinople — as Istanbul was then called — to fight for Jerusalem and Christendom. Many of the shopkeepers are Jews whose ancestors fled from the Spanish Inquisition in the fifteenth century, to be joined during the last fifty years by their persecuted brethren from all over Europe. Here and there, a broad-browed, bearded face recalled a more ancient lineage, for features like these are to be found on the stone friezes of the Hittites and the Assyrians who had their heyday in Asia Minor long before the Greeks arrived. Foreign tourists were easy to recognise by their attire and by the paraphernalia they carried about with them. Most of them were German or Americans. Then there were the international hippies who pass through the town on their way to and from India and Nepal. As they walked past our table we would catch snatches of their conversations. They were usually searching for the 'cheapest dive' in town or the chance of a hitch on a TIR juggernaut bound for Tehran.

The heat of noon would drive us from the streets to seek shade in one of the mosques. Prayers were in progress when we slipped inside the cool tiled interior of the Blue Mosque. An attendant handed us large soft slippers to wear over our shoes lest we should damage the priceless carpets and prayer rugs which cover the floor. Blue is the colour of the tiles on the floor and ceilings, and the light which floods in through the windows has a bluish tinge. Coming from the bustle and glare of the outside world one feels immediately an atmosphere of restfulness and peace. We relaxed on the soft red carpet and listened to the mullah chanting. It was surprising to see such a large congregation at prayer in the middle of the day, and it was not a Friday which is the Muslim's Sunday. It was, of course, a male congregation, and as the only woman present, I felt conspicuous, for women in Muslim countries say their prayers in the privacy of their own homes. When the service was over we met an old Turkish soldier who, with his white beard and martial bearing, might have been a Chelsea Pensioner if his uniform had been red instead of black. He told us through an interpreter that he had fought under Ataturk, and showed us with pride the gold medal he was wearing which he had received from the great man himself.

Although he died almost forty years ago, Ataturk's presence is felt everywhere in Turkey. He rides on horseback in the main squares of the cities; his profile is emblazoned in lights on towers and hilltops, and his face looks down from every public building and from the wall of every Turkish home. It was Ataturk, whose name signifies the head of the Turks, who welded together the fragmented Turkish nation after World War I and started off the process of Westernisation which is still in progress. He is venerated by all sections of the community, except perhaps by the mullahs who lost their stranglehold on the people when Ataturk made Turkey a secular republic. Some of them have reverted to using Arabic when they call their Muslim brethren to prayer, instead of Turkish as Ataturk decreed. In some of the more backward areas of Turkey there are women who persist in hiding behind their veils, in spite of the fact that Ataturk, who gave them the vote in 1934, recommended that they should face the world without them. Prostitutes, however, were exempted from this general rule and were required to cover their faces.

The Istanbul you see from the terraces of the Topkapi Palace is the Constantinople you have dreamt about; a city of domes and minarets.

The very names of the places before you conjure up the remarkable past. Looking over the Bosphorus you see the Tower of Leander where Hero, watched for her lover across the Hellespont and the Golden Horn, whose deep blue waters divide the old town from the new. At this distance, the mean back streets and alleys are hidden from sight and the whole city looks fresh and sparkling. The view is just as entrancing if you take a ferry boat across the Bosphorus and look down on the town from the hillside at Camlica, or climb up to the village of Eyup with its quaint wooden houses and famous white mosque. There is plenty to see in Topkapi besides the Sultan's Harems and the Treasury. The Archaeological Museum in the palace grounds contains one masterpiece, which alone would make a visit to Istanbul worthwhile. It is said to be the white marble sarcophagus of Alexander the Great with its superb relief of scenes from the hunt. Alexander conquered most of the Middle East in 333BC and his army got as far as the Indus. Our journey was to take us over much of the ground which he conquered and we were to see the destruction which he caused to Darius' Palace at Persepolis. Since our return I have learned that historians do not agree that this tomb belongs to Alexander the Great. After his death in Babylon, supposedly by poisoning, his body was taken to Alexandria but it is not known where he was buried.

There are nearly six hundred mosques in Istanbul but only a few are of special interest. There is one, however, which rivals the Blue Mosque in popularity with tourists — St Sophia, now a museum. It has had a very eventful history, which began in AD562 when the Emperor Justinian decided to build a church for Christian worship to equal Solomon's Temple in grandeur. And so the great Basilica of St Sophia, one of the largest churches in the world was constructed and decorated with gold mosaics and veined marble. Some nine hundred years later, the Basilica, which by now had lost much of its original splendour, acquired minarets and new interior decorations when the Muslims converted it into a mosque. Forty years ago, Ataturk whose policy was to foster religious tolerance, turned St Sophia into a museum so that it could be visited by people of all religions. Because it is a museum, it lacks the atmosphere of the Blue Mosque, but as a masterpiece of Byzantine architecture, it is well worth a visit.

On the other side of the Golden Horn lies Beyoglu, the fashionable part of the town where the large hotels are situated. We went to visit Turkish friends of ours who have recently moved back to Istanbul from London where they had a fur and leather business. Members of the wealthy Jewish community, they live in a smart modern flat not far from the Hilton Hotel, and although they grumble about prices and inflation, they are still able to afford a maid and a chauffeur. Mrs Kuraoglu made what she called a typical Turkish meal, but it was one of the most delicious meals we had on the whole of the journey, and proved to us how good Turkish food at its best can be. Hitherto, we had not been greatly enamoured with food in restaurants where kebabs with great mounds of plain rice or stuffed aubergines and peppers were the only dishes on the menu. At our friends' house we had a selection of hors d'oeuvres which included creamed aubergines, cod roe mousse and melon with white cheese. This was followed by savoury rice in vine leaves and pastry squares filled with meat and cheese. We rounded off the meal with fresh peaches, Turkish liqueur and coffee. It was such a pleasant change from our caravan diet of tinned food, for we were still very conservative in our cooking. Later on, when our store of tins was finished, however, we made some weird and wonderful menus using local produce and creating new recipes, which we now use to amaze our friends.

On the following day we squeezed into a dolmus, (a shared taxi) bound for the Galata Bridge where we and our Turkish friends took a ferry boat to Buyuk Ada, the largest of the group of islands which lies ten miles south of Istanbul in the sea of Marmara. In Buyuk Ada, life seems to have stood still for at least a hundred years, and only the arrival of the ferry boat with its raucous tourists shatters the peace of this little haven. The great ornate, white villas overlooking the sea, surrounded by tropical shrubbery and the dignified bearing of the inhabitants recall a more tranquil and leisured age. As no cars are allowed here we hired a canopied fiacre and set off, horse bells jingling, through the pinewoods on a tour of these beautiful islands. At the Akasya Restaurant we dined on mussels stuffed with savoury rice and peanuts, followed by baklava, which is a delicious Eastern sweet made of layers of strudel pastry covered with walnuts and syrup. Mrs Kuraoglu's daughter, Gunes, was with us. She was a very pretty girl of eighteen years of age, who, although, she had been educated in England, was like most Turkish girls very closely chaperoned by her mother. Mrs Kuraoglu made no secret of the fact that she was on the lookout for a suitable husband for her daughter. By the time we had finished our hors d'oeuvres she had invited a handsome young man, sitting on his own at a table nearby to join us. As it happened, he was an eligible bachelor with a jewellery shop in the Bazaar at Istanbul. Prompted by Mama, the young couple went off for a stroll along the shore while we waited in the restaurant. To tell the truth, we were glad to sit still as one or two glasses of raki had made us feel weak at the knees. By the time we reached Galata Bridge, the young man had been invited to our friends' house, but we do not know whether the romance ever blossomed as we had to leave the next day. At least, Gunes would be able to accept or refuse a suitor selected by her parents, a choice which is not often open to girls in the East, as we were to discover on our journey.

Göreme — Turkey

Didyma — Turkey

BLACK SEA
ISTANBUL
BOSFORUS
SEA OF MARMARA
BOGASKOY
BURSA
ANKARA
SIVAS
ARMENIA
TURKEY
MT. ARARAT
IZMIR
MEANDER RIVER
BINGOL
GOREME
MALATYA
TATVAN
VAN
TABRIZ
PAMUKKALE
ANTALYA
TARSUS
SIDE
ALANYA
MERSIN
IRAN
CYPRUS
SYRIA
IRAQ
MEDITERRANEAN SEA

Chapter Two

TURKISH DELIGHTS

It takes only a few minutes to cross from Europe to Asia by way of the magnificent suspension bridge which spans the Bosphorus. Until 1973, the only means of crossing was by ferry boat, and there were long queues and inevitable delays. Now, thousands of cars and international juggernauts stream daily across the great bridge which links Europe with Asia. Turks who live to the east of the bridge, in the part of the country which we used to call Asia Minor and which is now known as Anatolia, consider themselves to be Europeans. They certainly have inherited a great deal of Western culture, for much of Anatolia was colonized by the Greeks and Romans long before the arrival of the Turks. As we drove south from Istanbul along the shores of the Sea of Marmara and the Aegean we saw many signs of their occupations — walls, aqueducts, bridges and triumphal arches. In fact, many of the Greek and Roman sites in Turkey are as well preserved as those in Greece and Italy. Unfortunately, with the disappearance of their ancient and familiar names which have been changed to Turkish they have lost some of their magic. Hence searching for Troy, Smyrna, Pergamum and Ephesus, names we have known from our schooldays, we found Truva, Izmir, Bergama and Efes, names which somehow or other sound less romantic.

From Izmir to Bursa the road runs through fertile country where apple and peach trees grow in abundance and plastic-covered greenhouses shelter early vegetables. As we had decided to explore the West and South of Turkey before proceeding to Iran, we headed toward Izmir by way of Balikesir. The tomato harvest was in full swing and we shared the road with trucks laden with tomatoes on their way to the canning factories at Sugurçuk. Tobacco leaves and sunflower seeds lay drying in the sun by the roadside, and there were mountains of melons for sale in the villages. It was dark when we reached Balikesir and we parked in the corner of a large, empty car park. We could not believe our good fortune in having the place all to ourselves, but we might have guessed that it was too good to be true.

We were, however, surprised to find that the shops and cafés in that part of the town were open so late and even more astonished when passing a little restaurant a voice called out to us in English, "Come and join us in a cup of tea." We went inside and found a Turkish lorry driver who had been a chauffeur to an English family in Izmir. He was very keen to talk to us and to tell us about his country, of which he was extremely proud. He told us that 90% of the goods we saw in the shops were produced in Turkey. As a lorry driver, he received a wage of TL1.200 (£45) which is a substantial amount in Turkey. We asked him about Trade Unions and he told us that there are two main sections — one for distribution workers, and the other for workers in the manufacturing industries. "What about pay agreements?" we asked. He told us that these run for two years and are then re-negotiated. If workers are not satisfied, there is an independent body of local people who try to settle differences. If they fail, a committee of government officials acts as a mediator. Talking to our new friend, we had the impression that Turkey is making good progress with industrial relations and that the ordinary worker views his country's future with optimism. This impression was corroborated in subsequent discussions with Turkish people.

Around midnight, the café suddenly filled with people, and looking over to our parking spot we saw that our van was completely surrounded by sleek long-distance coaches. All night long there was constant noise and bustle as the buses came and went with their complement of noisy travellers. When we were knocked up about 4 a.m. and asked to move forward to make room for another coach, we reckoned that the time had come to continue our journey.

The first streaks of dawn revealed the stark face of Anatolia with which we were to become more and more familiar as we proceeded eastwards. Bare volcanic hills rose on all sides with not a tree or shrub in sight, and the cracked earth had consumed every blade of grass. Nearer Izmir where the land was more fertile, women were picking cotton in the fields, their bright tunics and pantaloons giving colour to the arid background. Some of the older women were wearing veils, the first we had seen in Turkey, which showed that Ataturk's attempt to free his womenfolk from the age-old custom had not been wholly successful.

Overlooking the beautiful blue Aegean Sea, Izmir is an attractive modern town, with wide streets, fine squares and parks. Little is left of the Smyrna of old, most of which perished in a fire in 1922. Only the old fortress, Kadifekale, perched on the top of Mount Pagos and the 'agora' or market place, remind us of the pre-Turkish era. An inscription in the agora tells us that the market was rebuilt after an earthquake by a grant from Marcus Aurelius. Only the rather battered statues of three Greek gods and a few marble columns remain where shops and arched galleries once stood. The Muslims made a cemetery here and the strange turbaned heads of stone which have been unearthed are quite as fascinating as the Greek and Roman remains.

In the little town of Selçuk near Ephesus, we were searching for a parking spot when we saw a man approach with what appeared to be a large slab of ice cream in his hand. It turned out to be a chunk of butter which, as it was a very warm day, was melting fast. Falling into step beside him so that we should not impede his progress, we asked him if he could direct us to a parking place. He answered in French, which is widely spoken amongst the educated classes, and bade us accompany him. We were almost out of breath when we reached our destination, our eyes fixed on the diminishing butter pat, but before our friend disappeared inside his house he had indicated a parking spot beneath some palm trees and had invited us to supper. When we visited him later we discovered, much to our surprise, that he was no less a person than the governor of the district and a very knowledgeable man. We talked about education in Turkey and he told us that about 65% of the children attend elementary schools. As the duration of their stay there, however, depends on their economic circumstances, there is a high level of illiteracy in the poorer country areas. Well-to-do parents, like the governor and his wife, send their children to boarding schools.

Next morning we opened our curtains just as the morning sun lit up the slender top of a tiny minaret in the village, transforming its colour from a dull green to a brilliant emerald. Kerry immediately began to entone a verse of one of his favourite poems from Fitzgerald's *The Rubáiyát of Omar Khayyám.*

> "Awake! for Morning in the Bowl of Night,
> Has flung the Stone that puts the Stars to Flight:
> And Lo! the Hunter of the East has caught
> The Sultan's Turret in a Noose of Light."

A few minutes later as I was laying the table for breakfast, I was startled by a grotesque face which appeared at the rear window and rubbed its nose against the glass. It was a camel expressing its disapproval of our presence in its palm grove.

Heaps of stones and rubble, lying half concealed by cotton grass, in a marshy hollow are all that remain of one of the Seven Wonders of the ancient world — The Temple of Artemis (or Diana, as she was known to the Romans). It is hard to believe that on this neglected spot there was once a mighty temple thronged with vestal virgins, priests and worshippers. Ephesus was a prosperous port and centre of culture long before St Paul came to visit his Christian brethren in one of the seven Churches of the Apocalypse. It was the cult of Artemis which made Ephesus famous and which prompted its inhabitants to drown St Paul's preaching with shouts of "Great is Diana of the Ephesians!" During the course of centuries as the port gradually silted up and trade moved away, the great Temple of Diana fell into ruins and marble from its walls was taken to build new basilicas and mosques. Some blocks of marble are said to have been taken to Constantinople to be used in the building of St Sophia, and much of the material for the construction of St John's Basilica and the Isa Bey Mosque nearby, came from the temple. St John is said to have died in Ephesus about AD95, and his tomb lies beneath the altar of the Basilica, of which only a few columns and paving stones remain. The Isa Bey Mosque is also a ruin as the result of an earthquake.

About a mile further on over the plain, sheltered by Mount Koressos, lie the ruins of ancient Ephesus. A small road runs past the remains of the gymnasium, the heating system of which is still visible under the rubble. Further on is the great stone entrance to the stadium where, under the gaze of 70,000 spectators, gladiators fought and died. On the Marble Avenue and the Arcadian Way, two streets in the town, we had the thrill of walking where saints have trod. From the walls of the Baths of Constantine we looked down on the spot where Cleopatra landed on her visit to the town. The port in now silted up and the sea has retreated beyond the horizon. The Marble Avenue leads to the Library and Reading Rooms where we saw the slots for the rolls of papyrus. Some of the earliest apartment blocks in the world — six storeys high — were built here by the Romans and were so well constructed that some of the upper floors are still intact.

We spent hours browsing through this part of the ruins, discovering baths, fountains, pillars and temples, and conjuring up the city as it was at the time of St Paul. "Is there a greater city than Ephesus?" he said. "Is there a more beautiful city?" Certainly few cities can surpass Ephesus in the beauty of its ruins. We did not feel energetic enough in the heat of the day to follow the path up the mountainside which leads to the House of Mary. It is said that St John brought Jesus' mother to Ephesus and that she lived and died in the little house on the hillside. There is no historical proof of this, but it was in Ephesus some 400 years later that the Ecumenical Council proclaimed that Mary was the mother of God.

By the time we reached the small market town of Söke, which lies south of the beautiful bay of Kusadasi, our stock of provisions was running low. We drew up not far from the town centre beneath a garden wall, and we were about to set out for the market when three smiling faces looked at us over the wall. "Hello, are you English?" said a pretty fair-haired girl who introduced herself as Lara. The other two were her young sister Denez and her mother who, although she did not speak a word of English, had the most welcoming of smiles. In next to no time we were sitting comfortably in their little villa sipping tea, brewed in a silver samovar. Lara, who had studied Economics at Istanbul University, was working in a bank, and Denez was an art student. Since the death of their father ten years previously, their mother had trained as a primary school teacher. The interior of their house was more Western in style than we had expected, except for the wood stove and the tapestry wall-hangings. These and the painted plaques with their Turkish motifs had been made by the girls and their mother who were very artistic. They were keenly interested in life in Britain, in our journey and in our impressions of Turkey and darkness had fallen by the time we rose to leave. We declined their invitation to supper but accepted their invitation to breakfast next morning. What a memorable breakfast it was: there was a great selection of home-made jam — strawberry, apricot, peach and cherry — slices of white cheese served with olives, boiled eggs and freshly toasted bread (they had an electric toaster) and cup after cup of tea.

For a day or two we lingered in this pleasant, friendly spot, sunning ourselves on the beaches nearby or amongst the flowers in our friends' garden. This taste of family life in Söke was a real bonus for us. We were extremely fortunate to have had this encounter with people to whom we could relate entirely, in spite of differences in culture, race, language and religion. It was a lesson we had to learn and re-learn throughout the whole of our journey. With the girls we visited Didyma to see the ruins of the temple dedicated to Apollo, the twin brother of Artemis. Didyma means twin in Greek. The temple, whose colossal scale is quite awe-inspiring, was started by the Greeks and completed some hundreds of years later by the Romans. Over one hundred fluted columns are still intact on their solid plinths of black marble. In the ancient world the oracle of Didyma was almost as famous as that of Delphi. We saw the hole in a chamber beneath the sanctuary where the oracle used to speak, his voice reverberating through the maze of stone corridors.

When we took leave of our friends, laden with gifts of food, we set off eastward toward Pamukkale, along the fertile valley of the River Meander, now called Buyukmenderes, where grapes, figs and olives grow in abundance. Near Nazilli they were bringing in the cotton harvest and the roads were crammed with tractors and lorries piled high with bales for the cotton and carpet factories. Other travellers have told us not to miss Pamukkale on any account and we were quite prepared to be amazed at one of nature's wonders. However, as we approached the area the sight which confronted us was much more spectacular than we had ever imagined. In a great hollow between the mountains we saw what appeared to be the frozen cascades of a gigantic waterfall. As we drew nearer we realized that these waterfalls and the enormous marble-like basins below them had been formed over thousands of years by crystallised lime-rich water. Beneath the terraces, the slowly dripping water has petrified into stalactites which hang like fringed curtains, incandescent in the light. The air is filled with the soft murmur of running water, as it trickles over the terraces and gushes in tiny streams down the grassy surface of the hillside. On the top of the plateau, above the limestone terraces, are a number of modern hotels with large swimming pools. We bathed in one of these pools which lies right on the edge of the cliff, and as we lay in the warm spring water, wafted by the mountain breeze we had the feeling that we were being slowly drawn towards the rim and that another puff of wind would carry us over the cascade below. The only drawback of this delightful bathe was the difficulty we had later of removing the limy water from our hair.

Above the limestone steps lie the ruins of the ancient city of Hierapolis which was famous as a spa in Roman times. Parts of the city walls survived the terrible earthquake of the fourteenth century. Much of the great theatre is still intact and part of the bath where wealthy Romans came to take the cure, for the spring water was supposed to have health-giving properties. Many of them died here and are buried in the vast necropolis which lies beyond the ruins. Although their elaborately carved marble tombstones have been defaced by the Muslims, we were able to decipher some of the Latin inscriptions describing the exalted worldly status of the deceased.

The road to Antalya and the Mediterranean runs through an arid, treeless plain edged by wooded mountain slopes. The Turks are, however, making an effort to stop further erosion of their soil in this area. Near Burdur, hundreds of workers were engaged in planting trees on the desolate hillsides. We stopped in a little village to buy crusty bread, white cheese, olives and bottles of fruit juice, but we had to drive for miles before we could find a shady spot to have our snack. High in the Taurus Mountains there is no vegetation and one can find shelter from the sun only in the shadow cast by a rock face or overhanging ledge. Our stopping place was near a tumble-down shack in front of which a woman and several ragged children were sitting. On a wood fire close by was an enormous black iron pot filled with wheat grains and water. As we approached with our cameras, the woman beckoned us to sit down on the mat beside her and one of the children brought us a tin can full of boiled wheat. We did our best to swallow some of this unappetising fare which had been so generously given to us, while little brown hands fingered our cameras and clothes and bright inquisitive eyes gave us a close examination. By pointing and counting on our fingers we elicited the children's ages, and they laughed uproariously when we tried to pronounce their strange Turkish names. Fortunately, we had brought with us plenty of packets of sweets and thus were able to give something in return for such a friendly reception.

At last the mountains gave way to the lush coastal plain, where cotton, apples and pears were growing and great mounds of melons were awaiting collection by the roadside. At Antalya, a large modern tourist resort, we made straight for the beach at Lara, anticipating a cool dip in the clear waters of the Mediterranean. However, the beach and the sea looked so uninviting that we gave up the idea. The Turks have not yet seen the necessity of making the most of their priceless tourist asset of sandy beaches by providing some trees and shrubbery on the fringes. Fortunately, along most of the Turkish coasts, nature itself supplies these amenities. After a cursory look around Antalya, we set out along the coastal road which skirts the turquoise waters of the Mediterranean. When we reached Side, the sun was setting like a glowing orange on the rim of the horizon, lighting up the dark ruins of the ancient town. The site was completely deserted as we wandered in the gathering dusk past crumbling walls, columns, porticoes, fountains and temples to the promontory looking out towards the sea. As we retraced our steps we resolved to come back in the morning to examine these wonderful remains by daylight — but, alas, that was not to be.

Following a sign directing us to a camp site, we took a small lane through a banana plantation. It was now quite dark and we could not see the way in front of us, only lights twinkling in the distance. Suddenly there was a great flash and a loud bang as the roof of the van struck something overhead. Darkness enveloped us. We leapt out and Kerry climbed aloft.

c

"Good gracious!" he exclaimed, "we have severed some electric cables and see what we have done." He threw down the head of a small palm tree which we had decapitated.

"Shall I go for help?" I said.

"Well" he replied, "since we have put all the camp lights out I think it would be wise to beat a hasty retreat."

So taking the coward's way out, we disentangled ourselves from the wires and slowly backed away from the scene of our crime. To this day, I feel guilty about this episode.

Some twenty miles from Side, in a shady grove by the sea, is the Alanya Mocamp where we awoke next morning to find ourselves in idyllic surroundings. Situated on a cliff above the sea, the camp site is fringed with olive and banana trees and planted with masses of rose bushes and cannas. Even the sides of the washrooms and toilets are covered with sweet scented white jasmine. Turkish mocamps at their best make our European sites look like army barracks. The toilets and shower rooms were spotlessly clean and there was plenty of hot water on tap. Soon we had washed all our clothes and bedding which dried in an hour's time under the tropical sun. The sea was as warm as it is in Spain in mid-summer and the little beach had rocks where we could shelter from the heat and soft white sand. As it was almost the end of the season there were few campers about and we had the mocamp facilities and the beach almost to ourselves. There was, however, one drawback, for although there was plenty of washing powder, Vim and Nescafé in the camp store, there was practically nothing to eat. As the shops were several miles away we had to make do with our own meagre rations — soup, dried meat and rice, sardines and an occasional egg bought from the little farms near the shore. How we wished we had had the foresight to purchase large quantities of aubergines, onions and green peppers in Antalya where they were plentiful and cheap, or had stocked up in Britain with more tinned goods, especially meat. Our supply of dried milk was now running low and long since we had exhausted our packets of crisp-bread and biscuits.

By now, the car was needing some attention as the bodywork was covered with dust and tar and the back reflectors were loose. Inside, the hinges on the sink unit and oven were broken and the carpet was full of grit. For a day or two we divided our time between these tasks and the beach. The night before we left we were disturbed by the noisy arrival of a Polish expedition to the Persian Gulf. A thirty-seater coach and a truck full of equipment came into the camp with much hooting and tooting in the early hours of the morning and parked next to us. As the new arrivals spent the rest of the night cooking and unpacking, we rose before dawn and watched the sunrise from the high corniche road. This road, winding its way along the coast at the foot of the Taurus Mountains, was one of the most spectacular routes of our journey. It reminded us of the Corniche roads in the French Riviera with their entrancing views of bays and beaches. Within a few years this part of Turkey will no doubt become a great holiday playground, rivalling the best in Europe. The road is bordered by great orange and banana groves where camels are used as beasts of burden. In this area both men and women wear Turkish dress, the women looking especially attractive in long flared dresses over their full trousers. At one place where we stopped to admire the view, a Turkish woman with her baby strapped to her back approached us and kissed my hand in greeting. She was a most beautiful creature with exquisite eyes and teeth.

For over a hundred miles the road winds its way along the coast fringed with fragrant pine trees through which, from time to time, we caught glimpses of endless stretches of sand with not a hotel or house in sight. Every inch of arable land was cultivated and the more arid patches were covered with the skeletons of greenhouses which would be enclosed in plastic later in the year and used to force vegetables and fruit. On this part of the route the houses were made of stone with flat, thatched roofs. Next to these houses were small erections resembling hides covered on top with dried branches and open at the sides. These are used by the peasants as extensions of their homes in the height of the summer. In some of these shelters women were at work sewing or grinding corn; in others, around noon, whole families were having their siesta, while beneath them on the ground, their cattle rested in the shade.

All along the coast, the ruins of great Roman and medieval castles rise above the sea. We had a bathe under the ramparts of the Mamuriye Castle which was built so solidly by the Romans that many of its squat towers are still intact. As we picnicked on the sand beneath the massive walls, Turkish children came to us with bunches of wild flowers which they had gathered on the shore. We did not accept their gifts, however, as the children expect money in return and this practice encourages begging and the harassment of tourists.

At the little market town of Anamur, lying amongst orchards and gardens, we tried to replenish our food stores with little success. There were plenty of grapes, however, which even after a good deal of hard bargaining were still expensive. Beyond Silifke we saw the ruins of Korykos, where Cicero was governor about 50BC, dwarfed by towering twin castles constructed by the Armenians seven hundred years ago. Near Mersin the mountains gave way to a wide, fertile plain with vast lemon and orange groves. Mersin is a large modern port with broad boulevards and parks but no camping sites. As darkness fell we drove into the port area and obtained permission from an official to park near to the Customs Office. We were surprised that he did not ask any questions and it was only later that we realised that he had assumed that we wished to catch the morning boat to Cyprus.

About six o'clock next morning there was an urgent knocking at our door and a voice urged us to hurry as the boat was about to leave.

We were amazed at the variety of goods on sale in Mersin and at the friendliness of the shopkeepers, many of whom spoke English fluently. We were able to find all the provisions we needed, apart from tinned meat and margarine. As fruit juices and fruit liqueurs were good and inexpensive, we stocked up with enough to last us until we reached Iran. Restaurant prices were reasonable as we discovered when we had a meal in a café near the port. For a little over £1 each we had bread, soup, rice with meat balls, tomato salad, stewed apples and two bottles of fruit juice.

It was in Tarsus, twenty miles east of Mersin that St Paul was born and which he described as "No mean city". Nowadays, Tarsus is an unpretentious little market town set amongst lemon and orange plantations. Although St Paul's house has long since disappeared, the wall and part of the courtyard have been preserved. We also saw the ornamental gate which the townsfolk built to celebrate the first meeting of Anthony and Cleopatra which took place in Tarsus. It is hard to believe that she sailed through the town in her barge as there is now no access to the sea. At this point of our journey if we had had some knowledge about the Hittites, we would have continued along the coast beyond Adana to visit the famous site at Karotepe. Unfortunately, it was only on our return journey through Turkey over a year later, en route to Ankara, we discovered, almost by accident, the ancient capital of the Hittites near Boğazköy. So impressed were we by the bold rock carvings of warriors, gods and goddesses, that we spent some time in the museum at Ankara studying the history of the Hittites, and one day we intend to return to Turkey to visit all the Hittites' sites.

Turning our back on the Mediterranean we struck off northwards towards Central Anatolia over the Gulek Pass. Alexander the Great and his army passed this way en route to Persia and he is said to have caught a chill in the icy waters of the River Cydnus. We made slow progress up the pass, tailing a long queue of slow moving trucks against a strong headwind. At the top of the pass the sky grew dark and lightning flashed over the mountains. As we began to descend on the other side, we were enveloped in a great, red dust cloud from which the rain gushed as if from a water spout. The wind caught us as we rounded the hairpin bends and we lurched dangerously near the edge of the deep ravine. Beyond lay a vast desolate plateau with miserable little villages scattered on its bare surface. All the women were shrouded in dark coloured yashmaks, and the only spots of colour on the brown landscape were the gaily painted donkey carts, the only means of transport in that area.

At Derinkuyu, we sought out the entrance to the underground city which is connected by a tunnel to a longer one seven miles further north. Unfortunately, the doors were closed so we were unable to visit it. Little is known of the origins of these subterranean towns, carved from the bowels of the earth on several levels. Hundreds of people were accommodated on each floor which had its own cooking facilities, ventilation system and even its own cemetery. It is thought that the inhabitants of this underground hideout were Christians, escaping from persecution.

Strangely enough, it was in Derinkuyu that we first encountered bands of pestering children who were to persecute us for the remainder of our trip through Turkey. In that small village, children were led by a shrew of a girl, aged about nine years of age. As we refused to buy the hideous rag doll which she tried to sell us, she and her tattered followers pelted our van with stones. At Nevesehir we had a similar experience. There, school children looking very demure in their neat black uniforms with white Peter Pan collars threw stones at us out of sheer devilment.

This was an answer to a question which had puzzled us ever since we entered Turkey, "Why do the overlanders have their windscreens and windows encased in wire?" Now we knew why. Kerry got out and chased one of the little boys who escaped into an alleyway, still holding a stone tightly and defiantly in his hand. Stone-throwing at tourists by juveniles is a game all over the East said the travellers we met at the Tusan Hotel in Nevesehir. Several motorists had had their windscreens and headlights shattered in Eastern Turkey where the children are most hostile. As it happened, we managed to escape lightly from these young persecutors acquiring only a few dents and scratches, although we lost our back reflectors and petrol caps.

We had come to this part of Central Turkey — the Cappadocia of old — to see the famous rock dwellings in the valley of Göreme. As was the case at Pamukkale, the spectacle was much more remarkable than we had anticipated. In a lunar-like landscape of stark white rock rise hundreds of volcanic cones, some sharp as needles, others blunted and twisted by erosion. Gaping holes reveal that these strange protuberances are hollow inside and were once habitations. About fourteen hundred years ago monastic Christian communities settled in this area and carved dwellings and churches for themselves out of the soft rock. There they remained for four or five centuries until driven out by the Muslim invaders or by the gradual decay of their fragile homes. We visited a number of chapels and with the aid of a torch examined the remarkable frescoes which these early Christians painted on the walls and ceilings. There are refectories with stone tables, niches for cooking and stores, stone slabs used as beds, holes for toilets and cisterns for water.

It is a three-day journey from Göreme to Lake Van over a monotonous and seemingly endless steppe, flanked by bald mountains. There is little to see for hundreds of miles apart from an occasional flock of sheep nibbling the stubble and little clusters of square mud houses huddled beneath a rock face. Although the asphalt surface was good for most of the way, we made slow progress because of the steep, winding road. To relieve the boredom of driving through this unvarying and unexciting landscape, we kept up our spirits by singing all the songs we knew and by making up rhymes about our recent experiences, laughing hilariously at our compositions. At Gurun, a miserable hill town, we spent the night in a petrol station next to a field full of enormous cabbages two to three feet in diameter. We planned to take a photograph of these on the following day to amaze our horticultural friends, but our plans were thwarted by an unpleasant little incident.

The next morning, the garage proprietor, a great hulking man stalked into the caravan, asking in a peremptory way for a pencil. We supplied one, thinking that he wanted to write something down. He pushed it aside and with uncanny accuracy went straight to the bookshelf where we kept our writing material and appropriated Kerry's Parker pen and two biros. He was going to walk away with his loot, had we not remonstrated and snatched back the Parker. Then there was an ugly moment of confrontation before he left still clutching the biro pens. With more important things than cabbages to think about, we left hurriedly in the direction of Malatya. For over three hundred miles the road switchbacked over the bare plateau with scarcely a village in sight. At the end of dusty tracks leading into the mountains, men and boys sitting on their haunches made signs as if they were blowing kisses in our direction. But this is no friendly gesture; it is the begging sign for cigarettes, used throughout the East.

Puny little children sat by the roadside holding out pitiful handfuls of tiny apples for sale. Here and there a dead donkey lay on the road verge killed by a car and left to the vultures. So far, we had seen very few birds apart from magpies, but now great flocks of swallows were passing overhead on their way south.

We stopped in Malatya for only a few minutes as we were mobbed by children and adults who hung on to the car shouting and grimacing in an unpleasant manner. There was little to buy except macaroni and a kind of red salami which was so full of chillies that we could not eat it.

That evening, however, we had a friendly reception at the Ofisi Petrol Station at Bingöl where we spent the night. The manager, resplendent in striped pyjamas invited us to tea with his family in a garden behind the station. Like most Turks, he was fiercely patriotic and keen to know whether we, too, had a good opinion of his native land. "Çok, çok," we replied, "very nice indeed." His wife offered us a room in their spotlessly clean house, but we declined, explaining that we slept in our van. It was obvious that other travellers used these facilities as floor rugs, pillows and blankets were piled up in readiness. Later in the evening, one of the children brought us a plateful of white cheese, rancid unfortunately, and a large water melon, which was most welcome.

Beyond Bingöl the road deteriorated and we had a bumpy ride over a vast plain which was moist and green in places. We were now in the area inhabited by the Kurds, tall, dusky men in turbans, tending flocks of sheep, goats and water buffaloes. In pools by the roadside, naked herd boys were having a wash and there were the usual groups of stone-throwing children. To distract them from their purpose, we waved frantically, a device which was very often successful, as the children would wave back still clutching their stones. Their response set Kerry thinking, "Why don't we make little packages, full of stones but looking like gifts and throw them out when we see these little blighters?" So we made dozens of little parcels and tied them up with string. When the next group of stone throwers came in sight, I leaned out of the window waving and throwing two or three parcels onto the road. The children scrambled wildly after them and we passed unscathed. And so we arrived at Lake Van which was quite unlike the description we had read in our guidebooks. It resembles a vast sea which is not surprising as it covers an area of 2,250 square miles and has a high salt content because of deep sulphur springs.

Fodor describes Tatvan, the small town at the head of the lake, as a "deservedly popular summer resort" and that may be so, but by the 1st October it had definitely lost its charm. We viewed the sombre waters and the desolate mountains beyond with a sense of disappointment, chilled by the wind from the lake which lies at an altitude of 6,000 feet above sea level. We had already discovered that the road to Iran, which skirts the southern shore of the lake, was in a poor condition and had decided to cross the lake by the steamer which plies between Tatvan and Van, a journey of about five hours.

As we had several hours to wait, we set off on a rough road which eventually led to a hamlet where women were washing clothes. I decided to follow their example and started to wash our smalls in a pail of water which I drew from the pump to the utter amazement of the onlookers. I immediately sensed their resentment and regretted my action, but it was too late to retreat. Later, recalling the incident, we were in no doubt that this was the most dangerous situation which we had to face during our overland journey. While I was busy at the pump, a crowd of people gathered round the van and one unpleasant looking youth began to re-adjust the side mirrors to comb his hair. Kerry remonstrated gently at first, then angrily, but without avail, so he came out of the car and pushed the fellow aside. Whereupon the latter shouted in Turkish, "These are the foreigners who are killing our people in Cyprus" — or words to that effect. It was the autumn of 1974 and the Turks had the impression that the British were siding with the Greek Cypriots.

There was a sudden tension in the atmosphere around us and we found ourselves surrounded by a hostile, threatening mob. If we had panicked and rushed off in the car, we would certainly have been stoned. Fortunately, Kerry kept calm. "I am not English" he said, "I am a Pakistani."

They scoffed at this remark, pointing to the GB on the car. Then one bearded old man decided to test whether Kerry was a Muslim or not "A illa ililla!" he chanted.

Kerry, recalling the answer from his youth answered correctly "Mohamad ay resull Allah!"

The reaction was instantaneous. The old man embraced him and there was back-slapping and handshaking all round. Some of the women even came forward to help me wring out the clothes and there were smiles on their faces. However, not wishing to chance our luck for too long, we took our leave and dried the washing on the mountain side above Tatvan.

That night we shared the steamer with several railway freight wagons bound for Iran, filled with butter from Bulgaria. The boat was scheduled to leave at midnight, but it was four o'clock in the morning before it moved away, like some ghost ship, with no passengers except ourselves and no members of the crew in evidence. As the sun rose over the bare volcanic hills, tinting the water with delicate shades of pink, our first unfavourable impression of the lake was erased. Perhaps the guidebook was right about Lake Van after all; it has the stark beauty of a moon landscape. In Van we tarried only long enough to collect a few stores — eggs, mince (an unexpected find), onions, melons and margarine, and we attracted our usual crowds of inquisitive onlookers. Further north, in the middle of the day, we watched a herd of buffaloes wallowing in the lake and thought that we, too, might enjoy a dip. Unfortunately, the sparkling, inviting water was icy cold, and we beat a hasty retreat before it reached our ankles. In the height of summer this area would be an ideal spot for camping and bathing, but snow on the crest of Süphan Daği (13,750 feet) already heralded the advent of winter. Some miles south of Erçis we saw what looked like a pretty little village by the lakeside and we branched off towards it.

As we drew nearer we realised that we were in the grounds of a school. It was in fact a Teachers' Training College. Before we had time to turn the car we had received an invitation to tea by a charming young teacher of French. Her living quarters had none of the comforts to which teachers in our county are accustomed, her only furniture consisting of a bed and a wood stove, but there was nothing lacking in her hospitality. She invited us to meet her colleagues and we had tea together and delicious Turkish Delight. We were introduced to the director who told us about the college. There were 700 trainee teachers, boys between thirteen and seventeen years of age who had come from poor families and had had a very limited education. The staff of twenty-seven teachers taught a wide range of subjects which included French and German, but not English. The classes were large, averaging forty pupils, and the facilities and amenities were extremely meagre. In fact we did not see any equipment and the classrooms and dormitories were bare and bleak. The director and his staff, however, were not in the least depressed by their surroundings, which by Turkish standards were probably quite satisfactory.

We were invited to stay overnight at the college and meet the staff later in the evening; an invitation which we readily accepted. No sooner had we parked the car by the lakeside, however, than we began to regret our decision. In a few moments the children of the college employees were swarming all over the van, hanging on to the side mirrors and tampering with everything. The little girls were worse than the boys, being especially defiant. However, they did eventually lose interest and we were able to enjoy the magnificent view of the lake and mountains in the setting sun.

The two hundred miles of road between Erçis and the Iranian frontier at Maku are dusty and unpaved, passing through one of the poorest parts of Turkey. The earth-coloured houses and their hayricks covered with baked mud are hardly distinguishable against the barren brown hills. The inhabitants are rough, fierce-looking individuals who make no secret of the fact that they resent the presence of foreigners. We hurried on, not daring to stop anywhere lest we were besieged by stone-throwing children, eager to leave them and the barren wastelands behind us. Suddenly, rounding a bend in the road we were met with a view which more than compensated for our recent frustrations.

Towering above us, to the height of 17,000 feet, rose the majestic form of Mount Ararat with its cap of snow glistening in the sunshine. 'Ararat', the very name has magic in it, bringing back childhood memories and beliefs. Some years ago a Frenchman claimed to have found the Ark beneath the snow, and he was not the first to make such a claim nor will he be the last. Whatever the reason, Mount Ararat held us in its spell until we crossed the Iranian frontier and its massive outline faded away and merged with the horizon.

Mosque — Isfahan, Iran

Bringing home the bread

CASPIAN
SEA
ARMENIA
USSR
TURKEY
TABRIZ
TEHRAN
MASHHAD
QOM
DASH-E-KABIR
HERAT
IRAN
ISFAHAN
AFGHANISTAN
YAZD
PERSEPOLIS
SHIRAZ
PERSIAN
GULF
PAKISTAN
GULF OF OMAN

Chapter Three

IN SEARCH OF ZOROASTER

We had plenty of time to watch Mount Ararat disappear from our view, as we queued up at the Iranian Customs behind a long line of transport trucks from all over Europe. They travel to Iran by the middle route through Erzurum, monopolising the roads, as we were to discover on our homeward journey through Turkey. There, the gorges and hillsides are littered with their skeletons, which lie upside down like stranded dinosaurs or gigantic centipedes. Truckers told us that these juggernauts are very difficult to handle on steep, winding roads, and if travelling fast, it only needs a gust of wind at the bend of a road to topple them into a ravine. We were to see many more of these wrecks as we travelled south towards the Persian Gulf.

The first Iranians we met, apart from the custom officials, were two university students at Maku, a few miles from the frontier. We had arrived long after dark and parked rather brazenly but prudently, a few yards from a police post in the Central Square. Two young men were pacing up and down between the lamp standards near the caravan, reciting something aloud. After an hour or two, our curiosity got the better of us and we inquired what they were doing. They explained in good English that they were medical students and that they were learning their textbooks by heart in preparation for their forthcoming examinations. Probably in their crowded homes there was no opportunity to study, and learning by rote as we were to discover, is the method used at primary, secondary and university level all over the Middle East and India.

The Iranian landscape with its monotonous stretches of barren tableland and its mud-baked houses differs little from that of Eastern and Central Turkey. The roads, however, are much better, and we made good progress to Tabriz, the capital of the province of Eastern Azerbaijan. We parked in the Shah Goli camp site, south of the town, a cool, shady spot by the side of a lake. There we rested for a few days and caught up with our household chores. As usual, the motor home was covered in dust, which had seeped into the cupboards through the air vents and central heating system. Fortunately, there was plenty of hot water on the site, which was clean and well maintained. There were other travellers in the camp, including an elderly English couple who looked thoroughly exhausted, which was not surprising as they had made the journey from Iran to India and back in the space of seven weeks. They had intended to proceed to Nepal, but the heat and the squalor of India had proved too much for them. "It is a dreadful place, India," they warned us. "Thousands of people lie on the streets and on the pavements. They even squat down brazenly in front of you to do their toilet. We can't get home quick enough." They also told us of a Norwegian doctor whom they had met in Agra, whose youngest child had become so dehydrated that he had to be taken to hospital. We were not dismayed by these tales and similar versions which we heard from other travellers, as we were well aware of the hazards which lay ahead of us in the Indian sub-continent. Besides, with our home comforts around us we felt sheltered from most dangers, but we were full of admiration for two elderly English women whom we met in the bazaar at Tabriz. They were travelling to India the hard way using local buses and finding accommodation and food as they went along. Undeterred by the rigours of their journey, they looked and felt they said "as fresh as a daisy", having just had a wash in the public baths.

It is more pleasant to shop in Iran than in Turkey as the Iranian shopkeeper does not usually badger you to buy his wares. We were able to stroll around peacefully and examine at leisure the bales of brightly coloured cloth, the cheap cutlery and plastic ware which fill the shops and stalls. We were intrigued by the method used by most shopkeepers to calculate the cost of their goods. Their simple abacus with coloured balls on wires was as effective as any expensive adding machine. We had expected to find plenty of fresh fruit for sale in the market but we could only find pomegranates and tiny, sweet grapes. As the pomegranates were very cheap, we purchased large quantities and laboriously extracted the tangy, purple juice with the aid of a lemon squeezer. After ferreting around and looking in the sacks in the shops, we realised that we should have been searching for dried instead of fresh fruit, as there was an abundance of raisins, dried apricots, almonds, walnuts and peanuts at a reasonable price. We stocked up with enough of these goods to last us for several weeks and we wished we had bought much more, as dried fruit was virtually unobtainable in India.

In Tabriz the shops which attract most tourists are those of the silversmiths, most of whom are Armenians and whose handiwork, although expensive is beautifully executed. They have a wonderful display of silver goods, from dainty filigree butterflies to massive presentation goblets. We watched these master craftsmen at work in their little booths and marvelled at their artistry and skill. We were fascinated by the bakers' shops and the various methods of making bread. Iranian bread — nane, (Indian naan) is quite unlike its Western counterpart and is scarcely recognisable as bread. You emerge from the bakers with your bread draped over your arm like an outsize tea towel, or held in your hand like a crudely shaped tennis bat. For this type of bread the dough is clamped on the end of a long pole, which is held for a few moments against the roof of the heated oven, or it is cooked on a layer of stones, which become embedded in the dough and have to be picked out of the bread. When it is newly baked, nane is quite palatable, but in less than half an hour it has the consistency and taste of cardboard.

If we had been less particular about hygiene we could have had some tasty snacks in the street stalls, which also sold pomegranate and carrot juice. Meals in the restaurants of Iran were on the whole a disappointment, as they lacked the variety we had found in Western Turkey. No matter which restaurant we visited we knew what the menu would be — a kebab (lamb, sausage or chicken) and a great mound of white rice, topped with a pat of butter. This would be accompanied by a sliced raw onion, a slab of nane and a lukewarm soft drink. It was only when we reached Tehran that we realized that there are other dishes besides kebab and rice in the Iranian cuisine. Until then we made do with or own fare of curried eggs and vegetables, with an occasional chicken to vary the menu, fresh fruit and rusks instead of bread.

Apart from the bazaar and the main shopping area there is little of interest for tourists in Tabriz. The Blue Mosque — which is listed as one of the sights of the town — is under repair, having lost most of the blue faience façade which made it famous. Like most towns of its size in Iran, Tabriz is doing its best to become a modern city as quickly as possible and in one respect it has already succeeded. The traffic flows more smoothly than in any other Iranian town.

As we filled up at a petrol station on our way south to Isfahan, two young men approached us and asked if we were English. "Will you help us, please? How do you put 'Who shut the door?' in the passive tense?" The question seemed so irrelevant that we would have burst out laughing had it not been for the earnest look in the eyes of the two students. "By whom was the door shut?" we replied after a little reflection. They thanked us profusely for our assistance. This eagerness to become proficient in English was a characteristic of most of the young Iranians we met and any excuse was good enough if it gave them the opportunity to speak English. In Iran, India and Pakistan, English has been accepted as the international language. Schools and colleges are quite unable to cope with the growing demand for lessons in English. At the camp site in Tehran there were several young Englishmen making a lucrative business from giving English lessons to members of the Iranian Air Force, and the British Council in the main cities is overwhelmed with requests for classes in English.

We fell in love with Isfahan at first sight and it will always be one of our favourite cities. The seven-hour drive over the arid plateau had been a monotonous one, with little to see except rolling hills tinted in shades of green, purple and beige by chemical deposits. The mud houses in the tiny villages have strange bulbous roofs with small ventilation holes which make them much cooler than their rectangular counterparts. Suddenly, the barren landscape fell away and we were travelling through the long, shady boulevards which lead to the centre of Isfahan. We made for the Maidan-I-Shah, the main square of the town, and were immediately enthralled by its beauty and peace. As it was a public holiday, the anniversary of the death of Mohammed's son-in-law, the mosques were closed and there were few people about. We strolled through the tranquil gardens, sat by the fountain, gazing towards the cupola of the King's Mosque which glistened in a cloudless sky. Everywhere you look in the Maidan there is beauty, symmetry and colour.

It was Shah Abbas the Great of the Safavid dynasty, who created what must surely be the world's most beautiful square. He made Isfahan his capital in 1598 and before he died thirty years later, the King's Mosque was almost completed as were the arcades and the imposing entrance to the bazaar. The gardens and the pool were commissioned by the father of the last Shah. In Shah Abbas' time there was a water channel around the Maidan which was little more than a great field where public executions took place and festivals were held. Polo was also played here and the stone goal posts are still in place at the ends of the gardens. From the terrace of the Ali Qapu Palace the Shah would look down on the various spectacles in the square, deriving perhaps considerable enjoyment from the executions, for in spite of his appreciation of beauty, he was reputed to be a harsh and cruel man. We became so attached to the Maidan that, over a year later on our return journey, we made a six-hundred-mile detour just to see it once again. We even had the audacity to park our mobile home for two nights under the trees in the square and wandered in the garden by moonlight with the great domes reflected in the silent pools beneath them. Never have we slept more peacefully and blissfully than in this little bit of earthly paradise.

The Maidan is not just a collection of beautiful buildings and souvenir shops. The brass workers' alley which leads from the square is a hive of activity. Sitting back on their haunches the men hammer, weld and beat the brass into every conceivable shape. There are enormous pots, six feet in diameter, ornamental tables, wall plaques and bowls. In tiny workshops behind the arcades we watched artists with minute brushes made of cat's hair painting miniature pictures of Persian scenes, exquisite in colour and detail. In craftsmanship and artistry there is not another town in the Middle or Far East to equal Isfahan and it is questionable that it can be rivalled anywhere in the world. A stone's throw from the gardens is the great bazaar which sprawls in every direction like an enormous rabbit warren. There are separate areas where you can buy cloth, slippers, carpets, brassware, in fact every conceivable commodity. Little bent men appear from underground caverns like dwarfs, bearing tremendous bundles on their backs and disappear again in the semi-darkness. Small boys sit at sewing machines in tiny booths: men using a chisel and a contraption like a bow are turning wood whilst others hammer out intricate designs on trays and tabletops. We followed our noses to another part of the market where all kinds of pungent and aromatic spices were for sale. Further on we saw sugar molasses being poured into moulds the shape of dunces' caps. We wandered for hours getting completely lost, emerging into the light of day half a mile from the Maidan, near the Friday Mosque, which is one of the oldest in Isfahan, its brown dome having been constructed in the twelfth century. Its muted colour and vaulted arcades make it a place of peace and it was one of the few mosques in Iran where we saw women at prayer.

One of the most tranquil and attractive spots in Isfahan is the sanctuary of the Madraseh ye Mader I Shah — the School of the Shah's Mother, a former theological college. When you leave the hustle of the town's main thoroughfare, the Chehar Bagh, behind you and enter the cool, green garden with its pool and arcades, you feel at peace with the world. The caravanserai next door to the sanctuary was also once a theological college, but is now a superb, luxury hotel, the Shah Abbas. North American and German accents echo in the foyer and beside the pool, but there is a little corner in the garden for less wealthy visitors, where you can recline on cushions and sip tea served with variegated sugar lumps.

At the government camp site, south of the town, we had a joyful reunion with French friends we had met in Turkey. Nicole and Jackie were a married couple who had taken a year off from teaching to make a trip to Nepal. They were accompanied by their friend, Prosper, an accountant in Paris. All three were highly intelligent and interesting and we enjoyed their company immensely. It was at Isfahan that we made the acquaintance of six new friends who were to be our companions on and off for the next four months. We were having a meal in the camp restaurant one evening, next to a Belgian couple with their two children and two women friends. We noticed Patrick at once, a bonny, chubby boy of about two, with a surprisingly deep voice. When they had finished their meal, he said loudly, in French "That was a good meal. I enjoyed it, we all enjoyed it," and pointing at me, "That lady over there enjoyed it too, didn't you?"

Everyone laughed and turned to look at me. So it was Patrick who introduced us to each other. His parents, Françoise and Albert, were teachers in Belgium and they were travelling to Nepal with Patrick and his sister, Véronique, a demure-looking five-year-old with a mind of her own. They were accompanied by two Michèles, one a teacher and the other a student, whom we called Mimi and Titi. This Belgium expedition was very well organised, each member of the party having his or her own specific task to perform. Albert and Mimi drove the two Dormobiles; Françoise did most of the cooking; whilst Titi was the mechanic, never happier than when wriggling under the cars covered with grime. Mimi also acted as a letter writer and reporter, sending back typed records of the journey to a local newspaper. We soon were fast friends and Kerry became for the children "Patapouffe", that friendly French elephant.

The camp site was a bleak spot, lacking in shade and privacy. Only the toilets and washrooms had been completed, but the plumbing left a great deal to be desired. Nevertheless, we did manage to plug in to electric light and our caravan became a meeting place for our travelling companions. We played chess, drank pot after pot of coffee and discussed every subject under the sun until the early hours of the morning. Together we went to visit the sights of the town, including the Shaking Minarets which are some miles out of the town, perched precariously on the roof of a small mosque. Jackie and Prosper squeezed into one of the minarets and began to rock it to and fro using their backs and knees alternatively. Whereupon the other minaret started to shake in unison and we all laughed and applauded. There is no doubt that this practice is a danger to life and limb and the authorities will do well to forbid it but it is still quite an amusing and lucrative tourist attraction.

Our attempt to have our gas cylinders refilled was another source of amusement. Every time we made enquiries about Calor gas we were directed to confectionery shops, which naturally enough only stocked sweets. After the fourth or fifth attempt we were in a state of hysterical laughter until we discovered that the word 'gaz' in Farsi (the main language in Iran) means 'nougat'. We never did find Calor gas in Isfahan and had to wait until we reached Shiraz, 300 miles further south before we could replenish our stock.

It was in Isfahan that we noticed that the fixture holding our water filter was broken so we went to a little joiners' shop to have it repaired. Kerry had made a sketch to show what was required and the worker nodded to show that he understood. "Can I have it tomorrow?" asked Kerry.

"No, tomorrow" was the answer.

Kerry persisted but could get no other reply.

On our way back to the camp, Kerry suddenly exclaimed, "It has just occurred to me why that fellow did not understand, he has confused the word 'tomorrow' with 'shumera' which means 'yours'. He was saying that he did not want to keep the fixture."

And so it turned out to be when we collected the finished article the next day. In his boyhood in India, Kerry had been taught some Persian and this knowledge was very useful to us. In addition, his ability to recite Persian poems earned him quite a reputation and obvious admiration.

The desert takes over on the edge of Isfahan and the road winds up and down through barren mountains. In this drab landscape the only touches of colour are those provided by the scarlet dresses of the nomad Qachquai women on their way south to their winter quarters near the Persian Gulf. The Iranian Government is doing its best to persuade the Qachquai tribes to forsake their nomadic way of life and settle down permanently, but so far, this plan has met with little success apart from the fact that a number of the children are receiving education. We visited a school for nomad children on our way to Shiraz and found seventy children of all ages being taught by two teachers. The teachers, who migrate with the tribe, live in white tents alongside the black tents of the tribes people. When we arrived, the children were standing in a long file in front of the teachers' tables. We asked what was happening. "We are taking the children's fingerprints for identification purposes," explained one of the teachers. There were no books or paper and the children learned by repeating what the teachers said to them.

About 250 miles south of Isfahan, we turned off the main road to visit the Tomb of Cyrus the Great at Pasargadae. There is something very moving about this massive tomb which stands alone in a vast and bleak plain. The huge sarcophagus of the first king of the Achaemenid dynasty is supported by blocks of stone arranged in the shape of a pyramid. There is no sculpture, no inscription to identify this as the last resting place of Cyrus whose kingdom stretched from the Aegean to India. For several centuries local people believed that it was the tomb of Solomon's mother and women used to go there on pilgrimage. Not far away are the remains of fire temples and palaces, but not even the stout black basalt columns have been able to withstand the ravages of time and they lie split and fragmented on the ground.

It is difficult to believe that at the time of Cyrus and his descendants this arid part of Iran, the Fars, was a very fertile and fruitful region, providing enough grain to feed vast armies. Because of these favourable conditions it was the cradle of the Persian nation, and its language, Farsi, originated here. Today all that remains to remind us of its past glory are the massive tombs of the kings and the ruins of Persepolis. The great rock face in which four of the Archaemenid kings are buried towers above the plain a few miles north of Persepolis. We visited the site with our French friends and hired a cassette with a recording of its history. The tomb of Darius I, who died in 485BC is the most impressive of all the burial places with its frieze of people symbolizing the twenty-eight nations that were his vassals. Carved on the rock is a speech attributed to the king in which he asserts that his power comes from God and that he loves justice. For centuries no one could decipher this text, until about 100 years ago, an English traveller let himself down in a basket from the top of the cliff. He made an accurate copy of the strange script and later helped to decipher it. Below the four rock tombs are sculptures depicting scenes in the lives of the Sassanid kings who ruled some 600 years after the Achaemenids. It was on the piece of sculpture which showed the investiture of Ardashir I (224-241BC) that we saw for the first time the winged figure of Ahura-Mazda, hovering above the head of the king. This figure of a man with the wings of an eagle, holding in his hand a beribboned tiara, caught our imagination and set us off on an exciting trail of research, a trail which was to lead us in a few days across the desert to Yazd.

It was dark when we reached Persepolis and camped beneath its walls. There was no moon and all we could see in the darkness was a forest of stone columns rising into the night sky. We could hardly wait for dawn to reveal what lay beyond. The morning light lit up the monumental staircase opposite which we were encamped. It was up these great flights of steps that the princes and representatives of the subject nations went in procession to pay homage to King Darius. At the top of the steps they passed through the Gateway of Xerxes, guarded by enormous stone bulls, two of which have wings and human heads. Thirty-six of the columns which supported the roof of the great hall are still standing, beautifully carved and fluted, decorated with various motifs. Here a bull was being torn to pieces by a lion; there King Darius seated under a parasol was receiving homage. The friezes on the ornamental staircases feature the parade of the vassals, each one in his own national costume, and each one bearing a gift for the king.

That evening we attended a Son et Lumière presentation of the history of Persepolis, narrated as it were, by Artaxerxes III who lies buried in the rock face behind the ruins. We heard how Darius I built Persepolis as a prestige capital. He had a least two others, a winter residence at Susa, and a summer capital at Ecbatana. Like King Solomon before him, Darius commissioned thousands of craftsmen to assist him with the construction. Never had there been such a splendid and grandiose royal palace, a fitting residence for the dynasty which ruled from Egypt to the Punjab. Each year at Nawruz, the New Year Festival, Persian dignitaries and vassal nobles gathered here to pay homage to the king in the great hall, the Apadana. For two hundred years the Achaemenids were the most powerful kings on earth, until Alexander the Great crossed the Tigris and defeated the army of Darius III. In the Son et Lumière performance we heard the conquering army approach the gates of Persepolis. Then the sky grew red above the town and soon the columns and gateways were engulfed in flames. Alexander the Great had destroyed the Achaemenid capital and put an end to the greatest period in Persian history. In 1971, the 2,500 anniversary of this remarkable era was commemorated in Persepolis where the Shah and his Empress received the world's dignitaries. The tent city (made of concrete) where the guests were housed in lavish splendour lies near the ruins and can be visited by tourists.

We followed a train of donkeys laden with pomegranates and grapes into the town of Shiraz which lies forty miles south of Persepolis, like a great oasis in the desert. If Isfahan is reputed for its beautiful mosques, Shiraz is famous for its gardens and literary heritage. We had the good fortune to be invited by the owner of one of Shiraz's private gardens to visit him. The Kalili Bagh (garden) lies on the outskirts of Shiraz, hidden behind high walls, and it had everything we expected to find in a Persian garden. Cool fountains were playing against a background of tall, dark cypress trees; shaded walks led to little arbours covered with bougainvillaea and clematis. It was very peaceful, the only sound being that of water trickling into the lily ponds and the air was fragrant with the scent of roses. The young owner told us that nightingales sing in the garden in the evening and we could not imagine a better setting for their song. Later, we visited other gardens in Shiraz and although some of them, like the Naranjestan, had orange groves and a splendid pavilion with mirrors and mosaics, none of them had the special magic of the Bagh e Kalili.

There is silver jewellery and marquetry for sale in the bazaar in the centre of the town, and brightly coloured rugs and blankets with geometric designs made by the Qachquais women. We saw many of these women in the market buying new finery, yards of gaudy red cotton with silver trimmings and coins for their earrings and necklaces. With their bright clothes and strong features they made all the other women look dowdy and plain. Not far from the bazaar is the shrine of the brother of Imam, Reza, who is venerated by the Shiite sect, to which most of the Iranian Muslims belong. Foreigners, and especially foreign women, are not usually allowed into this shrine but I was permitted to enter, enveloped in a voluminous chador (cloak). I followed the crowds which surged into the sacred place beneath its pear-shaped dome. The sight of the tomb seemed to make a great emotional impact on the viewers who fell on their knees before it, weeping uncontrollably and kissing the silver doors and mirrors which surrounded the shrine. In contrast to this hysterical scene, peace and calm reigned in the gardens which surround the tomb of two of Persia's most famous poets, Saadi and Hafiz. They lie buried beneath splendid modern memorials in gardens on the hillside above Shiraz. The Iranians venerate their poets more than any other literary figures, and during the last thirty years they have raised many beautiful mausoleums in their honour.

The camp site at Shiraz was delightful, set amongst green lawns and flowering shrubs, with excellent facilities and a clean swimming pool. As the weather was still very warm, we had a daily dip, accompanied by Patrick and Véronique. Véronique could swim a few strokes and Patrick splashed vigorously in his rubber ring. Mimi sat typing her reports under the large bright parasol they had prudently brought with them. Titi, and the men of the group, including Jackie and Prosper, spent most of their time under the cars, tightening up nuts and bolts and making minor repairs in preparation for the next lap of the journey. The Belgians were going to undertake the arduous three-day journey across the desert to Mashhad. The French trio were making for Tehran and the Caspian Sea and we were bound for Yazd. We were, however, very concerned about our tyres, which were to be our Achilles heel, and were already showing signs of wear. Two had developed large bosses and had to be discarded. Nevertheless, we were determined to cross the desert to discover the descendants of the ancient fire worshippers, the Zoroastrians.

To explain why an apparently rational middle-aged couple should make the perilous journey across a trackless desert without maps on what might be called a wild goose chase, I should perhaps digress a little into history. When the Muslims conquered Persia in the seventh century, they persecuted the followers of Zoroaster and tried to convert them. Many became Muslims, but thousands fled by sea to India and settled in Gujerat. Their descendants are the present-day Parsees. Some very brave Zoroastrians, however, defied the might of the Arab conquerors and kept their religion alive in remote places like Yazd in the desert where their descendants still live. One of the original fire temples where the sacred flame has been kept burning for more than thirteen hundred years is still standing and to find it was the aim of our journey to Yazd.

For the first sixty miles or so the desert road to Yazd was little more than an empty track across a waste of undulating sand, through which we ploughed raising great billowing clouds of dust. Then we lurched and rattled over a corrugated surface, pitted with holes and riddled with boulders before we reached a more reasonable stretch of road. It was a most terrifying journey. However, the scenery compensated for the rough ride with the stark beauty of jagged mountain peaks rising from the desert. In each tiny village through which we passed we discovered a fire temple located as we had been told is the custom, beneath a tall tree. All of these, however, were hidden by high mud walls and gates which were firmly locked.

When we reached Yazd and had rid ourselves of the layer of cement-like dust which covered us and every inch of the caravan inside and out, we set out on the trail of the Zoroastrians. We started our enquiries in one of the busy streets of the little town and made no headway until a shopkeeper who had overheard us came over and spoke to us in English. As it happened, he was a Zoroastrian and without more ado he closed his shop and accompanied us to the chief priest of the Zoroastrians. The Anjuman, as he is called, lived in a quarter of the town, inhabited by the members of the Zoroaster sect, in a neat stone house in a cobbled street. With the shopkeeper as our interpreter, we learned that there are about 40,000 Zoroastrians in Iran, more than half of whom are farmers. In order to keep their blood pure they do not intermarry with other Iranians. The Anjuman told us that the winged figure we had seen on the sculptures was not that of Ahura-Mazda, the Supreme Being, who was never depicted, but his symbol. This emblem is still used by the Zoroastrians in Iran and we saw it on the temple in Yazd and above other buildings. It is also the symbol of the Parsees in India where it is called 'Fravashi' or 'Fravahar'. We were to discover later that this symbol resembles the winged disk used by the Egyptians and the Assyrians. The beribboned ring which the figure holds in his hand, explained the Anjuman, may be a regal tiara or a love token. Some believe that this was the origin of the wedding ring. During our researches in Tehran we were given another explanation of the ring, namely that it represents the solar disk, venerated by the Indo-European ancestors of the Persian people. Another link with the Indo-Europeans is the symbol of fire used by the Zoroastrians and the Parsees. This is derived from the primitive worship of the sun which we find in the earliest religions in Babylon, Egypt and amongst the Incas.

As we talked, the Anjuman's wife, a good-looking woman, colourfully attired in a tunic with a cowl over baggy bloomers, served us with tea and cakes. We smiled at each other, but unfortunately we were unable to communicate. The Anjuman asked if we wanted to see the sacred flame and we jumped at the opportunity. Suitably garbed in a shawl (me) and in a white cap and vestment (Kerry), we entered the fire temple. There in a great bronze urn was the sacred flame fed with pieces of sandalwood which gives off a distinctive aroma.

I was very impressed and felt privileged but as I was to learn later, I was cheated. When I was with his wife, the Anjuman escorted Kerry to the really ancient fire, deep in the bowels of the temple, and permitted to be viewed by Zoroastrians of the male sex only. For the Zoroastrians, the fire itself is not the object of worship but represents the supreme being whom they revere in much the same way as the cross represents Christianity and God. We also visited a large, modern sports centre nearby which had been donated by Zoroastrians from abroad for the use of all the children of the area, including Muslims. Before we took our departure we obtained the address of the Chief Anjuman in Tehran, as we were eager to find the answer to several questions which still puzzled us. For instance, who was this mysterious Zoroaster? And what were the doctrines he preached? Why do the Zoroastrians deposit their dead in tall towers to be devoured by vultures?

The wealthy owner of a carpet factory near Yazd allows campers to park in his courtyard, free of charge, and he has provided toilet and washroom facilities. He came to see if we were comfortable and when he learned that Kerry was an electronic engineer he enlisted his help to solve some of his electrical problems in his house and in his factory.

Kerry, always eager to be of assistance, went with him at once. He did not return until the evening, in an exuberant mood. "I have had a wonderful day. Before lunch I solved some problems in the factory, where by the way, there are lots of young boys working. Then he asked me to come to his house. You should have seen it — a marble-floored mansion with fountains playing in the lounge."

"What did he want you to do there?" I asked.

Kerry burst out laughing. "I couldn't believe it," he said.

His problem was a new gadget in his kitchen, a microwave oven. In 1974 these ovens were comparatively rare in Europe, so it was surprising to say the least, that someone in this remote part of the world should possess one.

"Look," said Mr Ali. "When I switch it on I can't feel any heat."

"He had his hand inside the oven, imagine! I told him that had it not been for the safety device he would have burnt his hand to the bone and I explained the principles of this type of oven."

"Did he understand?" I asked.

"Of course, Mr Ali clapped his hands and a servant appeared with a large leg of lamb, which after some drinks we enjoyed for lunch, with rice of course, and mounds of vegetables."

I was quite envious and suddenly very hungry. But then there was a knock on the door. It was one of Mr Ali's servants bearing a large basket of peaches and pomegranates.

The next day Mr Ali invited us to see the mosque he was building near his house. Constructed in marble, using special Italian machines and craftsmen, with its palm-frond roof and mosaics etched in gold, this will be one of the most beautiful in Yazd. This truly magnificent edifice was going to cost him, he said, over two million pounds. "But that does not matter, it is for the glory of Allah." It will also ensure that Mr Ali's name is known to posterity.

The road to Qom runs for over three hundred miles along the edge of the Great Salt Desert, the Dasht e Kevir. In this desolate area, where large stretches of salt shimmer in the sun, there is no vegetation and few signs of human habitation. Even in this wilderness, however, man has managed to survive. Lines of small craters denote the presence of underground 'kanats' (canals), which generations of workers have hollowed out to bring to the villages the most precious liquid of all — not oil, but water. When we arrived at Qom we found the streets packed with people jammed with cars and buses. A kind policeman on a motorcycle came to our assistance and conducted us to a parking spot on a bridge in the centre of the town. It was the end of Ramadan and pilgrims had come in their thousands to Qom, the second most holy city of Iran, to celebrate the Festival of Id. Ramadan is one of the great Muslim Festivals when the faithful fast from sunrise to sunset. The end of the month of fasting is marked by the Festival of Id, when there is general public merry-making. The saints of the Shiite Muslims are the twelve Imams descended from Mohammed. The relatives of these Imams are also venerated, as we had seen at Shiraz when we visited the tomb of Imam Reza's brother. At Qom it is the tomb of Imam Reza's sister Fatima, which makes the tomb a place of pilgrimage. Floodlit above the town rose the golden cupola of the sanctuary with its slender minarets. The pilgrims were thronging towards the entrance to the shrine, where silver mirrors reflected the glow of thousands of lights within, but a notice in English forbade strangers to enter, so we dared not proceed any further. Jostled by the milling holiday crowd we wandered through the bazaar, admiring the intricate designs and dazzling colours of the silken rugs for which Qom is famous. These we resisted because of their astronomical price, but we found the delicious sweets which were on sale everywhere, irresistible. After midnight we managed to extricate our van from the line of parked cars and found a quieter spot for the night on the outskirts of the town. Even there it was far from peaceful and our sleep was disturbed by noisy bands of revellers returning from the festivities. It was a relief to be on the road again before dawn, heading for the capital city.

The Gol e Sahra camp site, eight miles south of Tehran was packed with cars, mobile homes, buses, trucks and tents of travellers from all over the world and we squeezed into a space in the dusty shrubbery next to a Land Rover. It belonged to three young Dutchmen, returning to Holland after a fourteen-month journey which had taken them through Africa to Mombasa and thence to India. The camp had an end-of-season look about it; the empty swimming pool was filling up with fallen leaves and there was a decided nip in the air. For the first time during our journey we donned our pullovers and plugged in our electric fire. However, there was plenty of hot water in the showers, the toilets were reasonably clean and the camp owner allowed us the use of his own washing machine, the last time we were to have such a facility for twelve months. As I hung out my washing, I caught a glimpse through the bushes of a black vehicle which looked remarkably like a hearse. It was a hearse! The occupants of this unusual home were a South American and his German wife, their small baby and two puppies. They had spent three years in India, hooked on Yoga and the free and easy lifestyle of Goa's beaches. Judging by their uninhibited mode of living and dressing and the clutter which surrounded them and the hearse, we surmised that it would be very difficult for them to settle down again in the West.

It was significant that most of the young British campers were travelling, not in private cars and motor homes, as did their counterparts from the Continent, but the inexpensive, hard way, crammed into buses and old army trucks. One such party of fifteen youngsters had been held up for a week in the camp, waiting for a new back axle to arrive by air. They were on their way to Kathmandu, sleeping in tents and cooking in the open air. Another group of thirteen people, including three children, were living in a converted bus. Having run out of money on their way to India, some of them had found temporary jobs as truck drivers to finance the next stage of their journey. One decidedly scruffy young man from this group, whom I discovered in the women's washroom, scrubbing his clothes, told me that he had found a job teaching English at the Iranian Air Force Base. That morning he had been sent back as his appearance and dress did not come up to the required standard. Parked at the end of the site was a large trailer which proclaimed itself as "Das Rollende Hotel". It was a German travelling hotel, housing over thirty people in tiny cubicles built into the side of the vehicle with just enough room for the passengers to slide into bed. This huge caravan was towed by a bus used for travelling and sightseeing. We met an English couple with a luxurious American mobile home which they were trying to sell in Tehran but they never found a buyer, partly because the mobile home is a comparatively new concept for Iranians, and partly because their Winnebago was an extremely expensive vehicle. The price of new foreign cars in Iran is exorbitant. Iranians working in Germany invariably return home with a smart Mercedes which they sell at double the purchase price. There were several foreign cars for sale at the camp and most of them were disposed of at a profit for the seller.

A maelstrom of traffic, surging in every direction, blocking the wide avenues, hooters sounding, taxis weaving in and out, stopping without warning, ignoring traffic lights and the police, that was our first impression of Tehran. In time we did discover some pleasant aspects of the city, but we never really warmed towards this soulless modern capital. From a commanding position beneath Mount Demavend (18,500 feet) which can at times be glimpsed through a heavy haze, Tehran sprawls southwards into the desert. On the northern side lies the pleasant residential area of Shemiran with gardens and clear mountain streams. After flowing in open gutters the whole length of the town, these streams end up in the poor quarter of the city as stagnant pools, where people wash themselves, their clothes and their vegetables. This busy squalid area, has a certain oriental charm, with its pavements piled high with oranges, pomegranates and vegetables, with its street vendors selling sweet potatoes dipped in syrup, braised sweet corn, kebabs and hot potatoes. Here and there, between the stalls are groups of skinny sheep and goats, bleating pitifully in anticipation of the fate awaiting them.

After much searching, we found a parking spot in a very appropriate place — Churchill Street, near the British Embassy. From this central position we were able to explore the centre of Tehran on foot or by the black and white 'collective' taxis which serve the main thoroughfare. Apart from the Gulestan Palace, there are few ancient buildings worth visiting in Tehran. Reza Shah, the father of the last Shah, demolished most of the old town to create the boulevards, squares and parks of the new capital. The Gulestan Palace is worth a visit because it contains the best along with the worst of Persian art. The lavish mirror mosaics at the entrance to the palace are gaudy and brash, but the splendour of the great sofa-shaped Peacock Throne is breathtaking. The Indians allege that this is the throne which was stolen from Delhi by Nadir Shah in the eighteenth century, but it is almost certain that this throne is of Persian not Indian origin. The whole surface is covered with intricate patterns formed of emeralds, sapphires and rubies which glisten under the lights of crystal chandeliers. The palace garden is pleasant and cool with its tiled pool and tall trees where flocks of green parrots have made their homes.

We went to see the Crown Jewels of Iran in the vaults of the Bank Markasi in Firdausi Avenue. There can be few countries in the world which can boast of such a magnificent collection of jewels. There are crowns, coronets and tiaras encrusted with pearls, diamonds and rubies, hundred of necklaces and earrings, golden egg cups studded with pearls, snuff boxes encased in turquoise and emeralds, rubies as large as pigeons' eggs, and a diamond one and a half inches long, which is one of the largest in the world. There is also another Peacock Throne almost as splendid as the one in the Gulestan Palace, said to be a copy of the famous Indian original. On view, too, are the queen's coronation robes of green velvet, embroidered with pearls and sapphires.

The journey back to camp was so slow and dusty that we vowed that we would rather live in the streets of Tehran than make the return trip again. We wavered in our decision when we realised that we would miss the facilities which we had enjoyed in the camp, the hot showers, the use of toilets and electricity and the companionship of other travellers. However, when we found the camp site full of TIR trucks whose transistors blared forth loud music all day and well into the night, our minds were made up. For the following week our address would be Churchill Street.

Before we left the camp we had one important task to perform, one which we were to repeat every two months for the rest of our journey. We called it 'Operation Marmalade'. We found foreign bread and rusks quite unpalatable without the addition of our favourite breakfast jelly. With the permission of the camp manager we had the use of a stove and a large pot; sugar and oranges were plentiful and cheap. Surrounded by curious staff and fellow travellers we boiled and set the golden liquid, producing pot upon pot of tasty marmalade. The next phase of 'Operation Marmalade', took place in Bombay, where we commandeered a relative's kitchen. With all the neighbours watching we carried out our ritual and started, I was told, a local craze for marmalade. Other marmalade boilings were to follow. We did one in the kitchen of Gandhi's ashram near Nagpur where oranges grow in abundance. Another took place on an open fire in Nepal within sight of Annapurna and we did one on a friend's stove in the hotel compound at Palgam in Kashmir. The chef insisted on having my recipe!

Back in Tehran, we sought an interview with the Chief Secretary of the Zoroastrian Society to find out more about that mysterious prophet, Zoroaster, who is also known as Zarathustra. Zoroaster is thought to have been born in Balkh, now a town in Afghanistan, in the sixth or seventh century BC. Little is known of his life and he is said to have been killed while praying in the fire temple at Nalkh. There is no doubt, however, that he was a great preacher and innovator. At a time when people everywhere believed in the existence of a number of deities, Zoroaster preached the existence of one God, the creator of the universe. Six hundred years before Christ, he transformed the chief sun god into Ahura-Mazda, the Eternal Spirit of Light. His ideas are contained in the Hathas, the sacred book of "Good thoughts, good words, good deeds". He stressed that everyone had the freedom of choice between the good path, that of Ahura-Mazda, and the wrong path, that of Ahriman, the spirit of evil.

In answer to our query about the Towers of Silence, the Chief Secretary explained that the branch of Indo-Europeans from which the Persians are descended, is believed to have come originally from the steppes north of the Caspian Sea. As the ground there was frozen for most of the year, the dead were not buried but left on the ice where they were devoured by birds of prey. Some months later in Bombay when we looked up reference books on this subject, we found a different explanation for this strange and gruesome practice. In the Zoroastrian code of ethics it was a sin to defile any of the elements, so the dead could not be cremated, immersed in water or buried under the earth. By enclosing the dead in the Towers of Silence where they are devoured by vultures, no elements are defiled and in addition the Zoroastrians performed their final act of charity by feeding the birds.

Zoroastrianism was not the only religion which interested us in Tehran. Kerry was keen to find out more about the Bahai faith which originated in Persia a century ago. The owner of the camp was a member of the sect and he introduced us to some of its leading exponents. The original founder, a Muslim, called the 'Bab', which means the 'Gate', was put to death because he proclaimed that Mohammed was only one of many prophets and that divine revelation continues from age to age. Bahais believe that their faith incorporates the best in all religions and it welcomes people of all creeds and races. We attended two meetings in private houses and came away very impressed and heartened by the possibility of one religion being embraced by everyone.

Shopping in Tehran was no problem as the city is well provided with large supermarkets stocked with the goods to which we are accustomed in the West — Swiss and French cheeses, German salami, English biscuits, etc. We purchased as much as our store cupboard could hold, including more than a dozen packets of Iranian rusks which were much more appetising than their 'nan'. Our breakfast time in Churchill Street corresponded with the Tehran rush hour, and we calmly ate our rusks and marmalade and drank our coffee as we watched the mad scramble for parking places around us. The restaurants in Tehran serve a much greater variety of food than elsewhere in Iran and at a more reasonable price. For as little as £2 each we had some excellent meals. We avoided Chelo Kebab Restaurants as we had had our fill of kebabs and rice, but we found plenty of modest restaurants, serving inexpensive Italian, Chinese or Indian dishes. We had only one extravagant meal at Leon's Russian Restaurant, where we sampled 'Kiev chicken' — rolled chicken breasts filled with butter, caviar and vodka.

What we missed most when we were living in the streets of Tehran was the facility to have a hot shower. We could have had a cold shower in the caravan, but the disposal of waste water was a problem in a busy thoroughfare. Besides, in the third week of October it was becoming too chilly to wash in cold water. We did discover a number of Turkish Baths (Hammam) which are very popular in Iran and are claimed as a Persian invention, but there were different hours of attendance for men and women. At last we found the Public Baths we were looking for in an imposing building with a façade of coloured tiles. The white-coated attendant showed us the sumptuous washrooms, all of which had two compartments, one a dressing room with a massage bench and hair dryer, the other with a bath and a shower. It was just what we wanted, with an abundance of hot water and spotlessly clean, but we did not know what was in store for us when we hurried back with our soap and towels and enquired if we could share a cubicle. "Yes," said the attendant. How were we to know that this was the only English word he knew! What happened afterwards was sheer pantomime.

I was under the shower and Kerry was undressing in the ante-room when suddenly all hell was let loose. Bells in the corridor started ringing, followed by loud shouts and a continuous banging at our door. I reached for my towel and clothes, thinking that it was a fire alarm, whilst Kerry in his underpants opened the door. Outside was a bevy of white-coated attendants screaming unintelligibly and obviously very angry. Someone took hold of Kerry and tried to pull him outside. He resisted vigorously and I began to dress to go to his assistance. It was some minutes before we realised what the commotion was about. In the eyes of the Muslims it is a heinous crime for a man and a woman to share a cubicle, and we had committed that crime. The furore subsided when Kerry departed to another cubicle with as much dignity as he could master, whilst I finished my toilet, feeling somewhat shaken by the extraordinary stir we had created.

The first lap of the six-hundred mile journey from Tehran to Mashhad took us northward over the Elburz Mountains to the Caspian Sea. It is a busy, modern road with numerous tunnels, hairpin bends and spectacular views. About sixty miles north of the capital, we caught a glimpse of the snow-covered Mount Damavend, and in the creases of the mountains, amidst autumn tinted poplars, we saw little villages with neat tin roofed houses. Near the coast, the mountains gave way to a wide plain with the first green grass we had seen since we left Austria, and a river flowing through swampy land towards the sea. North of Amol we made a detour along the Caspian Sea which looked dark and uninviting in the fading afternoon light.

Bordered with trees and well cultivated land, the road now ran due east, heading towards the mountains. Women were at work in the cotton fields with bright kerchiefs on their heads and their babies slung on their backs. It was pitch-dark long before we reached the Wildlife Park where we had hoped to spend the night. So we found a parking place in a walled compound near a petrol station.

Next morning before seven o'clock we were awakened by children's voices. Looking out we realised that we were stationed right in the middle of a school playground and judging by the expressions of amazement on the children's faces, we might well have been visitors from outer space. They scattered when we opened the door, and a rosy-cheeked woman, who appeared to be the teacher, came out of the wooden hut which was the school. In the Western world it would have been considered impertinent for strangers to park in school property, but it was obvious from her manner — unfortunately she spoke no English and we no Farsi — that she was delighted to have visitors. In Muslim countries, it is a duty to welcome strangers, and the 'misifir' (guest) is always received with due honour. She beckoned us into the school to have tea from her samovar, but we declined as gracefully as we could, wishing that we had brought more sweets to distribute to these bright-eyed youngsters. We were given a great send-off by the children, who climbed on to the school wall and waved until we were out of sight.

The rest of our journey to Mashhad was completed in a dust storm, with the wind whipping up the desert sand into gigantic whorls which careered across the plain before disintegrating. For mile after mile there was not a soul in sight, and the miserable mud villages looked desolate and abandoned in a treeless, arid waste. Then, suddenly, there were fields of sugar beet as far as the eye could see and groups of brightly dressed women loading the crop into trucks. For the next forty miles or so, we trundled behind a queue of lorries laden with beet bound for the sugar refinery. Every time we tried to overtake them we were prevented by a procession of empty trucks coming from the opposite direction. At one point on the road we were held up for an hour as two trucks had collided and the load of sugar beet was being shovelled off into the desert sand.

After crossing so many miles of desert, Mashhad appeared to be a mirage, an oasis in the desert and its avenues lined with golden poplars, its flowering parks and squares seemed to burgeon from the sandy waste which surrounds the town. As we stopped to consult our map under the trees, a car drew up alongside and two young men offered to assist us. We were touched by their solicitude, until we realised that their primary object in speaking to us was not to guide us to our camp site but to their carpet factory. On the days which followed we had endless offers of assistance from touts like these who were most insistent and sometimes quite unpleasant. On one occasion we were looking for a restaurant near the Kuh-Sangi Pool when a young man informed us that it was closed. He then accompanied us to an indifferent café owned by a friend of his and produced an English essay for us to correct while we were having our meal. Another young man offered to show us where we could take photographs of the sacred shrine. We drove around with him for an hour before we realised that we were being taken for a ride, as his only object was to entice us into a jeweller's shop belonging to a relative. On exchanging notes with other travellers we found that all of them had had similar experiences. Some had accepted invitations from friendly Iranians to dine with them, and then were badgered to buy carpets or turquoise rings. In the end, we suspected everyone who said "Can I help you?" which was a pity, as we did meet one or two genuine people in Mashhad who helped us without calculating their own advantage.

As we drove into the camp site on the edge of the town, two little figures came running toward us shouting "Patapouffe!" It was Patrick and Véronique, whom we had not expected to meet again. The journey across the desert to Mashhad had been a very arduous one and they had had to spend two nights in the middle of nowhere when the axle broke on Albert's car. It had been bitterly cold during the night in the desert where a sandstorm had added to their discomfort. We heard every detail of their exciting journey before we even looked round the camp site, but when we did we were agreeably impressed. Set amongst green lawns and flowering shrubs, this camp site was one of the best we visited. Unfortunately it was desperately overcrowded with several busloads of travellers who were housed in tents on the lawns and about twenty mobile homes and several Land Rovers. Looking around we saw a number of people whom we had met previously in Tehran and Isfahan, sunbathing on the grass or repairing their vehicles. It was as warm as in the height of an English summer, but the camp pool had already been emptied and we could not persuade the manager to fill it up again. However, there was plenty of cold and hot water on tap for washing-up. Until one has had the experience of washing dishes in a small saucepan of water with which one has also to wash clothes and the caravan floor, one cannot fully appreciate to the full the delight of clear running water.

In the East, any water which flows from a tap or a spring is a bonus to be collected whenever it is spied. When we saw a waterspout or clear running stream, we would stop the car, fill our water tanks by pail or hose pipe and wash ourselves and our dishes. Rarely, however, did we have this bonus all to ourselves; it had to be shared with others, usually Sikh truck drivers washing their hair and their turbans, and a motley band of sadhus (wandering monks) scrubbing themselves and their clothes. As we had decided when we left Europe never to drink untreated water, we had to resist the temptation of cupping our hands to drink from mountain streams. We filtered every drop of drinking water through our little Safari filter which did yeoman service and probably saved us from a multitude of ills.

The shops near the camp site offered the usual unappetising fare — tasteless white cheese, dry salami, rusks, yoghurt and rather wizened vegetables. However, a little further afield we discovered some delicious melons and pomegranates which were still very cheap and plentiful. When we returned to the camp we found our Belgian friends engaged in a heated argument with the manager about the security of the site. Françoise, who had been keeping guard near the washing line, as there had been several thefts from campers, looked up from the book she was reading to see a youth disappearing over the fence with her best pair of jeans. Albert gave chase but the thief had disappeared. I rushed to see if any of my laundry was missing but our baggy trousers and old fashioned shirts were still dangling on the line.

The people of Mashhad are extremely interested in Western fashions, probably because their own clothes are of poor material and style and on numerous occasions we were stopped in the street and asked if we had any garments for sale. The camp manager's wife came to the caravan and offered a good price for any dress or cardigan we wished to dispose of. We had brought very few clothes with us as we intended to have new ones made in India but I nearly lost my one and only corduroy jacket to a keen street trader. I was carrying it over my arm in the bazaar area of Mashhad when a youth snatched it from me and offered to buy it. I would have made a handsome profit, but I needed the jacket. There was another nasty and vicious habit practised by groups of teenage boys on the outlook for foreign women. They bump into them on the pavement or road as if by accident. It happened to me too often to be by chance. I had to restrain Kerry on several occasions when this occurred.

All the main avenues of Mashhad converge on the shrine of Imam Reza which dominates the town and makes it the most holy place in Iran. Mashhad means the place of the martyr and it was here that Ali Reza died, poisoned, they say, by his own son and successor. Of all the twelve Imams, Reza is the most deeply venerated by the Shiite sect of Muslims and thousands of pilgrims flock each year to his tomb beneath its gilded copper dome. As in the case of Qom, where Reza's sister, Fatima, is buried, non-Muslims are strictly forbidden to enter the sacred enclosure.

When we approached the sanctuary, the surrounding streets were thronged with pilgrims jostling their way towards the entrance. Mashhad was gay with flags and coloured lights, for it was the 26th October, the Shah's birthday and the whole nation was on holiday. What better way to celebrate, than to visit the holy shrine and to buy souvenirs from the shops near the mausoleum. In an endless stream of buses, the pilgrims poured in from the countryside — tall, turbaned peasants, stocky herdsmen with Mongolian features and Iranian men in Western attire with prayer beads round their necks. There were comparatively few women in the crowd and they were closely enveloped in their dark chadris. Squatting on the pavements with their red petticoats trailing in the gutter were bright-eyed gypsies selling rugs and embroidered caps. Stalls where grey and black prayer beads were for sale were doing a roaring trade, as most pilgrims bring these back as souvenirs, together with clay tiles on which to rest their forehead when they pray. Not for them the turquoise rings and bracelets and the inlaid coffee tables sought after by foreigners; they are content with plastic bangles and tin cooking pots. In the tiny restaurants in the back streets, kebabs and sheeps' heads seemed to be the favourite snack, washed down with gallons of tea from giant samovars. Less affluent pilgrims could only afford threepenny worth of salted melon seeds or a sweet potato cooked in syrup on a pavement brazier.

Tiring of the milling crowds, we set off for Tus, some fifteen miles away, which was the capital of Khorasan before it was destroyed by the son of Tamerlane. But it has another claim to fame, for it was here in the tenth century that one of Persia's best known writers was born — Firduasi, whose 'Book of Kings' is the best known epic poem of the East. His white mausoleum stands in a pleasant garden full of fountains and flowers. We were sitting on the marble steps reading one of Firdausi's stories aloud in English when a youngish man approached us. In fluent English he explained that he was a teacher in a small country town where there were few opportunities of meeting people from abroad. He invited us to have tea with his wife and himself in the car park. His wife, a vivacious dark-eyed woman, who unfortunately did not speak English, was sitting on a rug beside their car while a servant was preparing tea in a samovar. For an hour or two we sat cross-legged on cushions conversing with the husband, sipping tea and eating water melon.

Speaking about Trade Unions, he told us what we had already heard several times that they are not effective in Iran and that there are no unions for school teachers. To bring his wife into the conversation, I asked her for the recipe for 'Fasenjan', a well-known Iranian delicacy. With her husband as an interpreter, I wrote down the instructions:– cook the chicken and add to it a handful of crushed walnuts and a cupful of pomegranate juice. Continue cooking for a further ten minutes before serving. It is not often in a lifetime that one has a superfluity of walnuts and pomegranates, but we happened to have just that. So the following day we purchased a chicken and tried out the recipe. It was delicious!

Once again we said goodbye to our Belgian friends who set off for Afghanistan three days ahead of us. Everyday more travellers were arriving at the camp site with the result that the litter bins were overflowing. So too, was a waste pipe in the women's washrooms where water was ankle deep and it did not seem to be anyone's job to clear up the mess. The problem of the lack of maintenance in public and private buildings was one with which we were to become more and more familiar as we proceeded eastwards. The number of campers was further increased when a large party of young people, who had set out the previous day to Kerman by the desert route, had to return because of a faulty gearbox. They had to wait for several days until a replacement was sent by air from London. The party organiser was extremely worried as he feared that they might encounter wintry weather on their way through Europe in November. It was a cold prospect for a party which was sleeping in tents.

Early one morning, a young man with a crew cut hairstyle arrived at the camp in a taxi. As it was rather unusual to see someone on the site dressed in a lounge suit and carrying a suitcase, we followed his movements with interest. When he had arranged for accommodation in one of the tents, he sat down at one of the wooden tables where campers were having breakfast. Within a few minutes he was the centre of attraction, and we could see that he was enjoying the attention of his audience. We heard his story some hours later when he retold it for the umpteenth time. He had just completed a twenty-two month jail sentence for smuggling hashish into Iran.

"I had to bring the stuff from Afghanistan and leave it at a shop in Paris. Then I collected £5,000 from a chap in a café," he explained in a Midlands accent. "Getting out of Afghanistan is easy enough, but Iran has put the screw on."

He had made several successful journeys in his ramshackle car before being caught, but he had some money salted away in Switzerland. Apparently he had been well treated in prison, although food had not been too plentiful and he had lived a life of idleness, hatching up new schemes to foil the customs.

Later that day he was joined by two of his associates who had been in jail for the same offence and at once the three of them began to discuss quite openly their plans to resume smuggling. "There is plenty of cash in hash," they told us.

We went to Nishapur, not to see the turquoise mines for which the town is renowned, but to visit the tomb of one of our favourite poets — Omar Khayyám. An eighty mile stretch of desert separates Mashhad from Nishapur and there is little to see on the way except the skeletons of deserted mud villages and lone travellers on donkeys. As we had already noted, Iranians excel in the building of mausoleums and Omar's tomb was no exception. The white dome soars into the sky and through the fretted stonework the morning light and the moon, so beloved by the poet, shine on his last resting place. We wandered in the gardens amidst scented roses and carnations and visited the little museum where the portrait of Fitzgerald, who translated Omar's poetry into English, has a place of honour on the wall. As a souvenir of our visit we had hoped to buy a clear blue turquoise ring in Nishapur but the stones and settings in the shops there, were inferior to those we had seen in the bazaar at Mashhad and much more expensive. It was not until our return a year later that I bought my ring. It had a pretty green turquoise stone veined with grey and cost about £6.00. The clear blue turquoise stones cost at least three times that amount.

Before we set out for Afghanistan, there was a good deal of work to be done on the van. The hinges on the cooker top had worked loose again and the sink outlet pipe, which was constantly blocked, had to be replaced by a wider tube. Then, rather foolishly, we followed the example of our fellow travellers who were feverishly purchasing rolls of wire netting to fix over their windscreens. This anti-stone device made driving so difficult that we jettisoned it in Afghanistan, and apart from a large stone thrown at us in Pakistan and another in India, we escaped without damage. Not everyone was as fortunate as we were. But most of the shattered windscreens we saw were in Eastern Turkey, not east of Mashhad. During our stay in Iran we had enjoyed the luxury of cheap petrol but we knew that expensive days lay ahead for us in Pakistan and India where the price was about £1.00 per gallon, about five times more than in Iran. We therefore, purchased four twenty-eight litre cans of petrol and hoisted them with our friends' help onto the roof of the van. We calculated that we were saving £14.00 by our foresight. In the final reckoning, however, we lost more than £250.00 by our penny-pinching — but more of that anon.

One of our most precious possessions was our transistor radio as it enabled us to tune into the BBC's excellent overseas programmes and thus keep in touch with events at home and elsewhere. Being avid newspaper readers, however, we did miss our dailies, more than we had ever imagined. That is why the library services of the British Council were a godsend. In Mashhad there was a splendid British Council Library with a helpful friendly staff, and we spent many happy hours browsing through old copies of the *Times*. In Kabul, Islamabad, Bombay, Bangalore and Kathmandu, time stood still.

Tombs of the Kings Nakshi Rustam — Iran

MASHHAD
USSR
HINDU KUSH
HERAT
KABUL
AFGHANISTAN
ISLAMABAD
PESHAWAR
AZAD
KASHMIR
RAWALPINDI
FAHROD
IRAN
KANDAHAR
AMRITSAR
LAHORE
PAKISTAN
ARABIAN
SEA
INDIA
BOMBAY

Chapter Four

AS FAR AS THE HINDU KUSH

Anticipating a long wait at the Afghan border, we left Mashhad at dawn, but in spite of an early start and a good tarmac road, it was noon before we reached the Iranian frontier due to a delay caused by a puncture. We were now very worried about the state of our tyres. We were given a speedy clearance at the customs which we had cause to recall a year later when our van was very thoroughly examined. At the first checkpoint in Afghanistan, which was the medical one, however, we were aghast to discover that our health cards were not in order. The bumptious doctor on duty pointed out that although our GP had signed our cards, he had omitted to affix an official stamp. He told us to have our van cleared at the customs and then return to him. Knowing that the Afghans take a very firm line on inoculations we began to be worried. Customs formalities were cursory and speedy, as no one seemed to be interested in goods brought into the country. On returning to the medical unit we were referred to the Immigration Department before the matter of our health cards was dealt with. When we came back, the doctor, now wearing a grubby white coat, informed us that we would have to be re-vaccinated for smallpox and cholera and remain in the customs area for a further twenty-four hours. Kerry remonstrated angrily. "We have had our inoculations. We got them for our own benefit not for yours." But the doctor was adamant and he refused to give us either our cards or our passports. We sat disconsolately for some time in the dusty surgery where there was no water supply and no means of sterilizing medical instruments, wondering what to do next. Meanwhile, streams of travellers came and went and the sun dropped lower on the horizon. We remembered the dire warnings on the embassy wall in Tehran about the danger of night travel in Afghanistan where several British tourists have been murdered in recent years. Finally, in exasperation, Kerry requested the use of a telephone. "I am going to complain about your treatment" he said, "to a friend of mine in the Afghan Army, Colonel Quadir." Kerry told me later that he had made up the name and had almost said Colonel Gadaffi. His request was refused. So he made for the door "All right, I shall ring from the Police Headquarters."

"Come back," called the doctor hastily, throwing our cards and passports across the table. And that was the end of that little episode, except for the finale which took place later in Kabul.

There was no bank in the custom's area where we could exchange traveller's cheques into Afghan currency which we required to pay the road tolls between the frontier and Herat. However, there were plenty of touts willing to give us a very low rate for sterling, indeed for any foreign currency. It was when we were negotiating with these desperadoes that we met a charming young Pakistani couple, Jalil and Ghazala, returning from a holiday in England. Jalil advised us to change our money in Herat and offered us 200 Afghanis (about £20.00) to help us out of our temporary difficulties. This generous gesture was the beginning of a friendship which was to blossom when we visited Rawalpindi several weeks later.

It was nearly five o'clock when we left the frontier with seventy miles ahead of us, but the road was good and there was little traffic, so we were able to speed along, only to be delayed at the first toll barrier. Our vehicle, said the official, was not a 'car' but a 'bus' as it had four wheels at the rear. The road tax was therefore fifty Afgs, not twenty as we had anticipated. An argument ensued in the course of which we managed to persuade him that our van was a car, and now we had a receipt to prove it at the many other toll barriers in Afghanistan.

Darkness had already fallen and we had the flat road across the plain entirely to ourselves. We had already forgotten our fears of night-travel as the countryside around us looked peaceful and empty. Still, it was with some relief that we saw the lights of Herat ahead and pulled into the compound of the Park Hotel. Inside this rambling, old-fashioned hotel, which does not boast of a restaurant, a party of young New Zealanders and Australians were preparing a meal on Primus stoves. They were travelling home via Nepal with Hughes Overland Tours and we had already met some of the party at Mashhad. "Come and join us for dinner," was their greeting, when they saw us arrive. The invitation was only too welcome, as we had scarcely had a bite the whole day. Seated on packing cases we were treated to a tasty Western-style meal of mince, beans and cabbages, melon and coffee which may not seem particularly exciting, but was for us at that moment a veritable banquet. We also made the acquaintance of some of the friendliest travellers we had encountered and we exchanged tales until well after midnight.

Next to us in the hotel compound was a rather battered Volkswagen occupied by two long-haired Danish youths who told us of their plans to reach Mazar-i-Sharif by the desert route. They had already attempted the journey but had to turn back for repairs and for a permit which is required by foreigners. When we talked to them we sensed that they were not typical tourists, eager to see new places and faces and, as we had heard that Mazar-i-Sharif has the best hashish market in Asia, we could not help speculating on the purpose of their journey. Perhaps we did them an injustice.

We had planned to have a quick look around Herat, then set out for Kandahar by noon, but we had not reckoned with the town's banking system. It took us over two hours to get our traveller's cheques changed or rather short-changed, whether by accident or design, we do not know. Significantly, several members of the Hughes party had the same experience. We did discover as we proceeded through Afghanistan that, although the natives were courteous and friendly, they were not particularly honest. On more than one occasion at a petrol station the attendant obstructed our view of the dial in order to cheat us. We had also to bargain obstinately for every article we purchased and check our change very carefully.

You can stroll along the middle of the Shar-i-nau, the main street of Herat, without worrying about traffic, as there are very few cars and lorries about. For twenty to thirty Afgs you can hire a pony trap gaily decorated with coloured pompoms, ribbons and bells, to visit the bazaar and the Friday Mosque. There was plenty of good quality fruit and vegetables in the market, the grapes being especially delicious. The shops were full of leather goods, bags, sandals, jackets, etc., solidly if inelegantly made, and the usual cheap imitations of the jewellery worn by the nomads.

Much more interesting than the goods on display, were the people we saw in the streets. Afghan men with their flamboyant turbans and proud demeanour are splendid specimens of humanity, besides whom, their women, hidden behind drab chadris and tight fitting veils pale into insignificance. As they peer through the close lattice work which covers their faces, their view of the world must be as distorted as that of a horse with blinkers. It is a pity that they are not allowed to wear the 'yashmak' the half veil used by the women of more advanced Muslim countries. A water seller with the countenance of a biblical patriarch offered us a drink from his goatskin, and a bright little lad of about thirteen years of age pestered us to buy a live cock. Although this boy had never been to school, he had a remarkable command of English which he had picked up while doing odd jobs in hotels. It was when we were talking to this lad through the open window of the van that another urchin snatched the car keys and ran off with them. Kerry gave chase and the boy threw the keys into a bush. This game of snatch and run is apparently the method employed by the children to obtain 'buckshee' as the losers have to pay to retrieve their goods. Hitherto in our journey we had not encountered many beggars, but from Afghanistan eastwards the cry of 'buckshee!' was to grow louder and more insistent.

The Friday Mosque is the pride of Herat and it has a very imposing façade. In comparison with the mosques in Iran, however, we found it somewhat lacking in character and colour. I now realise that we did not fully appreciate the almost classical beauty and muted colours of this mosque because we were still under the spell of the glowing domes of Isfahan.

Following a dusty little road at the end of the town, we went in search of the windmills and minarets, which are distinctive features of Afganistan. We did not find any windmills but we discovered several ancient minarets. In most parts of the East, minarets are found only in conjunction with mosques; however, in Afganistan they often stand alone or in groups as in Herat. In spite of their peeling faience and general dilapidation, the minarets were quite impressive and we took out our photographic equipment to take some pictures. However, we were so harassed by a band of gypsy children who became very unpleasant when we refused to give them money, that we beat a hasty retreat and returned to the town.

The three hundred miles from Herat to Kandahar is an easy, if bumpy ride on a new cement road built and paid for by the Russians. This must be one of the most stark and barren landscapes of the world with ranges of mountains, ridged like the backs of prehistoric monsters, converging from time to time, then gradually sloping away towards the rim of the horizon. For mile after mile there are vast areas of sand where nothing grows, interspersed with patches of scrubland where herds of camels and shaggy goats are feeding. Ranging in colour from charcoal grey to pale cream, the camels with their statuesque poses reminded me of flamingos. Thin trails of smoke rose from the nomads' tents which were stuck to the desert floor like black limpets. Sheep, donkeys and camels were grazing nearby, and sitting around their cooking pots were the nomad women in their red full-skirted dresses. Most of the Afghan villagers live in mud fortresses with very high walls and when these begin to crumble the inhabitants make a new village a few miles away leaving their old dwellings to the mercy of the elements. On our way through Afghanistan we passed many gaunt, abandoned fortresses with gaping holes in the walls through which one could see the shells of houses and mosques. We broke our journey to Farah Rod, where a sign pointed the way to a modern hotel with a swimming pool. As it was very warm, the prospect of a refreshing swim and a cool drink was very welcome. The hotel which is one of a number built in Afghanistan by the Russians, was dusty and deserted and when we found the swimming pool it was covered with a thick green slime. A few days before we had had a similar experience in Mashhad when we went in search of the swimming pool at Kuh-Sangi, only to find a large weedy pond with gleaming aluminium ladders leading into its murky depths. It is not really surprising, however, that swimming pools are a rare luxury in a part of the world where oil is probably more plentiful than water.

Beyond Farah Rod, in the middle of a bleak plain, a group of men were gathered near the cluster of jagged stones which denote a Muslim cemetery. No polished headstones with inscriptions mark the graves of the departed; their only memorials are the pointed slivers of rock inserted beside their remains and a few tattered flags fluttering above the barren hillside. There seems to be little sentimentality connected with death in Muslim countries probably because of the element of fatalism in the religion of Islam and as a result, their cemeteries are usually overgrown and untended.

Most of the way to Kandahar we had the road all to ourselves, apart from a few gaily painted lorries bulging with goods and people. Passengers who could not find space to sit inside squatted on the roof or clung to the ladder at the rear. At the roadside, children would suddenly appear clutching in their hands eggs or branches of a silvery shrub which they were offering for sale. We did not stop to investigate as we had found Afghan children unpleasantly forward and persistent. Washing their clothes in puddles by the roadside were groups of nomad women who stared at us quite boldly but refused to be photographed. In a village near Kandahar, as the sun was setting, we saw about twenty men kneeling together in prayer with their faces towards Mecca. Afghan Muslims carry out their religious duties very meticulously, reciting their prayers five times daily, at the appointed hour, no matter where they are or what they are doing. They remove their shoes, spread out a clean cloth on the ground and prostrate themselves upon it. Religion in Afghanistan is the province of the male, as women do not enter mosques and are supposed to say their prayers in the privacy of their own houses. The majority of Afghans belong to the Sunni (i.e. orthodox) Muslim sect, as distinct from their neighbours in Iran and Pakistan who are mostly Shiites.

Kandahar's long avenues of trees are cool and welcoming and several of its hotels offer facilities for campers. We found one with a large garden, a clean swimming pool, showers and electricity for forty Afgs (£4.00) per night. Alexander the Great is said to have passed this way and left behind his name as a legacy to the town. Alexander is Iskandar in Persian, hence Kandahar. The town has had a historic past, standing as it does at an important crossroad through Asia, but there is little of real interest now for tourists, apart from the people and the bazaar. We hired a brightly painted bubble car to take us to the market where the stalls were heaped with vegetables and fruit. This is the most fertile region of Afghanistan and the town is surrounded by orchards and vineyards. In tiny booths, sitting cross-legged on raised platforms, men were drinking tea from large copper samovars. You could buy a plateful of sweet semolina from the street stalls if you did not mind the attendant flies. There were many Indian shops which sold cloth and a great variety of international goods like cigarettes, toilet paper, soap, Nescafé, motor oil, shaving blades. Afghan shops contained a jumble of rather tawdry antiques, crude leather work and dusty old jewellery but we were delighted to discover an excellent bakery, selling Western-style bread, apple turnovers and biscuits. The owner told us with some pride that he had learned his trade in a large hotel at Kabul which caters for American tourists. We noticed a number of beggars, mainly gypsy women and many people with eye diseases and other deformities, which are probably the result of the insanitary conditions in which the majority of Afghans live.

At the top of the 9,000 foot Ghazni Pass about eighty miles south of Kabul we caught our first glimpse of the Hindu Kush Mountains far away on the northern horizon. We felt elated at the sight, for the very name of "Hindu Kush" has magic in it and it was one of the objects of our journey to explore the secret valleys of this great range of mountains. Although we had left Kandahar at dawn, we had been delayed for several hours on the way by a deformed tyre. It was the third time that one of our tubeless tyres had developed a large bump on one side, and we were at a loss to know what was causing the trouble. An Afghan boy offered to assist Kerry to change the tyre, then made a dreadful fuss when his tip was less than he expected. We had another altercation at a lonely petrol station where the attendant asked Kerry to put the petrol nozzle in our tank in order to distract his attention from the dial which registered ten litres from a previous sale. Fortunately, I had my eyes glued on the figures, as we had been duped before and I screamed out in protest. This time, instead of losing, we actually gained a few litres.

For a capital city, Kabul is at first sight a rather disappointing untidy-looking town, sprawling inelegantly on the mountain side. We were not impressed as we picked our way over the holes in the pavements and straddled the wide open gutters filled with stagnant water. Yet, in a few days we had become quite attached to Kabul and its people, perhaps because of their very lack of pretensions and their refusal to pretty themselves up to impress outsiders. Rickety market stalls line the river bank where a slimy trickle of water makes its way through piles of onion skins and rotting vegetables. We saw small boys struggling through the mud to fetch buckets of filthy water to pour over the piles of fruit and vegetables. In one large puddle a group of men were washing their feet, prior to saying their prayers on the river bank.

In the main bazaar we jostled our way past bales of cloth, second-hand clothes, plastic buckets, baskets full of small birds and piles of aromatic spices. Squatting in the gutter, a small boy was having oil rubbed into his hair and an old man was having a shave. On the pavements, crouching in front of their hubble-bubble pipes, pathetic looking creatures, some of them Western hippies, were smoking hashish for a few Afghanis a puff. Hashish is offered for sale quite openly in Afghanistan and we could have bought kilos of the stuff in Kabul. On a rough wooden table in a side street, a youth with a mincing machine was making large quantities of mince which attracted all the bluebottles of the area. We had been looking for meat for our evening meal but we had no stomach for fly-blown mince. However, in the residential neighbourhood of Shar-i-nao where we had parked in the compound of a hotel we found a number of excellent supermarkets stocked with a great variety of Western food. Although most of the goods were expensive — tinned milk, coffee, chocolates, etc.; the meat, mainly frozen veal and chicken, was reasonable in price. There was also an abundance of good fruit and vegetables, and the bakers sold French bread, rolls, pastries and cakes. In fact, during the time we spent in Kabul we dined very well indeed, both in our caravan and on the few occasions we visited a restaurant.

We had another joyful meeting with our Belgian friends who had reached Kabul several days before us. We found Patrick and Véronique playing in their swimsuits under a water tap in the pleasant garden of the Hotel Gulzar. "You must see our new clothes," they shouted, as they ran off to fetch their embroidered sheepskin jackets and astrakhan hats. Then we had a detailed account of their adventure since we parted at Mashhad. It was like a family reunion.

It was the 1st November but the sun at noon was as warm as on a summer's day at home. By six o'clock, however, as darkness closed in, a chilling mist settled over the garden and we quickly exchanged our bikinis for trousers and pullovers. We were more fortunate than most campers as our electric cable gave us not only light but warmth, as we had brought a small fan heater with us. In spite of this, we both developed heavy head colds which would not respond to hot lemon and aspirins. It was for this reason and also to obtain an official stamp on our health card that we made the acquaintance of Dr Babur, to whom we had been recommended by the British Embassy. We had asked for an English-speaking doctor, but we were astounded by Dr Babur's remarkable command of our language.

Discerning a Scottish lilt in his diction, I asked, "How long were you in Scotland?"

"I was a medical student at Edinburgh University for seven years; one of the happiest periods of my life."

As he was quite elderly, probably seventy years old, I made a quick calculation and asked him, "Then you must have known an uncle of mine, Professor Brash, who was in charge of the Pathology Department."

Surprise and delight showed on his face. "Indeed I did and I believe that I was one of his favourite students. Look!" and he went to his bookshelf and took out a well-thumbed book which my uncle had written and showed us the inscription on the flyleaf. *"To my most diligent student, Akbar Mohammed Babur, signed James Brash."*

We had a long chat with this interesting man who had been a royal physician until the last Afghan monarch was deposed in 1973. When we parted he had signed our health cards without demur and prescribed a course of vitamins and tetramycin for our colds.

Not far from the centre of Kabul is a great stadium where in wintertime you can see the exciting game of buzkashi. We followed the crowds of men, there were no women apart from some Westerners, through the gates, only to find that tourists were required to pay for their tickets in dollars. However, after the usual heated argument which seemed to be a necessary preliminary of many transactions in Afghanistan, we were allowed to pay in Afghan money. Then, more by accident than design, we found ourselves in the VIP section of the stadium. A shabbily-dressed Afghan in a moth-eaten astrakhan cap and frayed suit moved over politely to give us seats and spoke to us in halting English. We were surprised and embarrassed to discover that he was the President of Buzkashi, the most important man in the stadium. We had had the temerity to sit amongst the officials who were presiding over the game, but everyone had been too well-mannered to direct us elsewhere.

Two teams of wild-looking horsemen, who could well have been part of Ghengis Khan's army, were lined up in front of us in the arena, waiting for the president's signal to begin the contest. "Buzkashi" means, "snatching the goat", said the president, who went on to explain the origins of the game to us. It is thought to have begun in far-off days when bands of thieves descended on the sheepfolds and rode off with some of the animals. The shepherds gave chase and the game was on. The 'boz', a dead goat or calf, with its head and feet cut off, lay in the middle of the stadium. When the sign was given, the riders dashed forward shouting, lashing their steeds and raising great clouds of dust. From this melee, one horseman emerged with the boz dangling from his horse's neck. Another with his whip between his teeth, following in hot pursuit, snatched it away, and the cavalcade thundered off in the opposite direction. The game was so fast and furious that it was difficult to follow the progress of the boz. Sometimes a rider was unseated in the struggle, and it seemed inevitable that he would fall under his horse's hooves. But every time this happened, the horseman, with almost superhuman strength and agility, regained the saddle and re-entered the fray. When the game came to a halt, the president explained to us that the referees were exacting a penalty for an infringement of the rules, but the delay did not last for more than a few seconds. Off they galloped again, yelling themselves hoarse, swerving, rearing and turning at an incredible speed. We shall never know which rider kissed the president's hand and received the coveted prize or which team scored most points, for chilled to the bone with sitting for hours on the cold cement steps of the grandstand, we slipped out before the end of the contest. We came away, however, with the greatest admiration for the daring and skill of these doughty riders and their powerful steeds.

Our Belgian friends and especially Patrick and Véronique, loved the Chicken Street Market in Shar-i-nao, and we used to go there together to look for bargains. The Chicken Street shops had the best buys in fur jackets and astrakhan hats, embroidered waistcoats and dresses. I bought two beautifully embroidered blouses for myself at a reasonable price. Unfortunately, they lost most of their colour in their first wash. It is a pity that so much time and skill are expended on poor materials. On our return journey we bought fur-lined jackets as gifts for children but these garments too, were poorly finished. There were lots of dusty, little shops filled with a huggermugger of antiques, old firearms, samovars and semi-precious stones. Western tourists were paying high prices for tribal jewellery discarded by the nomad women.

On our return journey we bought several pieces of lapis lazuli and agate, and a gold(?) ring offered to us for £20.00 which we purchased for £1.00. One of our fellow campers en route for New Zealand, whom we met again later in Nepal, bought an ancient firelock in Kabul. As firearms cannot be brought into Nepal he had to leave it at the frontier and make a 500-mile detour to retrieve it after visiting Kathmandu. Another couple with an antique business in England took the precaution of visiting Kabul Museum with their purchases to obtain a certificate stating that they were not 'genuine antiques'. Otherwise, since antiques may not be exported, the customs would have confiscated these articles.

One of the objects of our journey was to visit the Valley of Bamian which lies 154 miles north-west of Kabul. We had hoped to travel there in our caravan, but were deterred by other travellers' tales of rough roads and steep gradients. "You will break your springs," they warned, or "be blown over in the Shibar Pass." These hazards, as we were to discover, were greatly exaggerated. Later in Nepal and Kashmir our Ford Transit was to tackle successfully much more arduous and dangerous journeys. However, we decided to play safe and hire a car.

So one dark and chilly November morning muffled up in coats and pullovers, we waited in the hotel compound at Kabul for our taxi to arrive. We had parted with fifty dollars for the round trip to Bamian and as we did not have a receipt, we suspected the worst. Shortly before 6 a.m. however, a smart-looking Afghan dressed in Western clothes appeared, grumbling because he had had to walk ten kilometres to fetch his vehicle. His face brightened when we offered him a cigarette. "Ah, English," he exclaimed, obviously pleased with the brand and perhaps also with the nationality of his two passengers, as he spoke English fluently. "My name is Sangal," he said, as we sped along the blacktop (asphalt) road which leads to the Salang Pass.

By the first streaks of dawn we discerned that the bundles by the roadside were not sacks of grain but sleeping travellers wrapped in scarves and frost-covered blankets. "These are road workers' tents," said Sangal, indicating the tents where men were brewing tea over smoky fires. Further on, he pointed to the low black tents on the hillside surrounded by vast herds of sheep and goats. They were the tents of the tribals who would soon be moving east to spend the winter in Pakistan.

Soon we left the blacktop road for a bumpy dirt track which led toward the heart of the mountains. In fact, we were travelling on one of the most ancient routes in the world; the silk road from China to the West. On this road two thousand years ago camel trains travelled from India and China bearing loads of silk and spices. Also along the same route Buddhism spread from India to the Valley of Bamian. Now, regardless of the potholes and the billowing dust, we were racing along at fifty miles an hour to see the giant Buddhas carved in that valley by these early travellers.

Most of the square mud houses we passed had glass in their gaily-painted window frames, but we did see a number of dwellings with no windows, only holes in the wall stuffed with straw to keep out the winter's cold. Heaped up on the flat roofs were bundles of brushwood and gorse for use as fuel, and bales of cattle fodder, representing many a weary journey by donkey or camel, or more likely by the peasant himself, as everyone we passed was bent double under a heavy load. The fields and compounds surrounding these houses were so clean and tidy that I was prompted to ask Sangal what people did with litter. "Litter?" he said, not understanding the word. "Paper and old tins" I said. "Paper is used in shops," and I recalled that the stalls always sold nuts and sweets, etc., in old newspapers, and "tins are used in building. Look," he pointed to the walls and doors of the houses made out of the flattened sides of petrol cans neatly nailed together. The little villages on our route were hidden behind the high crenellated mud walls of 'qualas', the equivalent of English manors of old. Nowadays, these walls offer shelter to the villagers and their herds of sheep and goats not so much from marauding bands as from the fierce summer sun and winter winds.

After three hours' driving, Sangal announced that he was hungry as he had not breakfasted. So we stopped at a tehaikhana (teahouse) in the shade of a giant walnut tree. The locals sat cross-legged on the rough wooden tables, but we were given chairs. Sangal ordered tea, 'naun' (flat bread) walnuts and dried mulberries. Dried berries and fruits are considered delicacies by the Afghans but we preferred the walnuts which were the finest we had ever tasted. Then on we went again at the same furious pace along a road which twisted its way by a shining river towards the towering mountains ahead.

In a field near the river, a woman with a jewel in her nose and silver chains dangling from her ears was weaving a long red carpet with the aid of pegs and strings fixed in the ground. "That's an Uzbek woman," said Sangal. Most of the Uzbek women seemed to be afraid of strangers. They hid their faces and ran away when they saw the car. We watched them from afar throwing corn into the air and catching the grain in a cloth as the wind carried the chaff away. Sangal managed to persuade three ragged barefooted Uzbek children to pose for a photograph. They stared glumly into the camera and even the sweets we gave them did not bring a glimmer of a smile to their truculent little faces. "Ask them if they go to school," we said.

Sangal's question seemed to be beyond their comprehension. "Few of the country children go to school, but most of the town children do," he replied. There is no compulsory education as we understand it, nor for that matter is education free.

I admired the little girl's silver necklace.

"It will be part of her wedding dowry," explained Sangal. "Every year a new piece will be added to the chain."

The child, imagining perhaps that we had designs upon her finery, looked alarmed and darted off up the hillside.

At the foot of the Shibar Pass we met a group of nomads returning from the uplands with a great train of camels and donkeys. The camels came swaying towards us in great clouds of dust with their loads of bedding and cooking pots crowned with small children and squawking fowls.

Behind them walked strapping men in turbans looking like Old Testament patriarchs and handsome women in faded full-skirted dresses. "They resemble the Quachais we saw in Iran."

"No, they are Kushis" said Sangal, "on their way to Pakistan."

The road climbed steeply over the 10,000 foot pass where icicles hung over the streams and a biting wind blew from the snow-covered Hindu Kush Mountains. Then we followed the course of the river down through wild and narrow gorges until we came to a valley full of golden poplars where women were gathering fallen leaves into baskets. These are Hazara women, who, unlike the majority of tall and swarthy Afghans, are stockily built, with yellow Mongolian features. It was in the thirteenth century that the Mongol hordes from the steppelands invaded the country, leaving behind them utter desolation and numerous offspring who have since peopled these remote valleys. The Afghans seem to despise these Hazaras, chiefly because their branch of religion is slightly different from their own, being Shiite Muslims whilst the Hazaras are Sunnis.

Eleven miles from Bamian we stopped at the Red City, perched on a massive rock which towers above the road. Once a great Muslim stronghold, it was sacked by the Mongols and all that remains are the crumbling ruins of its turrets and battlements. But disaster came to Bamian four hundred years before the Mongols arrived. Until then, sheltered by the mountains and defended by successive rulers it had been an oasis of peace and prosperity, as well as an important caravan stopping place on the great silk route. With the establishment of Buddhist monasteries, Bamian became a great spiritual and cultural centre. The two Great Buddhas which were shaped from the face of the cliff attracted pilgrims from near and far. Hsuan Tsang, a traveller from China, visited Bamian in AD632, and recorded that its Buddha images were 'glistening with jewels and gold'. Then, in AD871, when the Arabs overthrew the Sassanid Kings of Kabul, Buddhism had to give way to Islam. The Muslim conquerors devastated the valley, defaced the great images and stripped them of their treasure.

From the terrace of the Bamian Motel we had our first, unforgettable view of the Buddhas, standing in their niches in the sun-baked cliff. Even at half a mile distance they dominated the landscape making the peasants in the fields below look like tiny flies. An hour later we were scrambling up the path which leads to the greater Buddha. Resting on his feet we gazed up at his disfigured face, 175 feet above, merging with the shadowy frescoes of the vaulted niche. There were pockmarks on the stone where jewels and draperies had been fixed and his limbs were broken, but in spite of these mutilations he transmitted a feeling of serenity and peace. As we sat beneath him in the autumn sunshine, time seemed to stand still. The spell was rudely broken by a group of Japanese who prostrated themselves at the feet of the Buddha, not in prayer, I must hastily add, but to take his photograph from an unusual angle.

The smaller Buddha with its rounder proportions (it is called Sher Mama, the Queen, by the Afghans) has little spiritual appeal. However, there are some interesting fragments of Indian frescoes on the crumbling chapels and cells which have been burrowed into the cliffs like rabbit warrens. We noticed that diminutive stone Buddhas had had their eyes poked out by the Muslims in the belief that human images were idolatrous.

Sangal was waiting for us in the bazaar where we found him bargaining for a Western-style jacket. There were plenty of garments on the stall and as all were marked 'not for sale' we suspected that they were sent to Afghanistan as part of the Aid Programme from the West and had been appropriated by black marketeers. Sangal had already purchased a multicoloured woollen blanket which he said was for his fiancée. "But you told us you had a wife," I blurted out.

"Yes, I have been married for five years, but we had only one child who died, so I am allowed to take another wife."

We plied him with questions. "Is she pretty?"

"Yes, naturally. She is a very pretty Pakistani girl."

"Does she speak the same language?"

"Yes we both speak Pushto." Pushto is the official language of Afghanistan which is also spoken in some parts of Pakistan.

"Are you required to supply a dowry?"

"Of course, I am paying 50,000 Afghanis for her."

We learnt later that a dowry is not purchase price, as such, but money kept in trust by the girl's parents in case it is needed by their daughter should she be repudiated by her husband. I wanted to ask Sangal what his first wife thought of his impending marriage but I contained my curiosity. Besides, as there is little communication between husbands and wives in this part of the world, I suspect that Sangal hardly knew what was in his wife's mind.

As we drove to the ruins of the old citadel of Bamian, Sangal told me the story of the Mongol's last assault upon the fortress, then in the hands of a Muslim king. The siege had lasted several months and Genghis Khan had lost many soldiers, some drowned when they tried to walk on the hay which the townspeople had carefully placed on the moat. As Genghis Khan was on the point of giving up all hopes of capturing the fortress, a stroke of luck came from an unexpected source. The king's daughter, Lala, angered by her father's intention to remarry, revealed to the enemy the source of the citadel's water supply, high up in the mountains. When this was cut off the townsfolk were forced to surrender and all were put to death. "This place is known as Shar-i-gholgola" said Sangal. "The city of sighs. Some people say they hear the moans of the dying when the wind blows through the ruins." The citadel was razed to the ground, but the princess's castle was spared. We climbed the hill to see the ruins of its vaults, battlements and domes. The remains of a finely carved porch showed how sumptuous the palace had been.

"What happened to the princess?" we asked.

"Genghis Khan grew weary of her demands, and ordered his troops to stone her to death." Pointing to a great heap of stones in the valley, he added, "That is where she lies."

When we returned to the hotel in the evening we saw a GB Bedford van parked near the Yurt tents which accommodate summer visitors. The van looked familiar and so did its occupants; an English couple in our age bracket, whose company we had enjoyed in Tehran. "Fancy meeting you in the back of beyond," we chorused. Little did we know that our next meeting was going to be in an even more unusual place. "Where is your motor home?" And we had to confess that we had chickened out of the rough ride. After supper we sat in their van wrapped in rugs to keep out the chill, fortified with a glass of brandy, exchanging travellers' tales which is one of the most pleasant pastimes of journeying.

The next morning at dawn we were on the road which leads westward from Bamian to the lakes of Band-i-Amir, fifty miles away. At first there was nothing to see as thick mist obscured everything except the stony, dusty road. Then the sun rose to reveal the empty desert with jagged mountain peaks on the horizon. Bored with the seemingly endless arid plateau, I had dozed off when Kerry's excited voice woke me up. Far below us, in a series of rocky gorges, with colours ranging from the palest blue to a deep purple lay the miraculous lakes of Band-i-Amir. The sunlight lay on the topmost lake and it shone like smooth silver, with the outlines of the mountains and rocks etched within it. The water spilled over a gigantic waterfall into the lake below, which in turn, overflowed into a lower basin, and so on to the bottom of the valley. Sangal repeated the strange names of the five lakes which strung together, sounded like a religious chant — Pudina, Aibat, Gulaman, Khaman, Panir and Zulficar. He told us of their miraculous origin at the hand of Ali, the son-in-law of Mohammed. But we were so overcome by the beauty of the scene before us, that we do not recall the details of the miracle. Our one regret was that we had no time to follow the winding road into the gorge below, as ten hours of hard driving lay ahead of us. Reluctantly we turned away from the pools of gleaming water and made our way back to Bamian.

Before we reached the motel, Sangal said "I hope you don't mind if we have an extra passenger; the hotel manager has asked me to take his uncle back to Kabul. He is a Sufi from Herat." We made no demur, knowing full well that the arrangement had already been made; besides, we were rather intrigued. Having failed to meet a Whirling Dervish in Turkey, we had hoped to meet a Sufi in Iran or Afghanistan, and here was the opportunity being presented to us. Sufis are Mohammedan mystics, and are generally supposed to be exceedingly wise and humble. So we looked forward eagerly to hearing this Sufi's views on religion and life during the long journey to Kabul. He was waiting for us by the roadside, an elderly man in his late sixties, wearing a white turban and thin white cotton trousers and tunic. We marvelled that he was able to withstand the cold in such summery attire. All his luggage was wrapped up in a handkerchief. In the course of the journey we asked him through Sangal, numerous questions about his concept of God and Mohammed and of the purpose of life. He gave us the short, pat answers which one would expect from someone who has never really given any thought to these matters. "God is everywhere." There was no spiritual depth in any of his observations, although he could repeat long passages from the Koran. We asked him what his duties were in the Friday Mosque at Herat, and he described his routine which was of a caretaker rather than that of a religious teacher. So we concluded that he was not a real Sufi after all, and that the hotel manager had given him that title to impress us, gullible foreigners.

During our two days' absence, the hotel compound had become quite crowded with motor caravans bound for India. We found a space next to a large Mercedes coach which was home for a German couple and their two young children. During the day the baby crawled about happily on a large Persian rug which was spread out under the trees. When she ventured further into the dusty garden, obliging campers put her back on the mat. Opposite our Belgian friends was a battered old Volkswagen with an Englishman and his French girlfriend. The young man with shoulder-length hair, long beard and white robe looked as if he had modelled himself upon paintings of Jesus Christ, so we nicknamed him J. C. The resemblance, however, stopped at his outward appearance, as there was nothing altruistic about him. In fact, he was quite a sharp businessman. "Can I help you?" he would say. "Do you need tyres, Calor gas, plastic padding, lapis lazuli, etc.? I can get them at a discount." He had been here before and he knew the ropes. Fortunately, we did not require his services. Five months later we met up with him again in Nepal, where he was wearing his hair in a top-knot, Buddhist-style, and had exchanged his white robe for a saffron one. He had also acquired a smart Mercedes motor home and a new girlfriend.

Our Belgian friends, who had not accompanied us to Bamian because they planned to visit it on their return journey, a journey they were not destined to make, were preparing to leave for Pakistan. On their last evening we finalised the arrangements for our next meeting in India, at Rishikesh on the Ganges. We had discovered that Albert and Françoise had been for several years members of the Belgian Yoga Society with close contacts with an ashram (Hindu monastery) in Rishikesh. They planned to spend two months there, studying Yoga under the direction of a guru. As the study of the religions of the East was one of the aims of our journey, we decided to join them by the Ganges at the end of November. So we parted once more and they set off through Pakistan to spend a week or two in Kashmir whilst we visited schools and universities in Peshawar, Lahore and Rawalpindi, as guests of the Pakistani Government.

We had still a few days left before our educational visits were due to start, but time does not hang on your hands in Kabul. We paid regular visits to the British Embassy on the outskirts of the town to fetch our mail and to the British Council Library in Shar-i-nao to catch up on home news. As Christmas was only six weeks away we dispatched one or two parcels of walnuts and pistachio nuts to friends in England and Scotland. Much to our surprise, as the Afghan postal service seemed singularly inefficient, all the parcels arrived safely. On the other hand, two of the parcels posted in India several weeks later did not reach their destination. I still grieve over the little silver spoons with elephants on the handles which I bought for a special friend, and which she never received.

Near the hotel we discovered a launderette and after months of washing in pails, it was a joy to heap our mounds of laundry into the machines and let them do the work. Everything now was shipshape, except for me. I happened to look in the mirror one day, which I did but rarely, and was appalled at the sight of my unkempt hair. Fortunately, I managed to discover a hairdressing salon, surprisingly well equipped, in the charge of an intelligent-looking woman in a miniskirt. She told me that her husband was a government official and as she cut and shampooed my hair, she talked about the status of Afghan women. "We have no freedom," she said, "should my husband decide to take another wife, I would have to accept it, and even assist in making the wedding dresses and the food for the marriage banquet." Then she added bitterly, "If Mohammed had been a woman, there would have been no stupid talk of four wives for one husband. The Koran says that a man may have more than one wife, if he treats them exactly alike."

"How is that possible?" we said.

She went on to say that there is now a school for girls in Kabul and they may now attend university classes. "Young women are becoming more independent — but only about one per cent will have a say in the choice of a husband."

"Whose fault is it?" I asked.

"It is all due to a religion which is for men only. Women have no part in it."

We talked about salaries, and she told me that even top government officials get no more than £150.00 per month and have often to entertain government guests without extra pay. The head of the Post Office gets about £15.00 a month and bribery is therefore accepted as a fact of life. Retirement pensions are about 80% of a man's wage, which seems quite generous, but since most men earn very little, it is in reality, a meagre sum.

"No, our country will not become communist," she said, in answer to one of my queries. "Our religion does not favour communism — but we got rid of our king because he was not democratic enough. Afghanistan is a rich country," she added proudly, "rich, I mean in mineral and other resources, petrol, for instance, but they will not allow us to develop them."

When I tried to find out who 'they' were, instead of answering, she abruptly changed the topic of conversation.

Before we left Kabul we paid a belated visit to the museum — belated because we would have had a greater appreciation of Bamian, if we had seen the exhibits before our journey to the valley. There is an interesting collection of magnificent photographs of the various sites which have been excavated during the last twenty years by a French archaeological team. The Nuristan section with its strange, wooden images inspired us with the desire to visit that area some day. The Begram room was perhaps the most interesting one with its treasure-trove of works of art — glassware from the first and second centuries, Chinese lacquer and Greek and Roman bronzes, inlaid ivory work from India. All these articles, some of them very fragile, had been discovered at Begram, formerly called Kapissa, and been brought along the rough caravan trail which linked the East with the West. For us, the most evocative object in the museum was much more ancient than other articles. It was a pebble found in the Palaeolithic strata with a face upon it, carved by some unknown artist, 30,000 years ago.

When we came out of the museum, we discovered that the caps of our petrol tanks were missing from the caravan which we had left in the road outside. It was infuriating. We had to go rummaging in motor shops in search of these covers which small boys in the East find irresistible. Our experience of losing car parts such as petrol caps and reflectors was by no means unique. When we were in Delhi, campers told us how they had lost all their hubs when they were in Kashmir. There, four cars had parked together to form a square which the occupants shared for cooking and dining but in spite of the fact that there was always someone in the area, all the hubs were stolen. When the articles were traced to a shop in Srinagar, the police would not allow them to be retrieved, as there was "not sufficient proof".

We spent our last day in Kabul stocking up for our journey, as we had been told that many of the goods for sale in Afghanistan were unobtainable in India and Pakistan. We filled our cupboards with washing powder, coffee, chocolate, cheese, tinned meat, dried fruit and walnuts, omitting fruit and vegetables which we knew we would find on route, and bread, as we still had packets of Iranian rusks. One commodity which we found almost impossible to track down was 'ice'. We had been fortunate in obtaining electricity for our fridge from the hotel in Kabul but we knew we were unlikely to have this luxury in our journey to Pakistan. After much futile searching we were directed to the local slaughterhouse where we filled our refrigerator with ice for five Afghanis.

Sheltering from the heat — Afghanistan

Chapter Five

BEYOND THE KHYBER

We had grown quite fond of Kabul and we were sorry to leave it and the pleasant compound of the hotel. A year later when we returned we found that the whole garden had been uprooted to make way for caravans and where the trees and shrubs had once grown there was nothing but a great slab of concrete. We followed the nomads on the highway which leads from Kabul over the mountains to Pakistan. Trains of camels, herds of sheep, goats and donkeys blocked our way and reduced our progress to walking pace, as we tried to avoid straggling animals and the clouds of dust raised by their feet. Suddenly, the mountains seemed to close in upon us and we began to climb by a series of crazy hairpin bends through a steep narrow gorge carved out by the foaming Kabul river, which roared 1,000 feet below us. This is the Tang-i-Garo Pass, one of the most spectacular places we saw on all our journey, surpassed in wild splendour only by some areas of Nepal and Kashmir.

Even though most of the nomads had left the road near the bottom of the pass to encamp by the river, or to proceed along stony tracks across the mountain side, we did not have the highway all to ourselves. Every few moments an old Bedford truck laden with goods would come hurtling round a bend at breakneck speed. The owners of these vehicles, determined to express their individuality, had decorated every inch of the bodywork with motifs of birds, animals and flowers in flamboyant colours and the fronts of the chassis were hung with bright tassels and ornamented with studs, sequins and coloured glass. We met very few buses but there were scores of small Toyota vans crammed with passengers, plying between Kabul and Pakistan. On the steepest part of the pass, a Chevrolet saloon car had broken down and twenty disconsolate passengers were sitting on the ground surrounded by a mound of crates and bundles.

When we regained the valley and the river, we picnicked by the water, now flowing peacefully between its banks. These lunch stops by rivers and lakes, in forests and on mountain sides, were some of the most pleasurable moments of our tour. After several hours of hard driving we would search for a suitable place to rest from the heat of the day, a place where we were not completely surrounded by inquisitive faces. On our long journey, whenever we stopped the car no matter how deserted the road and the landscape, someone would appear beside us in a few moments. Privacy in the East is a rare and priceless state. In Turkey and Iran, and later in Pakistan and India we considered ourselves fortunate if we managed to find a little shade beneath a tree or a rock. In Afghanistan, Kashmir and Nepal our aim was to find a running stream where we could dangle our feet and cool our drinks. I recall a precise spot by the Kabul river because it was perfect in every respect. Fanned by a breeze from a gap in the mountains, our feet in the clear stream, we nibbled the last piece of French bread and cheese we were to taste for another year, washed down with ice-cold pomegranate juice. There was no one around to disturb our privacy, no flies to settle on our lunch which was spread out on a clean flat rock. In the months which lay ahead, in the dust and heat of crowded India, we were often to remember and long for these idyllic conditions.

A warm wind met us as we drew near to Jalalabad which is 4,000 feet lower than Kabul and the valley widened into a plain, filled with palm trees and orange groves. We sought the shade in the garden of the vast Spinghar Hotel, Russian-built like the hotel at Farah Rod, and just as deserted. Although we were not able to get electricity, it was a very pleasant parking place with a water tap near by and use of the hotel toilets. Later that evening a Volkswagen arrived with a young English girl and her Indian husband. Kathie and Ranjit had a big problem. Since India and Pakistan were not on friendly terms, Ranjit, an Indian national, had not been able to obtain permission to cross the Pakistan frontier. The following morning he was returning by taxi, to Kabul 112 miles away, where he would fly to Amritsar in India. Meanwhile, Kathie would drive through Pakistan, to meet him. Kathie, who was quite a competent driver, confessed to us that she was scared to cross the Khyber Pass on her own in case she had a breakdown or met with unfriendly tribesmen; so it was agreed that we should travel with her as far as Peshawar.

Before leaving Afghanistan, we had to pass through two custom checkpoints, at both of which we had angry altercations with officials. On the shelf above our cooker, amongst an assortment of tins and jars, we had an unopened bottle of Vermouth. At the first inspection point, an Afghan official inspected the caravan and seeing the bottle, began to open it.

"What do you think you are doing?" shouted Kerry, retrieving the bottle and replacing it on the shelf. To our surprise the man made no demur. At the frontier another official repeated the performance. Only this time, not deterred by our anger, he took the bottle away and disappeared into his office. Enraged, Kerry hammered on the door, shouting "Give me back my bottle. This is robbery. You are nothing but thieves, etc." A more senior official appeared and suggested, in a conciliatory tone that we should give his colleague fifty Afghanis to have it back. "Not on your life," said Kerry. "You have stolen my bottle." Then he tried the tactics which had worked so well before. He strode over to the office phone, announcing, "I will ring my friend Colonel Quadir in Kabul." That did the trick. The bottle was returned to us forthwith and without further ado we passed over the frontier to Pakistan. There, although the custom formalities took a long time, we noticed at once that there was a greater air of efficiency, and that soldiers and officials looked much smarter than in Afghanistan.

After the wild Tang-i-Garo Pass, the Khyber was a great disappointment. History books had led us to expect an exciting, dangerous place with fierce Pathans lurking at every bend of the road. In reality it was no more formidable than some of the mountain passes in Switzerland. A smooth, modern highway took us past the great military forts, once famous in dispatches, and now stranded on the mountain side like huge dinosaurs. We saw many Pathan tribesmen armed with bandoleers and rifles, but they did not seem at all interested in us and looked peaceable fellows. However, we were in for a rude shock at the foot of the pass when we stopped at a road barrier. Suddenly, the face of a fierce-looking Pathan appeared at the open window and a pistol was thrust in front of our noses. 'This is it,' I thought. 'Death on the Khyber,' and I closed my eyes in sheer terror. There was a pause, then I heard a voice say "How much?" The fellow was after a few Afghanis, not a kill. We did not purchase his pistol although it was cheap at the price. The Pathans are excellent gunsmiths making pistols and rifles which are the exact copies of Japanese and European models. Before we left home we had considered buying small arms and had consulted a gunsmith. "How good a shot are you?" he asked Kerry.

"Fair to middling, I suppose," answered Kerry.

"Then a pistol will be no use to you. The other man will get you first and if he doesn't, one of his cronies will take revenge."

It sounded good advice.

As we proceeded through the pass, we were surprised to see on the hill tracks used by the nomads, great trains of donkeys bearing most unusual loads. They came struggling up the stony paths with lavatory pans and basins, plastic baths and tyres perched precariously on their backs. Where were they going? And why was it necessary to bring these goods on animals' backs over the mountains, instead of in trucks along the highway? We found some of the answers to these questions when we arrived at Landi Kotal, a little village at the end of the pass. At first sight, it looked like an ordinary mountain village and a poor one at that with tumbledown houses and a row of shops. What surprised us, however, was that the street was full of cars and trucks and every few minutes a taxi would arrive with passengers who were obviously not country peasants but townsfolk. "This gets curiouser and curiouser," we said, as we followed a group of new arrivals into the basement of one of the shops and along a dark corridor which opened out into a large underground cavern.

To our amazement, we found a veritable Aladdin's cave, where all the goods which we associate with the West were stored — washing machines, transistor radios, bathroom fittings, stoves, electrical goods, cameras, silks, etc. Most of the goods we saw came from Germany and Japan, but the whisky and some of the electrical appliances were British. The silks came from China and the cosmetics from France. Everyone was too busy making purchases to reply to our queries about the presence of these goods in this remote spot. Later, however, our friends in Rawalpindi explained the enigma. For the Pathans, smuggling has always been a way of life and the Pakistan Government tacitly allows them to pursue these illegal activities in return for their political support. Besides, it would be almost impossible to impose a ban on smuggling in the wild no-man's-land which lies between Afghanistan and Pakistan. Since most of the goods on sale at Landi Kotal are unobtainable in Pakistan, or are so highly taxed that they are beyond most people's means, purchasers come from all over the country. We met two ladies from Karachi, 600 miles away, buying sarees of Benares silk and later when we were in Rawalpindi, our friends proudly showed us their bathroom suite, bought in Landi Kotal.

We said goodbye to Kathie at Peshawar as she was eager to reach the frontier by the following day. A postcard received a few days later informed us that she had rejoined Ranjit at Amritsar. We settled down to spend several days in the compound of Dean's Hotel in Peshawar, rejoicing at having our electric fan, not to warm us as in Kabul, but to cool us down. We took an instant liking to Peshawar and this favourable first impression created in us a definite bias in favour of Pakistan. What was it that made us feel at home? The green lawns, the flowers and trees of the cantonment, a legacy of British days? The friendly attitude of the people we met, most of whom were helpful and eager to talk to us, or was it because English was spoken more or less everywhere and we were able to communicate? It is probably impossible to pinpoint the reasons why one is more at ease in one country than another, but there is no doubt that we immediately felt a kinship with the Pakistanis and later with the Indians which we did not experience in other countries on our route.

Dean's Hotel is built in the old colonial style, like an over-grown country cottage with wooden verandahs and balconies overlooking pleasant gardens. Old fashioned? – Yes, perhaps, but these old hotels, Dak Bungalows and Circuit Houses have a charm and spaciousness altogether lacking in the featureless box-shaped Hiltons and Inter Continentals which now tower above the cities of the East. The hotel servants seemed to assume that all our menial tasks were theirs and whenever I appeared with a bucket to fetch water, a white-robed figure would come forward to do the needful. "Memsahib must not dirty her hands." In the same way the tonga wallas (cabbies) waiting in the hotel compound with their ancient landaus and skinny nags were determined that we should not wear ourselves out by walking. One elderly Pathan wearing an elaborate tufted turban decided to adopt us as his clients and he would wait all day for us to appear. Then off we would go at a spanking trot, bells jingling, along the pleasant, wide avenues of the cantonment or through the crowded narrow streets of the bazaar. "Foreigners are always cheated," he said, so he did our shopping for us, as he had done many years before for his English master, purchasing kilos of grapes and oranges at bargain prices. When we went to the shoe bazaar to look for Pathan sandals, he brought piles of shoes to the cab for Kerry to try on. His delight in serving us was so obvious and genuine that it would have been churlish of us to refuse his assistance.

We made the acquaintance of a young man staying in the hotel who worked as a representative for the Japanese firm Toyota. Outwardly rather brash and self-assured, an impression given, unfortunately by many young middle-class Pakistanis, he was, in reality, sensitive and shy. We had tea with him once or twice in his room and one evening we invited him to dinner in the hotel. He came to the dining room, dressed in pyjamas and dressing gown, which seemed rather odd to us, although no one else raised an eyebrow. When we were about to order the meal, he explained with some diffidence that as he was accustomed to eating with his fingers, he would prefer to dine in the privacy of his own room.

The hotel manager, who as brigadier in the British Army had been decorated by King George after the Battle of El Alamein, invited us to supper with his family. That evening was a pleasant introduction to life in Pakistan, as the brigadier and his two daughters, one a student of

Political Science and the other a Lecturer in English, were very informative. I have another memory of that evening, for it was then that I discovered persimmons, a fruit shaped like a tomato with a delicious, juicy pulp which was served for supper with melon and ice cream.

Our first educational visit was to the Girls' Training College at Peshawar. In their sugar-pink tunics, worn over white trousers, the girls moved quietly about the corridors with a look of dedication in their earnest dark eyes. These students, aged between sixteen and eighteen were following a one-year training course for teaching, to which they had been admitted as a result of their good school examination marks. The principal, who had trained at the Institute of Education in London, did not appear to have introduced many modern methods. All the rooms were bare with no equipment on view, even in the Home Economics and Fine Arts Departments. We tried to talk to some of the girls but they were too shy to respond.

The Comprehensive School for girls, whose students were aged between twelve and sixteen, was housed in better buildings adjoining a small playing field where a game of volley ball was in progress. We soon realized that the word 'Comprehensive' does not have the same connotation as it has in Britain, since it denotes a school with a vocational bias. We were taken on a tour of the classrooms, and again were surprised to see no equipment apart from a skeleton in the Biology room. Everywhere, however, prefect order reigned and an almost unnatural stillness, so unlike the atmosphere in our schools at home, where the girls would have been whispering and nudging each other in the presence of strangers. "I am a teacher in London," I said. "Would you like to know something about English schools?"

After some hesitation one girl asked "What do English girls wear in school?"

This was not an easy question to answer as it would have been about ten years ago, but to simplify matters, I described the conventional navy blue or grey uniform with shirt and tie, thinking as I did so how much more charming these girls looked in their pink and white cotton suits.

There was a much livelier atmosphere in the Boys' Technical School. As we crossed the playground several of the boys came forward to talk to us and to offer to show us round. They were friendly and relaxed and spoke very good English. There was plenty of equipment in the Science rooms and in the Motor and Electrical shops and we sensed when we talked to the staff that the teaching was much more dynamic and practical than in the girls' schools we had seen. Of course, as a teacher, I am fully aware that tours of classrooms give only a very superficial impression of what is happening in a school. Our discussions with staff were more interesting and enlightening. Over innumerable cups of tea, accompanied by platefuls of sweet pastries, we discussed educational topics for hours on end. Considering the fact that under British rule, very few Muslim boys and none of the girls, received any schooling, the Pakistanis have made great strides since 1947. There are now more than 2,500 secondary schools preparing students for university education. Strangely enough the medium of instruction is usually English and the British educational system as it was at the time of partition remains the favourite model. However, there are now signs that American practices are beginning to gain favour. When we visited the Institute of Education at the University of Peshawar, we found that many of the staff had been educated at universities in the United States, to which they had obtained scholarships and they were gradually introducing American methods. We also noticed that most of the books and equipment used in the university came from America.

At Attock, about fifty miles east of Peshawar, an ancient metal viaduct guarded by sentries, carries the road across a wide expanse of grey water. This was our first encounter with the mighty River Indus after which the whole sub-continent was named. The original Persian name for the river was Sindhu which came to be pronounced Indus. Eight months later we were to follow its course through the gorges it has gouged out of the Himalayas in the north-east of Kashmir. There it was a turbulent, narrow river rushing headlong through the rocky valleys. By the time it reaches Attock, 800 miles further south, it has slackened its pace and spread out, and joined by four tributaries, it waters the whole of the Punjab — the land of five rivers.

Leaving the mountains of the North West Frontier Province behind us, we travelled over the green and fertile plain towards the new capital of Pakistan, Islamabad. There, on the outskirts of the town, we found a very pleasant camping area, set aside for foreign tourists. It seemed an ideal spot, with pine trees for shade, good toilet facilities, electricity and blissful peace and quiet. We remarked on our good fortune to an Australian couple parked nearby and they asked "Have you seen the camp kitchen?" So we went to have a look inside and found every sink filled with dirty pots and pans and scraps of food lying on the tables and floor. Then we heard about the German hippy with her children and two cats who had moved into the camp and appropriated the kitchen for their own use. Our conversation was interrupted by the arrival of the children who were attending a local school and who spent the rest of the evening playing

Tarzan games in the trees, screaming at the tops of their voices. Later we met their mother who came to ask us for some tea and sugar. A good-looking woman in her late thirties, neatly dressed in spite of the squalid conditions under which she was living, she had been well educated and spoke English and French fluently. We listened to her tirades against the camp authorities, Pakistanis and fellow campers, wondering how and why she had come to be in this plight. No doubt, like many Europeans whom we encountered on our travels, disillusioned with life in the West, she had come to the East in search of a happier mode of existence. Unhappily, most of them end up destitute on the steps of their home consulates. Another traveller in an even more desperate plight was living in the camp. We never knew his name, nor his nationality as he spoke to no one, spending the whole of the day curled up in the shade, 'spaced out' as the phrase goes. Emaciated and wan he had scarcely enough strength to stand on his feet, but he did manage to disappear mysteriously every evening, no doubt to obtain the drugs which were killing him. Other campers brought him cups of tea and bread and tried to rouse him from his torpor, but he refused every offer of help, preferring to die slowly and alone.

On the day after we arrived, another fugitive from the West arrived at the camp. He was an Italian lad in his early twenties, wearing a stylish white silk shirt over his jeans. It was neither his attire nor his gold earrings which intrigued us, but the fact that his only luggage was a cage containing a green parrot. Nor were we surprised to discover when he removed his jaunty flat cap, that all his hair had been shaved off, as we suspected that he had just come out of jail. Much to the German woman's annoyance, he took over a corner of the camp kitchen and made his bed on a window ledge. Thereafter, the din was incessant, as the cats declared war on the parrot who retaliated with ear-piercing shrieks. Meanwhile, his master lay puffing contentedly at cigarettes which filled the air with a sickly sweet odour. "That is the smell of hash" said the Australians knowingly. "He is probably a dope pedlar." We did not discover any more about him as he was very uncommunicative and did not mix with other travellers. We left him in the camp three days later 'waiting for friends to arrive'.

Fortunately, most of the camp's inmates were young people from all over the West with a healthy sense of adventure. Two huge army trucks arrived one night with a party of fifteen people from a Polish university. They were archaeological students on an expedition to the ancient sites of Harappa and Mohenjo Daro in the Valley of the Indus. The trip was a reward for their hard work and outstanding success in their examinations. One evening they invited us over for a glass of vodka and they told us in fluent English about their study projects. We were impressed not only by their enthusiasm and their friendliness but by their modern equipment which included a giant freezer containing their meat supply for the three months' tour. As a gesture of goodwill to their fellow campers, the Poles gave gifts of food from their stores and toys for the children. The poor drug addict was given a blanket which he kept for only a couple of days. We fell heir to a large tin of brown bread which we hoarded until we reached India where we savoured every crumb. It is surprising that British bakers have never thought of canning bread as housewives would find it useful as a stand-by and it would be ideal for campers.

After partition in 1947, Pakistan found itself with several large towns but not one suitable to become the capital city. The largest town, Karachi, is too far from the centre of the land and, Lahore, the cultural centre, is too near the Indian frontier. So a spot was chosen for a new capital, on a wide plateau about twelve miles from Rawalpindi. For twenty years the work of construction has been under way, but progress is slow since donkeys and not tractors move the soil; stones are cut by hand and women carry the cement in baskets on their heads. Viewed from a distance with its backdrop of high mountains and its abundant greenery, Islamabad is a pleasant modern town, but as one drives through the straight avenues, all identical and leading nowhere in particular, one becomes rather bored as there are no imposing features to hold one's attention. We turned into the gateway of the Shahrazad Hotel, the only hotel listed by Fodor's Guide (275 rooms and swimming pool), where we hoped to have a meal and perhaps a swim. To our surprise we found that this hotel is now used by the government as administration offices and we had to dine in a poky little café in one of the shopping precincts.

When we went to Rawalpindi to look up and repay the friendly couple, Ghazala and Jalil, whom we had met at the Afghan frontier, we had some difficulty in locating them. The main streets which had been named after famous British generals — Mayo Road, Dalhousie Road, Napier Road, etc., have recently received new titles, not yet recorded on official maps. However, we managed to track them down in the cantonment where they were living with relations. A servant opened the door and we introduced ourselves. Then the voice of an Englishman with an Oxford accent called out, "You are most welcome. Please step inside." The Englishman was in fact Ghazalas' father, Major Khan. Although getting on in years and infirm, the major was unmistakably an army man with his erect bearing and trim moustache. "My family served in the British Colonial Army for five generations," he told us with pride, "and at the time of partition I was a major in a British regiment. I still keep in contact with old army friends in Britain. Of course, most of them are now retired like myself." When we got to know him better on our return journey we were astonished at his knowledge of British history and current British affairs. He could also illustrate a point very aptly with a quotation from Shakespeare, Kipling or the Bible. It is fashionable to denigrate the legacy left behind in the East by the British, but one should not forget the love of English life and letters which men like Major Khan imbibed and have passed on to their children. Ghazala has inherited her father's love of English and History which she teaches at a girls' secondary school.

We got to know the Khan family very well, especially on our second visit during our homeward journey when we stayed for a week near our friends who had moved into their own house. There we enjoyed the luxury of ice-cold drinks, showers and long siestas under a cooling fan. Our favourite cold drink was 'Lassi', which is made of yoghurt diluted with water to which sugar or salt is added. Salt instead of sugar is often served with fruit. 'Chat', for instance, is a fruit salad with lemon, salt and pepper added. For afternoon tea — the English habit still lingers on — we had green tea with cloves and cardamoms or jasmine tea accompanied by sweetmeats and pastries. Ghazala's aunt, an amiable country woman who was staying with them, did not drink tea, but smoked a hookah, as we sat in the garden.

It seemed to us that middle-class people in Pakistan have quite a pleasant life. For less than £80.00 a month our friends lived very comfortably. All the menial tasks were done by a young servant, a daily washerwoman, and a jobbing gardener. For the servant, a boy of twelve, they paid his father £3.50 a month and for this sum he was on duty from dawn to dusk. We got an inkling of the different mores prevailing in Pakistan and the great gap between the educated and the non-educated by a casual remark made by Ghazala. She told us that her servant's brother, a lad of fifteen, had just got married and as part of the wedding deal he had given his eleven-year-old sister to his bride's brother. This, according to Ghazala, was not an unusual arrangement since even amongst Westernized Pakistanis, very few choose their own wives, who are still selected for them by their parents. When a son does choose to exercise his own choice, his parents still go through with all the formalities. It is the wife's parents who pay all the wedding expenses which are very heavy as celebrations usually last for at least three days and parents are also expected to provide most of the furniture and jewellery. The latter item is the costliest in the wedding budget as the bride's status is reflected in the amount of gold which she receives. The question every bride is asked by her friends is "How many grams of gold did you receive?" Ghazala had received one pound of gold in gifts, and since their marriage, she and her husband continually add to this amount by buying necklaces and rings. On their way through Turkey, Jalil bought his wife a gold necklace costing £70.00. "It is not really surprising," he said to us jovially, "middle-class Pakistanis seldom have more than one wife. We just can't afford them!"

One very expensive item in Pakistan is the motorcar. We were told that the duty on a new Mercedes car is more than £4,000 and even if you purchase a second-hand one abroad you have to pay £1,000–£2,000 in duty. Notwithstanding the cost, we saw a great many Cadillacs, Mercedes and Toyotas in the towns as well as hundreds of Ford Transits from Germany and Morris Minors which are used mainly as taxis. As the hotels and restaurants we visited, which we found expensive, were well patronized, we concluded that there was quite a lot of money about, in the towns at least. Pakistani women are becoming quite hair-conscious and many of them now wear hair-pieces, and have their hair permed and hair-dressing salons are flourishing in spite of high prices. A shampoo and set cost £6.00, which is not cheap but understandable when one considers that all the materials, hair-setting lotions, etc., are imported by air from Hong Kong. We saw very few beggars in Rawalpindi, but one day when Ghazala and I were shopping we were followed by a persistent whining beggar woman. Finally, exasperated, Ghazala rounded on her in Urdu "You have no money to feed your children," she said. "All right, you can earn the money; come home with me and lend me a hand in my house." The woman quickly turned about and disappeared into the crowd.

There was plenty of dress material available — cotton, chiffon, satin, nylon, etc., at reasonable prices. Silk, however, which is imported, cost about the same as it does in Britain. Most Pakistani women wear a tunic over bloomer-shaped trousers, although for weddings and other festive occasions the saree is worn. I bought satin for a blouse for eleven rupees (about 50p) and went to Ghazala's tailor to have it made up. He was sitting on the wooden floor in front of his sewing machine in a dark little booth into which I had to peer to distinguish him from the mounds of cloth heaped around him. The blouse was finished next morning, expertly made for ten rupees.

As for food stuff, fruit and vegetables were cheap, and goods like Nescafé, biscuits, toilet rolls and washing powder cost about the same as they do at home. Very popular were the 'take away' food shops where you could buy succulent chicken kebab, hamburgers, curry, rice, etc., at all hours, at reasonable prices. We had several meals in Chinese restaurants, situated in the poor quarter of the town on the other side of the railway line, which were better and cheaper than their Pakistani equivalents. Near the railway station were the shabby hotels and lodging houses used by Western hippies who come in search of hashish. We saw some of these youngsters sitting around on the pavements looking vacant and lost. Driving in Rawalpindi after dark was a nightmare, as there were dozens of cars without lights or with lights in the rear or front only. None of the cyclists had lights nor were there any on the bullock carts. Most pedestrians walked in the middle of the road and refused to move when we hooted.

Our conversations with various members of the Western community revealed two very divergent points of view. There were those who were convinced that things had gone from bad to worse in Pakistan since the British left. One elderly Catholic priest we spoke to, claimed that academic standards in secondary schools had gradually deteriorated, but others were more optimistic. We met an Irish woman who had been teaching for more than twenty years in a private school where almost all the girls were Muslims. She told us that most schools had been nationalised some years ago, in great haste, without proper buildings or staff but her school was exempted for the time being and did not suffer from excessively large classes, as was the case in state schools. In spite of these changes, together with poor administration and the lamentable position of women, she was convinced that Pakistan was definitely making progress, "I do not wish to return to Ireland," she added. "This is my home now."

The Muslim religion exercises almost as strong an influence in Pakistan as it does in Afghanistan, except that the women are not obliged to wear the veil. Ghazala's family belong to the Shiite sect of Muslims, unlike most Pakistanis who are Sunnis, but there did not seem to be any animosity between these two branches of Islam in Pakistan. Although the women in the Khan family did not go to the mosque very often, they spent a good deal of time at their prayers. Ghazala, who said her prayers five times a day, said she would have liked to go to Mecca, adding sadly, "But it is not possible."

"Because of the expense?" we asked.

"Oh no, we could afford to go but Father, who is not very religious, has never been to Mecca."

"Surely that should not prevent you from going."

"Yes, the rule is, that unless the parents have made the journey first, the children may not go."

Once, when we were buying cloth in the bazaar, the assistant asked us to wait for a moment. Thereupon he fell on his face, amidst the bales of cloth, to say his prayers, before proceeding without any confusion or explanation to measure our cloth.

We discussed with Major Khan the possibility of visiting the remote valley of Hunza which lies about 125 miles north of Rawalpindi. He told us that to visit Hunza, where people are said to live to the age of Methuselah, a special permit is needed; also that it was far too late in the season. The following September we made several attempts to fly to this part of Azad Kashmir (free Kashmir), but unfortunately, all flights were cancelled due to flooding and bad weather. We shall never forget the sad, middle-aged American who was waiting in the airport lounge every time we went to enquire about the flights. On our last visit he came over to us and asked "Have you been to Gilgit?"

"Not yet; we are trying to get a flight."

"I have been waiting to go for more than a week," he said. "I must get there somehow." He looked so tense and anxious that we felt it must be a matter of life and death. Then he added, "You see I am hoping to get news of my son who was last seen over a year ago in this lounge making a reservation for a flight to Gilgit." We have often wondered what this poor man discovered when he eventually reached Gilgit.

"As you are interested in history, you must visit Taxila," said Major Khan. "It is only twenty-five miles from here and is one of the most ancient sites in Pakistan. If my old legs were a bit stronger, I would accompany you. Go to the museum first, then ask the curator to recommend a guide to take you to the ruins." We followed his advice and were soon on the way to the oldest part of the site, Bhir Mound with an elderly man as a guide. His English was fluent and he told us that many years ago he had worked with Sir John Marshall who was in charge of the excavations. It was in 1913 that British archaeological teams began to unearth the history of this ancient town which dates from about 2,000BC. Alexander the Great's conquering army took Taxila in 326BC, but it survived as a commercial and university centre on various sites until the fifth century AD when it was devastated by the White Huns. It is interesting to reflect that when our ancestors in Britain were emerging from the Stone Age this urban community was flourishing in the valley of the Indus. In Bhir Mound only the foundations of the streets remain, although the museum has a collection of household objects and coins found amongst the ruins. A few miles away at Sirkap, we visited Taxila which the Greeks built on a plateau overlooking a river, and at Jandial we saw a strange tower (a Ziggurat) thought to have been connected with Zarathustrian fire worship.

As we wandered along the ancient streets and climbed over the mounds of rubble, we were followed by a persistent band of pedlars, selling small statuettes and other objects which had allegedly been unearthed in the ruins. Some of these images were well made, but most of them were both crudely executed and highly priced. Convinced that all these objects were copies of statuettes we had seen in the museum, we told these men repeatedly that we were not interested in their goods. Nevertheless, they continued to harass us and as we had not yet learned to ignore their tactics, we abandoned our visit out of sheer frustration.

Beyond Islamabad, the road climbs steeply into the mountains and winds its way through Alpine scenery to the height of 8,000 feet, where in Murree, affluent Pakistanis take refuge from the summer's heat. The tradition of hill resorts was started by the British over a hundred years ago when they established rest centres in the mountains for their troops during the hot season. When we reached Murree late one afternoon, we found ourselves faced with an unexpected problem. Perched on the mountain side with narrow twisting streets, Murree had no parking facilities and no space large enough for us to turn the car. We made several attempts to drive into the compounds of hotels but the entrances were either too narrow or had not sufficient headroom for our large vehicle. Finally, however, at the very end of the village, we managed to manoeuvre our way into the garden of a small hotel. There, from our high viewpoint we could see the whole of the little town lying beneath us. With its frail-looking wooden houses clinging to the mountain side and its solid church steeples, Murree is a cross between a Tibetan and English village. But there is nothing English about the bazaar with its hotchpotch of stalls selling carved walking sticks, embroidered jackets, baskets and nuts. Most of the male population seemed to spend their time sitting back aimlessly on their heels at the side of the streets. There were few women to be seen apart from a few aged crones sweeping the dust from their doors.

By dusk, there was mist in the air and a hint of frost in the wind, so we were glad to connect our heater to the hotel's electric supply. An old servant brought us our meal on a tray as the hotel did not boast of a dining room. He had worked for eighteen years with the former owner of the hotel, an English woman. "We, poor people, were much happier under the British," he said.

There was frost on the tall hollyhocks in the hotel garden when we set off next morning wrapped in our winter woollies for a walk to Kashmir Point. On the hillside we passed a fine English mansion, which now belongs to President Bhutto and the soldiers on guard directed us to the gap between the hills where we saw in the far distance the snow-capped mountains of Kashmir. Before partition in 1947 one could reach Srinagar, the capital of Kashmir, in a few hours as it is less than a hundred miles from Murree as the crow flies. Now you have to make a detour of more than five hundred miles via Lahore and Jammu to get to Srinagar for the beautiful state of Kashmir has been carved in two, one half owing allegiance to Islamabad and the other to Delhi. As we retraced our steps downhill we heard church bells ringing and realised that it was Sunday. In a little chapel on the hillside, an Anglican service was in progress. We peeped inside and saw a congregation of Pakistani schoolgirls in pink and white tunics and an English woman who was reading one of St Paul's Epistles. The school, St Denys, is close by, and as we learned later, is attended by about one hundred and fifty fee-paying girls from good families whose whole ambition is to be successful in the Cambridge 'O' and 'A' level examinations. As we came back into the village we met groups of people carrying picnic hampers, who had come by bus from Islamabad to spend the day in Murree. We remarked to each other how nice it was to see family parties enjoying themselves together when we noticed that, although there were several children, there were no women in these groups.

The time had now come for us to leave Major Khan and his family who were as reluctant to part from us as we from them. With promises to return the following year we set off laden with gifts of fruit and nuts on the road to Lahore. Hitherto our progress along the main highways of Pakistan had been fairly speedy, but now we were forced to proceed much more slowly as there were so many obstacles in our way. Herds of water buffalo would appear from nowhere to wander across the road, and no water buffalo is ever in a hurry. Undeterred by our horn blowing, bullock carts would remain obstinately in the middle of the road, as did bicycles carrying two or three people and as many bundles. On one stretch of road where we had gathered a little speed, our view was suddenly obscured by a great black object which hit the windscreen with tremendous force. Fortunately, the glass withstood the shock and looking back we saw that a huge vulture had come to grief against our car. In one little village we were held up for nearly an hour behind a queue of buses and tongas. Bystanders told us that some of the inhabitants were going to Mecca and people from far and near had come to wish them well. Being a less competent and less confident driver than Kerry, I confess that I usually took the driver's seat on the easy stretches of road. In Afghanistan where the roads are mostly new, wide and flat, I did most of the driving as I had done on the long lovely stretches of road in Eastern Turkey. More skilful driving was required in Pakistan and India where frequently only the middle of the trunk roads was asphalted; one had, however, to be on the outlook for lorry drivers, usually Sikhs, whose main aim was to drive all other vehicles off the hard centre into the dusty sides of the road.

In Lahore, where we were the guests of the Education Authority for five days, we were given a pleasant parking spot on a university campus and our hosts had arranged for us an interesting programme of educational visits to various schools, training colleges and to Lahore's two universities. What impressed us most during these visits was the enthusiasm of the members of staff and the initiative shown by the authorities in coping with their problems. In spite of the enormous numbers of children to be educated, a serious lack of qualified teachers and inadequate funds, everyone we met was working hard to improve the quality of state education. The staff shortage was most acute in primary schools and in an effort to remedy this deficiency the Education Extension Centre was giving in-service courses to experienced teachers to enable them to become 'master teachers' who would train the unqualified staff in primary schools. Financed by American money, the Institute of Education and Research which has a model school attached is investigating a number of primary school topics, including one on basic vocabulary and another on the reasons for dropouts in elementary education between the ages of six and eight.

When we had visited the schools in Peshawar we had been informed that the lack of equipment was due to the high cost of importing teaching aids and at the Education Equipment Centre at Lahore we saw the measures being taken to overcome this problem. Glass-blowers, using foot bellows were making science beakers of all types and sizes out of old florescent light tubes. We saw scientific and other charts being copied for use in schools and intricate drawings of balances and spectrometers being made so that these items could be constructed by illiterate workmen. So skilfully were these executed, that it was impossible to distinguish the home-made from the expensive imported goods. In the paint-shop, casts of kidneys and hearts for use in Biology classes waited their turn next to enormous pink ears and blue eyes made of plaster. There were also packs of flash cards for the teaching of Urdu and English.

Much remains to be done, however, to improve the status of teachers and in Pakistan, as in most countries, status is linked with salaries. There, a graduate starts his teaching career with a salary of about 350 rupees (£17.00) which rises to £23.00 per month if he takes a further degree. No wonder that most of the teachers we met had to spend their leisure hours tutoring private pupils. When we visited the University of Engineering and the University of the Punjab, we discovered in our discussions with the vice chancellor and others that they had the same problems as their Western counterparts. During the last few years there has been considerable student unrest and some of the staff were very unhappy about the concessions which the university has been forced to give to "hot heads". Some professors believed that their promotion prospects depended entirely on the students' likes and dislikes. A greater problem, however, and one with which we in the UK are quite familiar, is the difficulty of retaining well qualified members of staff, especially in the Science and Engineering faculties. Experts in these fields are being attracted to countries like Saudi Arabia and Libya where salaries are much higher and facilities and equipment more up-to-date.

We obtained some interesting sidelights on the position of women when we talked to the principals and the teachers of the women's colleges. Although these ladies were very well educated and appeared to be what we in the West call 'emancipated', they admitted that they would not go walking or shopping on their own. "It is not the custom," they said. If they pay a rare visit to a cinema or a restaurant, they do so in the company of a woman friend and not with their husband. We discovered too, that women are prevented from having normal social contacts by numerous religious taboos. At the end of our week's stay in Lahore we invited Dr Popelsai who had accompanied us on our visits to have dinner with us in a restaurant. Although we were parked close to his back door, we had not met his wife, so we asked him to bring her with him. He explained that his wife had had a baby two weeks before and could not leave the house for forty days, as is the custom. As an orthodox Muslim, he would never have dreamt of questioning this practice. With a degree from the Sorbonne and having travelled extensively in the USA and in Europe, Dr Popelsai, was very well informed on current educational practices in the West and as well as being extremely competent, he was charming and considerate. Early every morning on his return from the mosque, he brought us a can of buffalo's milk and a newspaper and we discussed the day's programme.

One morning, he said "Do you mind if we call at the railway station before we start our visits?" On the way, he explained that his elderly parents were going to Mecca in a few weeks' time, taking the train to Karachi where they would catch a plane to Saudi Arabia. This religious pilgrimage, which is called 'Haji' is an expensive trip and our guide, as a dutiful son, was paying most of the costs which amounted to £800.

"That is a lot of money for a few days in Mecca," we said.

He agreed. "In addition to the transport costs and hotel expenses each person has to pay for a goat which is sacrificed during the religious ceremony and the Saudi Arabians charge exorbitant prices for their animals."

"What happens to the goats after they are slaughtered?"

"Most of the carcasses are donated by the pilgrims to the poor people of Mecca."

Considering that from Pakistan alone more than 5,000 pilgrims attended the Id Festival on the 25th December, we reckoned that the inhabitants of Mecca must have dined well over Christmas.

On his university salary, Dr Popelsai could afford neither a car nor a servant and when he had completed the payment for his parents' journey, he had to start saving for even greater outlays. He had the misfortune, although he did not use that word, of having four daughters and only one son. He told us that professional people like himself are crippled by the tremendous cost of weddings.

We were reminded of his dilemma some months later when we attended a Muslim wedding in Kashmir. In a vast pavilion of brightly coloured canvas we sat down to afternoon tea with some 200 other guests — all men; I was the only woman present. No expense had been spared by the bride's family to impress their new in-laws and friends. Later that evening the same company sat down at tables groaning under mountains of rice and platters of mutton cooked in fifteen different ways. The bridegroom, dressed in white and garlanded in flowers was very much in evidence, but we did not catch a glimpse of the bride, who with the other women relatives was confined to the house, where, no doubt, she was showing off her dowry of gold and her score of new dresses.

During our stay in Lahore, Kerry, who is a Justice of the Peace in England, having obtained an introduction to the Chief Superintendent of Magistrates from Dr Popelsai, paid a visit to the Magistrates Court. We had already learned that in Pakistan and India, the title 'magistrate', is synonymous with 'judge', that there is no jury system and that penalties are cut and dried and very severe. When Kerry arrived at the court he was extremely surprised to be asked to take a seat on the dais, but he had an even greater surprise in store for him. A few minutes later the presiding judge turned to him and said, "I am handing the next two cases over to you and we shall conduct the proceedings in English."

"But I can't do that" protested Kerry. "I have not been sworn in."

"Oh, that is all right," was the answer.

Without more ado, Kerry found himself in the seat of judgement. The first case was that of a man accused of murder. The offence had occurred two years before, but, such is the delay in courts, it had taken that time for the action to be brought. He was remanded for three months. The next case was that of a girl of ten who had stolen a goat. She was convicted of the crime and Kerry had no option but to pronounce the statutory punishment of three months' imprisonment. Disgusted, he handed the rest of the cases back to the judge. During the whole of these proceedings there was a total lack of the formality and decorum to which we are accustomed in our courts. Witnesses interrupted each other and made direct appeals to the judge, and as there was no clerk of the court to regulate matters, the accused, lawyers and witnesses, crowded round the dais vying for the judge's attention. "My case should have been taken first, judge." "You didn't consider this point, judge" and so on.

Later in chambers the judge said, "I know that you disagreed with the judgement in the case of the girl and the goat."

"Naturally," said Kerry. "It is a barbaric sentence."

"Ah, but you do not understand the full implications. It is winter here, this child has no home and sleeps on the street, now she will have a reasonable life for three months and be looked after." He concluded by saying "You are not a better man than I am, Gunga Din."

Most of the Westerners who travel overland to India make a beeline through Pakistan, with at the most a one-night stop at the camp site in Islamabad. The reason for this unseeming haste is the paucity of suitable parking facilities for vans and motor homes. There are, of course, in most of the large towns, hotels which allow you to park in their compounds, but their fees are usually quite high. Thus, arriving at the outskirts of Lahore, most travellers take the Circular Road which avoids the town centre and speed on to the frontier of India without casting a glance at the Mogul splendours within. The Circular Road, jam-packed with bullock carts, tongas, bicycles and pedestrians encourages one to flee from the town. Creeping along at a snail's pace, one has the almost claustrophobic fear of being hemmed in for ever by a solid mass of humanity. Once within the confines of the town, in the Mall, for instance, or in one of the leafy avenues adjoining it, there is order and spaciousness and the familiar sight of English church spires on the horizon. We explored the town in the evenings, and as in the case of Kabul, the longer we stayed the more reluctant we were to leave it.

It was in Lahore that we first became interested in the fabulous and fascinating dynasty of the Great Moguls who ruled over India for over two hundred years. In Kabul we had seen the Tomb of Babur, the founder of the line and a descendant of Genghis Khan, hence the title Mogul or Mongol. He lies buried in a garden in a hillside, a fitting resting place for a conqueror who surrounded himself with Persian gardens and who, during his campaign in India, longed for the hills and streams of his homeland. In Lahore, you cannot go very far without encountering either a tomb, a mosque or a fortress which owes its existence to one of the Great Moguls. Akbar, grandson of Babur, and the most famous of his descendants, built the Fort of Lahore about 1566 and it was enlarged and embellished by his grandson, Shah Jahan. We entered this vast fortress with its medieval bastions by the Elephant Passage; it was up this long staircase that the elephants carried the emperor to the royal palace (Shish

Mahal), and it was in this palace that the famous Kohinoor diamond was handed over to the British in 1849 when they annexed the Punjab.

In residences lavishly decorated with mosaic and inlaid with precious stones and marble marquetry, the Great Moguls lived in splendour. Even their summerhouse had floral designs in lapis lazuli, agate and jade. We saw the magnificent colonnaded chamber where Shah Jahan gave public audiences and the beautiful Pearl Mosque (Moti Masjid) where he said his prayers. This tiny sanctuary is reminiscent of his greatest creation, the Taj Mahal. The women of the harem lived in separate apartments in an adjoining courtyard and their garden is one of the most pleasant features of the fort. Here, paved walks lead off in all directions around a small lake fringed with shrubs and potted plants.

We visited this part of the fort one evening at sunset, expecting to see a programme of son et lumière, but found it had been cancelled because of a rehearsal for a fabric exhibition. Model girls dressed in shimmering sarees or brilliantly coloured tunics and trousers were going through their paces in the garden. The arc lights, shining on the water, reflected the dazzling colours of the garments as the girls moved gracefully along the narrow paths leading to the centre of the lake. From time to time, the taped background music was rudely interrupted by the voice of the director on the loudspeaker, asking Hamida or Fatima to 'get a move on', or to 'look more animated'. I could not help wondering what the ladies of the harem would think of this display, could they but emerge from the shadows of the past to be witnesses? Would they be bewildered, shocked or amused? On the other hand, since they were no doubt familiar with the episodes of the Arabian Nights, they might not have been too surprised.

It was Shah Jahan's son, Aurangzeb, whom history has branded for his ruthless treatment of his father, who commissioned the building of the beautiful Badshahi Mosque. An architectural marvel in pink sandstone and white marble, it faces the fort across the square of Hazuri Bagh. We were about to take off our shoes, as instructed, at the bottom of the great staircase, when a diligent attendant persuaded us to don a pair of overshoes. So in contraptions like giant goloshes, we climbed the steps and crossed the vast courtyard, which must be one of the longest in the world, for they say that as many as 60,000 prostrate themselves here in prayer during religious festivals. The mosque has had a chequered history. The Sikh leader, Ranjit Singh, who conquered the town in 1799 used it as a warehouse. Then the British converted it into an ammunition store and troops were garrisoned in part of the old 'medresse' (koran school). Today, however, restored to its former glory, the mosque has an almost pristine freshness. Abandoning our goloshes, we climbed the 204 steps of the spiral staircase to the top of one of the minarets and gazed over the city. In the square below the mosque is an unpretentious sandstone building containing the tomb of one of the most famous Muslims of this century, the poet philosopher, Allama Iqbal. It was Iqbal who first put forward the proposal that the Muslims of India should have a separate homeland.

The view to the west is spoiled by Ranjit Singh's white mausoleum which looks like the top of an elaborate wedding cake and is quite out of place in its Mogul setting. To the east, above the clutter of narrow streets of the old town rise the shining minarets of the Mosque of Wazir Khan, who was Shah Jahan's grand vizier (prime minister). To the west, beyond the River Ravi, just visible above the trees are the bulbous domes of the tombs of Shah Jahan's father, Jehangir, and his favourite wife, Nur Jahan. Nur Jahan had been married before to an Afghan prince who defied the Moguls and after his death she was taken as a captive to Delhi. However, she did not remain a prisoner for long as she captured the heart of the emperor who made her empress with the title "Light of the World" (Nur Jahan). There is another tomb in Lahore which has a sentimental link with Jehangir. In his youth he fell in love with a beautiful young woman attached to his father's harem, Anarkali, (pomegranate flower). It is said that his father, Akbar, who had inherited the ruthlessness of Genghis Khan, put an end to the romance by having the girl buried alive. Years later, Jehangir had a mausoleum erected to Anarkali's memory. We tried to locate her tomb in Lahore, but no one seemed to know anything about it. First of all we were directed to the Anarkali Bazaar which commemorates the unfortunate girl and then to the grounds of the Government Secretariat where the doorkeeper disclaimed any knowledge of the tomb. So Anarkali, remains in death, as she was in life, a mysterious, elusive figure.

People the world over who had never heard of the Great Moguls and Shah Jahan, are nevertheless aware of the existence of the Shalimar Gardens which are his creation. The word 'Shalimar' conjures up a picture of fountains, flowers and voluptuous women. However, as we waited for a ticket at the shabby entrance off the dusty Grand Trunk Road we wondered whether Shalimar after all was a figment of the imagination. Within the walls, the canals in the terraced gardens were empty; the flowers were dry and withered. There were several couples wandering hand-in-hand under the trees, but they were males. Men and women do not hold hands in the East. To capture the charm of the Shalimar Gardens in Lahore you have to use your imagination, to see them in their original splendour with water flowing in the basins, fountains playing and the royal retinue relaxing on cushions in the pavilions listening to music. Six months later we were fortunate to see the Shalimar Gardens as we had always imagined them, when we visited Kashmir. It was here, by the side of Dal Lake, that Shah Jahan constructed his first water garden. That Shalimar, sheltered by the mountains and by the massive plane trees so dear to the Moguls, with its waterfalls and brilliant flowerbeds, is a little earthly paradise.

On the eve of our departure from Lahore, as we were waiting in a garage for our car to be serviced, we started talking to a young woman and her son. I noticed that she was reading a book by Enid Blyton, and I may have looked surprised for she said, "You are wondering why I am reading a children's book. Well, I retell these stories in very simple language to my children."

"In Urdu?" I asked.

"Of course not," she said almost scornfully. "All my children are at English medium schools." Her son, aged about twelve, was sitting beside her, busy with his homework. "Ali, show the lady and gentleman your school books," she said.

Ali handed over his Science book which was written in English. In another notebook he was answering a series of questions in English, in connection with Social Studies. One question was "What was the state of the common man before the Muslims came?"

It was this little encounter which crystalized our impressions about Pakistan which we had gathered from many sources. There is a very deep desire amongst literate and middle-class Pakistanis to belong to the Western community and as the English language is considered the password, every effort is being made to assimilate it. In this process of assimilation much of the culture and technology of the West, and more especially of America has been absorbed. On the other hand, the Pakistanis are very conscious of their Muslim heritage which provides them with their motive force and separates them from their Indian neighbours and rivals. Between these two aspirations, the one cultural and economic and the other religious, there is an underlying contradiction which was pointed out more than forty years ago by Iqbal. With poetic fervour he urged them to forsake the materialism of the West and to pursue an independent course, guided only by the tenets of Islam. Their enthusiastic response to his appeal led to the partition of India and the founding of the State of Pakistan. The older generation is still confident that Iqbal's philosophy is the right one, but there are signs that the young, with their addiction to Western ways, are finding the strictures of Islam increasingly irksome.

As we made our way slowly out of Lahore towards the Grand Trunk Road, we passed a sad little funeral procession. A father was carrying in his arms the body of his child which was wrapped in a white robe for burial. Four of five mourners, all men, walked behind him. There was no coffin, no flowers and no priest in attendance, for death in the East is accompanied by little pomp and circumstance, and no headstone would mark the spot where that child was laid to rest.

Custom formalities at the Pakistan border took only a few moments as the officials appeared to be interested in only two things. "Have you any Pakistani newspapers?" asked one.

"Yes, we have this morning's paper" we replied.

"Give it to me, please. You are not allowed to take any newspapers with you into India."

When two other customs officers approached, we expected that they had come to inspect the caravan, but not a bit of it. One leaned over and whispered in Kerry's ear "Have you any *Playboy* magazines?" His face registered utter astonishment and incredulity, when Kerry answered that he had never heard of that particular magazine.

We had plenty of time to reflect as we waited our turn at the Indian frontier and it occurred to me then that a study of custom officials and regulations would serve as a very good introduction to the country about to be visited. Our experiences in Afghanistan, for instance, had confirmed our first impressions, formed at the frontier, where officials had tried to filch our bottle of Vermouth. As far as the Afghanis are concerned, foreigners are fair game. On our return journey through Afghanistan we had another indicative experience at the frontier. We were asked to put our car on a ramp where a very youthful customs official examined it underneath, tapping it with a small hammer. Then he came into the van and said in a confiding tone "Tell me how many kilos of hashish you have brought with you and I won't say a word to anyone."

Kerry blew his top off. "You have a nerve to insinuate that I, a respectable citizen, am carrying hashish. What right have you to ask these questions? How old are you, anyhow?"

The boy admitted to being fifteen.

"Well, I am almost four times your age and I have I trust, four times as much sense."

"I was only joking," said the lad making a quick getaway.

We were convinced, however, that it was not a joke but a confidence trick, for we had heard of travellers, who, knowing that it is not an offence to possess hashish in Afghanistan, foolishly divulged to officials the amount of the weed they were carrying. They did not realize that their confession would result in a telephone call to the Iranian frontier and the consequent discovery of their hoard. It served them right — but no doubt the Afghan customs officers did not go unrewarded.

When we crossed the border into Iran we found the custom office full of flies. The burly officer in charge remarked to us in all seriousness, "These flies come from Afghanistan. It is a filthy country."

The Bulgarians make it even more obvious that they consider their neighbours, the Turks, to be unclean and insanitary by providing a large trough of disinfectant through which incoming vehicles must pass. In fact, we found the Bulgarians just as unscrupulous in their dealing with foreigners as the Afghans. Their frontier soldiers make money on the side levying fines on tourists who fail to stop at specific points. We missed a 'Stop' sign and drew up a few yards further on. Whereupon, a soldier with a sten gun appeared, demanding ten levas — about £5.00 for our disobedience. We said we had no levas to spare, so he asked for Deutschemarks, and then for English liras! It took Kerry sometime, exercising his considerable skill at cajoling, with frequent use of the words 'brother', and 'comrade', to dissuade him from his piracy.

At the Indian border we were at once confronted with their bureaucratic system, inherited from the British. All travellers have to list in triplicate, equipment such as radios, transistor sets, cameras, projectors, etc., and take the lists and the articles to the customs office. Since we had all these gadgets with us, it was a very lengthy process. As we waited our turn, we noticed the German couple in front of us slip six cans of beer under the official's desk. "For me?" he said. The answer was an affirmative nod. He opened a drawer and put the gift inside.

"Now watch!" I said to Kerry under my breath, suspecting that where there is bribery there is also corruption, "he is not going to inspect their van." But I was mistaken. He proceeded to inspect their van with the utmost thoroughness, and he made them bring all their equipment into the office. During the year we were in India, although we heard many tales about corruption in high places, we did not come across one single example of malpractice amongst government officials.

Customs formalities completed, we passed through the final barrier which separated us from our destination. After three months of travelling we were in India at last. We both felt a great sense of elation mingled with relief that, in spite of private fears, and open misgivings on the part of our friends, we had successfully completed the first lap of our journey.

Gurus at the ashram — India

CHINA
KABUL
AFGHANISTAN
AZAD KASHMIR
SRINAGAR
LEH
KHYBER PASS
KASHMIR
PESHAWAR
JAMMO
RAWALPINDI
AMRITSAR
HIMALAYAS
LAHORE
RISHIKESH
LHASA
SIMLA
DEHRADUN
NEPAL
MT. EVEREST
PAKISTAN
DELHI
ANAKRNA
KATHMANDU
BHUTAN
AGRA
LUCKNOW
JAIPUR
GORAKHPUR
ASSAM
BENARES
PATNA
KHAJURAHO
BANGLADESH
GAYA
UDAIPUR
INDIA
BARODA
BROACH
NAGPUR
SURAT
SEVAGRAM
BOMBAY
HYDERABAD
ARABIAN SEA
PANAHI
GOA
BAY OF BENGAL
MANGALORE
BANGALORE
MYSORE
SRI LANKA

Chapter Six

LIVING IN A YOGA ASHRAM

Two days after we crossed the Indian frontier at Amritsar we were sitting on a wooden bench on the verandah of the Sivananda ashram outside the secretary's office, waiting to be interviewed. From time to time the door opened slightly and a yellow robed swami disappeared inside, leaving his shoes on the threshold. Above our heads was a notice in English stating that no foreigner would be accepted in the ashram unless written permission had been received from the secretary at least six weeks before the proposed visit. An hour passed and we wondered whether we were wasting our time, as it was most unlikely that we would gain immediate admittance. Surely it was presumptuous of us to expect it. Perhaps we should slip away quietly and forget the whole project. We were puzzled, too, by the fact that Albert and his family, whom we had hoped to find here, had not arrived and were not on the list of expected visitors. Three weeks before this when we had parted from them in Kabul, they were planning to arrive at the ashram on the 26th November and it was now the 28th November. They may, of course, have been delayed on the road from Kashmir where early snowfalls had blocked the Banibal Pass. Or had they changed their plans and gone somewhere else? These thoughts and queries passed through our minds as we waited our turn in the queue. We were also mulling over our recent experiences as we were still very confused by the conflicting impressions we had formed of India since our arrival.

In the frontier town of Amritsar, the streets appeared to be more squalid than their counterparts in Pakistan and beggars and people with deformities surrounded the car whenever we stopped. Abject looking women in tattered, faded sarees were cleaning the streets with straw brooms, scavenging amongst the rubbish and lifting up the dust and cow dung with their bare hands. Yet the majority of the male passers-by, mostly Sikhs, looked neat and trim in bright turbans and Western suits. The young boys with white mobcaps on their heads looked intelligent and alert, but it was the middle-class Indian women who attracted our attention most. They appeared so much more confident and poised than their Pakistani counterparts. None of them were veiled and they went about their business freely and independently as women do in the West, walking and shopping on their own. We saw a number of schoolgirls on bicycles and we even saw a woman driving a car. There were, however, very few private cars to be seen, but hundreds of cyclists blocked the streets through which we proceeded at a snail's pace to the Golden Temple.

The contrast between the drab, dirty streets of Amritsar and the sparkling brilliance of the Sikh's Mecca was both unexpected and astounding and when we passed through the marble portal the scene with which we were confronted was like a scenario for the Arabian Nights. The shining temple, covered in gold leaf, lay in the centre of a pool which reflected its shimmering image. The marble pathways which lead towards the temple were crowded with Sikh pilgrims carrying offerings of food and flowers. An elderly Sikh, speaking excellent English and wearing a suit which might well have come from Saville Row, offered to escort us. Inside the temple the pilgrims were moving around a central enclosure where prayers were being chanted and into which coins and marigolds were thrown. As we left the sacred place we were offered sweetmeats and our companion explained that these were provided for the pilgrims who had come to celebrate the birthday of the most famous of all the Sikh saints, Guru Nanak, the founder of the Sikh community. We noticed that there were no beggars in the temple precincts and that teams of women were constantly at work, scrubbing and brushing the beautiful inlaid marble floors. In spite of their efforts, however, swarms of flies, attracted by the heaps of sweetmeats, buzzed around us and settled on our bare arms and legs.

I was thinking of our visit to the Golden Temple and wondering what the differences were in beliefs and rites between the Sikhs and the yogis of the Sivananda ashram when our turn came for an audience. Instead of the solemn, elderly swami we had expected the secretary to be, we found a long-haired bearded young man in a white robe, looking for all the world like Jesus Christ. His face wore the sweetest expression I have seen on any man and his dark eyes beamed with intelligence and friendliness. In a soft voice and perfect English he questioned us about our request to stay in the ashram, asking why we were interested in Yoga and why we had come to India. We told him how we had found our way to the Sivananda ashram and he listened with interest in what we had to say. He told us that although his family had come from India he had been born and brought up in South Africa and that his name was Nathan. He was not able to give us permission to stay in the ashram as that was the prerogative of the president or his deputy, but he would present our case in a favourable light. In the meantime, as we were bound to be hungry as it was well past noon, he suggested that we should dine in the ashram refectory when the bell rang for the second sitting.

A guru took us downstairs to a dimly lit, stone-floored basement where we removed our shoes and washed our hands under a tap. Swamis and gurus, some of them clad in loincloths, were filing silently into the refectory where they squatted cross-legged on strips of matting, arranged in lines across the room. I was about to take a seat on the floor beside Kerry when the only other woman present, an Indian lady in a saree, took my arm and piloted me to the other side to sit with her. Men and women in ashrams do not sit together. She also indicated by placing her finger on her lips, that no word should be spoken. I sat down on the matting wondering how I would manage to convey the food from the tin platter on the floor to my mouth without the help of a spoon or a fork. It was a cold, dingy dining room, unadorned except for these words written large in English on the walls:- Meditate, Love, Realize, Do Good, Be Good, Serve, Purity. On one side of the room in a large glass case was the life-size bust of the founder, the benign-looking Sivananda. The swamis and gurus opposite sat with impassive faces absorbed in their own thoughts. Then everyone started to chant in a pleasant, melodious fashion, before falling silent again, waiting for the food which the kitchen staff began to dish out from large iron pots. Dollops of boiled vegetables, dhal (lentils) and rice were ladled into the tin trays in front of us, together with one chappati (thin pancake) and our tin goblets were filled with water. I had great difficulty in getting the wet, mushy food into my mouth, without losing it halfway, although I tried to copy the others who rolled it deftly in a piece of chappati. I was covered in rice and confusion, and what is more, after only a few minutes, I found the cross-legged position almost unbearable. Kerry appeared to be managing very well, enjoying his meal and quite at ease in the cross-legged position. He indicated that I should not drink the water from the goblet, which I had been tempted to do, as I was extremely thirsty. When everyone had finished, with second helpings for most people, there were more prayers, ending with the melodious note — OM — before we filed out into the daylight. I was wondering how many meals I could endure sitting cross-legged and forcing myself to consume large quantities of rice which is not one of my favourite foods. However, I concluded, philosophically, that both my limbs and my appetite would gradually accommodate themselves to the circumstances.

Outside, a guru was waiting to take us to the deputy president's room where we and a number of Indian visitors were received in audience. We removed our shoes and sat on the floor while the others bowed low in obeisance with their foreheads touching the ground. Krishnananda, an elderly swami with bright, quizzical eyes, asked us our reasons for coming and probed into our religious beliefs. Kerry spoke of his keen interest in the ideas of Gurdjieff, which were derived from the East and a rapport was immediately established between the two of them. Permission for our stay was granted and we felt strangely relieved and elated at the prospect of spending several weeks in the peaceful environment of the ashram. We would, of course, have been less enthusiastic if we had been obliged to live under the Spartan conditions experienced by the other members of the community. The tiny cubicle we were given afforded only the most rudimentary comforts. It had one wooden bench with a straw mattress, a straw trunk for our worldly possessions and two stone pots for water. There was nothing else. No chairs, cupboards, floor matting, only bare walls and a cement floor. In a space adjoining the room was an Asian (floor) toilet, a cold water tap and a bucket for showering. The room which was both cold and dark was covered with dust and had obviously not been cleaned out for many days. Fortunately, we were allowed to park the car in one of the upper courtyards and to connect our cable to an electric point, so apart from using the toilet facilities of the cubicle we continued to live in our motor home and enjoy all its comforts. Judging by the amazement on the faces of the inmates it was the first time that such unorthodox arrangements had been permitted, and judging by the stir we caused, it was the first occasion that a motor home had been seen in the ashram. Everyone we met wanted to look inside our vehicle. So for the first few days a continuous procession of swamis and gurus filed through the caravan, staring uncomprehendingly at our strange possessions. They all asked the same question, "Where do you sleep?" and when we explained that the sitting area became a bed, they looked incredulous, because for them a bed was a hard wooden board on the floor.

The Sivananda ashram is a very large institution and its buildings stretch from the edge of the Ganges to the crest of a small hill. The main residential buildings are arranged around courtyards connected by long flights of steps. Here, too, are the library, lecture room, temple and mausoleum of Sivananda, who, in a little shrine above his tomb, rotund and cross-legged like a Buddha, presides over the institution he founded. Every day he is garlanded with a fresh chain of marigolds. In the temple nearby, the crudely painted statues of the Hindu gods and goddesses — Siva, Rama, Krishna and the black goddess Kali, are similarly garlanded.

The main road which leads to Gangotri, the source of the Ganges, divides the upper part of the ashram from the lower section which contains the office, refectory, medical department and publicity shop of the ashram. From our vantage point on the hillside we could look down on the River Ganges and at the foothills of the Himalayas beyond. We had our first glimpse of the great river that morning when we drove through Rishikesh on our way to the ashram. As I had expected to see a vast expanse of murky brown water I was not prepared for the sight which confronted us. From a cleft in the high green mountains comes a stream of turquoise blue water, rippling over white boulders, as clear as spring water and sparkling in the sunshine. This was the mighty Mother Ganga, fresh from the snow of the Himalayas, wending her way towards the plain and Benares, where we were to meet her again under quite a different guise.

That evening, before the eight o'clock meeting, we strolled along the banks of the Ganges and discovered that the opposite side above the bathing ghats (steps) was lined with Hindu temples and ashrams. A ferry boat, free of charge, plies to and fro between the two banks, laden with saffron-robed pilgrims. Near the landing stage twenty or thirty ragged beggars lay in wait, crouching on the ground with their begging bowls in front of them, motionless and mute, like survivors from the Belsen prison camp. They did not wait in vain, because even the poorest pilgrim gives alms. In rickety stalls by the river's edge you can buy chappatis and samosas cooked on the spot in large iron pots over charcoal fires. We managed to buy a couple of eggs, no larger than those of a pigeon, but there was no bread and no milk on sale anywhere. It was now after five o'clock and the sun was beginning to disappear behind the mountains, leaving trails of burnished red in the sky and transforming the blue river into a mass of molten gold. The valley was hushed and still and as we climbed up to the ashram we experienced a feeling of peace and serenity.

The secretary had given us a programme, outlining the daily routine of the ashram and a set of rules which we were expected to follow. Every evening there was a Satsanga (musical get-together) at eight o'clock in the lecture hall. Our first Satsanga was not a great success. The session lasted from 8 p.m. to 10.30 p.m., and as we were not accustomed to sit for so long on hard boards, we were extremely uncomfortable by the end of the evening. What is more, although it had been pleasantly warm during the day, it became very chilly in the evening and we were shivering with cold. The discourse was in Hindi, therefore, quite unintelligible. There was, however, one compensation, the music was extremely pleasant to listen to, and although the chants were in Hindi, they had a catchy, lively rhythm. Most of the forty people present were saffron-robed devotees, but there were six other Westerners. The women sat together at one side. I sat down beside an Indian girl and a middle-aged European lady who sang all the hymns with great gusto and appeared to feel no discomfort in the cross-legged position. I wriggled about continuously, crossing and uncrossing my legs in an effort to find a comfortable position. Thus it was with the greatest relief that I realized that the last 'Om' had been sung and that I could sink down on our own soft cushions in the caravan.

Our routine began in earnest soon after five o'clock next morning. Kerry fetched hot water from the boiler house where it was heated over a wood fire and we had a quick wash before we joined the Yoga exercise class. There was no illumination in the hall, apart from candlelight, so it was difficult to see what our instructor was doing, but he gave directions clearly in good English. There were four or five other Westerners and three Indians, all of whom appeared to be adept at the exercises. Being absolute novices, Kerry and I made a very poor showing, as neither our limbs nor our breathing apparatus would respond to our will. Nevertheless, the instructor spoke encouraging words to us, propping up our sagging bodies and urging us to greater efforts. How we envied the lithe fitness of the others, whose limbs seemed to be made of India rubber. After an hour we were quite exhausted, but having realized how badly in need of training we were, we were quite determined to persevere in our endeavours.

After a quick breakfast in the caravan we were back in the main hall for a lecture by an elderly, scholarly swami on the Bhagavad-Gita. Nelicurtananda had been Professor of Sanscrit at an Indian University before he gave up his post to live in the obscurity of the ashram in a cell about eight feet square. Although we did not make a great deal of progress in our study of the ancient, holy texts, he took a liking to us and we to him and he became one of our most frequent visitors. His first discourse sounded to me much like the sermons I used to hear in my childhood in Scotland, with the minister stressing six important points for good living — truth, purity, fortitude, service, love, humility — only Nelicurtananda was quoting not from the Bible but from the Gita. Our understanding of his lecture was hampered, however, by the fact that we did not know the meaning of many of the Sanscrit terms which he used to describe the various stages of enlightenment, but this lack we remedied by frequent visits to the ashram library where we consulted books on Yoga practices. At the end of Nelicurtananda's lecture there was a little ceremony which we were to see repeated on many occasions. Two devotees stood in front of a small shrine containing the image of Saraswati, the goddess of learning and repeated the hundred and one names of God. After pronouncing a name they threw marigold petals over the shrine which they later baptised with flowers dipped in water. Incense burners were then lit and everyone present was given sweetmeats and pieces of banana.

That day in the refectory, having secreted a spoon up my sleeve, I managed to eat my meal more decorously and I was also hungry enough to consume a whole mound of rice and its attendant vegetables and dhal. Sitting cross-legged was still a penance as my limbs were stiff after the morning's exercises. Yet we were so much more fortunate than the others, as we had our padded seats awaiting us in the caravan and the prospect of a cup of coffee after our rather unappetising meal.

According to our programme, we were free from 1.30 p.m. to 4.30 p.m. However, in the course of the afternoon, our Yoga instructor, Krishnananda, came to invite us to a session of exercises on the roof where his little cell was situated. This yogi, whom we nicknamed, the monkey swami, was the most friendly and cheerful of all our instructors. In spite of his fifty-nine years, this small Keralan was as supple as a teenager. An excellent exponent of Yoga, he had been photographed many times in various postures to illustrate books published by the ashram. He showed us these pictures with childlike pride, also many of the letters and photographs which he had received from former students. The cubicle where he had spent the last twenty-two years of his life was no larger than a fair-sized cupboard and, as it had neither windows nor a fan, it must have been unbearable in the summer. We spread out the blankets which we had brought with us to soften the impact of the cement and for an hour or so we panted our way through the various exercises, stopping only when our instructor called out, "Now, take rest!" Never were words more welcome to our ears. The late November sun had still enough warmth to make us feel uncomfortably hot and we were glad to lie still and watch the other two students go through their paces. They were Brazilians, a man and his wife in their thirties who had been several weeks in the ashram and had been doing Yoga exercises for years. When the session was over, Krishnananda volunteered to accompany us to a stall where we could buy fresh milk, which was very difficult to obtain. So together we went to the river bank where we purchased a half pint of milk for the equivalent of 12p.

On the way he informed us that there would be no meals in the ashram that evening as there was an eclipse of the moon.

"What connection is there," said I, "between no food and the eclipse of the moon?"

"Don't you know," he replied, "that evil influences emanate from the eclipse and must be avoided, therefore we must fast this evening and pray from 7.15 to 10.45 when the eclipse will be complete. You must observe these rules."

I must confess that we failed to follow his instructions, as we made ourselves a meal of boiled eggs and tinned cherries after our Hindi lesson, before we went to Satsanga at 7.30 p.m. This time we wore our warmest clothes and took cushions with us, so the evening was much more enjoyable. There was the usual chanting and music and readings in Hindi from the Gita. Then a very impressive looking swami whom we had noticed in the refectory because of his striking appearance, a South African, Chankrananda by name, read extracts from the life and work of Guru Nanak and commented on his ideas. His English accent and pronunciation were so faultless, his remarks so penetrating, his personality so powerful that he became our favourite lecturer and henceforth we looked forward eagerly to his discourses. We had first heard the name of Guru Nanak in the Golden Temple and again in Dehra Dun on our way to Rishikesh. There we had found the streets so packed with people that we could not proceed any further, so parking the car we went to investigate. We were met near the bazaar by a great procession of children, some carrying banners, some on the backs of camels and others crammed into lorries decorated with streamers. They sang as they passed through the streets, scattering marigolds as they went. The children were followed by men with long staves who staged what appeared to be a mock fight, but which may have been some kind of a dance. We asked the bystanders, all in cheerful, holiday mood, what the festival was about and were told that the festivities were to celebrate the birthday of Guru Nanak. As we approached Rishikesh we stopped to photograph a beautiful, new Sikh temple and as we did so a white-robed Sikh came forward and invited us inside where we were shown a shrine covered with marigolds, in front of which devotees were at prayer. "Today is Guru Nanak's birthday," they said, "and we are honoured by your presence on this auspicious day."

By this time our interest in Guru Nanak was thoroughly aroused and we were very keen to discover more about him. Born in the second half of the fifteenth century, Nanak had been a humble Hindu storekeeper before he became a preacher. Throughout his life his chief concern was to heal the divisions in Indian society, created by the rival religions of Hinduism and Islam and by the rigid caste system. His plea for a more egalitarian society had a powerful appeal to the artisans and low caste groups who were despised by the high caste Muslims and Hindus. They became his disciples and founded the Sikh religion after Nanak's death. Later, the adherents of this religion adopted a number of symbols to emphasize their separateness from Muslims and Hindus. Thus every orthodox Sikh carries five Ks — Kanga (a small comb), Kara (an iron bangle), Kirpan (a small dagger), Kacha (special underwear) and Kesha (uncut hair). Whether Nanak would have approved of these symbols, however, is open to doubt, as he always emphasized that his followers should not isolate themselves from their fellow countrymen.

We had already made the acquaintance of several of our fellow students, novices like ourselves, and they used to come to see us between lectures and in the evening. There was Hamish, a blond New Zealander, looking for all the world like a young Apollo in his white guru robe. He had come to the ashram to study manuscripts left behind there by a famous Australian swami who had died two years previously. Hamish, who had been four months in the ashram, had an extensive knowledge of Yoga theory and practice and had travelled all over India where he had many friends. We found him a delightful companion. Murt was an American psychiatrist in his mid-thirties who had studied Yoga for years. He was able, he said, to shut himself off and meditate in any situation, no matter how distracting. On one occasion he had sat cross-legged in the middle of bustling Kennedy Airport and meditated for half an hour, to the great amazement of other travellers, who no doubt imagined that he was the screwy, hippy type. He was certainly no hippy, and unlike Hamish, his hair was short-cropped and he wore a neat blue safari suit. He was more of an intellectual than a mystic and we had many interesting discussions with him. One constant visitor was the wiry Belgian lady I had seen on the first evening and who astounded us by her facility for headstands. She was sixty-eight years old and belonged to a Yoga society in Belgium with close links with the ashram, where she had been many times before. On several occasions she had acted as a nurse in medical missions which the ashram had organized in various parts of India. One of the swamis was her special guru and she spent several hours daily receiving instructions from him and practising Yoga alone in her cubicle. Now and then, she would drop in on us for a long chat, either about Yoga or about Macrobiotics which was another overriding interest of hers. She had learned all about this subject from a Japanese who had cured her of arthritis of the neck twenty years before. When I happened to mention a stiffness of my knees and fingers, she at once put me on a diet. I should eat only rice and chappatis, no fruit or sugar, very few vegetables. I should take salt with food but drink very little, so that, the fluid would come out of my joints. She may have been right about the diet, but as I was keen on neither rice nor chappatis and very fond of vegetables and fruit, I felt that the cure would be worse than the disease.

As the Brazilian couple kept to themselves a great deal we did not get to know them well, nor did we become acquainted with several other

Europeans who did not come to lectures and only attended Satsangas. One was a very pale, handsome French woman, always dressed in an immaculately white robe, who had been in the ashram for several years and had taken out Indian citizenship. During the Satsanga she sat completely motionless and abstracted, joining only in the closing prayer. There was a young Australian girl, rather dishevelled, in tatty clothes, who was so absorbed in her study of Hindi and the Gita that she had neither the time nor the inclination to talk to anyone. There was only one Western swami, a youngish Frenchman whom we saw only fleetingly as he crossed our courtyard. We would have liked to talk to him, but he had taken a vow of silence for ten years, and soon after we arrived he left the ashram to set out on a pilgrimage throughout India, dressed in his saffron robe and carrying only a staff. For the next few years he will wander from ashram to ashram, speaking to none, receiving alms on his way from devout Hindus. During our stay in India we were to see thousands of swamis and gurus like him on the highways and byways. Some were young and lithe, but most of them were gaunt and elderly, wearing tattered robes which barely covered their bony frames. Nothing seemed to deter them from their pilgrimage, neither the burning midsummer heat on the plains, nor the winter's storms on the mountainous road to Kashmir. They pressed on regardless, never deigning to beg for food or drink, and such is the esteem which ordinary people have for their holy men, that poor, peasant folk with hardly a 'paisa' (penny) to bless themselves with, would stop them in their tracks with offerings of bread and money.

There were, of course, a number of Indian novices in the ashram. The Indian lady who was my regular companion in the refectory had been in the ashram for several weeks with her husband who was a doctor. After a Satsanga she told me that her husband wished to remain in the ashram permanently, but she wanted to return to her family in Madras. We met another Indian who was a self-confessed alcoholic who returned to the ashram from time to time when his weakness got the better of him. He attended neither the lectures nor the Satsanga, and only appeared in the courtyard occasionally, when we tried to avoid him as he was both garrulous and incoherent. There were many other devotees, elderly swamis who seemed to spend their lives inside their cells and we only caught glimpses of them when they emptied their buckets in the open drain near the caravan, or hung up their faded robes on the washing line. In a remarkably short time we had settled down to the routine of ashram life, adapting our pace to its calm and unhurried tempo and feeling wonderfully relaxed and contented. It is true that we were not as assiduous in our duties as we ought to have been. According to our list of spiritual instructions we should have meditated for two hours from 4 a.m, when we heard the bells and the footsteps of the swamis hurrying through the courtyard but we stayed in bed. Some of them were engaged in laughing sessions as part of their training and we would be startled by loud outbursts of hysterical laughs, as we stumbled along in the darkness to our Yoga lessons. For the first few days I made no progress with the exercises and was almost in despair, when, as my stiffness disappeared, I sensed a little improvement. Our kind instructor, noticing that I was having difficulty in bending my left knee, suggested that I should seek advice from the ashram's doctor. The ashram has excellent services which are freely available to the public. A doctor is always in attendance and all types of medicine are available in the dispensary. My trouble was diagnosed as due to anaemia, and I was given a prescription for a daily dose of an 'ayurvedic' potion. Ayurvedic remedies, which are mainly herbal, are derived from ancient prescriptions dating from the time of the Vedas. They are very popular in India where a number of universities, e.g. Benares, have ayurvedic medical departments. My mixture seemed to be composed of black treacle and herbs and not unpalatable. The monkey swami urged me to drink the water of the Ganges which he assured me had special medicinal properties. When I looked rather sceptical, he told me of tests which Indian chemists had carried out on samples of the water. These samples were found to have no bacteria whatsoever and were therefore safe to drink. It was also, he went on to add, sacred water and that was why it was imbibed by the swamis and gurus in such quantities. My faith, however, in the chemists and in the sacred river was not as great as theirs and I never drank a drop of it unless it had first been filtered and boiled.

Important as the physical exercises are and the training in breathing which accompanies them, these practices are only one aspect of Yoga — Hatha Yoga, as it is termed. Our main purpose, however, in visiting the ashram was to become acquainted with the theory and practice of Raja Yoga, in order to gain control not only of the body but of the mind and the emotions. The word 'Yoga' comes from a Sanscrit root 'Yu' which means to join. By the practice of Yoga, the individual soul is united with the Supreme Soul, thus Yoga, means union with God. This was explained by Nelicurtananda in one of his lectures on the passage in the Gita, which points out that Salvation, Self-Realisation and God-Realisation mean the same thing. Chankrananda's discourses dealt with the subject of self-control which is the core of the Yoga philosophy and as we were already familiar with Gurdjieffian doctrines of self-remembering we found his instructions easy to follow. We also tape-recorded part of his lectures.

"Most of us," he said, "go through life in a state of sleep, unaware of our real motives and our real selves. Most of our responses, our anger, hates, loves, etc., are mechanical and are due to subconscious and uncontrolled urges within us which rise to the surface like bubbles from a deep murky lake. We create false personalities and make ourselves believe that these are our true selves, forcing ourselves into moulds. We have, however, a potential far beyond these narrow limits, but we shall never know who we really are until we are able to control our 'prana' (life force). When we have achieved this 'parinama' (modification of the mind) we shall perceive ourselves from without, as it were, and be able to assess our faults and shortcomings."

"This is a familiar doctrine to us," we said.

"Man know thyself, but it is extremely difficult to be aware of oneself." Chankrananda agreed. "It takes most of us a lifetime to have even a glimmer of awareness, but this is where the practice of meditation is helpful."

We had already had some advice on meditation from Guru Nathan and had spent some hours in the quiet room which was available for that purpose. We usually went in the morning when the doors were closed at eleven o'clock and no one was allowed to leave before twelve o'clock. We, Westerners, sat cross-legged on the floor but the gurus sat in the lotus 'asana' (posture) throughout the hour. The room was completely silent. Everyone was absorbed in his own thoughts and the outside world ceased to exist. We had been instructed to concentrate our thoughts on an external object, so, on the first occasion, I stared at my sandals which I had removed and which lay near the doorway. Although I tried hard to fix my thoughts upon them, within a few moments, my mind had wandered to the events of the past days, to the dust on the floor and to the rays of bright sunlight filtering through the high narrow window. My eyes strayed to my companions — the gurus, with the soles of their feet turned upwards, sitting upright, staring straight ahead, motionless, not appearing to breathe. I felt irritated and frustrated because I was unable to fix my thoughts on any object for long. On the second occasion, having decided that my lack of success was due to the fact that I was taking too narrow a view of concentration, I fixed my thoughts on an apple — not one particular apple, but all apples. I thought of the various colours, textures, shapes, the seeds, pulp, and the countries where apples are grown. I thought of the Golden Apples, Eve's Apple, the canker in apples, and so on, allowing no thought but of apples to enter my mind. This time I was much more successful in my efforts to concentrate and I actually learned something about apples during that hour and even more about my own lack of awareness. Of course, the ability to concentrate is only the first step toward meditation. After three weeks I felt that the practice of concentration had induced in me a change of approach to the world around me by opening up new avenues of thought which I could explore in an effortless and unemotional manner. I also began to understand something which Nathan had indicated in his advice about meditation, "You don't go to meditate, meditation comes to you."

One day at the beginning of our stay we took a tonga to Rishikesh to replenish our food supply and to buy cloth for a white tunic and trousers (a guru suit) for Kerry. We bought bread and vegetables, aubergines, onions and potatoes and after a great deal of searching, four tiny eggs. When we were buying the cloth, we learned from the shopkeeper that Indian men are allowed to buy eight metres of plain white cotton for 'dhotis' (Yoga style robes) each month at the reduced price of one to two and a half rupees per metre. As the exchange rate was eighteen rupees to the pound this seemed extremely reasonable. Strangely enough the same facility is not available for women. During the following lunch break we took the ferry boat across the Ganges, accompanied by Guru Nathan who had volunteered to take us to the dherji (tailor), whom we found sitting on the floor beside his sewing machine in a stall no bigger than a cupboard. He promised to make the suit by the next day, also a curtain out of an old sheet for the caravan door. We needed the curtain to deter the monkeys from entering the caravan whenever the door was left ajar. The trees around the courtyard were full of these chattering nuisances, waiting for an opportunity to snatch any food in sight. Once a large grey monkey with a baby on her back and a menacing look on her face leapt onto the steps of the caravan and Kerry had to drive her off with the help of a plastic bucket.

There are about eighteen ashrams on the other side of the Ganges, including the Maharishi's 'pad', which was often in the news a few years ago when it was frequented by the Beatles. As it lies off the beaten track some way from the river, we did not visit it, but we looked round several others, including a very imposing and prosperous looking ashram. There, in extensive and well laid out grounds, were dozens of cage-like structures containing life-size plaster cast images of various Hindu gods and goddesses. We saw baby Krishna in his cradle, who must have been one of the earliest "blue babies" as he is always painted blue; Siva dressed in a tiger skin and encircled by a serpent sat on Nandi, the sacred bull. We were beamed upon by friendly Ganesh who has an elephant trunk, and scowled at by Kali with her garland of skulls. All these familiar deities, crudely painted in harsh bright colours, attracted crowds of pilgrims who gathered round them, and showed their appreciation and piety by throwing money at the feet of their favourite gods.

As we sat on the steps of the bathing ghats (terraces) which front the Ganges waiting for the ferry boat, we watched a group of Indian women drying sarees which they had washed in the river. Working in pairs they held the long strips of silk and cotton up to the sun and wind, and in the space of ten minutes the garments were dry and uncreased. The blue-green waters were seething with shoals of large fish which were so tame that they swam around the ferry boat and leapt out of the water to seize the titbits which the pilgrims held out to them. These fish, like the waters they swim in, are considered to be sacred and the Hindus would no more dream of eating them than they would eat the flesh of a cow. Thus, hundreds of miserable beggars starve to death within a few yards of these well-fed fish. We loved to stroll by the Ganges just before sundown, watching the changing colour of the water and the many river birds darting from rock to rock. Our favourite was a small dark bird with flame-coloured feathers on the underside of its wings which flashed across the water like a sunbeam.

The 3rd December was a very special day for the ashram, as it was the thirty-first anniversary of its founding and the event was celebrated by a procession through the town. At the head of the procession went four gurus carrying a little shrine containing the image of Sivananda fixed on poles and decorated with banana leaves. Behind them came a group of children carrying banners, then the swamis and gurus and finally the novices like ourselves. After visiting the temple we set off on the road to Rishikesh, singing all the way "Hare Rama, Hare Krishna . . ." (hare means praise). As the weather had changed overnight and it was now bitterly cold, we were wrapped up in our woollies, yet the gurus in their thin cotton robes seemed oblivious of the chilly wind. We wondered what would happen when we reached the town with its narrow streets crammed with tongas, bullock carts and stray cows, but we turned back on the outskirts and retraced our steps to the ashram where a service was held and sweetmeats were distributed to all the participants. Later that day our Sanscrit lecturer came to call on us, as he often did, to discuss with us and to hear our views on his last discourse. We had grown quite fond of this scholarly man whose childlike frankness was so disarming. "Did you enjoy my lecture?" he would ask. "Don't forget to come to the next one, at 4.30 tomorrow, when I will talk about Rama and Lakshmi being attacked by an evil spirit in the forest . . . How long do you meditate each day? Hm — one hour is not enough. You must spend longer on that exercise. Tell me, how do you meditate?"

We told him of our difficulties and he nodded sympathetically.

"You can't expect instant meditation."

Then I introduced a more controversial topic. "Since you believe in the existence of a Supreme Being, why is it necessary to have the ashram temple filled with gods and goddesses?"

"That is kindergarten stuff" he replied, "not intended for people like you and me. Simple folk need to focus their attention on an image, on Vishnu or Siva, for instance. Those who hope for worldly success pray to Ganesh and Lakshmi; young girls love Krishna and Rama and his wife Sita; and there are many who fear Kali, the goddess of destruction and try to propitiate her with gifts of food and flowers. The yogi, however, although he names these gods in his prayers, fixes his thoughts on the Almighty." Then he quoted from the Bhagavad-Gita, "He who performs all actions without motive, for my sake, regarding me alone as Supreme — such a person comes to me, O Arjuna." With a hint of reproach in his voice, he added, "Don't you remember what I said last week about God — realisation and self-realisation being the same thing?"

Our secretary friend, Guru Nathan, was a regular visitor. Sometimes we discussed Yoga and sometimes we listened to tapes which he had recorded of sitar and tablas players. One day he brought a recording of a speech by Chidananda the President of the Ashram who was on a visit abroad. "You must meet him," he said. "He is a very remarkable man."

We were very impressed with what he had to say, and I copied down a passage from his discourse which dealt with the brotherhood of man. "Any unity or oneness of mankind, established upon mere economic, social or political foundations, will not last. Only through the means of awakened religious sense do we link up with one another at the deepest levels."

One afternoon, Nathan came to ask us to assist the officials in despatching the magazine, which is printed in the ashram and sent to the members of the Divine Light Society — the official title of the Sivananda ashram. We joined the other volunteers in a lower courtyard where we had to fold the magazines and affix an addressed label. There were mounds of magazines but very few helpers. Standing nearby, however, were several young boys, aged about eleven or twelve, whom we had seen doing the menial tasks of the ashram. They fetched the water, removed the garbage, swept the floors and so on, and we assumed that they were 'Untouchables', or as they are now called 'Members of the Scheduled Castes'. Most of them were sad-faced little fellows, grimy and ragged, but there was one intelligent-looking lad who attracted Kerry's attention. Using signs he asked him if he would like to help. It was evident that he was dying to assist but afraid of what the swamis would say, as he looked rather fearfully over his shoulder. Finally he was persuaded to sit down next to Kerry who showed him what to do. He did it perfectly and we proceeded happily and speedily with our pile of work. The swami who was in control of operations looked very disapproving and when the time came for sweetmeats to be distributed, he gave us two but none for the boy. "He will get his later," he said.

When Kerry offered the child a piece, he refused to take it, realising that these titbits were not meant for him.

The next time our friend Nathan called on us, we asked him to explain the attitude of the yogis towards the 'Untouchables' and in particular towards these small boys who are given neither education nor training.

His answer was rather surprising. "Today," he said, "I have not come to answer your questions but to ask some about conditions and problems in Britain."

So the subject of the 'Untouchables' was taboo; he did not wish to discuss it. When we put the same question to Nelicurtananda he referred us to a passage in the Bhagavad-Gita which points out that — "Our past thoughts or desires determine our present birth, and our present thoughts will determine our future lives." Although there is a great deal in the Yoga philosophy which we are prepared to accept and practise, we could not give credence to a system which condemns countless beings to an unending cycle of misery. However, we did not argue with him on that score nor with Chankrananda with whom we had a special interview about this time to discuss various points. He emphasized that our chief concern should not be with problems such as those of the 'Untouchables' but with ourselves. Our main task was to get rid of emotions such as anger and hate which dissipate our energies, and for this, constant practice and not theorizing, was required. To us, Chankrananda seemed to be the epitome of everything he preached. He had a powerful personality, a great intellect and he was obviously very self-controlled and self-sufficient. Disappointingly, however, he was not at all interested in his students as persons.

The monkey swami was the most approachable of all our instructors, and he bubbled over with curiosity. "Where have you been?" he would ask us. "What have you been doing?"

We did not discuss with him the philosophy of Yoga, because it was obvious that he was not concerned with this, and the exercises which he performed so perfectly seemed for him to be an end in themselves. He had come to the ashram from Kerala to be Sivananda's personal servant and his love and admiration for his late master were unbounded. One of the first things he did was to give us a conducted tour of Sivananda's abode which has been left just as it was when he lived there. The verandah looks over the Ganges and one of the gurus sleeps there on a mat every night, keeping guard. We were shown Sivananda's study where our guide kissed the bunk bed and Sivananda's picture in its frame on the wall. Although he had more space than is allotted to other swamis and the only Western toilet in the ashram, Sivananda had had few personal possessions and comforts and his rooms must have been very cold and damp in winter.

It was when we were looking over Sivananda's house that the monkey swami announced that he had an idea. "I like to take my Yoga students on a day's outing. Would you be interested?"

"Of course, we would love to come."

"Then, we shall need your vehicle to take the party to Dehra Dun."

Thus it was arranged that eight of us would visit the Forest Research Institute a week later, with the monkey swami providing all the food as he worked in the ashram kitchen and could arrange for a meal to be provided in containers. Until then we had not realized that he had duties other than the instruction of Hatha Yoga. In fact, he worked in the ashram kitchen from 4 a.m. until 5.30 a.m., after two hours of meditation. It was a strange motley group which set out for Dehra Dun that Saturday morning. There was Hamish, the New Zealander in his white guru robe, the monkey swami and a friend in bright saffron, the Brazilian couple, swathed in blankets as they felt the cold, Murt, the American, and the two of us. A few miles out of Rishikesh one of the bench seats collapsed under the weight of the passengers and we had to prop it up with pieces of wood. Then we had a long delay at Dehra Dun where the swamis disappeared into the bazaar to do some shopping. As such outings for them were very rare they made the most of the opportunity to look around the stalls. By the time we reached the grounds of the Forest Institute it was nearly three o'clock and we were ravenous. The monkey swami produced a stack of metal containers which are called 'tiffin tins' and are used all over India in place of sandwich boxes. As no meal in India, not even a picnic one, is complete without curry, dhal (lentils) and rice, something more copious than a sandwich box is required. We sat cross-legged on the grass, eating with our fingers and a piece of chappati. As I was still having difficulty in conveying the rather fluid curry to my mouth, I wished I had had the foresight to bring a spoon. It was during our picnic that the monkey swami asked us what we ate in the evening when we did not dine in the refectory. "Eggs, usually, with fried onions and other vegetables."

His eyes opened wide in horror. "Eggs and onions," he repeated. "Don't you know that these things are completely forbidden in the ashram."

Shamefacedly, we had to admit that we had not studied the rules very carefully.

"Where have you put the eggshells and the onion skins?"

"In a bucket outside our cell," we replied.

"This very night you must remove them and bury them outside the ashram. Now don't forget. This must be done."

So that same evening, late at night, Kerry took the bucket with its damning evidence and buried the contents amongst the bushes over the wall. Then we studied the rules appertaining to dietetic discipline and discovered that eggs, garlic, onion, chutney and mustard were strictly forbidden, and that "Eating for enjoyment is a sin". Nevertheless, we all enjoyed our picnic food — the two swamis no less than ourselves.

During the afternoon we toured the Forest Research Institute, which must be one of the largest research units in Asia. It is an imposing, colonnaded building, established by the British over forty years ago. In the museum there were specimens of every type of tree, cereal, insect and pest to be found in India. What was surprising and alarming, however, was the fact that not one item or specimen appeared to have been added since the British left India in 1947 and all the tests and research papers referred to the period before partition. It was the same story in the pleasant little botanical garden adjoining the institute, which like the museum, was well maintained and had been left exactly as it was in British days.

It was dark when we set out along the narrow, winding road which leads through the forest to Rishikesh. There, in the glare of the headlights, we saw a bicycle weaving to and fro across the road and as we approached the cyclist fell off and lay quite still. Thinking that the man was ill, Kerry stopped the car and opened the door. As he did so, the man, who was either dead drunk or under the influence of drugs, caught hold of the door and tried to force his way inside. He was a wild-looking creature, immensely strong, but we managed to push him away and close the door. Then he took hold of one of the side mirrors and wrenched it from its socket, breaking it in pieces. As we moved forward, he threw himself down in front of the car wheels shouting at the top of his voice, defying us to proceed. Murt and Hamish jumped out, and after a struggle they managed to drag him off the road into a ditch where they held him down until we were at a safe distance. We were quite shaken after this incident, realizing that the accident could have been staged and the man could have had accomplices hiding in the bushes, ready to pounce when the car stopped. It was fortunate, however, that we were not alone, but we decided never to travel at night and to curb our charitable instincts in future.

A few days later we were reading in the library when someone touched us on the shoulder and, looking up, we saw to our surprise and delight that it was our Belgian friend, Albert. Over a coffee in the caravan we learned that he and his companions had been in Rishikesh for about a week, staying in an annexe of the ashram two miles away. After leaving us in Kabul, his family and their two friends had gone straight to Srinagar, Kashmir, where they had remained longer than they had intended, entranced by the beauty and majesty of that part of the country. Then, delayed by an early snowfall, they had made a perilous return journey over the icy mountain roads. Albert had been surprised to see our van in the courtyard as he had not expected that we would gain admission to the ashram at short notice. We were busy catching up on the news of our erstwhile travelling companions when a swami friend of Nathan's called to accompany Kerry on a strange quest to an ashram on the other side of the Ganges. There they would be given a very special list containing the names and addresses of the six most 'enlightened' yogis in India, the saints of the Yoga fraternity, who through vigorous training and selfless actions have achieved freedom from the cycle of rebirths. Albert went with Kerry and they returned several hours later with the prized list. We studied this with interest, noticing that it did not contain the name of Maharishi yogi, whom his peers consider to be too commercial in his methods and we decided to visit some of these enlightened swamis on our way through India. That afternoon they learned from one of the gurus that an elderly swami, one of the most venerated in the area had just died, or rather had "reached Samadhi" which is the highest state of Yoga bliss. As holy men are not cremated he was wrapped in a white robe and placed on a raft which was carried away by the sacred river.

During this visit to the other side of the river, Kerry had collected from the dherji his cotton guru suit, the second one which had been made for him. The first suit which took a week, not a day, to complete made him look like an overgrown schoolboy. I laughed hilariously when he tried it on as the tunic was too tight and the trouser legs too short.

Nathan was with us at the time and he commented, "Didn't you give the dherji eight metres of cloth?"

"That's right," said Kerry.

"Then, let's go back straightaway and see him."

The dherji, looking aggrieved, protested that the material had been barely sufficient to make the suit.

"But you measured the cloth in our presence and it came to eight metres," said Kerry.

"That is true, sahib," he replied, raising his hands in a helpless gesture.

"Is there any cloth left?" asked Nathan.

"None swamiji, you know I am an honest man."

"Have you any material like this?"

The dherji rummaged amongst his bales of cloth and produced material which was identical.

"Cut me a piece of eight metres," said Nathan. When this was done, he asked the tailor to fetch a pair of scales. He placed the cloth on one side, and on the other, he put the guru suit and the scraps of material. They registered almost half the weight of the uncut cloth. There was no need for further argument as the tailor's duplicity had been proven beyond doubt.

"The suit will be ready tomorrow," said Nathan briskly, and the little dherji, for whom I now felt a twinge of pity, nodded resignedly.

The second suit fitted perfectly but Kerry never wore it in Rishikesh, as a sudden change in the weather made it an unsuitable garment and it had to wait until we reached Bombay before it had an outing.

The following afternoon we set off on foot along the river bank to the Swiss Cottage annexe where our friends were staying. We passed the beggars, motionless in front of their empty begging bowls and further on amongst the rocks, lone yogis deep in meditation. One of these, a strange looking fellow with long matted hair, seemed oblivious of the chill wind blowing through the valley as he was wearing only a loincloth to cover his nakedness. Three hours later when we returned, he was still sitting on the same rock, in the same rigid pose, staring into space. On the lush green sward by the river flocks of cranes were feeding, undisturbed by our presence. At this point in the valley, the Ganges spreads out and ripples over the pebbles up to the white sand which lines the water's edge and, as it is full of mica, glistens in the sunshine. When we drew near to the ashram we discovered that our way was barred by a wide ford through which we would have to wade. As we were about to remove our shoes we were hailed from the other side by a truck driver who was washing his vehicle in the stream. Before we realized what was happening, he had driven the truck across the ford, picked us up and deposited us on dry land on the other side. It was unexpected and spontaneous acts of kindness like these, which we encountered frequently on our journey, which endeared the Indians to us and made us feel both grateful and humble.

Since our arrival in Rishikesh, we had already had two unexpected invitations. Crossing in the ferry boat one day we met a retired brigadier who had served with the frontier forces before partition and had received a DSO from King George VI at the end of the Second World War. Like many of these veterans he was an ardent Anglophile and very keen to talk about old times under the British. He was having a reunion at his home in Pauri and he invited us to spend the weekend with him and his guests, an invitation which we were tempted to accept but we decided to stick to the Yoga regime which we had just started. A few days later in Rishikesh we met an advocate from Bombay who was spending a few days in one of the ashrams; he, too, was very pro-British and he invited us to stay with him in Bombay which we did later on our way south.

It was good to see our Belgian friends again, specially the children, Patrick and Véronique, who had plenty of adventures to relate. Both of them were much paler and thinner than they had been a month ago as they had caught severe chills in Kashmir. The facilities in the annexe were meagre, to say the least, as all they had was a place to park and a water tap. There were no toilets and, as they had run out of Calor gas, all their cooking had to be done on a wood fire for which Titi was the main stoker, as her blackened face and hands testified. In spite of these difficulties, however, they were all happy to be settled in one place for a couple of months, since they were tired of being on the move for so long. Every day, one of the yogis gave them instructions in Hatha Yoga, the children joining in with the others. At the mention of exercises, Patrick and Véronique insisted that we should watch them go through their paces, so Françoise put a blanket on the ground and both performed very creditably, especially Patrick, who, at the tender age of two, put the two of us to shame.

As Françoise and Albert were very keen to spend several days in the main ashram, attending the lectures and Hatha Yoga classes, they decided to ask the secretary if this could be arranged. The children, of course, would have to remain with Mimi and Titi at Swiss Cottage. So a few days later we were joined by Françoise and Albert who were given a small room near the river. Apart from a mat to cover the stone floor, the room was completely bare, but we were able to lend them mattresses and being seasoned campers they had brought sleeping bags with them. We breakfasted together after the early morning Yoga classes and had supper together in the evening when Françoise and I concocted a number of tasty dishes; spinach with white cheese, vegetable stews containing cauliflower, aubergines, turnips and potatoes, flavoured with Indian spices, compotes of dried apricots and small cakes made of dried milk, oats, molasses and the remains of a packet of muesli. Françoise brought us a tin of corned beef, which was a great treat as we had had no meat, tinned or otherwise for a very long time. We spent many happy hours discussing our experiences and the meaning of the Yoga philosophy. The monkey swami was delighted to have such agile students, as both Françoise and Albert were teachers of physical education and had practised Yoga for years.

One day, Mimi and Titi brought the children to visit us, or rather to visit the monkeys, which were a far bigger attraction. A large colony of them lived in the trees in the courtyard where they chattered incessantly, swinging from branch to branch and hanging by their tails to get a closer look at passers-by. The children soon realized that they were not the pleasant creatures they had imagined them to be. Patrick was watching the antics of a baby monkey, when its large grey mother advanced towards him, snarling. Patrick clutched the apple he was eating and ran, but the monkey was too quick for him; Patrick was bowled over and robbed of his apple. Resenting the indignity of the assault more than his loss, he howled with anger and that was the end of the monkey's popularity. Thereafter, Patrick never failed to shout some uncomplimentary remark every time he encountered a member of that species.

On their second visit to us we all crossed the river by the ferry boat and walked upstream towards the village of Laximjula. It was a beautiful afternoon with the sun shining on the blue water of the Ganges and the fringe of white sand. The path led us through a wood where hermit yogis live in dilapidated shacks. Many of them have turned to begging for a living and sit cross-legged by the pathway, hollow-eyed and pathetic, with their begging bowls. One of them lay almost naked on a bed of nails, looking so emaciated and wretched that the children were horror-struck thinking that he was being tortured. Munching the peanuts we had bought them, they could not understand how we could calmly pass by so many needy people without assisting them.

"Will they die?" they asked anxiously. "Why have they no clothes and no food?"

"Why don't they work?" said Véronique.

We had no ready answers to their questions. And now, a year later, after much reflection on the immense problems of poverty in India, we have no solutions to offer. Perhaps it would be honest to admit that on that sunny morning we, the adults, were probably less concerned with the beggars than the children were, since to protect ourselves, we had hardened our hearts towards them. The sound of temple bells in the distance indicated that we were approaching the village of Laximjula where ashrams line the little streets and saffron robed swamis seem to be the only inhabitants. Above the village, the Ganges flows through a narrow gorge spanned by a suspension bridge from which we looked down on the deep blue water and the green valley below. Behind us, the horizon was blocked by the great mass of the Himalayas with summits wreathed in snow. The way to the sacred source of the Ganges, Gangotri, was closed until the spring and the last pilgrims were returning along the mountain pathways. When we crossed the bridge we saw the familiar figures of the beggars by the roadside. A passer-by informed us that they were lepers, belonging to a colony further upstream, so we hurried past the line of pale, ghost-like creatures while Patrick and Véronique, panic-stricken, ran ahead to look for a tonga to take us back to Rishikesh.

One day after the morning Yoga class, we played truant and slipped away to visit Mussoorie which lies on a ledge of the Himalayan foothills, at the height of 6,000 feet. Like Murree, in Pakistan, Mussoorie was one of the hill stations established by the British and has become one of the favourite summer resorts of well-to-do Indians. It took us two hours to cover the twenty miles, between Dehra Dun and Mussoorie — a spectacular drive on a road which spiralled steeply upward through a countryside splashed with autumn colours. When we reached the little town, which is perched precariously on the mountain side, we encountered the same parking difficulties we had experienced in Murree. In the little crooked main street the van got jammed against a roof, dislodging some of the wooden tiles, but we pacified the angry proprietor with a few rupees and inched our way forward into a parking spot near the army barracks. The wooden bungalows where British subalterns used to spend their leave, now shabby and dilapidated, are being replaced by hotels and smart private houses. The town has a more prosperous air than Murree, although the goods for sale are the same as in its counterpart over the border — carved walking sticks, woven baskets, embroidered and woollen jackets, etc. We bought a beautifully made walking stick for only 6.50 rupees (35p) and some fruit for our lunch snack; then we climbed further up the hill beyond the town to Gun Point, hoping to catch a glimpse of the Himalayan giants beyond. We were not disappointed. In fact, my first view of the Himalayas was an almost mystical experience, enthralling and unforgettable. There on the horizon, some eighty miles away, in frozen splendour rose the white peaks of the Central Himalayas — Bandrinath, Kedarnath, Sonera Parbat, magical names for summits which tower over 20,000 feet in height. Time seemed to stand still as we gazed at them in wonder and studied them in detail through a telescope. Indian visitors came and went, the women posing in front of the mountains in gay peasant dresses lent by the cameraman, but we remained with our eyes on the far distance till a chill wind drove us back to the valley.

Sometimes, we spent the afternoons listening to and recording the music of tablas and sitars. Two of Nathan's friends were expert players and we used to visit them when they were practising for the evening of Satsanga. During our recording sessions in one of the guru's cells we were often joined by one of the lady swamis (there were three of them in the ashram) who had a beautiful voice. We spent hours sitting cross-legged on the floor, listening, to the playing and singing without feeling any discomfort. In most ashrams and Sivananda's was no exception, music plays a very important role. This is not due to the love of music but to the conviction that certain vibrations have a spiritual value. On our first day in the ashram we had realized that the sound 'Om' which is entoned at meal times and in the Yoga and Satsanga session, has a very special significance. Nelicurtananda explained to us that 'Om', being the symbol of God, is a much more comprehensive word than the Christian 'Amen'. "By entoning 'Om'," he said, "we are brought into harmony with God." One of our twenty spiritual instructions was that we should repeat a 'mantra' (invocation) from 108 to 1,600 times daily as an aid to meditation. These mantras such as 'om', 'om tat sat', 'om shanti om', are extremely pleasing on the ear, and when repeated over and over again have an almost hypnotic effect on one's mind, inducing calm and tranquillity. Whenever I try to define in what way I benefited by my stay in the ashram I think first of this feeling of infinite serenity which pervaded the atmosphere and which I absorbed.

We had now been in the ashram for more than three weeks and we planned to stay until the president returned from his tour. However, that was not to be. Nathan came to tell us that the president's return had been delayed, and that he would probably not be back before Christmas. He had other news for us too. He had decided to return to South Africa on the 28th December, a date which he said had been revealed to him three months before during meditation.

"What are you going to do in South Africa?" we asked.

"I shall, of course, continue my Yoga training, but I hope also in some way to help young people to lead more purposeful lives."

We were glad to hear this as we had formed the opinion that many of the yogis were so intent on self-realisation that they had neither time nor thought for others. Nathan, however, combined the finest qualities of the yogi and the Christian in practising self-control and service to others.

We began to make plans for our departure with some reluctance as we had felt very happy in the ashram and had enjoyed the company of the swamis and gurus.

Nelicurtananda was quite shocked when we told him of our decision and he tried to persuade, first Kerry, then me, separately to change our minds. "Yoga needs long practice," he said. "You must spend a whole year here if you wish to make progress, and as you are past middle age, you have no time to lose." The monkey swami begged us to stay over

Christmas when there would be a special service with carol singing, but we remained adamant. After all, we had come to see the whole of India and not just one corner of it. We went to our last Yoga Asana class on the morning of our departure and promised the monkey swami to continue to practise the exercises. Impassive, as ever, Chankrananda said goodbye gravely, looking beyond us into the distance. The librarian presented Kerry with a book on the practice of Yoga and the youngest lady swami gave him a packet of sesame seeds for mending her fuses. Only the Belgian lady and the two Brazilians were remaining in the ashram over the Christmas period, as Murt had left on a trip to Tokyo and Hamish had been invited to stay with an Indian family in Lucknow. It was with a profound feeling of sadness that we dismantled our electric cable and closed the doors of our cell for the last time. A grey mist covered the valley and hid the river from our sight as we drove past the main ashram buildings where we stopped to say a last word of farewell to Nathan who was waiting patiently on the steps. "Would we ever meet anyone of his spiritual stature again?" we wondered as we headed for Rishikesh where Titi was waiting with her rucksack to accompany us to Delhi.

The Taj Mahal — Agra — India

Chapter Seven

IN THE REALM OF THE MOGULS

Not far from Rishikesh is another place of pilgrimage, Hardwar, with its bathing ghats stretching for miles along the banks of the Ganges. Devout Hindus believe that the stones on these terraces bear the imprint of the feet of the god Vishnu himself, and thousands of pilgrims flock here to gaze at these wonders. At seven o'clock on a grey morning, Hardwar, with its shabby guest houses and down-at-heel ashrams, looked a most unlikely stopping place for a god, and indeed, we would not have tarried there for a moment had we not been very short of petrol. When we finally found a pump at the end of the town and had roused the sleeping attendant from his cocoon of blankets, there was a long delay before the pumping mechanism was made to function. By now, of course, we had used up the precious stock of petrol which we had purchased so cheaply in Iran and had stored in cans on the roof of the van, so we were shocked to find that we had to pay £l per gallon for petrol in India. We resolved to travel at thirty-five miles per hour in order to save our fuel, and as it transpired, this was no hardship as there were few stretches of road where one could travel with impunity even at that speed.

By the time we left Hardwar the low mist had cleared from the roadway and we were soon travelling through pleasant cultivated land, past rivers, canals and small villages where there was an abundance of fruit and vegetables. About forty miles from Delhi we stopped in one village to buy guavas and sesame cakes (a speciality of the region), to sustain us before we reached the capital, and it was just as well that we had fortified ourselves with some nourishment as our entry into the city was painfully slow. The Grand Trunk Road was blocked with queues of bullock carts, bicycle rickshaws, trucks, pedestrians and stray cows; a sight with which we were by now familiar and which we were to find in and around every town in India. Had we approached the capital from the south, passing such splendid monuments as the Qutb Minar, the Purana Qila, and the Jama Masjid, even on a grey day, our first impression of Delhi would have been a very favourable one. As it was, we got bogged down and lost in the drab, narrow streets near the railway station, before we reached our camping place at Kashmiri Gate.

The camp, lying in the shadow of an enormous bus station, did not look very prepossessing from the outside, but once within its walls we were agreeably surprised to discover a well laid out garden, toilets and showers, a grassy space for tents, and a paved area for cars. The toilets were European style, and although the flushing mechanism did not function, they were kept scrupulously clean. At one end of the site was a small restaurant which served hot drinks and snacks, and a shop which was open for several hours each day. Titi, our Belgian friend, who had accompanied us to Delhi with the sole purpose of collecting mail from the American Express, was despatched in a taxi to Connaught Place, while we set off on foot in the gathering dusk towards the Jama Masjid which we could see outlined against the horizon. We pushed our way through the crowds, along pavements covered with stalls and charcoal braziers, past railings draped with carpets and garments for sale, stumbling over piles of bedding belonging to homeless families who sleep in the streets. It was almost dark when we reached the precincts of the great mosque where the air was filled with the bleating of goats. Proceeding further, we found the whole area in front of the mosque filled with tents around which were tethered hundreds of scraggy goats, being offered for sale in preparation for the Muslim festival of Id. The cries of the vendors were almost as loud as those of the animals, and to add to the general din, from the inner courtyard came the sound of chanting as Muslims joined in their evening prayers. Deafened by the noise and harassed by beggars, we slipped into a side street which led eventually to the Chandni Chowk, the main bazaar area of the town, where we were engulfed by the milling throng in the maze of streets around the market. There is something very exciting about these bazaars of the East, especially at nightfall, when little lamps and candles twinkle on the stalls and the charcoal fires glow in the darkness. Shadowy figures stand over huge iron pots where samosas and puris are cooking, and savoury odours assail the nostrils. As elsewhere in the East, shops were grouped together in categories, giving the customer a wide choice of wares. All the sweetmeat shops were close together, and Kerry, who has a very sweet tooth, was in his element, sampling the various mithais and hulvas. In the first market we purchased some pawpaws, which, sprinkled with lemon and sugar, are one of our favourite breakfast dishes. We wandered down one street where tinsmiths were hammering away at their pots and pans, and up another where tailors were crouching in front of their sewing machines in semi-darkness.

We sought out the area where motor parts are sold, looking for a side mirror with a socket to replace the one which had come to grief in Rishikesh, but although there were plenty of mirrors available, as well as every other car accessory, there was no socket to fit our vehicle. During our search we came upon a workshop where a man was fixing linings to brake shoes with the help of Araldite.

"That's just what I have been looking for," said Kerry, who had parted with his last tube to mend Albert's petrol tank. "Where can I find it?"

The man looked surprised and explained that Araldite was on sale everywhere. In fact, it had become a household word in India, mainly because of its slogan "Araldite mends everything except broken hearts!" When we explained why we wanted it, the man offered to make a new socket for the mirror and to deliver it to us at the camp on the following evening.

As we were leaving the workshop, there was a commotion in the street outside and we heard the sound of military music.

"It is a Hindu wedding procession," said our new friend, as we joined the crowd of onlookers.

Proceeded by torchbearers with acetylene lamps, came a band of musicians in red uniforms, making a fearful din with drums and wind instruments. Behind them on a white horse, decorated with white beads and silver trappings, sat the bridegroom, his face hidden by a fringe of tassels. A small, pale-faced boy was also seated on the horse, with his arms clasped tightly around the bridegroom's waist.

"Every groom is accompanied by a small boy," said our informant. "He is the symbol of fertility; they are on their way to the bride's house."

Attracted by the noise and the prospect of the money and sweets which are sometimes distributed on these occasions, the children of the neighbourhood came running from the dark streets to swell the procession. Out of curiosity we followed on behind until we saw ahead of us, at the end of a narrow alley, a blaze of coloured lights and heard the raucous blaring of loudspeaker music. Adjoining a shabby little villa, with stucco peeling from its walls and pillars, stood a large, multicoloured tent in front of which a crowd of men in white tunics and dhotis was awaiting the arrival of the bridegroom. We were about to slip away into the darkness when an elderly man, who turned out to be the bride's grandfather, invited us to come inside and witness the wedding ceremony. Naturally we accepted as it was too good an opportunity to miss, and in fact, we could scarcely believe our good fortune in being invited to a Hindu wedding on our first evening in Delhi.

As we took our place, cross-legged on the carpet inside the tent, no one seemed to mind that we were rather scruffily dressed, and that I was the only woman present. The bridegroom, with garlands around his neck, was seated on an elaborately carved chair raised on a small dais near the entrance to the tent. One by one, his friends and relatives approached him and pinned rupee notes on his tunic. In the middle of the tent was a little arbour supported by wooden posts and decorated with banana leaves and marigold flowers. Kneeling on the floor inside were two priests making a fire in a metal container with paper and sticks, chanting as they did so. Whenever we sat down we were offered cigarettes and a mixture of tangy seeds — aniseed, cardamom and betel nuts. Then, as we waited for the ceremony to start, tea was served on trays, and we ate our way through a plateful of piping hot samosas and a mound of jalebis, dripping with syrup. The priests poured ghee (liquid butter) on the sacred fire, in front of which all Hindu marriages are solemnized and as the flames shot up, the bride and the female members of the family made their entrance. The bride was resplendent in a red and gold saree which covered her from top to toe so that only her eyes were visible. When she sat down by the side of her groom in front of the fire, her headgear slipped, revealing the pale, scared-looking face of an immature girl with a large red and gold ornament inserted in her nose. For more than an hour the bridal pair sat before the sacred fire while the priests continued to pour libations on the embers and to mumble prayers to which the couple had to respond from time to time. Meanwhile most of the guests, paying scant attention to the ceremony were engaged in their own conversations, or wandered in and out of the tent, chewing pan (leaves stuffed with hot spices), drinking water or sampling the remains of the cakes. The young children, belonging to members of the family, ran to and fro amongst the guests, laughing and talking loudly, but no one paid any attention to them either. As our companions showed their eagerness to talk to us by asking us all the usual questions, "Where do you come from? How many children do you have?" etc., we took the opportunity to find out something about Hindu marriages. The young man sitting next to Kerry was the groom's brother and he told us how his parents had found this bride. First of all, they had looked around in the families of their friends and acquaintances for a suitable girl. Unfortunately, none of their horoscopes corresponded with that of his brother.

"Are horoscopes so important?" I asked.

"Yes, you see each child has a horoscope cast for him at birth, and throughout his life he refers to it when he wishes to find the most auspicious days for new ventures. Since people are born under different influences not all horoscopes are compatible."

"I suppose your family put an advertisement in the newspaper in order to find a bride?" said Kerry.

We had derived great amusement from the wedding advertisements we had seen in the *Times of India* — e.g. "Wanted for handsome B. A. Khatri engineer, homely virgin, wheatish complexion must be vegetarian," etc.

"Yes, and we had a great number of replies, but not all were found suitable when we took up the references. Some girls belonged to the wrong sub-caste and others were not sufficiently educated. There was one very well-educated girl, but she was too dark. You can see that our family is fair-skinned, and my brother is a graduate in engineering. However, the family thinks that this girl is just the right one for Ranjit. She was at an English medium school, and she is quite pretty, isn't she?"

We nodded in assent, glancing at the pair who were gazing rather vacantly into the sacred fire.

Before this ceremony, they had probably only exchanged a few words with each other, and then not on their own but in the presence of others.

"These weddings must be costly?" queried Kerry.

"Of course," said our informant. "Today's ceremony, with tent and food and all, will have cost the bride's parents more than 1,000 rupees (£500), and the engagement party which took place a month ago must have cost at least 500 rupees. Then there is the dowry."

He did not specify a sum for that, but went on to say that his family would have preferred a very simple wedding, but it was a matter of prestige for the bride's family to do things in a big way.

"Well, perhaps they can afford it," said I.

"No," he assured me, "the bride's father is a government clerk, earning less than 800 rupees (£40) a month."

It was the same story we had heard from Muslim parents in Pakistan with families often living in penury and even becoming bankrupt in their efforts to provide for their daughter's future, so it is little wonder, that both Hindu and Muslim parents give a bigger welcome to a baby son than to a baby daughter.

After what seemed to be an interminable time, the bride and groom stood up and walked around the fire several times. This seemed to signify the end of the ceremony, because everyone got up and the young wife disappeared into the house. However, we were told that, although the wedding ceremony was over, festivities would continue for several days longer at the house of the groom. When the women of the family began to lay the tables for the marriage banquet, to which we had been warmly invited, we took leave of our kind host and made our way back to the camp through the drab unlit streets.

The following day, Titi, who had spent the night in our caravan, sleeping in the bed above the cab, returned to Rishikesh with her rucksack bulging with Christmas presents from Belgium. We were sorry to see her go as she was a helpful, jolly companion, who, although only eighteen years of age, was a seasoned traveller, able to cope with any contingency. Since she and her friends planned to go to Nepal in February, we did not expect to see them again until after we had returned home. However, just in case they decided to visit Bombay, we gave Titi our address there and the date we proposed to leave for the south of India; then we accompanied her to the bus station where the comfortable, long distance coach to Hardwar left on schedule and was not overcrowded. At the time, we took this for granted, and it was only later when we made bus journeys in other parts of India that we realized how efficient the Delhi bus system was. Elsewhere, coaches left only when every seat was filled and the gangway jampacked with passengers, and when those who had failed to find a space inside had climbed onto the roof or were clinging to the rungs of the ladder in the rear. Wedged in one's seat it was practically impossible to extricate oneself during the journey as the exit was blocked by a solid mass of bodies and bundles. All this is bearable during the winter months, but the summer heat transforms a long bus journey into a test of physical endurance.

After Titi's departure, we set out to explore Delhi in a motorcycle rickshaw to which we clung tenaciously to prevent our heads from being battered against the canopy. As every rickshaw in Delhi seemed to be engaged in a race against other competitors and against time, the pace was fast and furious as we weaved through the traffic and around obstacles. The sun shone warmly on us as we made our way past the great sandstone walls of the Red Fort and the onion-shaped domes of the Jama Masjid. This was Delhi as I had imagined it to be, full of Mogul splendour. However, as we approached Connaught Place, we could see from the neoclassical outlines ahead of us that we had left the Delhi of the Great Moguls behind us, and were entering the Delhi of the British Raj.

It was in 1920 that Sir Edwin Lutyens began to design a new Delhi with its state buildings, Viceroy's House, hotels and mansions set amongst gardens and tree-lined boulevards, and you can call it poetic justice or the irony of fate depending on your point of view, that the British completed the building of the new capital on the eve of their departure from India. Lutyens gave the new city three focal points from which great avenues radiate in all directions — the circular shopping centre of

Connaught Place, the domed Viceroy's Palace and lofty India Gate, which is a war memorial arch resembling the Arc de Triomphe in Paris. Nothing could be in greater contrast to the Indian bazaar than Connaught Place with its colonnaded shops and quiet uncluttered streets. No bullock carts, no tongas or rickshaws are allowed near these select precincts where well-dressed shoppers haggle discreetly over the same goods as are available in the downtown areas. We did not see any beggars, although there were a few fortune-tellers about who do little more than beg for a living, and the inevitable touts who are always at hand to show visitors where they can purchase goods at bargain prices. There are so many good hotels and restaurants in this area that we had some difficulty in deciding where to have our lunch as every eating place was clean, well appointed and served both Indian and Western-style meals at a reasonable cost.

Leaving Connaught Place behind us, we set off in a rickshaw down the Janpath towards the Diplomatic Enclave which lies some three miles south-west of the centre. That drive revealed to us the full glory of Lutyen's design which has made New Delhi one of the most spacious and elegant capitals of the world. The vista along the Rajpath, the great avenue which connects India Gate with the Presidential Palace, is a majestic one and has probably few equals in the world, for there can be few capitals where the planners have been able to leave so much open space in the city centre. 'But is this really the heart of the city?' we wondered as we sped along these wide, almost empty boulevards. To be sure, New Delhi contains the state and presidential buildings, the nerve centres of the land, but these fine monuments scarcely contribute a beating heart; that lies in the pulsing, congested streets, in the crowded bazaars and slums of Old Delhi; for beautiful New Delhi has an alien face, grafted on the body of a much older city. Historians claim that during the last thousand years, no fewer than eight cities have shared this site on the banks of the Jumna river and Hindu and Muslim dynasties had their capitals here for five hundred years before the British Raj transferred his seat of power to Delhi from Calcutta in 1911.

We found the British High Commission in very pleasant surroundings off Shanti Path where most of the foreign embassies and diplomatic residences are situated in spacious tree-lined gardens. We were eager to collect our Christmas mail which we had had forwarded to the High Commission, and although, strictly speaking, it is not part of the British Foreign Service's duties to look after tourists' mail, we were given every help and assistance. It would be true to say that our journey would have been much more difficult and less agreeable had it not been for the advice and help we received from British Foreign Service officials in all the countries we visited, and we formed a high opinion of the work being done abroad by our diplomatic corps. As we were hoping to attend a session of the Lok Sabha and the Rajya Sabha — the Lower and Upper Houses of the Indian Parliament — we asked a High Commission official if a visit could be arranged within the next few days. In spite of the short notice, arrangements for our visit were made while we caught up with home news in the High Commission's Library. Since we had not seen a British newspaper since we left Kabul, this browse through old copies of the *Times* was a special treat.

That evening, our friend from the garage, brought the new mirror socket as promised and it fitted perfectly. Over and over again during our stay in India we were amazed at the skill and ingenuity of native workmen, and their calm acceptance of tasks which no one would dream of attempting at home. In Kashmir, for instance, we required a special thread adapter to enable us to have our Gaz cylinders fitted with Propane gas. With the aid of a little sketch drawn by Kerry, a metal worker made us one to fit and asked for mere pittance in payment. In Bombay, friends of ours needed a new gear box for their Land Rover, and a garage hand made a replacement which enabled them to return home safely to Germany.

As it transpired, our friend from the garage had an ulterior motive in giving us such good service, for he wanted our help and advice on behalf of his son. "Can you find a place for him at a university or polytechnic in England?"

Pleas such as this from anxious and ambitious fathers were to become commonplace as we proceeded through India.

A few days later the owner of the camp restaurant made a similar request to Kerry when he invited him for a meal. Indeed everywhere we went we encountered people who wished to come to Britain either to train or settle permanently, and they expected us to assist them.

That night it rained heavily, the first rain we had had for three months, and we were awakened by cold water falling on our faces. As we viewed with dismay the steady drip from the ceiling, the full extent of our folly in overloading the roof with petrol cans began to dawn on us. Buckets had to be placed on the bed to stem the stream which became a torrent, and we spent the rest of the night mopping up and emptying pailfuls of water. Fortunately, the sun shone brightly the next day and we were able to dry out the beds and the blankets. Kerry sealed the cracks with plastic solution and we thought that the problem had been solved; but we were wrong. Two days later there was another downpour in the middle of the night and the water gushed in again. Once more we were driven from our beds and had to sleep on the floor of the caravan.

These moments of discomfort, however, were quickly forgotten when we sallied forth on our exploratory visits to the capital. I had become so engrossed in the history of the Great Moguls that it was the Red Fort which first claimed our attention. It was built by Akbar's grandson Shah Jahan, who also shared in the building of the fort at Lahore, which it closely resembles. The passageway along which elephants carried the Mogul princes and their retinue, leads to a large lawn — once a great courtyard — where the Hall of Public Audience is situated and it was in this magnificent chamber, seated on a raised marble throne, that the Great Mogul used to preside. Bernier, a seventeenth century French traveller, visited the court of Aurangzeb, Shah Jahan's son, and described the splendour of the public rooms with their walls inlaid with precious stones. The courtiers stood with their eyes cast downward and their hands crossed before the dazzling figure of the Great Mogul; a figure to strike terror, for a frown meant death. The Hall of Private Audience was even more magnificent, for its ceiling was of solid silver which reflected the sparkling image of the Mogul's most precious possession, the Peacock Throne. This fabulous object, estimated to have been worth twelve million pounds in the seventeenth century, was appropriated by Ahmed Shah Durrani when he sacked Delhi in 1761. No one knows for certain what happened to this throne, but historians are positive that it is not the one which graces the Gulestan Palace in Tehran, as the workmanship of that throne is of Persian and not of Indian origin. The royal bathroom with marble basins in the shape of lotus flowers, the gardens with their pavilions and cascades, and the Pearl Mosque, which is almost an exact copy of the one in Lahore, reveal the artistic genius of the Mogul emperors. As we wandered back to the main entrance which is filled with stalls selling knick-knacks for tourists, we wondered what the Mogul princes would have thought of the silver and bejewelled baubles produced by present-day craftsmen.

Parliament House in New Delhi is a handsome circular building, surrounded by an open colonnaded walk. Although we were in possession of permits, we had to be vetted in the reception office before we received passes to attend parliamentary sessions. We went first to the Rajya Sabha, which resembles the American Senate and comprises representatives from the various Indian States. There we spent an hour or two listening to a very interesting debate on the nationalisation of textile mills. The debate was conducted entirely in English, and such was the clarity of speech and the proficiency of the speakers that, had we closed our eyes we might well have imagined that we were in the House of Lords. One left-wing senator from Bombay put forward the view that the owners of the mills did not deserve compensation as they had mismanaged their businesses by squandering the profits and by not investing in new machinery; it was the workers, he asserted, who should receive compensation as they had suffered by losing their livelihood. We had lunch with this senator in the Members' Dining Room after the debate and he invited us to visit him in Bombay. The debate in the Lok Sabha, the equivalent of our House of Commons, was much less interesting as it was about whether a bill concerning a matter which was sub judice could or could not be brought in. There was much quoting of precedents from the latest Erskine May book of reference, which is also our Parliamentary guidebook, and a great deal of quibbling about interpretations. As some speakers spoke in Hindu and some in English, and as little attention was paid to the Speaker or Presiding Officer, as he is called, it was difficult to follow the proceedings. The gentlemanly restraint and scholarly eloquence of the Rajya Sabha were lacking, especially when tempers became frayed, just as is the case in our own House of Commons. Nevertheless, considering the difficulties faced by this vast country, divided by more than thirty different languages and by so many diverse customs, we were impressed by the proceedings in the Indian Parliament. We noted too that most of the public gallery space was occupied by parties of college students, girls as well as boys, who listened very attentively to the debates. It is heartening to know that Indian schools and colleges are ensuring that their students have some knowledge of how government affairs are conducted.

That evening for supper, I made a large pot of soup which was just coming to the boil when our supply of Calor gas ran out, and as we had no other means of cooking we were in something of a predicament. However, Kerry took the soup in the pot to the little camp restaurant where the obliging manager finished the cooking for us and boiled a kettle of water for our evening cup of coffee. As we had already discovered that Calor gas is very difficult to obtain in India, and as we had been able to connect our cable to a supply of electricity at most of our stopping places, we decided to purchase an electric stove and an immersion heater, and although we did manage, after several forays, to have our gas cylinders filled in Delhi, thereafter we used our gas very sparingly and relied on electricity for light and cooking.

All available space in the camp park was filled with vans and motor homes, many of them belonging to Australians on their way down under. Most of them had planned to sell their vehicles in Nepal and fly home, but as there had been a tightening up on entry regulations into Australia, many travellers were preparing to hand over their cars to the Indian customs and to take any plane available before the first of January. One Scottish couple, who were emigrating to Australia, came to ask us if we would like a dog. They had taken pity on a stray mongrel in Isfahan and since they could not take it with them, were trying desperately to find a home for it. Although we felt sorry for them and the stray — a shaggy affectionate beast — we decided against adopting it. I have often wondered what they did with the dog as few Indians keep animals as pets and there are no homes for strays in India. I recall a conversation I had in Bombay with a professor with whom I was discussing the cult of the sacred cow, he said "I don't know who are more ridiculous, people who worship cows and stone dogs, or people who eat cows and keep dogs as pets." We had other callers, mainly Sikhs, who would pop their turbaned heads through the caravan door, enquiring whether we had any goods for sale. They told us that they would give us a high price for anything we wished to dispose of, but they seemed to be mainly interested in electrical goods, transistor radios, photographic equipment and Western clothes. As they were rather pushing fellows who refused to take 'no' for an answer, we found them very tiresome and told them so. However, other campers, especially the Australians about to leave India, found their services very useful, as they were able to dispose of all their belongings and make a handsome profit.

The weather had now become very chilly and damp, and for several days heavy clouds had obscured the sun and although we had not seen half the sights we had hoped to see in Delhi, we felt that the time had come to escape from the cold to the warmth of the south. We had no plans to return to the capital, and we were resigned to the fact that we would not see it again during our present trip. However, fate decided otherwise.

Four and a half months later, when the summer heat was reaching its peak, we returned to India after a month in Nepal and learned from the customs officials that the permit for our caravan was valid for only one month longer. As we had planned to remain in India for a further four months, this was a very serious problem. Of course, we were aware that the permit for the caravan was for six months only but we had assumed, rather naively, that having taken our car out of India to Nepal, we could remain for a further six months. We were told that this was not the case, and that there were no exceptions to this rule. The penalty for keeping the car in India longer than the stipulated period is a severe one, and in our case would have meant the forfeiture of the £8,000 indemnity which we had to deposit with the Automobile Association in Britain. The Indian Government requires a substantial guarantee from motorists, in our case it was twice the value of the vehicle, in order to ensure that the car is taken out within six months and is not sold in India. So we set out on a frantic paper chase in search of a permit, which made us retrace our steps and took us to unexpected places.

The Tourist Office in Lucknow had not the slightest idea how we should proceed to obtain an extension to our permit, but as no one in India will ever admit to ignorance, we were sent hither and thither on fruitless errands. We were directed to the police station and to the Customs Department in Lucknow, and then to the Area Customs Department in Kanpur, fifty miles away, where it looked as if we were going to be successful. The Area Commissioner, a very helpful individual, dictated a letter to his clerk granting us the extension and asked us to return within half an hour to collect it, so we sighed with relief and began to study our maps to find the shortest route from the sizzling plain to the mountains of Kashmir. Our elation was short-lived, however, for, when we returned to pick up the letter, the Commissioner informed us that he had realized that he had no authority to grant an extension; power to do this was vested only in the Ministry of Finance in Delhi. Fortunately, however, he knew Mr Singh, the Deputy Finance Minister, and he telephoned him to arrange an appointment for us.

The following day we were on our way to Delhi, our heads and necks swathed in towels soaked in water from the refrigerator in a vain attempt to keep cool during our dash over the plain. At Bareilly, we looked longingly at the road which branched off towards Naini Tal and the Himalayan foothills, the route we had hoped to follow. Then, bathed in sweat and pursued by the relentless sun, we sped on towards the capital. In Delhi we went straight to our senator friend, whom we had visited frequently in Bombay, to ask for advice. He was prepared to come with us to the Minister of Finance, but Kerry wanted to 'go it alone' and to enlist help only if he failed. Our friend shook his head, knowingly. "You will either have to give them a substantial bribe, or wait for three months. The choice is yours." In fact, it looked as if we had no choice, since Kerry refused to bribe on principle, and we had only one month left.

First of all, we had to find an air-conditioned room and a parking place, as it was far too hot to sleep in the caravan; in fact, the heat was so intense that we could have fried an egg on the bonnet. We found a room in a modest hotel in New Delhi about three miles from Connaught Place. It was air-conditioned and would have been very comfortable, had it not been for the frequent cuts in electricity which occurred regularly during the afternoons and evenings. At these times, there was neither relief nor refuge from the heat, and we had just to sweat it out in the hotel bedroom.

Early next morning, Kerry went to the Ministry of Finance to see Mr

Singh, who was rather dubious about our chance of obtaining an extension, but listed Kerry's reasons for the request and even suggested some extenuating circumstances which could be mentioned in the application. Kerry then had the problem of having his letter of request typed in triplicate. He was going to go to a bank when he saw that there was a court across the street. From previous experience he knew that lawyers usually have their "offices" on the pavements outside courts where private petitions are written and typed and cases are prepared, so he was able to have his application typed and there was no need for him to say 'in triplicate', for that is the normal procedure.

Mr Singh, who was surprised at the speed at which Kerry had moved, produced three more forms for Kerry to complete, which he did straightaway anticipating that after all this paperwork the permit would be within his grasp. "Leave the matter with me," said Mr Singh, "and I will let you know."

Fearing a delay of three months, Kerry asked him what would happen next.

"The most difficult task is still to come as I require the signatures of the Permanent Secretary and of the Minister himself in addition to my own."

"But you can add yours now" said Kerry, "and I am sure that the Permanent Secretary is a friend of yours."

Mr Singh signed a little reluctantly and vouchsafed that the Permanent Secretary's Office was on the fifth floor.

"Why don't we see him now?" said Kerry.

After some hesitation, Mr Singh accompanied him to the Permanent Secretary, a much harder man, who was not accustomed to sign on the spot; he had to think it over, consult regulations and so on.

But Kerry is very persuasive, and he finally emerged triumphantly with the second signature. "And now the Minister?" said Kerry, with incorrigible optimism.

Mr Singh paled visibly at the suggestion, as it was more than his job was worth to approach the Minister directly on this matter. "The Minister is a very busy man; we will have to wait for an opportune moment. I will do my best," he assured us. "You will have to be patient."

Time did not hang on our hands as we waited for our permit. There is plenty to do in Delhi and we had still many places of interest to visit. We used to rise early and make use of the cool hours before the heat became unbearable. Pursuing my interest in the Great Moguls we went to the Tomb of Homayun, the son of Babur and father of Akbar. Clever but indolent, Homayun almost lost the empire his father had won, and it was more by luck than by good judgment that he had a part of his kingdom left to hand over to his son. Our rickshaw driver set us down in front of a neglected garden, where, on a raised platform, stood a crumbling tomb from which most of the red sandstone facing had fallen away. Surely this forlorn spot was not the last resting place of a great emperor. On consulting our guidebooks we discovered that this was the Tomb of Isa Khan of the Lodi Afghan dynasty which ruled over Delhi before the coming of the Moguls. Wandering further, accompanied by a crowd of ragged urchins, shouting "Yek paisa" (One penny), we found ourselves in a beautiful garden full of flowering shrubs, where in front of us, resplendent in red sandstone, with white marble domes, stood the royal tomb. This was the Mogul magnificence we had hoped to find, reminiscent in style and setting of Akbar's tomb in Sikandra and of the Taj Mahal in Agra. As it was a Friday, which is to Mohammedans what Sunday is to Christians, and entry to places of interest is free, Muslim men and women with their children were streaming into the gardens carrying tiffin tins and cans of water. Soon the shady spots beneath the trees were splashed with colour as groups of women in silken blouses and men in white dhotis spread out their bright rugs on the grass. Meanwhile the children in their Friday best, the little girls in silver tinsel dresses and the boys in white suits, were rolling over and over ecstatically on the lawns. No one appeared to have the slightest interest in the great tomb, lying in the full glare of the sun. Perhaps within it, the Great Mogul was turning in his grave at the realisation that these Muslims had come, not out of reverence to him, but to relax and frolic in the beautiful garden. On the other hand, since he was a scion of a race who created beauty and loved gardens, he might well have felt deeply satisfied.

The most remarkable monument in Delhi is the Qutb Minar, a tower begun in the twelfth century by the first Muslim sultan and completed three hundred years later. Like the Tower of Pisa it has a list, caused by an earthquake which fortunately did not damage the shell of the tower with its finely carved quotations from the Koran. The letters have been so skilfully graded that, from a distance, they appear to be of the same size. At the foot of the tower lie the ruins of the first mosque ever to be built in India, and its carved pillars with designs of dancing girls and animals are thought to have been taken from earlier Hindu and Jain temples. The faces of the girls, however, have been mutilated, since Islam forbids the representation of the human form in its places of worship. In the courtyard of the mosque stands the famous Iron Pillar, twenty-four feet high, erected by a Hindu king, fifteen hundred years ago, and which, for some unaccountable reason has remained completely free of rust. Because of the mystery surrounding it, Indians have endowed this pillar with magical qualities. It is said, for instance, that if you can join your fingers as you stand with your back to the pillar, clasping your arms around it, your dearest wish will be fulfilled. After watching other visitors struggling without success to bring their fingertips together, Kerry managed to do so without any effort. If he did make a wish, I am sure that it concerned the permit we were seeking, and it may have been the Iron Pillar, and not his persistence, which was working for us.

It was at the Qutb Minar that I had a strange encounter. While Kerry was parking the van, a bearded, elderly man, dressed in a turban and a long white robe approached me, looking intently at me, he said, "I know your father's name."

I ignored him and turned away. From the corner of my eye I could see him write something down on a piece of paper which he screwed up and put in my hand. Kerry, who had joined me by this time, indicated that I should throw the paper away, but I was intrigued.

"Don't look at it," said the man. "Now spell your father's name." He wrote the name on a piece of paper, along with a number of irrelevant details such as my favourite flower, my lucky number, my birthday and so on. He folded this paper neatly saying "Now place your paper on top of mine."

Kerry and I kept our eyes fixed on my piece of crumpled paper lying in the palm of his hand.

"Open your paper," he said, and when I did so, I found the name 'Thomas' my father's name written boldly upon it.

We had been fooled, of course, by his sleight of hand, and for this trick, he demanded the sum of thirty rupees (about £1.60). When we gave him two rupees he protested loudly, claiming that he had been robbed.

"All right," said Kerry, "tell me my father's name and I will give you some more money," but the old fellow would have none of it, and he quickly disappeared into the crowd.

Sometimes we spent the evenings with our senator friend, who invited us to his house on a number of occasions, and from him we learned a great deal about Indian politics and Indian problems from the point of view of the left wing, or as he preferred to call it, the "progressive" point of view. When we had talked with him in Bombay, he was obviously shocked to hear that we had spent several weeks in an ashram.

"I believe," he said, "that Hinduism is one of the factors which is hindering India's progress. In the past, the Brahmins (members of the sacred caste) gave a good example to the people by leading austere and blameless lives, but nowadays they keep the lower classes in subjugation by inspiring fear of retribution in the next re-incarnation. Modern capitalists are just as blameworthy since they foster the trappings of Hinduism, the rituals, visits to shrines, etc., to keep the minds of their employees off their rights as individuals."

When we discussed family planning, an area in which the government was at that time spending a great deal of money in an effort to limit the population, our friend again blamed religion for the lack of progress. "Most Muslims and Hindus believe that it is their religious duty to produce progeny, preferably male, of course."

"But surely" countered Kerry, "the main reasons for large families are economic. The children are an insurance against bad health and old age, and since many children die in childhood, parents need to rear a large family to have a big reserve."

"The number of children dying in childhood is diminishing every day," our friend informed us. "Medical facilities have improved enormously and now even sickly children survive to swell the number."

We mentioned that we had been surprised that so many people in India speak English, and asked him whether he approved of this.

"The use of English," he averred, "brought together the Indian intelligentsia and furthered the 'Quit India Movement' — but it also created a gulf between them and other Indians. That gulf still remains between those who are educated in English medium schools, i.e. the upper and middle classes, and those who have no knowledge of English. Gandhi was right in insisting that Hindi should be adopted as the national language of India, but I believe that each child should also learn the language of his own province."

"And what about English?"

"Well, it is now the main international language and our schools must continue to teach it, but our official language must be Hindi."

The most emotive subject which we discussed was that of the 'black market', which our friend saw as the canker in India's economy. He claimed that the black market operates at all levels of society. Landowners hoard cereals and prices rise because of the scarcity; but those who make most money are the traders and not the producers, which results in the lack of incentive to produce. Watchdog committees have been set up to ferret out corruption, but members who reveal the truth fail to get promotion or are transferred elsewhere. The poor, and that means more than half of the population, do not benefit from the black market, also some professional people whose salaries and work have no connection with trade, but anyone who gains a living by selling, whether it is manufactured goods, food and drink, medicine, licences, tickets, etc., gain money on the side. "I will give you some examples of what is happening," he said. "New firms are set up with government grants to make, for instance, diesel engines or soap, etc., but nothing is produced. Instead, the promoters re-sell, at an inflated price, the materials what they have received from the government. Recently, I had a tip-off that grain was being stored in a large garage in Bombay, and I had the greatest difficulty in getting the police to take action. India has sufficient grain to feed its people, but it is badly distributed and hoarded. Prices are soaring, and we are living beyond our means. The crunch is bound to come."

"Can't parliament do something about it?" we asked.

"Members of the Congress Party are involved in black market dealings, just like other sections of the community, and remember there is no real opposition party in parliament. The second largest party is the Communist Party and it numbers about fifty members out of a total of more than five hundred."

We enquired about Jaynarayan Prakash whose activities were much in the news at that time.

"He is a Fascist, supported by funds from big business concerns in this country and in America. I do not always agree with Indira Gandhi, but when it comes to a showdown between her and J.P., she will have my support and that of members of all left-wing groups."

The showdown which he predicted, took place barely one month later, when all the left-wing senators supported the prime minister — but more of that anon.

It was during our discussions with our senator friend that we learned of an exciting new project about to be launched by the Ministry of Education through the National Educational Research Institute in Delhi. The scheme, the first of its kind in the world for educating people in backward areas, uses a broadcast system which is produced centrally in Delhi and relayed by a satellite dedicated to educational purposes. Every village in the chosen areas has been provided with a special dish aerial and a television set which is usually kept in the local school. When we visited the Research Institute, the Public Relations Officer explained the purpose of the project, the main aim of which is to keep children in school and to make lessons more interesting for them. At present, 60% of the children between the ages of six and fourteen drop out of school — a large percentage, when one considers that nearly 70% of the population is illiterate and receive no education whatsoever. The satellite programmes are intended for children of nine to ten years of age living in certain backward areas. Science has been selected as one of the main subjects to be taught and, in order to stimulate interest in the topics dealt with in the programmes, science kits and science booklets have been issued to the schools. We were not able to see any of the science films which were due to be broadcast in the autumn of 1975, but we did have a preview of two short films which formed part of the teacher training programme to be transmitted during the summer holidays. There are not nearly enough teachers especially in rural areas, and even if more were available, state authorities could not afford to employ them, thus the programmes we saw were intended to give the teachers, most of whom have had very little education, new and stimulating ideas. One of the programmes showed how to make the teaching of numbers interesting to children, how to encourage them to handle the various objects to be enumerated, how to group them in pairs, in sets, etc., and how to hold their interest with songs and rhymes. The other film dealt with the teaching of the letters of the alphabet using straws to form them and games with words beginning with each new letter learnt. Although I felt that there was not sufficient content in these programmes to justify the considerable sums of money spent on producing them, they did represent a great step forward in primary education. Up till now, all over India, children have been taught by rote, committing their lessons to memory without any real understanding of the content. In addition to the programmes for children and teachers which were broadcast during the day, there were evening broadcasts for small farmers which showed them how to make the best use of their land, and there were also programmes dealing with health and hygiene which were of special interest to the women of the village.

After the series of programmes started in August 1975, we read with interest the comments of teachers and others in the columns of the *Times of India*. There had been the usual teething troubles, most of which were of a technical nature; for example the TV sets broke down frequently, and as each village had only one apparatus, the whole series of broadcasts were disrupted. Since there are very few technicians capable of repairing the sets there have been long delays during which the children and teachers have lost interest in the programmes, but it is to be hoped that these difficulties will soon be overcome and that this brave educational endeavour will succeed.

In addition to our educational visits and our political discussions, we had other distractions in Delhi because Kerry had re-discovered a long-lost cousin living with his family in Delhi, and we spent several happy evenings with them. As is the case in the West, middle and upper-class people in India reside on the fringes of large towns in pleasant garden suburbs, and there are a number of these situated on the south side of Delhi with well designed modern villas set amongst flowering trees and shrubs. Most of the people who live in these housing estates, or 'Colonies', as they are called, are professional or business people who can afford a car, a TV and a servant. Our relations live in the Kailash Colony which is about four miles from the centre of Delhi and their lifestyle is very similar to that of a professional family in the West. Hoshi, his wife, Alu, and their three children reside in a spacious house with all modern amenities, including air-conditioning, a TV set, a car and a daily servant. However, to pay for these extras, both Hoshi and his wife work full time — Hoshi, as a manager of an American firm, and Alu as a teacher in a private school. Their house costs them about £37 per month in rent, which is cheap compared with prices in this country, but it must be remembered that salaries are also low; especially those of teachers. Alu complained that there was nothing one could do about it as there are many unemployed teachers waiting to take her place. Her kindergarten school, which was run previously by Irish nuns, now replaced by Indians, is fee-paying and therefore exclusive. Alu is in favour of this as she dislikes state schools, but resents the fact that funds for school activities are very short and have to be supplemented by the proceeds of fetes, jumble sales and concerts, organised by an energetic Parent-Teacher Association. Alu's brother and parents have emigrated to America where they have prospered, and it is her greatest ambition to join them to ensure a happy and secure future for her children. Both she and Hoshi see a long troubled period ahead for India, and like many educated Indians we met on our journey, they would like to escape to the West.

Their two teenage girls, dressed in jeans and stretch tops, and their young son, would fit happily into any upper or middle-class family in Britain or America. Educated in English medium schools they are bilingual, speaking Gujarati and English with equal fluency and in their choice of clothes, books and hobbies there is nothing to distinguish them from their Western counterparts. In some respects, however, these children, have in our eyes, some very definite advantages over most European youngsters. They have delightful manners, move with poise and grace and seem to have a very friendly and happy relationship with their parents; qualities and circumstances which are comparatively rare in the West. On our second visit to their home, a tailor had taken up residence for a few days and was busy stitching pants, tops and long dresses for the girls who were going to Bombay for their summer holidays. Visits from tailors, still common in India, are now quite beyond the means of most of us in the West.

Nine days after our arrival in Delhi, we rang up as usual to find out whether our permit had been granted, and a triumphant Under Secretary informed us that we had been successful and had permission to keep our vehicle in India until the end of September. We were overjoyed, and when we told our senator friend he could not believe that we had achieved this favourable result so quickly without pulling strings or giving some inducement. We can put on record, however, that at no time during the whole transaction did any of the officials hint that they expected a 'backhander', and that everyone we approached acted in accordance with the best traditions of the Indian Civil Service.

Here I must pick up again the thread of the account of our first visit to Delhi which ended on Christmas Eve, 1975. The Delhi we left on that day was a very different city from the one we were to revisit in blistering heat five months later; for when we set out for Agra in December, feeling chilly in spite of our winter clothes, a wet fog lay low over the town, and for an hour we drove without seeing anything but the stretch of road ahead of us. By that time we had left the capital behind us and were travelling through a dismal, damp countryside, where the peasants were going to work, wrapped in blankets and with scarves around their heads. In the villages, the day's work had not yet begun, and groups of people were huddled over smoky braziers. Conditions have probably changed very little during the last three hundred years since the Great Moguls followed this, the royal route, between Delhi and Agra where they held court. We turned off the main road to visit Mathura, one of the oldest temple towns in India, made famous by the cult of Krishna. Legend has it that Krishna, the cowherd god and eighth incarnation of Vishnu, was born here, and for that reason the town is held in special reverence by the Hindus. Mathura has another claim to fame; because it was here, in the first century AD, that there was a flowering of religious sculpture which lasted for a millennium. Thousands of images of the Hindu gods and of Buddha were fashioned here in stone and found their way all over India. However, on that morning in December when we visited Mathura the mist obscured the bathing ghats on River Jumna and the streets looked deserted and forlorn.

It was not far from Mathura that the box on our roof rack suffered its first, and by no means its last, calamity. This container had been made by Kerry before our departure from stout pieces of wood with a lid of aluminium. It held two spare tyres, camping equipment, climbing boots and an assortment of other bits and pieces. I was driving at the time along a narrow stretch of road where lorries laden with sugar cane were drawn up on both sides. It was, as we realized later, a checking point for truck loads, in front of which a wooden pole, used as a barrier, hung at an angle over the road. Unfortunately, I misjudged the height of the pole which caught our box, sheering off the lid and splintering its wooden sides. Kerry bound it together with rope and string and we proceeded very soberly to Sikandra, six miles north of Agra with me feeling very chastened by the thought of my own carelessness. This mood was soon dispelled, however, when I caught sight of the great red sandstone gateway, topped by minarets which leads to the mausoleum of Akbar the Great. We were back in the realm of the Moguls, in a world of fantasy and splendour which has for me an irresistible appeal. We parked the car in front of the entrance which was guarded by an army of large, grey monkeys. Nearby a small boy with a cobra twined around his neck was playing the flute and a snake charmer was sitting cross-legged in front of a basket from which protruded the heads of a number of evil-looking snakes. Viewing these tourist attractions were crowds of visitors, including a bus load of Australians on a Swagman tour whom we had already met at the camp site in Delhi. According to the inscription above the gateway at Sikandra, the mausoleum was erected by Akbar's son, Jahangir in 1613. It lies in a huge garden, which we approached along an avenue of palm trees, scrutinized by the beady eyes of black vultures which were resting on the tree tops. Inside the vast, turreted building, dimly discernible in the semi-darkness, lie the tombs of Akbar and one of his wives. They are exquisitely carved and bear the inscription 'Allah-o-Akbar' (God is the greatest), as well as the ninety-nine names which the Muslims use to describe the Almighty. It is said that a marble pedestal in the burial chamber once supported the famous Kohinoor diamond, which Akbar's grandfather, Babur, seized when he captured Agra. When we had finished photographing the mausoleum and the vultures, we set out our tables and chairs to have our lunch in the open air, as it was now sunny and warm. However, we had not reckoned with the monkeys who were determined to snatch our food, so we retreated into the van to eat our scrambled egg on toast, entertained by the antics of the monkeys and the gyrations of the snakes.

As there is no camp site for tourists in Agra, or for that matter, anywhere else in India apart from Delhi, we found a parking spot in the garden of a private house which was recommended by the Tourist Office. Mrs Framjee, the owner of the bungalow, provided us with a space for our car and toilet facilities for the modest sum of five rupees, with two rupees extra for electricity. So eager were we to see the Mogul's greatest masterpiece before nightfall that we did not even wait to fix up our electric cable to the house supply or to wrap up warmly against the evening's cold. As we rode in a bicycle rickshaw through the cantonment area, we debated whether the Taj Mahal was likely to come up to our expectations, and as we alighted at the red-stone portal I braced myself for a possible disappointment. We hurried through the great gateway, and there was the famous Taj, white and shimmering, perfect in proportions and beauty, a sight for which alone it was worthwhile making the long journey to India. We photographed it from every conceivable

L

angle, capturing its lovely reflection in the water channel which flows in front of it. Then removing our shoes we followed the throng of tourists onto the great terrace which supports the white marble edifice and through the high archway which is the entrance to the mausoleum, where, under the great dome of the Taj Mahal lie the tombs of Shah Jahan and his wife Mumtaz.

Mumtaz, who is reported to have been both beautiful and wise, was the niece of Jahangir's wife, Nur Jahan, and the second wife of Shah Jahan. She bore him fourteen children and when she died in childbirth at the age of thirty-nine, Shah Jahan was broken-hearted. He vowed that he would erect a memorial to her which, would surpass in beauty every building in the world, and no one can gainsay that he succeeded in his aim, for few dispute that the Taj has an equal anywhere on earth. Skilled craftsmen were brought from all over the world, and together with twenty thousand labourers, they toiled for seventeen years to complete the building. Only a Mogul emperor, and a romantic one at that, could have conceived such an exquisite memorial to his beloved. The workmanship on the tomb of Mumtaz is beyond belief. The designs, inlaid with precious stones, have been done so skilfully that the flowers and leaves look as if they have been carved from one piece, although someone has counted thirty-five different varieties of cornelian in one carnation leaf. The royal pair do not lie in the white sarcophagi behind the marble screens, but in the crypt beneath, as this was the usual custom in royal mausoleums, to ensure that no one would be able to walk over the graves.

By the time we returned to the caravan we were shivering with cold after our drive in an open rickshaw and as it was now dark, Kerry had some difficulty in fixing the electric cable to the house supply where the plugs and wiring were in a poor condition. It was while we were struggling to sling a line over the courtyard that the realisation suddenly dawned on us, that it was Christmas Eve.

"Let's celebrate," said Kerry, but our cupboard was bare, and as we did not fancy the modest meal which Mrs Framjee supplied to her boarders, we set out in search of a 'super meal'. We found one in the Kwality Restaurant where we were served with very tasty Mughlai dishes. "Mughlai" food, as the name implies, owes a great deal to the Moguls and it is popular in this part of the country. After mulligatawny soup, I had 'rogan gosh', a spicy mutton curry, with a dish of dahi (curd) to cool it down, and Kerry had a chicken biriani, which is a sumptuous dish consisting of a whole chicken covered with rice, garnished with oranges, nuts and grapes. We finished off with a halva which is a sweet pudding made of semolina and spices. We had ordered so much food that we were not able to eat two large slabs of fresh nan (bread), which we wrapped up in serviettes and kept for breakfast. There was a decidedly wintry nip in the air as we went home to bed and a hot-water bottle, dreaming of Christmas at home.

In the early hours of the morning I was awakened by the sound of music, and for a moment I thought that I could hear Christmas carols being sung; but it was only the Muslims chanting their early morning prayers.

We had to spend several hours in the Street of the Carpenters to have our box mended, with Kerry keeping a close watch on the joiner as this was the only way to have work done to one's satisfaction. When I had washed the breakfast dishes and tidied up the caravan, I sat and watched what was happening in the street outside. From the large rear window of the van I had a cinematic view of ordinary life in a downtown area. The shops on either side of the road were no more than straw-covered shacks, standing on earth between tall trees, and in front of these stalls was an open gutter, full of stagnant water and decaying vegetation. Groups of children were gathered around charcoal fires trying to keep warm, and there was a constant procession of women passing to and fro with large copper pots upon their heads. One poor old woman, who was scraping the dirt and refuse together with the aid of a straw hand-broom was almost bowled over by a bony cow which ran across the road to join a hog rooting in a pile of rubbish. Tired of sitting around I sallied forth to explore, and was rather peeved to be greeted by an old man with "Good morning, Sir". Now I was wearing slacks, a woollen pullover and Kerry's old golfing hat, but somehow I had imagined that I was recognisable as a female. Later on, I did discover that 'Sir and Mister' are usual greetings for ladies from people who know little English. This particular old man was teasing out cotton on a foot treadle, just as I had seen women do with wool in the Outer Hebrides.

Further along the street, a man dressed only in his underpants, was sitting on a stone pouring bucketfuls of cold water over himself. This is quite a familiar sight in India at any season of the year, and belies the notion that Indians rarely wash themselves. In fact, in spite of the shortage of water, Hindus and Muslims are very particular about their toilet, and are continually washing both themselves and their garments. At the end of the street was a cemetery where four young women were sitting on a charpoy (string bed) between some tombstones, singing cheerfully and playing on sitars. When they saw me they called out something in Hindi and waved in a friendly manner, and I wished that I had been able to converse with them.

Opposite the cemetery, stood a large, old-fashioned house with ornate balconies and verandahs, and as I paused to look at it, a pleasant looking man in a long mandarin-style coat approached me. "Would you like to come and see my house?" he said.

I was completely taken by surprise, and scarcely knew what to answer since I did not wish to cause offence. I replied that I would be delighted and that I would fetch my husband to accompany me. When we returned he was waiting for us in front of the house and ushered us into a large room full of antiques.

'It's a museum,' I thought to myself, a little disappointed as I had imagined that it was a private house. There was a large collection of ancient clocks from all over the world, several beautifully carved sofas of Portuguese workmanship, a bed with embossed silver legs, numerous ornate daggers and swords, and strangest of all, a black old-fashioned English stove. It was a puzzling assortment, and it was only when our host showed us a silver scroll which had belonged to his father who had been a high court judge, that we realized that this strange collection was indeed a private one, belonging to a very rich Muslim family. As we went from room to room, each furnished with priceless works of art, our friend explained that this was a very special day for him and his family, as it was Id, the Muslim Festival which in 1975, coincided with Christmas Day. He was wearing ceremonial clothes to welcome strangers into his home on this auspicious day, according to tradition. We were taken into the women's room, which is rarely shown to strangers. It was completely bare except for a beautiful carpet on which two elderly women were seated, busily sewing a length of silk. In another room a servant brought us each a dish of a sweetmeat made of milk, sugar and some sort of cereal which is served only on Muslim special days, and here we were shown a number of jade plates, dating from the sixteenth and seventeenth centuries. In those days, explained our host, Indian grandees took their own plates with them when they were invited to a banquet, partly for reasons of hygiene and partly to ensure their lives against a possible attempt at poisoning. These jade plates had very special properties as they were made in such a way that should there be poison in the food served upon them they would break in to pieces. I thought this story rather improbable but did not voice my doubts as our host was so sincere and genial.

By this time our box had been mended, not entirely to our satisfaction, as the lid did not fit. However, we accepted it as it was, not wishing to have any further delay. After viewing the Taj every tourist goes to see the fort at Agra which is a most fascinating building both from the point of view of its history and for its artistic merits. Three of the greatest Moguls held court here, dividing their time between Agra and Delhi.

Each of these — Akbar, Jahangir and Shah Jahan — has left the imprint of his personality on the great fort. Akbar built the mighty battlements and a palace which is now in ruins. The palace he built for his son, Jahangir, is the first building you see when you come through the main entrance. In this ornate, gilded residence with its blend of Hindu and Mogul architectural styles, Jahangir and his wife, Nur Jahan, held court. By all accounts, he was a much weaker and less liberal monarch than his father, and it was his wife, a very forceful woman, who held the reins of power. The great bath which stands near the entrance is called Jahangir's bath and was carved out of one block of marble, probably as a christening gift from his father. The cruel streak which was a feature of all the Moguls' characters, is illustrated by the way they disposed of their enemies. We were shown the entrance to the underground pit into which many unfortunate victims were dropped to be engulfed by the flood waters of the River Jumna.

The most beautiful buildings in the fort are, as one would expect, those which were constructed by the most artistic of the Moguls, Shah Jahan. It was he who built the Moti Masjid, perhaps the most beautiful of all his pearl mosques, the throne room in the Hall of Public Audience with its wonderful mosaics, the Hall of Private Audience, and, of course, the jewel of the fort, the Khas Mahal, Shah Jahan's private palace. Nowhere in the West do we see buildings of such lavish magnificence, and although the walls have been stripped of the precious stones which were embedded in the floral patterns, the turreted marble palace has the beauty of a fairy-tale. Alas, the fairy-tale love story of Shah Jahan and his Mumtaz had an unhappy ending. Not only did the emperor lose his beloved one, but for the last seven years of his life he lost his freedom, held captive in the fort by his son, Aurangzeb. He died in the Musamman Burj, the octagonal tower which he had built for Mumtaz, attended by his faithful daughter, Jahanara. It was a miserable finish to a great reign, but it must be remembered that Aurangzeb in removing his father from power, was doing no more than follow his father's example, for at his succession, Shah Jahan had all the male descendants of his brothers and uncles executed. In the eyes of most Hindus, Aurangzeb was a villain, and this was the verdict we heard of him all over India, especially in Benares. Being a very orthodox Muslim, he lacked his predecessors' liberality towards members of other religions and he had inherited their ruthlessness.

As the sun was setting we returned to the Taj which, in the warm glow of sunset, appeared even more ethereal than in broad daylight. We waited until all the colour had drained from the sky, so reluctant were we to take our departure. Then we walked through the village nearby, the Taj Ganj, built by Shah Jahan to house the labourers who worked on his masterpiece. There in tiny workshops craftsmen were making plates, trays and models of the Taj, decorated and inlaid with precious stones. A power failure occurred when we were in the village, but soon candles were alight everywhere, twinkling through the gloom. There was still no electric power when we reached Mrs Framjee's so we cooked our vegetable stew by Calor gas with the aid of a torch. In retrospect, it was a somewhat dismal end to a Christmas day, but at the time we were so enthralled by the sights we had seen that we completely forgot the significance of the date.

There was still one Mogul pilgrimage which we had to make, namely to the amazing ghost city of Fatehpur Sikri which lies about thirty miles west of Agra. One day in 1566 Akbar came here to visit a Muslim holy man — Shaikh Salim Christi, to beg a boon from him. Although he had been married for several years and had three wives, Akbar had no son, and he desperately wanted an heir, so he asked the holy man to pray that his wish should be granted, as indeed it was with the birth of a son, who was named Salim in honour of the saint, although later known by the name of Jahangir. Three years later Akbar decided to transfer his capital from Agra to Fatehpur Sikri, where for fourteen years he ruled in such a magnificent style that the fame of his court spread throughout the Western world. Then, abruptly, Akbar abandoned his new capital and the city has been completely deserted ever since. There seems to be some mystery surrounding Akbar's decision to leave the town so suddenly, although most historians claim that he did so because the water supply dried up.

When we visited Fatehpur Sikri, we took a guide whom we shared with two Indian tourists from Fiji. Outside the Hall of Public Audience we were shown the stone post where the elephant which acted as the Lord High Executioner was tethered. It was this animal's gruesome task to trample all wrongdoers to death, a sight which the Mogul courtiers are said to have enjoyed. The status and importance of these elephants can be judged by the elaborate tomb which one of these beasts was given just outside the city walls. In the Hall of Private Audience, I climbed into the gallery to be photographed in the seat where Akbar used to sit to receive important dignitaries. Those exalted thrones were constructed so that anyone approaching the emperor should look up to him and he down upon them; but Akbar was no ordinary despot since he had many liberal ideas and showed so much tolerance to people of other religious persuasions that his fellow Muslims looked upon him as a heretic. He must have needed all his tolerance, since one of his wives was a Christian, another a Muslim, and his favourite wife, Jahangir's mother, was a

Hindu. For each of these wives Akbar built a separate palace, that of Jodh Bai, his Hindu wife, still being the most magnificent, even though thieves have removed its sandalwood panelling and the gems which were encrusted in its walls. Amongst the carved decorations on the outside walls of these palaces we discovered various religious symbols including the star of David, the Muslim crescent, and the swastika-like sign used by Hindus. Judging by the princely house which Akbar built for the court jester, the latter's status must have been considerable and he must have contributed to the gaiety which pervaded the court. We were shown one building decorated with stone monsters where Akbar is said to have played blind man's buff with the ladies of the harem, and we also saw in one courtyard an area laid out like a chessboard where Akbar played backgammon, using slave girls as pieces.

The great mass of the Jama Masjid Mosque dwarfs the white marble shrine of the Muslim holy man, Christi, which has become a place of pilgrimage, and childless women from all over India and even from further afield come here to pray to be blessed with children. When we visited the shrine we watched a number of women tie threads purchased from the attendant to the lacy marble screen around the tomb, expressing as they did so the wish to have a child. If the wish is granted it is the custom for the fortunate women to return to the shrine to untie the thread. Some of these women bring gifts with them, and our guide showed us a magnificent blue velvet cover embroidered with silver thread which one grateful mother from South Africa had donated to the shrine. Our guide also informed us that the area of the town near the tomb belongs to the descendants of the saint, and they have the right to be buried here. Lying in the shade of Akbar's triumphal arch, which was the main entrance to the town and is said to be the highest arch in India, their little graves look pitifully small.

As we were proceeding on our way towards Jaipur, we saw a signpost to the Keolado Ghana Bird Sanctuary and on the spur of the moment we decided to go there, as we were fond of bird-watching and the prospect of spending some time in peaceful, natural surroundings attracted us. It is one of the great advantages of travelling in a motor home that changes of plan occasioned by sudden whims and fancies present no problem; so in next to no time we were installed in a very pleasant parking spot near a well-appointed forest rest house which provides toilet and washing facilities for tourists at a very reasonable cost. The sanctuary covers an area of twelve square miles and a maze of narrow roads lead through the marshes where countless water birds breed and nest. In warm, bright sunshine we wandered along the edge of the swamp, identifying its inhabitants — painted storks, kingfishers, cranes, grey lags, egrets, white ibis, spoonbills and many others to which we could not give a name. As we sat amongst the tall reeds quietly contemplating these wonders, a herd of black deer came splashing through the water towards us. They shied away when they heard the click of the camera, and later we identified them from the pictures in the rest house as swamp deer which are found only in India. According to the warden, a great many of the birds we had seen had come to over-winter from as far afield as Siberia.

We had been surprised at the existence of this sanctuary which had obviously been established for many years, until we realized that it had been part of the Maharajah of Bharatpur's game reserve and we discovered huge stone plaques detailing the number of birds bagged by various shooting parties between 1900 and 1946. In some seasons, the viceroy or another dignitary with his guests, had accounted for five to six thousand water birds. It was an appalling massacre. Strangely enough, partition, which unhappily resulted in the death of countless Indians, led to the preservation of the wildlife of India since the estates of the maharajahs were nationalized and many became game reserves and national parks. There are now more than twenty wildlife sanctuaries and national parks in India with accommodation for tourists. Five months later we were on our way to one of the largest of these reserves — the Corbett National Park, near Nainital when our permit problems forced us to change course for Delhi. Some day, however, we hope to return to India to see the last remaining Indian lions in the Gir Forest Sanctuary in Gujarat, and the Peryar Sanctuary in Kerala with its wild elephants and herds of sambar and gaur.

In the late afternoon, on our way back to the rest house, we saw a Western couple studying the birds through binoculars. They looked familiar. "It can't be," I said. "Yes, it is the Marshalls" confirmed Kerry, and we hailed our erstwhile travelling companions whom we had last seen in the Valley of Bamian. Bruce and Phyllis Marshall had been in the sanctuary for several days and were so happy there that they intended to remain for several weeks before setting out on the long trek back to Britain.

That evening we had a happy get-together, recounting our experiences and exchanging our impressions of the places we had visited. Had it not been for arrangements we had made to be in Bombay by Christmas and were already a week behind schedule we would have been very happy to linger longer with our friends in the bird sanctuary.

Next morning, awakened by the babble of birds at dawn, we resumed our journey through Rajasthan towards Jaipur. The people of Rajasthan must surely be the most colourful inhabitants of India; the men in their pink or yellow turbans, and the women in their full skirted dresses in dazzling colours. We stopped several times near wells and pumps where women were waiting, their brass pots, anklets and gold necklaces glistening in the sunlight, but we were thwarted in our attempts to capture the scene with our cameras, since the women, unwilling to be photographed, turned their backs on us, and naturally we respected their wishes. These Rajputs are strong, proud-looking people, renowned for their martial qualities and feats of valour. For centuries they fought against the Muslim invaders, preferring to die rather than surrender. The women showed just as much courage as their menfolk, by throwing themselves on burning pyres when faced with overwhelming odds. It was only when Akbar married a Rajput princess that this warlike race was persuaded to join forces with the Moguls.

The shortage of water is one of Rajasthan's problems, and in the dry season it is a veritable dust bowl, for centuries of drought and erosion have made great tracts of land barren and useless. Near Jaipur we made a detour to see the mighty fort at Amber, which for hundreds of years was the capital of Rajasthan. Standing on the crest of a hill overlooking a lake, the fortress is an impressive sight, and we were tempted to see it at close quarters on the back of one of the elephants provided for tourists. However, we resisted the temptation and pressed on to Jaipur.

Our first impression of Jaipur was a disappointing one, as it was scarcely the idyllic place of unspoilt Oriental charm which our guidebook had led us to expect. Its pink stone walls, covered with graffiti, old posters and cinema advertisements, instead of glowing in the sunlight, looked faded and discoloured. However, the Tourist Bungalow offered us good facilities at a very cheap rate (2 rupees for parking and 1 for electricity), and there was now a welcome warmth in the sun which had been lacking further north. The centre of the town, enclosed by a high crenellated wall, is one great oriental bazaar, swarming with people and bicycle riskshaws. It was the best shopping place we found in the whole of India and the range and quality of goods for sale was amazing. In one area there were several streets where tie-dyed sarees in the most gorgeous colours billowed from the shop fronts like sails in the wind. In another part of the bazaar it was the sparkle of precious and semi-precious stones which caught our attention, and there was also an abundance of cheap fruit and vegetables, and mounds of white jasmine and marigold petals. For the equivalent of £8, I purchased two tie-dyed sarees, one cotton and one voile, two pairs of embroidered slippers, two necklaces and some uncut pieces of amethyst. Had we but known that goods were more expensive further south, we would have been much less penny-pinching and would have bought all our presents in Jaipur. We were so fascinated by the colourful displays in the bazaar that we had little time to explore the rest of the town, but we did visit the extraordinary Palace of the Winds which rises in the centre of the city like a magnificent five-tiered wedding cake in fretted stone. Another landmark we saw in Jaipur was the ancient observatory which stands in the middle of the bazaar and was erected by Maharajah Jai Singh who was a distinguished astronomer. It was this Jai Singh who founded Jaipur (pur means town) in 1727, when he transferred his capital from the citadel of Amber.

On the road to Udaipur, women in brilliant sarees vied for our attention with the peacocks which strutted over the fields. Their menfolk in enormous turbans were almost as colourful and just as handsome. Red was the predominant colour of this area; the red of the sarees and turbans, and the red of the chillies, acres of which were spread out to dry in the sun. We grieved that time did not allow us to visit the famous places to which the signposts pointed — Jodhpur, famous for its horsemen who have left us their 'jodhpurs' as a legacy; Mount Abu with its Jain shrines, and Chittorgarh, where, four hundred years ago, thousands of Rajpur women hurled themselves into a furnace rather than be taken captive by the Muslims.

In contrast to the arid uplands to the north, the surroundings of Udaipur are lush and green, and at first sight, the town seemed to float on the deep blue waters of Lake Pichola. We made straight for the lakeside, eager to see the famous Lake Palace Hotel which once belonged to the maharajah (or maharana as he was called), and which is now one of India's most select hotels. We crossed the lake by ferry boat and had tea in the luxurious surroundings, savouring for a brief moment the lifestyle of the former inhabitants. The hotel was full of tourists, mainly Americans, who had come here to spend the Christmas season. Bathed in afternoon sunshine, in a garden full of fountains and flowers, we sipped our tea and contemplated the marble wonders of the Palace. Two cups of tea and two 'bhujias' (savoury balls) cost us about £3, but we felt it was worth the price, just to see the Palace. Should we inherit a fortune some day, we plan to return for a holiday in these splendid surroundings. However, the Tourist Bungalow, very modest by the Lake Palace standard, offered us all the facilities we needed, namely toilets and electricity, and there we met a pleasant group of Geology students from Delhi University and dined with them at the Kwality Restaurant.

Next day, as we wandered through the bazaar of the old town, we were pestered by small boys, following at our heels, shouting, "Good morning! What is your name?" etc. One small urchin actually snatched off my hat and made off with it, but dropped it when Kerry raced after him. The bazaars were less colourful than those at Jaipur and the goods were more expensive, but there were many picturesque corners to explore along the lakeside and we also visited an ancient ornate Jain temple in the middle of the old town. It is in this part of India that most of the Jains are to be found. These are members of a small quasi-religious sect who believe in non-violence; some of them being so fanatical in their belief that they cover their mouths with a white cloth to prevent them from breathing in and destroying small insects. Jainism was founded in the sixth century BC by the teacher Mahivira who is referred to as Jina which means conqueror — hence the word Jain. As is the case with Buddhism, the popularity of Jainism has waned during the past centuries and it is now adhered to by a very small portion of the population.

That evening we had one of our marmalade-making sessions with oranges, limes and sugar bought at the market, but as we had no means of measuring quantities, it was not a great success, and the finished product, although still palatable, was so stiff that we could cut it with a knife. For supper, we followed our usual practice at Tourist Bungalows by ordering meat dishes from the canteen. Thus for the equivalent of 50p we had a meal of mutton curry and 'puris' (fried pastries), which we supplemented with our own cooked vegetables and fruit.

Next morning when dawn broke, suffusing the sky with the most delicate shades of pink, we had been on the road for over an hour and were travelling through the barren and empty uplands of Rajasthan. Here and there, however, the pervading brownness of the region was relieved with splashes of colour formed by women's bright garments. We caught up with a group of pretty young girls dressed in sarees who were striding along the road with copper trays balanced gracefully upon their heads. "What were they going to do?" In this arid land there was neither flowers nor fruit for dainty maidens to pick. Then we realized that there was nothing very dainty and feminine about the task which these girls were engaged in. Their work was to gather up the dung from the highway with their bare hands and take it back to the village. Everywhere in India, gathering dung is the job of women, and they do not seem to consider this task to be demeaning, for in fact, it affords them scope for their artistic skill. As we passed through Indian villages we often paused to watch the women, squatting in front of piles of dung, patting it into pancake or saucer shapes which they laid out in neat rows or circles to dry in the sun. When the dung was dry they shaped the piles into rounded or pointed stacks which looked like miniature hayricks. Whereas in the north of India we had observed that the dung was often roughly plastered on house walls to dry, the further south we proceeded the more elaborate were the patterns and shapes which the women fashioned from animal manure. In the East, dung is a very precious commodity as it is used in the same way as we use coal or coke. In most villages it is the only fuel available and even in towns we saw it being used to supplement charcoal. Indeed cow dung is a most versatile material, as it is used mixed with mud, in the construction of floors and walls, and it must also have some hidden significance as we have seen holy men plaster it over their matted locks. We could not help thinking that it should have been used to make the soil more fertile, but Indians would not dream of 'wasting' this precious material on Mother Earth. In addition to these elegant scavengers we saw other people at work on the bare hillsides, lone women, scratching the ground with a piece of sharp metal, clawing roots from the dry earth. We never discovered whether these roots were for human or animal consumption, although we suspected the former as this region was too arid to support crops of any kind and we saw no animals, apart from an occasional camel.

We took a short cut to Baroda via Rampur and Madosa on a rough road, fringed with hedges of cacti, where the milestones were as unreliable as the people we asked about distances. "It is two furlongs to the next village," they would say. After much calculation, having forgotten our tables, we worked this out at a quarter of a mile. As the village would inevitably be several miles away, we fully concluded that by Indian measurements eight furlongs do not constitute one mile. When we stopped for lunch we realized that our water supply was almost exhausted and we went in search of a well or a village pump. However, for mile after mile there was not a drop of water to be found, so in desperation we called in at a military barracks not far from Baroda, where a gardener who was watering the lawns offered to fill up our tanks with his hose pipe. Unfortunately, this water was so contaminated with organic material that our valiant little Safari filter could not cope with it and gave up the struggle; so that evening we had to flush out the tanks and refill them with purer water.

In Baroda we had the good fortune to be allowed to park in the pleasant garden of the Circuit House. Circuit Houses throughout India are intended primarily to accommodate important government officers and VIPs on official business, but occasionally tourists are allowed to stay there or to park their cars in the compound. At Ambala on our way to Rishikesh, our request to be allowed to park in the grounds of the Circuit House had been refused and we were referred to the Tourist Bungalow, where we were given toilet and shower facilities. Tourist Bungalows are to be found in most towns in India, and they offer the basic amenities and simple meals at a very reasonable cost. Later on we were to sample the humble facilities of the Dak Bungalow, the oldest institution of its kind in India, where the conditions are more Spartan than in the Tourist Bungalows and bedding and meals are not always provided, but you can enjoy the luxury of a cold shower from a bucket of water. On many an evening after a long day's drive our spirits would rise when we recognised the low pitched roof of a Dak Bungalow ahead of us, feeling pretty certain that we would find there the security of a compound, clean toilets and water, and we were never disappointed either with the facilities or with the service we received. Compared with its poor relation, the Dak Bungalow, the Circuit House at Baroda was very palatial, with spacious villas set in a garden full of hibiscus and bougainvillea. It was now as warm as it is at the height of our summer and we felt dusty and travel worn. However, a servant gave us the key to the bathroom of one of these residences, and we had a wash in luxurious surroundings. In the meantime, the 'dhobi' ironed one of my sarees and Kerry's tropical suit, so we were able to discard our crumpled jeans and jacket and emerge looking like respectable tourists.

Baroda is a large modern town with wide avenues and fine buildings, dating from the era when the Maharajah of Baroda was the head of a princedom. The city walls, however, are much more ancient, and it was from these that Akbar sallied forth with his army to secure the busy port of Surat. In the days before partition, the state of Baroda was one of the most progressive in the whole of India — now, swallowed up by the huge state of Gujarat it has lost much of its glamour and style; but Baroda is still a pleasant, interesting town, well worth a visit. Our main reason for making a halt there, however, was not to visit the town, but to call on one of Kerry's cousins who is a dentist. Posing as a patient, Kerry went into the waiting room, and then into the surgery when summoned by the bell. He sat down in the dental chair and started to relate a tale of toothache when Homi recognised him and burst out laughing. Kerry was pleased to know that he had not changed too much during the twelve years since he had met his cousin in London. That evening we dined with Homi and his wife who had just moved into a new home in a pleasant part of the town. Their villa with its floors and staircase faced with marble, its modern bathrooms with sunken baths, is a sample of the type of house now being built by India's professional and business classes. South of Baroda, a modern highway fringed with palm trees runs through maize fields and banana plantations. It was in this region near the old ports of Broach and Surat that the Zoroastrians, fleeing from the religious intolerance of the Muslims in Persia, made their homes in the seventh and eighth centuries AD. Their first settlement was on the island of Diu, in the Gulf of Cambray, and from there they gradually moved to the mainland where they were called Persis or Parsees — people from Persia, and adopted the language of Gujarat-Gujarati, which is still the main language of most Parsees. Often referred to as the Jews of the East, the Parsees, like the Jews, have retained their ancient customs and religion, and through hard work and innate intelligence have risen to the top of the business and professional worlds. I had two very good reasons for being interested in the history and background of the Parsees. Firstly, because Kerry's family is Parsee, and secondly because I wanted to pursue my study of the Zoroastrian religion which is still the official cult of the Parsees.

As we passed through the ancient town of Broach from which Kerry's family originated, we suddenly decided to go in search of his uncle's house which Kerry had visited as a small boy. He remembered vaguely that it was near a clock tower which stood above the town, so we drove through the narrow twisting streets to a high point overlooking the River Narmada where we found the old tower just as Kerry had described it. As we got out of the car a middle-aged man approached us, and to our great astonishment, addressed Kerry by his name. Since the man was a complete stranger to us both, we were at a loss to know how he knew our name and how he was able to recognise us. However, our puzzlement was of short duration when the man explained that he was one of Kerry's second cousins and that recently he had attended a family marriage in Bombay where he had heard the news of our coming. A mobile home is such an unusual sight in India that it was this which gave him the clue to our identity. He was obviously overjoyed to see us and so were other relations who welcomed us as if we had been close members of the family circle. Most of these relations were elderly and remembered Kerry as a small boy. The women wore the same sort of clothes — long tunics over midcalf pantaloons — which we had seen the Zoroastrian women wear in Yazd in Iran. In one home we visited, the lady of the house was busy with her devotions when we arrived, and for the first fifteen minutes of our visit she continued to read her holy book and mumble her prayers, swaying back and forward on a wooden swing in the middle of the room. These swings, suspended from the wooden beams of the ceiling, were a feature of all the houses we visited in Broach, and provide a very sensible way of keeping cool in a hot climate.

Several hours later, replete with sweetmeats and many cups of tea, we set off to complete the journey to Bombay, two hundred and twenty miles away. A fast road took us along the coast of the state of Maharastra where the inhabitants have their own distinctive mode of attire — the women in colourful sarees tucked up between their legs like tight pants, and with sleek black hair decorated with flowers; the men in wide-legged white shorts or in 'dhotis' (skirt-like garments) beneath a tunic. It appeared to be a prosperous area with few signs of poverty, but it was exceedingly hot, and when we stopped at a roadside restaurant hoping for a cool drink, we were offered lukewarm Coca-Cola. We were to discover that cold drinks were only available in large towns in India. By dusk we were switchbacking over the Western Ghats (hills), and night had fallen before we saw the lights of the great city of Bombay sparkling ahead of us.

Parliament, New Delhi — India

Chapter Eight

LIVING WITH THE FAMILY IN BOMBAY

It was with very mixed feelings that I watched the lights of Bombay draw nearer for I was about to meet for the first time a host of new relatives. I wondered if I would be able to adapt myself to their customs, to their food and to their way of life; would they like me and would I like them. Although Kerry and I had been married for nearly thirty years, I had never visited his native land. Now I experienced a very strong feeling of regret, of guilt even, that I had not made the effort earlier to meet his next of kin. The only members of the family with whom I was acquainted were his brother's eldest daughter, Gulistan, currently studying at the Institute of Education in London and a nephew, Nozer, student at the University of Strasbourg. I faced an exciting and intimidating prospect.

We crawled into the city behind queues of heavy vehicles, through dimly lit streets, until we reached Mahim, several miles from the town centre where Kerry's brother and sister live with their families. Here we were given a tremendous welcome, so warm that from the very first instant all my doubts were dispelled as I was enclosed within a close and affectionate family circle. The fact that everyone spoke English as if it were their mother tongue was a great help to understanding, but even if there had been a language barrier, I would have quickly and happily accepted my Indian relatives.

Everywhere we went we were given the traditional Parsee welcome which is a quaint little ceremony. First of all the outline of a fish was made in chalk upon the floor and over this was placed a tiny wooden platform decorated with coloured fish. On this we stood in turn while the lady of the house, holding a tray with small silver dishes put red tikkas (marks) on our foreheads to which she fixed several grains of rice. Then a garland of sweet-smelling flower heads was hung around our necks and everyone in the company came forward to embrace us. The fish, the rice, the chalk marks and the flowers are, of course, symbols of good fortune and prosperity. In addition to these good wishes we were also given gifts; not ordinary small tokens but substantial presents — brass candlesticks, embossed copper vases, silver serving spoons, table mats, etc. Their generosity was overwhelming. The ceremony of welcome was followed by a bumper meal, with tables covered with savoury dishes such as stuffed fish, curries, pilaus and dahi (curd) and a great variety of sweetmeats.

For the first few days after our arrival we were caught up in a whirl of meetings and celebrations, and it was only when life began to assume a normal pace that I was able to look closely at our surroundings. We were parked next to Kerry's sister's flat in the compound of a large block of apartments occupied by Parsee families. All over Bombay there are flats like these, grouped in 'estates' or 'colonies', owned by Parsee trusts and built for the adherents of the Zoroastrian religion. Our in-laws, Perin and Manchi, live in a small flat on the ground floor, for which they pay about £5 per month. We slept in our caravan and had our main meals in the flat where we also had the use of toilet and washing facilities. Kerry fixed up our electric cable to Perin's kitchen so that we could use a fan during the night to keep the caravan cool. During the day, when the sun beat down relentlessly on the tarmac of the open courtyard converting the caravan into an oven, we took refuge in the flat with its cool, tiled floors and shuttered windows. After sunset we sat outside on the verandah, enjoying every puff of wind which came our way.

There we were joined by Kerry's brother Jal and his wife Nerghish and by some of Kerry's old acquaintances. Reminiscing went on till the small hours. Brother Jal has a carpentry business in the centre of Bombay to which he travels every day by train. Brother-in-law, Manchi, has had a rather unusual career. Before the advent of colour on cinema screens he earned his living by hand-painting black and white films. It was a tedious and laborious procedure, involving countless hours of painstaking work to ensure that there was no discrepancy in colour from one frame to another. However, as he was well paid, Manchi was able to retire early. His wife, Perin, coaches children privately and works voluntarily in a school for disadvantaged children.

Every morning we were awakened very early by the strident calls of hawkers who came into the courtyard to sell their wares, and by the cries of the blind beggars who came tramping along the nearby street, tapping with their staffs and chanting loudly: "Allah ye diga," "Allah ye diga," which means 'God will reward you, that is, if you are charitable to us.' Then came the Marathi fish-wife and the rag-and-bone woman, both of whom had very shrill voices. "Pomfret. Pomfret" (a flat-fish), and "Batli bai. Batli bai", (bottles), they would shout alternately. Close on their heels came the fruit and vegetable seller and the milkman with his jingling metal cans. By about 7.30 a.m. when we pulled back our curtains, people were setting off to work, the men, well-groomed in neat business suits, the women, looking very attractive in their colourful sarees and smart hair-dos. Gradually, the cars parked next to us disappeared, leaving us in splendid isolation.

As we ate our toast and marmalade at our picture window we had a panoramic view of the goings-on outside, which were much more entertaining than a cinema or pantomime show. In one corner of the compound a cobbler would take up his usual position, squatting on a mat in front of his box of tools, and soon his customers would come in ones and twos with shoes and chaplis (sandals) to be mended. There were other visitors who used to arrive at this time every morning and whose presence reminded us that rural India was just round the corner. An old bent woman regularly drove her water buffalo into the courtyard to scavenge for food in the rubbish bins. None of the inhabitants of the flats seemed to mind this intrusion, any more than they heeded the skinny rats which streaked across the tarmac and disappeared up the drainpipes. By the time we had finished breakfast the children would have gone to school in their grey and navy-blue school uniforms, looking very much like children do in Britain, carrying bulging leather satchels and waving to their mothers watching at the windows. It was about this time of the day that the dhobis (washermen) used to appropriate the centre of the courtyard, piling up mountainous heaps of dirty linen, which they had collected from the flats. Then off they would stagger like gnomes, bent double beneath the weight of great mushroom-shaped bundles. We never did discover where the washing was done as there was neither a stream nor a public washhouse in the vicinity, yet the dhobis would be back the following morning with neat piles of smooth, snowy white linen. Sometimes, a little later in the morning, we would be entertained by a family of acrobats who used to visit the compound. Mother, father and three children, the youngest of whom was no more than one-year-old, would juggle, somersault and perform a variety of balancing acts. The finale was quite hair-raising with the baby being whirled aloft like a monkey on a stick. To reward them for their efforts coins were thrown down by onlookers on the balconies, and Perin and her neighbours donated clothes and food for the children.

Meanwhile, in Perin's house, the 'gunga' (servant) was busy at work, doing all the menial tasks about the house. With her faded tinsel saree tucked up between her legs, as is the custom with Marathi women, she squatted on her haunches in the kitchen in front of a wooden board, rolling and pounding the spices for the day's curry dishes. There was ginger root, turmeric, cardamom seeds, cloves, chillies and fresh coriander, which she reduced to a brown aromatic paste. Then she rolled out a great pile of paper-thin chappatis which are the Indians' equivalent of bread and an indispensable aid for those who eat with their fingers. The gunga does not cook the chappatis, however, as this is done by the woman of the house who also does the shopping, although her servant often accompanies her to carry the purchases.

After her early morning cup of tea, a habit which is more prevalent in India than it is in this country, Perin's first task was to decorate the corners of the living room and the front steps with chalk patterns. This is a Parsee custom, a kind of daily house blessing. I have already described the fish motif which is considered a very lucky one, but there were many others, such as flowers, bells and leaves which are auspicious and are used on certain days. To make these decorations, powdered chalk is sieved through a perforated mould in which a design has been pricked out. Sometimes two or three colours are used and the patterns are quite elaborate. We often visited homes with such magnificent chalk pictures on the doorsteps that we hesitated to walk on them. When news reached my brother-in-law's family that their elder daughter had obtained her PhD degree, the younger daughter spent hours on the doorstep making a scroll of honour in many shades of chalk. An artistic sense of colour and design seems to be innate in Indian women and is perhaps best displayed in their choice of dress and jewellery which I will refer to later on.

Like housewives everywhere, Perin spent a great deal of time in her kitchen, which contained a strange mixture of modern and traditional devices. There was an outsize refrigerator, a gas stove and sink, and in one corner, separated by a low wall from the rest of the area, was a tiled cubicle with a cold water tap. It was here on the floor that the dirty dishes and pots were piled up to be washed and scrubbed by the gunga who sat on her heels with the water swilling over her bare feet. As I washed up our breakfast things in the sink I wondered why it was necessary for her to work in such an uncomfortable position. At the same time, the gunga, unbeknown to me, was wondering why her mistress's guest should be busy in the kitchen when she was there to do the work. Was she not good enough? Could she not be trusted to do the memsahib's washing-up and smalls? She voiced her feelings to Perin who suggested that I relinquish these tasks to her maid, which needless to say, I did willingly, as the intense heat made even the slightest exertion quite exhausting.

Sometimes I helped Perin with the cooking, frying the chappatis and parathas (pastry rounds) on a griddle and puris in deep fat. The latter, which swell up like small Yorkshire puddings, are delicious when newly made but become like bits of leather in a matter of minutes. I tried to discover the secret of making Indian curries, the flavour of which is so much more subtle than my own home version. Perhaps the use of ghee (clarified butter) makes a difference, but the key to good curry seems to be in the skilful blending of freshly ground spices. Cooking took up a good deal of time because we had many special meals and large family gatherings. On these occasions the top of the stove would be covered with huge pots full of rice or dhal (lentils), and the oven would be full of appetising dishes of dhansak (a Parsee speciality made of spiced mutton and lentils), baked pomfret with curried stuffing, or meat and vegetables wrapped in vine leaves. This food was often too hot for me and I relished the cool thick yoghurts, the hulvas and the firnee puddings made of rice flour decorated with nuts, raisins and edible silver leaf. Some of the ingredients and combinations were most unfamiliar; for instance, there was a pudding made of milk and red pumpkin and a sweet made of sweetened lentil puree baked in flaky pastry. One sweet dish is served only on birthdays, anniversaries and for special celebrations; it is called 'save' and is made of thread-like vermicelli, cooked in butter, blended with sugar and spices. I have added a number of these recipes to my own collection, together with those for a wide range of chutneys made from carrots, limes and mangoes which are very popular in India.

When we accompanied Perin to the nearby market we filled our baskets with shining pawpaws and aubergines, ladies' fingers and peas, green chillies and bunches of coriander. Meat, being expensive, was rarely purchased so most of our food was of the vegetarian variety, supplemented with eggs. As oranges and limes were cheap and plentiful we bought a large quantity to ensure the continuity of our marmalade stocks. To our surprise, our relatives had never tasted marmalade and they enjoyed ours so much that for several days Perin's kitchen was transformed into a jam factory. I acted as supervisor while two of my sister-in-laws and a neighbour sweated over their steaming pans. Being a thrifty Scot, I thought I wasted nothing, but these Indian ladies taught me a trick or two. They used the skin and even the pips of the oranges to make a delicious savoury chutney. For my part, I was gratified to learn that marmalade has become a very acceptable item on our relatives' table, not at breakfast, but at tea time.

When we went to fetch the month's ration of rice, we could carry little else. Perin and Manchi's entitlement was ten kilos and this was just sufficient for their needs, since they, like most Indians consume a great deal of rice. They claimed, however, that this rice was of a very poor quality, being full of impurities which had to be removed before cooking.

It is a familiar sight in India to see women seated on their doorsteps or on the ground, picking over and cleaning trays of rice. But rationed rice is cheap and therefore within the means of poor families. People who can afford to pay a little more for their food engage in a system of barter which we considered to be very strange. Vendors, black marketeers, in fact, made regular visits to the compound to sell the best quality rice at about double the price of the rationed variety. In part payment for their superior product they were willing to accept the inferior rice, and the housewives gladly paid the difference in price. This strange method of barter was taken for granted by everyone engaged in it, for Indians, like people everywhere, have learned how to 'beat the system'.

Since most of our time in Bombay was spent meeting people and attending functions, dressing-up was an important part of my life. Middle-class Indian women are just as dress-conscious as their counterparts in the West, and they devote a good deal of time to bathing, brushing and combing their hair, and attending to their clothes and accessories. In the West, when we want to feel really clean, we believe in having a good soak in a hot bath. In India, however, they scorn the idea of a bath. "Fancy sitting in filthy water!" they exclaimed in horror when we discussed the practice. On the other hand, a shower is quite acceptable to them, as the dirty water runs away. We discovered, however, that few houses had showers, and if there was one, it was rarely in working order. Almost everywhere the ancient, traditional method of bathing by bucket and jug was the rule. I was initiated into this mode of washing at Perin's house. The bathroom was a small room with tiled walls and floors, containing a hand basin and a slotted wooden board such as one finds in bathing cubicles. One poured the warm water from a large tin bucket over one's head using a small plastic container. Unpractised bathers like myself showered the whole room with water instead of channelling it into the nearby drain.

It was while I was shedding water around me that I recalled an incident related to me some years previously by an indignant Kensington landlady whose tenant was a student from a provincial town in India. Having no knowledge of Western customs, the poor fellow had imagined that the bath was an outsize bucket and that the bathroom tumbler was intended for scooping out the water. So he filled up the bath with hot water, and, standing on the bathroom floor, he proceeded to shower himself liberally with water, with disastrous consequences to the landlady's living room. The latter, being as benighted about Eastern customs as her tenant was about those in the West, sent the "heathen packing".

After the daily bathe came the dressing-up session, and here I was fortunate in having an almost unlimited supply of sarees to choose from, since all my female relations in their generosity, offered me the pick of their wardrobes. They would bring me their exquisite sarees straight from the dhobi who laundered, pressed and wrapped them in tissue paper for a few rupees. Then they decked me up in their finery including their jewellery. Sometimes the saree would be made of the finest cotton with formal or flower patterns; for more festive occasions the garments would be of nylon or silk, embroidered, plain or coloured, bordered with bands of silver or gold tinsel. The art of putting on and wearing a saree is not at all as simple as it looks, as I realized to my cost after some embarrassing moments, including one when my garment began to unwind itself as I was boarding a bus. Indian women, of course, have no such difficulties as they have learned from childhood how to pleat the material into neat folds and fix it firmly into the band of the underskirt. There is no one way of putting on a saree. For instance, the Hindus wear the end of the silk over their right shoulder, whereas the Parsees have it on the left and Marathi women tuck it up between their legs. Even the patterns of the sarees in the different regions can identify the wearer as belonging to a certain part of the country. I just love wearing a saree; it is such a sensible garment for a hot climate, cool and elegant, adjusting itself to every figure. It was, however, quite unsuitable for life in a caravan, and particularly for driving. I noticed too, that even for housework Indian women prefer to wear short European-style dresses, which they exchange for sarees when they go shopping or visiting. I had brought with me several denim safari suits, but they were far too warm to wear in the heat of Bombay. However, in next to no time, my kind sister-in-laws had made me a complete new wardrobe of cotton dresses, skirts and blouses to wear about the house and when we went on picnics.

The family picnic is one of the Indians' favourite pastimes, and the Bombayites seem to be especially keen on these excursions. Every weekend, buses, trains and cars are packed with family parties heading out of town for the beach or countryside, laden with baskets and tiffin tins. We had several memorable picnics at Juhu Beach and at Vihar Lake on the outskirts of the town. With as many as fifteen people crammed into our van, we would set off on a Saturday or Sunday afternoon to Juhu Beach which lies about ten miles north of Mahim. Before our first visit I had been looking forward to a bathe in the Arabian Sea, and in my mind's eye I had pictured a beach like some of the idyllic ones we had visited in Turkey. Instead of a dazzling white beach fringed with palm trees, we found a wide muddy-looking stretch of sand, frequented not by bathers in scanty bikinis but by thousands of over-dressed day-trippers. Undeterred by the crowds and by the fact that there were no other bathers, Kerry and I sallied forth to have a swim. We caused quite a stir. People rushed down to the water's edge to catch a glimpse of two crazy foreigners disporting themselves in the sea. We would probably have reacted in a similar manner had we been in Brighton in mid-winter and seen people bathing. Although it is as warm as it is in Britain in mid-summer, January is a winter month in India, and one just doesn't go swimming at that time of year. It was a most unsatisfactory bathe as we had to wade far out over oily mud flats before we could find enough water to cover ourselves. Needless to say we never repeated the performance.

We discovered that the charm of Juhu lies not in the sea but on the beach with its motley crowds, balloon sellers, coconut vendors and weird and wonderful entertainments. We sampled the spicy savouries sizzling in large pots of oil — crisp samosas, pakoras and puris, which were my particular fancy. Our nieces preferred 'grams' (small nuts) toasted on charcoal braziers. Indians eat nuts as we do sweets and chocolates, and nut sellers with their trays and baskets are a familiar sight in the streets and bazaars. Kerry always made straight for piles of coconuts heaped up on the sand as he is very fond of the juice of green coconuts, which is a very refreshing drink. Fortified with these goodies we could wait for our big meal from the tiffin tins, which was seldom produced before the sun had set and the moon had risen. In the meantime, we would stroll along the shore in search of entertainment. Children would be queuing up, not for donkey rides, but for an amble on a camel. There were two ancient beasts of burden, one of whom was obviously on its last legs and had to be belaboured before it would rise with its load of young passengers. Attracted by children's laughter we would linger to watch a Punch and Judy Show, given by two rather bedraggled-looking monkeys. There were the usual antics which children love so much, Judy armed with a stick chasing Punch, the reconciliation and happy ending with a white wedding. There was one entertainer on the beach, however, who never failed to attract our attention although the only part of him we ever saw was his skinny brown arms raised above the sand in which he was entombed. A notice nearby informed us of the number of hours he intended to remain buried — usually five or six hours. As we could not discover any means by which this man could continue to receive a supply of air, this feat had a great fascination for us. Although his face was at least six inches below the surface of the sand, he was able to hear and answer questions.

Someone would shout, "How long have you been buried?"

He would raise two or three fingers of a bony hand.

"How old are you?" and he would indicate thirty with his hands.

He was probably a yogi who had learned through long practice to reduce his breathing to almost nothing. His feat, whether genuine or faked, was certainly a very paying proposition since the spectators rewarded him for his effort by showering coins on the sand above him.

One day we went on an excursion with Perin and Manchi to the Aarey Milk Colony which lies near Thana, twenty miles north of Bombay. It is this large, modern farm-cum-factory which provides the townspeople with pasteurized milk. Most of the milk comes from the farm's huge herd of water buffaloes, but local farmers also bring in milk to be processed. When we were shown round the plant we were informed that the bottles supplied to the citizens of Bombay contain only 7% of real milk, the remainder being made up of powdered milk.

"What happens to the cream?" enquired Perin.

"We make ghee from the fat" said our guide.

This information made Perin very indignant. "Ordinary people and children, in particular, need the fat which is contained in milk," she said, "and the price of ghee is so high that average families cannot afford to purchase it."

Our informant agreed with her, but he pointed out that it was much more profitable for the farm to sell ghee than milk, and money was needed to finance the school for farmers, New Zealand House, which forms part of the colony.

It was so hot outside that we lingered in the cool room, where the bottled milk is kept as long as possible before we emerged into the noonday heat. We did find some shade, however, under the trees in the national park adjoining the farm, where we had our picnic with not a soul in sight, a blessing which we rarely enjoyed in India.

It was on the day we visited the Kanheri Caves, which lie in the park, that my interest in Buddhism was aroused. My first encounter with Buddhism in the Valley of Bamian, although it had been an unforgettable experience, had not roused my curiosity sufficiently to make me want to delve into its history. This visit to these massive caves, carved out of hard black rock two thousand years ago by Buddhist monks, made me want to find out everything that is known about Buddha and his followers. We found that most of the caves, which number about 100, were inhabited by large bats which flew around us, making such a din that we quickly retreated. One cave, however, was very impressive as it contained a huge vaulted hall rising above tall pillars topped with sculptures of elephants. This is the Chaitya, or prayer hall in front of which are two images of the Buddha, twenty-three feet high. The channels which supplied the monks with water are still intact and we followed them to the spring in a wooded ravine where women were filling up their brass pots and battered petrol cans. As we rested under the teak trees, a ragged little girl came running towards us with her hands outstretched. I thought she was begging, but no, she took my hand and babbled something in Marathi.

"She wants to know your name" said Perin.

I told her and she produced a piece of newspaper and asked me to write my name down. Then she wrote her name, Kamal, which means Lotus Flower. She lived in a dilapidated shack near the caves with a host of brothers and sisters who came forward timidly to observe us. When we left I noticed that Perin gave the children some money.

After our visit to these caves, we were no longer interested in picnics at Juhu or at Vihar Lake, a favourite haunt of Sunday visitors, disfigured by colossal figures of the Wizard of Oz, Humpty Dumpty, etc., in black concrete. Instead, excursions were planned to the caves on Elephanta Island and to those near Lonavla. Unfortunately, however, the visit we arranged to the most famous of all the caves in India, at Ajanta and Ellora, was destined not to take place.

The boat for Elephanta Island leaves from under the shadow of the Gateway of India, the great triumphal arch built by the British, and crosses the busy harbour which is filled with tankers and ocean liners. Although we had caught an early boat to be ahead of the crowds, it was very warm as we toiled up the long flights of stone steps which lead to the rock temples. These are of a much later origin than the Kanheri Caves and were hollowed out, not by Buddhist but by Hindu monks, between the sixth and eighth centuries AD. It was about that time that there was a renewal of interest in Hinduism and the influence of Buddhism began to decline. The creators of the Elephanta Caves, about whom little is known, were inspired by the worship of the Hindu God, Siva. Outside the main cave a pillared entrance, flanked by stone elephants, leads to a great hall, dominated by the presence of Siva. On all the walls we see him portrayed in his various manifestations; Siva with his consort Parvati in a scene of domestic bliss; Siva on Nandi the bull; Siva contemplating on a lotus; Siva the multi-armed cosmic dancer. These images, however, are dwarfed by the sculpture in the central recess which represents the Hindu Trinity. The three faces of this figure — Brahma the creator, Vishnu the preserver, and Siva the destroyer, remind us that for the Hindus, God is one and many at the same time. The details and workmanship of these sculptures are of the highest order, and in spite of the damage which they suffered at the hands of the Portuguese, they are in a good state of preservation. Incidentally, it was the Portuguese who named the island Elephanta after their discovery of sculptured elephants near the caves.

By midday, people were streaming onto the island — foreign tourists, youths with tablas and other musical instruments and parties of school children. We retreated with our picnic basket to the shade of the great trees which overhang the bay, where we were besieged by an army of monkeys so intent on snatching our food that we had to arm ourselves with sticks to protect ourselves. The monkeys retreated to the tree tops above us, which were bare except for great clusters of brilliant red blossoms. The aggressive creatures tore those apart and scattered them upon us to signify their disgust and frustration.

Although Bombay cannot compete with Delhi from the point of view of sightseeing, we found a great deal even in our immediate surroundings to interest us. Mahim is a rather drab suburb with monotonous rows of grey cement blocks of flats, built about forty years ago and poorly maintained. However, within a few minutes walk is a small port, filled with ancient fishing vessels. During the day there is nothing extraordinary about the spot, but sunset brings a magical transformation. As the bright disk of the sun slides down behind the dark masts and timbers of the fishing boats, the sky is suffused with gold which spills over into the sea and glints on every ripple.

One evening just before sunset while on our evening walk to the port, we found the streets lined with people looking expectantly towards the road which leads to the airport.

"Mrs Gandhi is coming," they told us.

We waited, and in a few moments a black limousine came into view, and the prime minister smiling graciously passed within a few feet of us. Automatically I clapped, but I was the only one to do so. No one shouted a greeting and no one cheered. This was no reflection on Mrs Gandhi's popularity, for we had seen the same reception given to Mr Bhutto in the streets of Rawalpindi, and to the President of India when his motorcade proceeded down the Rajpath in New Delhi. As a rule, Indians are undemonstrative, unless they are involved in a game of cricket, when their excitement can reach fever pitch. We witnessed this phenomenon towards the end of January during the tour of the West Indian cricket team, when the whole tenor of Indian life was disturbed; a bank holiday was put forward by one day at short notice; post offices were closed, school children were sent home from school, and university classes were cancelled. In fact, very few people went to work, and shops and restaurants were almost empty, while everyone sat at home by the radio, sweating it out with the home side. When the Indians lost the series, their downfall was regarded as a national calamity as well as a personal blow to every individual.

Sometimes, in the cool of the evening, we would walk to Shivaji Park which lies at the edge of the sea. There, we would wander along the beach or sit on the sand watching the sun disappear into the sea. As the light faded from the sky the little lights of the charcoal burners glowed under the palm trees and the darkness hid the sleeping beggars. One day we went to a Rose Show in a marquee in the park and saw all our special favourites — Ena Harkness, Peace, Fragrant Cloud, making a brave show in spite of the heat. Looking round the marquee at the blooms, flower arrangements and critical spectators, we might well have been in England. Indian householders and flat-dwellers are becoming increasingly interested in flowers, and from our compound we could look up and around at bougainvillaea and hibiscus trailing over the balconies.

To reach the centre of Bombay with its massive Victorian buildings, reminiscent of St Pancras Station, we had to travel either by bus or train. As trains were overcrowded and stuffy we usually took the bus to go shopping at Crawford Market or Colaba. As we passed through the poor quarters of the town we saw the pavement dwellers like those we had seen in Delhi, old people and families with a tribe of children clutching their pitiful bundles of clothes and bedding. All day they sat on the pavements afraid to move in case they should lose the space they needed for sleeping during the night. As there are few, if any, public toilets, people have to use the gutters instead and the stench is far from pleasant. Huge posters on the walls urge people not to urinate in public by posing the questions "Do you need an audience?" But these remonstrances appear to have little effect, and will be of no avail until there are better toilet facilities and unless a campaign for greater hygiene is instituted throughout the land. Efforts should be made to stop the nasty habit which so many Indians have of spitting in the streets and on the pavements, which are covered with unsightly splotches of 'pan' juice. The reason for this ugly mess is the Indians' fondness for a concoction of spices and betel nuts enclosed in green leaves, which is sold everywhere in the streets. It would also be a great help to hygiene if people could be encouraged to use handkerchiefs, but unfortunately, handkerchiefs would be quite beyond the means of the worst offenders.

It is a far cry from the downtown slums of Bombay to the smart residential areas of Marine Drive, Malabar Hill and Bandra; it is in fact, another world, a world of privacy, comfort and style. We were introduced to an Indian family, living on Malabar Hill, not far from the Hanging Gardens, where all the houses are mansions, built during the British era, set in large gardens with views over the sea. Our new friends were most surprised that we did not drink whisky, which is the favourite drink of upper and middle-class Indians. They travelled abroad every year to Britain or Europe, and as they were very knowledgeable about foreign and domestic affairs, we found their conversation most stimulating and enjoyable. We also renewed our acquaintance with a friend of ours who had married an Indian chemist some twenty years ago and settled in Bandra, a suburb north of Mahim. After her husband's death our friend had purchased an apartment in a luxury block of flats overlooking the sea. She sent her chauffeur-driven car to collect us and we had a bathe before lunch in the private pool attached to the apartments. With the help of three servants she led a very pleasant and comfortable existence far removed from the pitiful struggle of the pavement dwellers.

To return to these poor unfortunates for a moment. When I first encountered them in the streets of Delhi, I kept asking, "Why doesn't someone do something about them?" It was only gradually that I became aware of the enormity of the problem. Most of India's problems are of a scale which is difficult to envisage. These destitute people are not to be numbered in thousands; there are millions of them eking out an existence by begging or stealing in the streets of Bombay and in the shanty towns around the city. In addition to having no means of subsistence, a great number of these people suffer from mental and physical handicaps. Many are blind; many have gross physical deformities; many are lepers. Whenever we stopped the car or were held up in a traffic jam, an unfortunate creature would appear from nowhere and thrust the stump of an arm or a fingerless hand through our window. Frequently women would stop us in the streets and hold up to us an emaciated child saying, "Baba bucha," (Baby is hungry). Some months after we left Bombay an attempt was made to remove the beggars from the streets. Thousands of them were taken to a village some distance away where provision had been made for their accommodation and training. Immediately there was an outcry in the *Times of India* by liberal-minded people who felt that this action was an attack on the rights of individuals, and in a very short time most of these beggars had returned to their old haunts in the town. The problem of the lepers is the most intractable of all. More than two million people suffer from leprosy in India, and twenty per cent of these are reckoned to be infectious. Their presence in the cities exposes a vast number of people to the risk of contracting the disease. There are numerous leper colonies throughout India but most lepers prefer to live in the anonymity of the great towns rather than in some secluded spot in the country. Besides, there is an almost inexhaustible supply of alms, since Hindus, Muslims and even minor religious sects like the Parsees, believe it to be their duty to give a part of their earnings to those in need.

I never saw an empty begging bowl, and almost every Indian we knew tossed a coin to a beggar on his way to work.

On the crown of Malabar Hill beyond the Hanging Gardens, high walls enclose what appears to be a jungle of date palms and banyan trees. Inside, amidst the trees, are six low stadium-like enclosures which, are known as 'dokhmas', towers of silence, where the Parsees leave their dead to be consumed by vultures. It was Perin who pointed them out to us one day when we were visiting the Kamala Nehru Garden, named after Nehru's wife, adjacent to which, two modern tower blocks are only partly occupied although they were completed several years ago. This we found surprising since there is an acute shortage of flats in the city. Perin explained that prospective buyers discovered that the interior of the towers of silence was visible from the top of these high-rise blocks, and they were horrified with what they saw. The dokhmas had been constructed in such a way that when the bones had been stripped by the vultures they would fall into the lime pit below and disintegrate. It appears, however, that vultures are not so hungry nowadays, and piles of shrunken corpses are clearly visible from the windows of the apartments. Higher walls are now being built to hide these unpleasant sights and Parsees are considering other ways of disposing of their dead. Ordinary cremation is not possible, as this would profane their sacred flame, but cremation by electric ovens is a possible solution as this method would not pollute the elements of water, earth and air.

Living as we did in a Parsee community, we were closely involved in their religious festivals and ancient customs. Most Parsees adhere closely to the traditions which they brought with them from Persia more than twelve hundred years ago. We were privileged in being allowed to take part in the ceremony of 'Novjote', which signifies 'the new life', at which a child is initiated into Zoroastrianism. Rustom, aged ten, Perin's neighbour's son, was at the centre of the ceremony we attended in a building specially built for initiations and weddings. Rustom sat on a high dais covered by a canopy, with his name emblazoned in marigold petals behind him. Wrapped in nothing but a white sheet he sat surrounded by four priests who chanted passages from the Zand Avesta, the Parsees' holy book. The chief 'dastur' (priest) was also in attendance as Rustom's family was well known in Parsee circles, and as the ceremony proceeded he explained the significance of each action, for the benefit of non-Parsee guests. The white sheet was removed to be replaced by a 'sudrah' and 'kusti'. The sudrah, a white muslin shirt, represents purity, and it has a small pocket for 'good deeds'. The 'kusti' is a slim girdle, made of woollen strands, which is wound around the waist three times, a reminder of good words, good thoughts, and good deeds. The four knots with which it is secured represent the elements from which the world was created. For the rest of his life Rustom will wear these two articles which symbolize his Zoroastrian faith. When the chanting had finished, and Rustom had been blessed and garlanded by the chief dastur, his parents and friends came forward to congratulate him and to give him gifts of money, clothes and toys. The ceremony had brought back old memories to Kerry who had been initiated in the same way at an early age. He recalled that he was so bored with the long and tedious chanting of the priests that he amused himself by pulling the beard of the elderly priest who was officiating to the latter's indignation and the disgust of his parents.

After the Novjote we were treated to a bumper meal, served on long tables, with banana leaves as plates. First we had fish stuffed with chillies, followed by chicken, pilau and meat, chutney, pickles and chappatis which we ate to the accompaniment of American tunes played by an Indian band.

I noticed that Novjote and wedding ceremonies always took place in the evening after sunset. The reason, I was told, dated back to the time when the Parsees arrived as refugees in India. The Hindu ruler of what is now the state of Gujarat imposed certain restrictions on the newcomers relating to religious observances. He instructed them to hold all their festivities either before sunrise or after sunset so that they would not clash with those of his Hindu subjects.

In this country we think of spring as the time for weddings. In India, however, winter is ring-time and most weddings are arranged between November and the end of February. As this period coincided with our visit, we were fortunate in being invited to two Parsee weddings. The first wedding we attended was that of Nellie's younger sister. Nellie is engaged to Perin's son Nozer, who is studying for his PhD at Strasbourg University. We were given the best seats in front of the raised dais which was gaily decorated with flowers. I sat next to Nellie's father who astounded me by quoting at length from the poetry of Robbie Burns as we waited for the ceremony to begin. Then the band struck up, "Here comes the bride" and the bride and groom appeared, only to disappear a few minutes later.

"What's happening?" I asked my neighbour.

"They have gone to show the dastur their sudrah and kusti to prove that they are true Zoroastrians," he replied.

A few minutes later the couple mounted the steps of the little platform, the groom wearing a little round hat and carrying a bunch of ferns in his hand. The bride, dressed in a pale blue saree, had a bouquet of flowers in one hand and a coconut in the other. They were accompanied by several relatives who acted as witnesses of the ceremony and by their mothers who have an important part to play in the wedding ceremony. It is they who ward off the evil eye from the bridal pair by making signs above their heads, and invoke good fortune by offering them an egg, a coconut, rice and garlands of flowers. When these rituals were completed, the two priests who officiated chanted lengthy prayers during which they showered the couple with grains of rice. Then they put the question, "Pasande Kardam? Do you take this person as your wife? Do you take this person as your husband?" When they gave their assent a silver paper ball suspended above their heads opened up and strewed them with flower petals. The formal ceremony was over and the band struck up, "Celebration". Friends and relatives came forward with their congratulations and with envelopes containing gifts of money. We did not stay for the wedding banquet as we had already consumed our share at lunch time. In an effort to curtail expenditure on weddings, the Indian Government has set a limit to the number of guests who can be entertained at a wedding. As Nellie's family had invited more than the statutory hundred, there were some including ourselves who could not partake of the feast. However, the meal was delivered to us in tiffin tins at midday, when we had fish in chilli sauce, chicken and potatoes, rice, dhal and meat, and a coconut-flavoured sweet. It was very tasty, but somehow it seemed less appetising on a plate than on a banana leaf.

The other wedding we attended was in a very grand private house on Malabar Hill. Our host was Dr Gilder, one-time Health Minister of India who was held in detention by the British with Gandhi in 1943. It was his grandson who was being married and there were several hundred guests. When I was introduced to Dr Gilder, now over eighty, I would have loved to have asked him about Gandhi and about his period in detention, but realized that it was neither the time nor the place for such questions.

We had many invitations from relatives and their friends to birthday parties and family celebrations. At those gatherings, food played a very important part, although we sometimes found the sequence of dishes quite surprising. For afternoon tea the cream cakes and buns were usually served before the savouries, and after a cup of tea we might be offered a glass of 'puffed milk' (whipped milk and gelatine). For us, the main pleasure of these meetings was in getting to know some very interesting people. I recall a kind-faced lady in her seventies who had been a primary school teacher and was having to subsist on a monthly pension of 80 rupees, (£4). Fortunately in India relatives stick together and share accommodation and resources. Unmarried daughters are looked after by their brothers or by another male relative when their parents die, although this custom is changing now that women are able to find jobs as secretaries, bank clerks, etc. Twenty years ago there were few opportunities in employment for single women, and in middle and upper-class circles it was considered demeaning for them to go out to work; even today there is little if any accommodation for single women apart from that available in the family home. Kerry's younger sister Sheroo, is one of these lone single women. After a lifetime of caring for her aged parents and other relatives she lives with her brother, Jal and his family.

One of the most interesting persons we met was Homi Schroff who had given up a good career as an engineer to found a home for orphan children. He and his wife purchased a plot of ground near Poona and toiled for several years to establish the orphanage which now cares for twenty-two children, aged between three and nine. They had to dig a well for water and erect the buildings, using their own money to finance the project. They also planted fruit trees, tomatoes and strawberries which they sell to enable them to buy food for the children. Now they have a small government grant and all the children have obtained places in good schools where they are doing well in their examinations, explained Homi with a father's pride. He does, however, ensure that all the children have some training in farming and horticulture. Hard work has taken its toll on Homi and his wife. At sixty they are worn and gaunt, but their eyes shine with happiness.

I have already mentioned our friendship with a Bombay senator and the interesting discussions we had with him on political and economic topics when we were in Delhi. The acquaintance we made with Doctor Framboze Bode opened up to us new avenues of religious thought. As one would expect from a co-worker of Gandhi and Rabindranath Tagore, Dr Bode, although he is a Zoroastrian high priest, is liberal and forward-looking in his religious views. We met him on several occasions, and when he discovered our interest in Zoroastrianism he invited us to his home and gave us several books and pamphlets which he had published on this subject. He claims that Zoroaster, whom he calls Zarathustra, was the first to propound the philosophy of 'self unfoldment', and it is in the evolving of spiritual awareness on a universal level, untrammelled by dogma, that he sees the future of religious thought.

Our interest in the history of Zoroastrianism brought us also into contact with Dr Hakkim, a Parsee doctor working in Iran on research into cancer. An amateur historian, Dr Hakkim had very many interesting views on the religious customs of the Achaemenids whose tombs we had visited near Persepolis. He claimed that the winged symbol we had seen there, which the Zoroastrians call the 'Fravashar', originally possessed an eagle's head. The theory is that the primitive ancestors of the Persians

N

thought that the spirit of man was borne away on an eagle's wings after death. Ten months later, when we were visiting an ancient Hittite shrine in the north of Turkey, we were astounded to discover on a rock face, the same symbol with the head of an eagle. It had been carved there about a thousand years before the death of Darius. It was Dr Hakkim who told us about the efforts Iran is making to attract educated Parsees back to Iran and how many thousands have already left for remunerative posts in their former homeland. This loss of professional people — doctors, scientists, architects and lawyers, etc. — is a serious one for India which badly needs their services but cannot afford to pay for them.

Sometimes when we went shopping in Bombay, we would seek refuge from the heat in the air-conditioned foyer of the Taj Mahal Hotel with its atmosphere of comfort and luxury so lacking in its more modern counterparts. Seated on a red plush sofa we used to watch tourists and foreign businessmen passing to and fro. American visitors formed the bulk of the hotel's clientele, but the Japanese were much in evidence as tourists with expensive cameras over their shoulders, and as commercial agents with bulging briefcases. There were also a number of Russians and Germans whose presence in Bombay appeared to be for business rather than for sightseeing. One day as I was waiting for Kerry in the lounge, a pleasant-faced Western woman sat down beside me. We soon struck up a conversation and I learned that she was a Baptist missionary from America who had been working in Darjeeling for the last thirty years. In a matter of fact way and without self-pity she told me her story. She had come to be treated for cancer and had just heard that her case was a terminal one. Her husband, also a missionary, was due to join her soon on furlough, and they would stay not at the Taj, which was beyond their means, but at the Salvation Army Hostel where she had a bed in a dormitory. It was difficult to believe that this cheerful pleasant woman was doomed to die quite soon, and what surprised me even more was the calm and courageous way she was prepared to meet her fate. From her conversation it was obvious that she was sustained by a strong Christian conviction, reinforced by years of close contact with the fatalistic philosophy of the East.

When it came to encountering remarkable people, however, there was no need for us to travel further than our own doorstep — or rather Perin's doorstep — for she has a very unusual neighbour. For five days a week, Jal Ameria is in charge of a small printing press, but on Wednesday afternoons and Sunday mornings he exchanges his blue overalls for a doctor's white coat to practise as an osteopath and naturopath. Although he is an orthodox Parsee, Jal has as his guru a venerable Hindu, renowned for his skill in healing, who has taught him all his secrets; but first Jal had to promise that he would never take money or gifts in payment of his services.

On Sunday mornings the queue of patients would begin to form before eight o'clock and by mid-morning, more than fifty people would be waiting at the surgery door. Some came in wheelchairs, others were carried or assisted by their friends; all were obviously in pain. From our vantage point at the caravan window, we watched the bent and the crippled disappear through Jal's door, to emerge, some time later, considerably more agile and cheerful. His patients came from all levels of society, and included Hindus and Muslims; the rich as well as the poor.

One day, the arrival of a particular patient, caused quite a stir in the neighbourhood. On hearing a commotion, I looked out of the window and saw a crowd of teenagers approach a good-looking youngish man who was waiting his turn in the queue. We discovered later that he was one of India's most famous film stars whose face should have been familiar to us as it appeared on all the cinema hoardings. Kerry witnessed one of Jal's 'cures'. The patient was a middle-aged man who was brought in on a wheelchair. After a preliminary examination, he was laid on his side on the floor and, as two assistants held his feet and shoulders, Jal gave a very sharp jerk to his hip. Without any further manipulation the patient was able to hobble away without the help of the wheelchair. We were therefore not surprised when the chief pathologist at Breach Candy Hospital told us that he was one of Jal's patients and that he always advised sufferers from backache to attend the latter's surgery.

There was another occupant of Jal's house, who deserves a mention here, as she was a remarkable little person in her own humble way. We first caught sight of Hira early one morning, as she sat on the doorstep, combing and brushing her long, black tresses. She was an attractive child of about ten years of age, and as she was invariably cheerful and smiling, we nicknamed her 'Sunshine'. She was the Amerias' gunga; she did all the menial tasks about the house, and helped Jal in his surgery. Sometimes when Perin's gunga was ill, Hira came to us to wash the dishes, make the masala, and scrub the floors. As the idea of child labour was abhorrent to us, we immediately began asking questions. "Where had she come from?" "Why was she not at school?" etc. We discovered that Hira, and a number of young girls like her, who were also in service in Mahim, had been brought from a poor farming community in the north of Gujarat State. Her parents, who had too many mouths to feed anyway, were only too willing to part with their daughter in exchange for money. Hira never talked of her home or her brothers and sisters, and seemed very happy with her lot. Naturally, she was much better fed and cared for than she would have been in the country. Ruttee, Jal's wife, made pretty cotton dresses for her, and gave her regular pocket money, and she could even watch television. Television sets are still a novelty in India, as few can afford them.

"But what about her education?" we asked.

"Hira does not wish to attend school," was the reply.

However, efforts had been made by my sister-in-law, Perin, to teach the child to read and write; efforts which had come to nothing, since Hira had shown no interest in her studies, and had made no progress. Yet she was a bright little thing, very competent in her household tasks, in answering the telephone, and in running errands. She had even picked up enough English to understand what we said to her and to make some reply.

"What is going to happen to her when she grows up?" we enquired.

"Her mother will come and fetch her when she is thirteen years old, and she will be married to someone of her own caste in her home village."

"This is monstrous," we said, "after the life she has led in Bombay. Can't you keep her with you?"

"Unfortunately, not," Ruttee explained sadly. "You see, parents have their rights, and, besides, this is the accepted custom. We can do nothing."

Although we felt sorry for the child, fortunately, she was not in the least sorry for herself. She sang and hummed to herself as she sat in the courtyard, topping and tailing piles of Bombay duck (small dried fish). Sometimes she played childish games on the doorstep with other little gungas who were allowed to come from time to time to play with her. What would the RSPCC do, we wondered, in cases like these, where the only reprehensible act was to give a child happiness and security for a few brief years? Like so many problems we encountered in India, the fate of little Hira and her playmates cannot be solved satisfactorily at this moment in time. Efforts are being made by the government to discourage early marriages, and it is to be hoped that soon there will be enough money to enforce primary education for all children.

Since our relatives, like most Indians, did not possess a television set, their chief enjoyment was a visit to the cinema. This fondness for films, which amounts to an addiction is shared by almost everyone in India who can afford the price of a seat. In the large towns, and especially in Bombay, one is confronted everywhere by huge posters advertising the current films. As there are comparatively few top actors and actresses, the same faces stare down from all the hoardings. Pink and white cheeked heroines and burly suntanned heroes appear to represent the Indians' ideal of womanhood and manhood, and they crowd into the cinemas to adore them. We went with members of the family to two Hindi films, in which there was no real acting, only a hotch-potch of actions. There were earthquakes, battles, fires, floods and murders, interspersed with songs and dances by coy Indian maidens. The sound was deafening, and as there was no air-conditioning, prohibited by law we were told, it was most uncomfortable. We left halfway through the second film, and declined further invitations except to one film about Akbar, which I could not resist. Although this film was nearly forty years old, it was infinitely superior to the films we had seen.

We had had the intention of remaining in Bombay for three to four weeks before moving on to explore the south of India. However, an unexpected and unfortunate turn of events delayed our departure for a month. When we were in Delhi, Kerry had complained of a pain in his side and he assumed that he had strained a muscle while struggling to unload our large cans of Iranian petrol. By the time we reached Bombay the pain had become insistent and the doctor he consulted diagnosed a hernia and referred him to Breach Candy Hospital. There, the surgeon, the eminent Dr Dastur, confirmed the diagnosis, and pointed out that although there was no immediate need for an operation, difficulties might arise if the hernia became strangulated in Nepal or Afghanistan, where medical facilities are sadly lacking. So Kerry resigned himself to his fate and the operation was fixed for the 20th January. In the meantime, as he had lost two and a half stones since we left England, he had to make an effort to regain some weight and improve his blood count. Abandoning our plan to visit Ajanta and Ellora, we decided to spend a week away from the heat and bustle of Bombay at Lonavla, a small hill resort near Poona, accompanied by Perin and Manchi.

The Government Holiday Camp at Lonavla is a collection of small bungalows, pleasantly situated under shady trees. When the camp was set up fifteen years ago, it must have been very attractive, but unfortunately it has suffered from general neglect and the lack of maintenance. There were several broken windows in our grimy kitchen, and the flushing system of the 'Asian' toilet would not function. However, we could not grumble at the cost, which was a mere 60p per day, plus 20p for parking, a small dining room, a double bedroom, a shower room (with a tap and bucket), a kitchen and outside toilet. We slept in the caravan and ate, cooked and washed in the bungalow where Perin and Manchi were living. There was a canteen on the site from which we ordered food in the evening to supplement our own rations — dishes of mutton or vegetable curry, bowls of spinach or rice, puris and potatoes, and the inevitable green chillies of which Manchi was so fond and which he usually had all to himself.

The rattling of milk cans outside the door woke us every morning. The jovial milkman, in turban and dhoti, was a rogue, although we did not realize it at first. We paid three times the standard price for his buffalo milk until Perin discovered his exorbitant demands. Her vehement denunciation surprised me, almost as much as the speedy refund which followed it; but we learned our lesson too, and were more careful in parting with our money in future. After breakfasting on fresh pawpaw, coffee, toast and marmalade, we would set out on a walk over the plain which lay around us, past the new country houses belonging to prosperous Bombayites, across the fields into the little villages where life had changed little in a thousand years. In the green water under the trees, the buffaloes wallow in the mud, and on the path to the well, the village women pass to and fro, balancing their shining brass pots on their heads. The shacks where they live, made of wood and straw, look scarcely habitable with their twisted roof supports and crooked walls, and yet from these miserable dwellings, school children emerge looking clean and neat in their blue uniforms, bound for Lonavla, four or five miles away. The soil in this area is poor and infertile, thinly covering the volcanic rock which protrudes like bare, bleached bones. On one of these stony patches we came across a young farmer who was using the technique of soil-less culture (hydroponics) to grow crops on the stones which covered most of his land. He proudly showed us the well he had sunk and a dam he had constructed to contain the water used to irrigate the tiny plots of fertile land where he was growing aubergines, chillies and peppers. We were not surprised to learn that he had been well trained, having spent four years in an agricultural college, and it was good to see what can be done in the most difficult circumstances with knowledge and hard work. As the sun rose to its noonday height, we would return to the bungalow by pathways overgrown with thyme, above which hovered clouds of butterflies; black and white, and every shade of blue.

Beyond the plain, at several miles distance, the horizon is edged with low, dark hills where, during the first century AD, Buddhist monks chiselled deep into the black rock to make their cells and temples.

Early one morning, leaving Perin in the caravan, we toiled up the steep path which leads to the Karla Caves. Part of the track had fallen away, and women were busy carrying soil and stones in baskets on their heads. In most construction sites in India, it is the women and not the men who do the labouring jobs. As we passed by, beggars squatting by the pathway called out for alms, and stallholders urged us to purchase garlands and coloured chalk to sprinkle on the shrines. Manchi took a guide, or rather a guide took him, but as he could not speak English, we left them to explore on their own. There are about four caves, constructed in the same manner as those at Kanheri, with cells and meeting places. The main chaitya with its ribbed ceiling of teak beams and its carved pillars, reminded me of an ancient cathedral, only it has a dome-shaped stupa at one end, instead of an altar. What is truly amazing about these caves is that the monks carved from the top downwards, starting with the ceiling and finishing with the floor. Outside the prayer hall is an Asoka pillar with four lion heads, and the façade is adorned with sculptured elephants and dancing girls. This imposing entrance, however, has been disfigured by the erection in front of it of a small Hindu temple, hideously painted and full of gilded shrines and jangling bells. Strangely enough, it was this temple and not the Buddhist caves which most of the Indian tourists had come to visit, and they streamed inside with their gifts of flowers and food. One young girl was carrying a beautiful bunch of lotus blossoms which I was tempted to smell, had I not recalled the advice which Perin had given me. She had warned me never to smell the garlands or petals which were being taken as gifts to the gods, as this action would defile the offering and make it unfit for presentation. Near the caves, in small recesses on the hillside are a number of blackened and bedaubed rocks, dedicated to Hindu gods and goddesses and covered with decaying garlands and fly-blown sweetmeats, which present a startling contrast to the unadorned stupa within the Buddhist cave.

When we returned from our excursion, exhausted by the noonday heat, we found a tasty meal awaiting us in the caravan. Perin had prepared a savoury omelette, which was followed by fruit salad and glorious cold water. As we had been permitted to connect our cable to the bungalow's electrical supply, we were able to enjoy the luxury of cold drinks.

The track to the Bhaja Caves rises from the centre of a small village about a mile from the Tourist Camp. After half an hour's walk up a steep valley, we reached the great mass of black rock where early Buddhist monks, or in this case possibly nuns, lived and worshipped. There are about eighteen caves, most of which are small, dark and unadorned. In the chaitya, the pillars and the ribbed wooden ceiling had been painted gold, and there are holes in the floor where the paint has been mixed. The finest cave has remarkable carvings of hunting scenes, and there we found two women photographers, one Greek and the other American, who were making a very detailed record of the sculptures. They were being financed by the Indian Government, which we were glad to learn, is continuing the wonderful work which the British began on these ancient sites.

In addition to its ancient caves, this part of Maharashtra has another claim to fame, for it was here in the seventeenth century that the almost legendary Shivaji battled against the Moguls. The ruined forts which crown the hilltops in this area — there are two near the Bhaja Caves — changed hands many times in the course of his struggle with the Muslims. At the Lion Fort near Poona, Shivaji's Maratha soldiers are said to have used giant lizards to carry ropes to the top of the walls; then, climbing stealthily under cover of darkness, they stormed the fortress and put the members of the Mogul garrison to the sword. Shivaji was born in Poona in 1627 and his battle cries of "homeland" and "cow" (religion) sparked off the flame of nationalism which burned brightly for more than fifty years. When Shivaji died in 1680 he left a powerful new nation behind him which gradually extended its boundaries. But the Marathas, whose tactics as guerilla fighters had been so outstanding, were tyrannical overlords and they eventually lost the support of other Indians.

Nevertheless, Shivaji is still remembered as one of India's great national heroes and his statue has pride of place in city parks and gardens.

I had been looking forward to visiting Poona, which is an hour's drive from Lonavla, and I was not disappointed with this pleasant town, reminiscent of Baroda, with its tree-lined streets and flowering parks. Many of the buildings recall the one-time presence of the British. Poona University was formerly Government House, and the Engineering College which has one of the best reputations in India, was set up in pre-Independence days. Crossing the river, which runs through the centre of the town, we visited a spot where less favourable memories of British rule linger, the Aga Khan's palace, which has become a memorial to Gandhi. It was here, from 1942 to 1944, that the Mahatma was imprisoned with his wife, Kasturba, his secretary and several other colleagues, including the Dr Gilder whom we had met in Bombay. In the garden behind the palace, we removed our shoes to visit the samadhi (tomb) of Kasturba and of Desai, the secretary, both of whom died during their period of imprisonment. We were shown Gandhi's room, which, although small, was far from being a prison cell, and we also saw an exhibition of photographs which depicted his long struggle for Indian freedom. What I remember most of this visit, however, is the life-size sculpture which stands in the entrance hall of the palace, and portrays Gandhi with hands outstretched towards a young "harijan" (outcaste) road sweeper.

Poona, which might be considered as one of the more "snooty" of Indian towns, has nevertheless its seamy side. On the outskirts of the town, we saw huge clusters of ramshackle huts, where hundreds of people were living in the most pitiful squalor. A muddy stream trickling past the doors, served as a sewer, washing-up place and drinking trough for stray cows. Outside the railway station we saw a large family who had taken up residence underneath a tree, with their bedding and cooking utensils spread around them. One girl was catching lice in her sister's hair just as we had seen the monkeys do to each other in Rishikesh.

Every evening after supper we had a game of Scrabble, and Manchi and Perin who had never seen the game before became very keen players; so the time passed quickly and pleasantly. Indeed this week at Lonavla would have been idyllic had we not been constantly engaged in a major struggle with rats in the kitchen. On the very first afternoon, I disturbed two rats which had been crawling over our food and dishes, covering everything with droppings. Ugh! As there were no cupboards, we transferred everything to the dining room table, kept the doors closed and stuffed a mat underneath, to keep out marauders. But our precautions were to no avail; on returning from a walk we found that everything on the table had been overturned, our halva had been eaten, our tomatoes nibbled, and the floor was strewn with bits of paper. The rats had found their way through a gap under the eaves; and they had not been the only trespassers; two striped tails, disappearing through the hole betrayed the presence at the feast of tiny tree squirrels. There were also several lizards which did not try to escape but remained rooted to the ceiling, but they were probably only interested in the flies. Thereafter, our utensils and everything edible were kept in the caravan, and we thought that the problem had been solved, that is, until we returned from the Bhaja Caves.

We were enjoying the lunch which Perin had made for us when Manchi remarked laconically, "You have got a rat in the caravan."

"What!" we chorused in horror. "Where?"

"I saw it disappear behind the fridge."

We poked with sticks; we rattled and shook the kitchen unit but nothing emerged, so we convinced ourselves that Manchi had been mistaken.

After a day had passed without a sign of it, we breathed a sigh of relief, but the following night I was sure that something ran over the bed. We searched but could find nothing. However, before we fell asleep we heard the unmistakable sound of a small creature, scratching about behind the larder. The next morning our worst fears were confirmed when we found rat droppings on the floor.

At breakfast time we drew up a plan of attack. We would go to Lonavla and buy a trap, and as a second line of defence, we would request the local authority to give us some rat poison. In the bazaar we purchased a large, wicked-looking wood trap and listened patiently to the vendor's gratuitous advice. "You must set a bait with a piece of coconut and a few coriander leaves. Remember to roast the coconut, and the coriander leaves must be fresh, etc., etc."

An officious fellow at the Town Hall replied to our request for poison with a peremptory, "Where are you living?"

"At the Tourist Camp near Malavli."

"Sorry, that lies outside our jurisdiction. We cannot supply you with poison."

"Which area do you serve?"

"Only the town of Lonavla."

"Good," said Kerry. "We have come to the right place. Would you mind stepping over to the window."

Looking puzzled, the man complied.

Pointing to our caravan in the street below, Kerry explained. "That is where we live, and that is where the rat is. So?"

Armed with the trap and the poison, we returned to the bungalow, and lay in wait for our enemy. I remained awake for hours, expecting at any moment to hear the trap go off, but there wasn't a sound, and early in the morning the bait was still untouched; then, as I dozed off again, there was a sharp report like a pistol shot. Our little foe was caught. The disposal of the creature caused quite an argument in the family. Kind-hearted Manchi and Perin pleaded with us to let the rat live, and release it in a nearby field. We thought that there were quite enough rats in the neighbourhood and decided that it should die as soon as possible, lest we should begin to examine our motives too closely, and as was always the case, when it came to unpleasant tasks, it was Kerry who was the executioner.

Shortly after our return from Lonavla, Kerry was admitted to Breach Candy Hospital which stands at the edge of the sea, surrounded by pleasant gardens. The matron, a friendly, rosy-cheeked English woman, kindly allowed us to park the van in the compound, and there I resided for the next nine days. Kerry had a private room on the second floor, overlooking the sea, and he was so well cared for, that when the operation was over he felt as if he was having a rest cure in a luxury hotel. His menu card, for instance, gave him a wide choice of Western and Indian dishes for lunch and dinner and was presented to him each morning by a charming young receptionist. As for me, I was able to take advantage of the fringe benefits. Since it was very difficult to dispose of waste water in the hospital car park, I used to sneak upstairs and use Kerry's private bathroom. It was a splendid arrangement, but there was one very embarrassing moment, when I emerged from the shower room with my head swathed in a towel, just as the matron came into Kerry's room. To her credit she neither raised an eyebrow, nor made a comment, but I was much more careful in future. Soon I had made friends with some of the nurses, including the staff nurse who allowed me to keep my milk, butter, fruit, etc., in one of the refrigerators. This was a great boon, because I had no electricity, and I could scarcely have asked for our cable to be connected to the hospital supply. There are limits! At visiting hours our relations and friends came in crowds, filling the room and overflowing into the corridor. I did feel that it would have been better for Kerry if fewer people had come and for shorter periods, but our friends wanted to show their interest and were anxious to prevent the patient from becoming bored.

Certainly the time did not hang on my hands, for beyond the hospital gardens lies the magnificent Breach Candy Swimming Pool — a private club but available to members of the public for about 50p. It still retains that exclusive air which it had in British days when only Europeans were admitted, and its lawns and shrubberies are well tended. There in the heat of the day, I used to relax after a swim, in the shade of a palm. As for meals, I was well provided for, since a good friend brought me my lunch and evening meal every day in tiffin tins. So, while Kerry was having his four-course meal, I was sampling tasty dishes — egg curry, mince balls, cold meat, rice, vegetables and various sweets. There was only one occasion when my appetite failed me and that was when I opened the tin to find a cold stew of pig's trotters. Sometimes in the evening I was invited to the home of a lady doctor who lived nearby. Being a lonely woman and keen to know about life in the West, she was pleased to have my company. One evening when I arrived, she was very upset, almost in tears. A few days before, she had had installed by a local carpenter, at considerable expense, a European-style wall unit which she had filled with her best (foreign) crockery. Unfortunately, since the plugs used to fix the cupboard were not sufficiently strong, it had collapsed, smashing all her precious china.

This fondness, or rather craze, for foreign styles and products, is very prevalent in India amongst the well-to-do classes. In fact we discovered that it is the dream of many Indians to make a 'haj' (pilgrimage) to Britain simply to fill up as many suitcases as possible with goods from Marks and Spencer. These imported goods are not only prized for their value, but they enhance the owner's status and importance. This conviction that the foreign product is superior to its Indian counterpart, can best be illustrated by a story which Dr Dastur told Kerry about one of his patients. The latter, a wealthy businessman had to undergo a small operation and Dr Dastur suggested that he should have a local anaesthetic.

His patient reacted angrily, "A 'local' anaesthetic, Doctor. What can you be thinking about? Local, indeed. You know I have means, and that I can well, afford to have a foreign one!"

Perhaps I should add that Dr Dastur has a London Degree and is an FRCS.

It was during this week that I encountered Krishnamurti, whose name and fame had been known to me for many years. He was the protege of Annie Besant, the celebrated Theosophist, who considered him to be the new Messiah. It was therefore with high expectations that I attended the first of two open-air lectures, delivered by this great man in the grounds of the Art College. Dressed in white, seated cross-legged on a table, Krishnamurti looked very distinguished and venerable. His high domed forehead and penetrating gaze seemed to reveal an outstanding intellect and great wisdom. I had taken my tape-recorder with me, and, ignoring notices, which requested the audience not to make recordings, I taped every word of his ninety minute speech.

His main theme was an attack on organized religion. "When you worship God, you are worshipping yourself," he said. "People should make up their own minds and yet be aware that thought and memory prevent the discovery of spiritual truth." When he talked of meditation he said, "Meditation is to be aware of thought and of every feeling, and out of this awareness comes silence and in that state of mind you may come upon the thing called truth."

I played the tapes over to Kerry in hospital that evening, and although the loud cawing of rooks spoilt the recording, most of it was audible. We agreed that Krishnamurti's message was muddled and contradictory.

Still hopeful I attended the second of his lectures, which was packed to overflowing as the previous one had been. Indians have a great affection for gurus of every religious persuasion.

Krishmamurti repeated much of what he had said in his first talk, and I came away with the feeling that he was a very frustrated man, hitting out at established institutions.

"All authority is evil," he proclaimed, but he had nothing to put in its place.

Eight days after his operation, Kerry, still a little weak, left Breach Candy Hospital. His expenses came to just over £250 — a very modest sum considering the excellent medical attention which he had received. Fortunately, we had had the foresight to take out a substantial insurance before we left on our journey and this covered the cost of the operation. Dr Dastur advised Kerry that, although he would be fit enough to drive within a month, he would be wise to hire a chauffeur for a month or two. This suggestion was not so extraordinary as it first appeared, since a chauffeur's services cost comparatively little. However, on one point the doctor was very firm; there was to be no pony trekking in Nepal or elsewhere during our present trip, which was very disappointing news.

Soon after our return to Mahim, we collected from the American Express, a letter which surprised and delighted us. Our Belgian friends, having abandoned their plan to visit Nepal, had arrived in Bombay and were parked at Juhu Beach. As they had lost our address they had written to the American Express. Unfortunately, ten days had elapsed since the letter had been written and there was a possibility that our friends had moved on in the meantime. However, full of hope we set out at once by bus for Juhu, and searched in every parking lot in the area; but alas, there was not a trace of them anywhere. Reluctant to give up hope, we returned with a letter for Albert to the American Express where we learned that one of our Belgian friends had come to collect mail that very morning. So the hunt was still on.

In the meantime, we had begun a round of visits to schools and colleges, arranged by Mr Naik of the British Consulate. We went first to a secondary school in Gorgeon, a suburb twelve miles north of Mahim. All the pupils in this school were children of Keralans who had come to work in Bombay factories. In spite of the fact that the buildings were quite inadequate for the number of pupils, up to fifty of whom were crammed into each classroom, it was clearly a well-organized and hard-working school. The children sat in complete silence, giving their full attention to their teachers and to their books. Each child had to learn three languages, including English which was the medium of instruction. The other two languages were Hindi, the national language, and one of the following: Tamil, Gujarati or Marathi. The other subjects in the curriculum were; Science, Mathematics, Social Studies and a modicum of Physical Training, of the 'knees-bend' type, since there were neither facilities nor equipment for games. We were shown round by the principal and a member of the local education committee who explained that he and three other colleagues met in the school every evening from 9 to 11 p.m. They controlled and supervised the running of the school and provided funds for books and equipment. I wondered how our head teachers would react if their powers were usurped by an education committee. This school was fee-paying, the cost to parents being about £5 per term, plus the cost of books and seventy per cent of the pupils went on to further education. In another secondary school in the same area, the children were being taught in the medium of Marathi, their mother tongue, and they also learned Hindi. This was a state school and therefore 'free'; for this reason it was much shabbier than the fee-paying school and even more crowded, but it had the advantage of having a large, pleasant compound, fringed with trees. In the Botany class, where the children were drawing leaves, I asked the teacher whether he ever took his pupils into the compound to look at the trees. He shook his head, surprised at the suggestion.

As was the case in the first school, apart from one laboratory, there were no specialist rooms, and Music, Art and Craft had no place in the timetable. We pricked up our ears when the headmaster spoke of work experience, but found that consisted in teaching the girls how to make biscuits. Judging from what we saw in these two schools we concluded that the efforts and talents of many Indian children are being needlessly dissipated in acquiring two or three languages, when what they really require is instruction in practical and technical subjects and a more liberal curriculum. Of course, the root of the problem is lack of money. Specialist subjects like Engineering, Electronics, Arts and Crafts are much more costly than language books. One encouraging aspect of education in Bombay, however, is the increasing involvement of local people in the schools and colleges in their own areas. When we were invited to the opening of a new chemistry laboratory at a polytechnic college, we discovered that it had been donated and equipped by a group of businessmen and members of the local Lions' Club.

There is a third type of school in Bombay, which plays an important part in the sphere of education, and which might be compared to the 'Grammar' school system in this country. Typical of this kind of school is the 'Scottish Orphanage', built by Scotsmen a hundred years ago to house and educate the progeny left behind by Scottish soldiers. Although it no longer has any Scottish connections, its architecture and the pulpit in the school hall betray its Presbyterian origin. It is well equipped with specialist facilities and the boarders' sitting room has a large TV set. This school, which is fee-paying, together with a number of former Roman Catholic schools in the city, are reputed to give a very good academic education to the children of affluent parents. In neat school uniforms, well mannered, but not inhibited, the pupils spoke English as if it were their mother tongue and all of them, girls as well as boys, confidently expected to have a career in one of the professions.

About a week after our abortive visit to Juhu, there was a loud knocking at Perin's door, rousing us from our afternoon siesta. To our surprise and delight, who should we find on the doorstep but Titi and Mimi, clutching a large bouquet of pink roses. We welcomed them with open arms, and listened to all that had transpired since we last met. For various reasons, including concern for the children's health, they had decided to return by boat to Belgium. They had moved from Juhu to Andheri and were living in a Catholic ashram, where they had been given a large shed in an over-grown garden.

A few days later we paid them a visit. As we were having a meal together, there was a commotion on the tin roof above us, and Albert exclaimed, "That's the rats squealing. Something must have given them a fright." We rushed to the window, just in time to see a huge, green snake slide down from the roof and glide along the branches of a tree. It was at least eight feet long, thicker than a man's arm with a tail, which looked razor-sharp.

"To think that the children have been playing in the shrubbery every day!" gasped Françoise. "But, never again. Do you hear Véronique and Patrick?"

The children who were following the snake's movements with horror and fascination, readily agreed.

The ashram specialized in the teaching of Indian Classical Dancing, and a group of their students was about to set out on a tour of Europe. Our friends were taking lessons there, and Véronique gave us a demonstration of some of the head and hand movements which she had learnt.

"We are going to Goa at the end of February," said Kerry. "What about joining us, Albert?"

And it was agreed that if they did not find a cargo boat by that time, they would accompany us to Goa; a decision which made Mimi and Titi wild with delight, as they were in no hurry to return home.

We now began to make preparations for our departure, and as we had now completed about half of our journey, 13,000 miles, we considered that the car needed a complete overhaul. However, we had some doubts as to whether we would be able to find a garage competent to carry out the work. Fortunately, we discovered one which was first class, with a chief mechanic with a BSc in Auto-Engineering. He checked every detail of our vehicle, and together with a number of minor repairs, he advised us to have the back springs replaced. The snag was that for this major repair the car would have to be left in the garage overnight. As we were rather reluctant to do this, there was only one solution; we, too, would have to spend the night in the garage. The manager gave his consent, pointing out that the doors would be closed after dusk when the 'chowkidar' (watchman) came on duty. It was a rather uncomfortable, claustrophobic experience. About 10 p.m. the night watchman closed and bolted the great iron gates of the garage, and stretched himself out on his string bed. We were wedged in a corner surrounded by broken-down vehicles and as there was no ventilation, we were overcome by the heat and almost suffocated by the stench of diesel oil and petrol fumes. Once or twice we were tempted to wake the sleeping attendant and ask him to unbolt the door, but we decided to stick it out till the morning. You can imagine our feelings of relief when we heard the doors clang open and felt the cool fresh air rush in.

It wasn't just the car which needed attention; looking critically at myself in the mirror, I decided that my hair required a new perm. As most Indian women are content with their smooth, straight hairstyles, they have no need for hairdressers, and there are very few salons even in the big cities. They are to be found, however, in luxury hotels like the Taj, and here in a very smart salon, the girl assistant looked doubtfully at my lank hair and murmured something about taking a test sample. She put a lock of my hair in the perming solution, then proceeded to crop my hair short. When she went to examine the test sample, I heard her gasp.

"What is the matter?" I asked.

"Your hair has completely disintegrated," was her reply, as she produced the dish with its muddy-looking contents.

I was appalled by the thought of what might have happened to the rest of my hair.

"Our solutions are too strong for your type of hair," said the poor girl, lamely.

But I was congratulating myself on a lucky escape, for although I was shorn, I was not completely bald.

When the moment of departure came and the last garland had been placed lovingly around our necks, we felt sad at parting with so many dear friends. Everyone we knew, including the gungas, had risen early to see us off. Our niece, Yasu, was in tears, but we cheered her up with the promise that she should join us in Nepal during her annual holiday. Sheroo, Kerry's youngest sister, was crying too, but I don't know why, because she was coming with us to Goa. Maybe she was apprehensive at leaving her family for the first time. However, as the outline of Bombay disappeared on the skyline so did her qualms, and when the sun rose, so did our spirits as we proceeded merrily along the road to Goa.

With Perin and Manchi at the Elephanta Caves — Bombay

Sheroo, Elizabeth and Michèle — Goa

Chapter Nine

IN THE HEART OF INDIA

Some forty miles east of Bombay, a narrow road forks right from the main highway to Poona and runs due south along the coast. This is the route to Goa which we took that February morning with the sun shining brightly out of a cloudless blue sky. We were happy to be on the move again after spending two months in the confines of the city, and like birds released from a cage, we sang until our throats were parched with dust and heat. It was an uneven, bumpy road which had lost most of its tarmac surface and was pitted with potholes. We headed first through low, scrub-covered hills, then over the Ghats to the coastal plain where rice was being planted in the paddy fields. In contrast to the brown, dry region we had left behind, there was an abundance of water everywhere, flowing in sluggish, green rivers to join the sea. Here the houses in the villages were raised on stilts above the swampy ground, with rickety verandahs lined with wattle. Our destination for the night was the small town of Chiplun, about 185 miles from Bombay and halfway to Goa, and it was there, in the Dak Bungalow, that we had arranged a rendezvous with our Belgian friends. We parked in a shady spot under the trees and booked a room with a shower and a toilet for Sheroo. Although the facilities were primitive, the cost was only a few rupees, and considering that nine members of our party shared the amenities, it was an admirable arrangement. We had tea ready for our friends when they arrived hot and dusty, and when the children had been put to bed, we sat for hours on the verandah listening to the cries of the parakeets in the trees above us.

The next morning we got off to a slow start as the air in our tyres was low and we had to drive for fifty miles before we found a garage; then our progress was retarded as we weaved our way past potholes and crept cautiously round frequent hairpin bends. By midday the heat was intense and the little fan which we had had installed in the cabin in Bombay was of no assistance, as it merely churned the hot air round and round. The landscape, filled with palms and luxuriant banana plantations, had now become quite lush and tropical and when we caught sight of the neat, whitewashed bungalows with their verandahs entwined with flowers, we knew that we had reached Goa, for these dwellings bore the unmistakable stamp of the Portuguese.

It was early in the sixteenth century that the Portuguese obtained a foothold here on the Malabar Coast and further north on the small islands of Goa, Daman and Diu. They were the first Europeans to arrive on the Indian scene, attracted by the lucrative trade in spices for which this area was famous. For 450 years the Portuguese held sway in Goa establishing their language, their way of life, their religion and culture, which, together with their intolerance, effectively cut off the Goanese from their Hindu neighbours. All religions except Christianity were forcibly discouraged, and those converts who defected, were subjected to the terrors of the Inquisition. The first foreigners to come to India, they were the last to leave, having watched the French and the British depart with a semblance of dignity, they waited until they were virtually hounded out in 1961.

When we caught up with our Belgian friends at Calangute Beach near Panaji, they were looking decidedly glum. "There is nowhere we can park in the shade," complained Albert.

"Just listen to the noise of these jukeboxes," said Françoise.

Off they went to have a look at Vaga Beach some miles away. Our dreams of a palm-fringed paradise faded as we looked around Calangute, where the approach road to the beach was lined with makeshift stalls selling tawdry goods and where in seedy-looking restaurants, hippies seemed to be the only customers. On the seafront stood the large, modern, State-run Tourist Resort Hotel with a tiny compound where we were allowed to leave our caravan; but on making enquiries for a room for Sheroo, we found that the hotel was fully booked, apart from a few rooms which were reserved for VIPs. Disconsolate and weary we wandered down to the beach, expecting to find another Juhu swarming with people, and there was a glorious sweep of white sand stretching for miles in each direction, lapped by the bluest of blue seas. What was even more surprising was that the beach was almost empty with only a few strollers in sight, and there were no ugly stalls, no striped umbrellas, only the great black hulks of the natives' fishing boats and their nets lying in the sun. A dip in the cool, clear sea revived our flagging spirits and wiped away our feelings of disappointment and as the sun set in a great blaze of gold over the Arabian Sea, the magic of Goa began to take effect.

Our friends returned from Vaga Beach, which is much smaller and quieter than Calangute, unable to find a place in the shade for their vehicle, as all the space under the palm trees had already been appropriated by Western travellers. Over a meal of fried shark, in a small beach restaurant, we discussed the problem and decided to send an expeditionary force next morning to investigate the possibilities of Colva Beach some thirty miles further south. We found a room for Sheroo in the hotel, with a shower and toilet attached and a verandah overlooking the sea; then we settled down for the night, but not before Kerry had persuaded the manager to allow him to connect our electric cable to the hotel supply, which was just as well, for only with our fan working throughout the night were we able to sleep comfortably.

The prospectors returned late the following afternoon after an unsuccessful trip. The beach at Colva was very beautiful with dazzling soft, white sand, but there were no trees, no refuge from the sun, only a few modest government bungalows which were fully occupied. We investigated the possibility of renting and sharing a bungalow in the village, but the houses to let had been left in such a filthy state by hippies, that even though the price was very reasonable, about £5 per week, we could not contemplate living there. Besides, none of the dwellings had running water, and we knew, having watched the native women who brought their own ropes and pots, that it was a laborious business drawing water from the wells. Had we not been so dependent on the comfort afforded by our vehicle we could easily have rented a room in one of the wooden shacks amongst the sand dunes — without any facilities, of course — for about £7 a month. Our friends set out again for Vaga Beach, where they had found a parking spot in the shade, but we decided to stay in the hotel compound where we could get electricity. Mimi, who was exhausted by the heat, did not go with the others, preferring to stay at Calangute and share a room with Sheroo. This turned out to be a very happy arrangement which lasted for three idyllic weeks. Sheroo and Mimi had their meals with us in the caravan; we used their shower and toilet facilities and I was also able to wash our clothes in their hand basin and hang them out on their balcony. After lunch, when heat made the caravan unbearable — there was no electricity in the afternoon — we, 'girls', had a siesta in the hotel bedroom, while Kerry dozed on the verandah. Of course, there were some disadvantages in being parked so close to the hotel. As the caravan was only a few feet away from the kitchen, we were roused very early every morning by the clatter of dishes and by loud strident voices; but we were amply compensated for our rude awakening, by the sight of the golden sun rising behind the distant palm trees. By the time the girls arrived for breakfast, the porridge was ready and Kerry had been to the market to buy pawpaws and fresh rolls. A milkman called each day with a can of buffalo milk which we boiled thoroughly before using, and this with fresh fruit and vegetables formed the basis of our main meals.

We discovered that Sheroo was a very discerning shopper and an excellent cook. I marvelled at the skilful way she could mince an onion, holding it in her left hand and chopping it finely with a knife. We had delicious omelettes spiced with coriander and served with fried onions and potatoes, plain and curried vegetable stews, containing cauliflower, potatoes, onions, aubergines and green mangoes. To supplement these dishes, we purchased items from the hotel menu — mutton cutlets, keema (curried mince meat) and prawn and chicken dishes, at the reasonable cost of about 30p per portion. We also made salads of tomatoes, cucumber and eggs, served with tinned sardines or mackerel, and for dessert we had grapes, pineapple or banana flambé. Most of the time, in spite of constant interruptions in the electricity supply, which the cooks often disconnected inadvertently, we were able to have cold drinks which are such a luxury in a hot country like India. Since soft drinks were expensive, we usually made do with our own filtered, boiled and chilled water. Occasionally we made 'falooda' a cold drink which we had enjoyed in the ice-cream parlours of Bombay, the basis of which is Issabgod seed, a packet of which Perin had given us before we left. These are left in water to expand, then cold milk and rosehip syrup are added to make a very refreshing drink.

We spent a good deal of our time cooling down in the sea. For Sheroo, who had never had a sea dip before, it was a wonderful new experience, although neither she nor Mimi ventured very far, preferring to lie at the edge and let the waves wash over them. Usually there were very few people on the beach and most of them were Westerners. From time to time, however, coach loads of Indian tourists would arrive and troop down to the water's edge. There they would sit in the blazing sun, watching the sea and the bathers until it was time for their coach to set off again. As yet, swimming is not a very popular sport in India, especially with women who consider that a bathing suit is too revealing and a bikini positively indecent. Older women keep their sarees on when they go for a bathe, and they emerge looking very bedraggled to sit in the sun until their garments are dry. Of course, they would never dream of actually sunbathing on the beach, since in their estimation, a suntanned skin is not beautiful, and they would willingly exchange their dusky complexions for the pale, 'wheatish' coloured skin, which according to the marriage advertisements, most men consider to be a very desirable attribute of a bride. So, on the beaches of Goa and elsewhere in the East, only Western palefaces lie in the sun endeavouring to acquire the shade of brown which the native people find so unbecoming.

On the great beach of Calangute it was never dull for there was always something to attract our interest. Vendors would come to tempt us with great baskets of fruit, with trays of nuts and barley sugar and with tepid soft drinks. Our favourite snacks were 'bughias', onions fried in a crisp batter, sold on a stall near the beach. One of the local 'characters' was an enterprising fellow who made a living from removing wax from tourists' ears. He tried to impress us with the complimentary references he had received from satisfied customers from all over the world but we did not avail ourselves of his services as he was decidedly grubby and we were convinced that he was a rogue.

Near the steps leading to the Tourist Hotel, a small group of women in worn and faded sarees were engaged in an activity which made the gargantuan task of painting the Forth Bridge seem like a day's work. Their job was to pass the sand — miles of it — through a coarse sieve, and remove litter such as cigarette ends, sweet papers, peach stones, etc. Toiling from dawn till dusk, they managed in the course of three weeks, to clean a patch of about fifty square yards. The beach was, however, remarkably clean, not because Indians are litter-conscious, they are not, but because India is still in the pre-package age, and cellophane covers, plastic containers, etc., are seldom used. We could walk for miles along the shore and not be confronted with the sight of plastic bottles bobbing up and down at the water's edge, as is the case along the coast of the Western Mediterranean. Moreover, Indians are much more thrifty with newspapers which are rarely thrown away, as they are sold to shopkeepers who use them to wrap up all kinds of goods from fabrics to bughias.

If there was a blot on the beach of Calangute it was that caused by the presence of Western hippies and their Asian counterparts. I hasten to add, however, that contrary to general belief, most hippies, far from being depraved, are docile, peace-loving individuals, who have either lost their sense of direction, or are trying to find a new one. We saw plenty of this type in Goa, sleeping on the sand or in rude shacks which they have erected, or in organised colonies. Layabouts and nudists they may be, and smokers of hashish, but, nevertheless, they are pretty harmless, and the Goanese tolerate their bizarre lifestyle. There is, however, in Goa a small group of international hippies whose dependence on drugs and drink makes them ruthless and vicious and Goanese people blame them for recent increases in crimes of robbery and violence. Many hippies are destitute and have to beg for a living. We made the acquaintance of one, a German in his twenties, well educated and well spoken. Late in the morning he used to extricate himself from his sleeping bag in a corner of the beach, and beg from everyone in sight, including the Indian tourists who are always more generous to beggars than Westerners. We tried to reason with him and he invariably agreed with us that it was a 'bum's life' that he was leading and he intended to give it up, but by the afternoon, he would be lying completely tipsy, having drunk large quantities of toddy, laced with gin. This toddy is the juice of the palm trees, tapped daily by collectors who shin up the trunks, with tin cans fastened to their waists. When it is fresh, toddy is not particularly potent, but when it ferments, which it does very rapidly, it is very intoxicating. Incidentally, one of the attractions of Goa for a certain type of traveller is that liquor is freely available, whereas in many Indian states, Maharashtra, for instance, the sale of alcohol is severely restricted. Some hippies drank themselves into a state of almost permanent stupor from which one or other would rouse himself from time to time to go on a rampage along the beach, tearing off what little clothing he had. In their state of nakedness it could be seen that their legs and arms were covered with suppurating wounds, caused no doubt, by dirty syringes, and only half concealed by filthy bandages. Strange to relate, some of these unsavoury characters had as appendages quite presentable-looking girls, over whom they seemed to exercise an almost hypnotic spell.

We got to know one of these young women as a result of a little incident which occurred one day on the beach. We were drying off from a bathe one morning when we observed three young Sikhs engaged in a heated argument with a Western girl who was sitting by the edge of the water, wrapped in a large towel. It was a one-sided argument, however, as the girl sat silent, gazing into the sea. Then we saw one of the youths snatch her towel and run off along the beach, leaving the girl stark naked in the sand.

Before we could go to her assistance two of the young men came over and explained what had transpired. "While we were bathing in the sea, she took one of our towels and refused to part with it."

"She is one of the hippies who sleeps here on the beach" said the third youth who had rejoined his friends. "That is her sleeping bag over there, she doesn't seem to have any other possessions."

We went over to talk to her, meeting first of all with no response. Then we discovered that she was an English nurse in her mid-twenties who had left a responsible job in the Midlands to come to Goa with her French boyfriend. When her money run out, he had gone off with someone else and she tagged along like a stray puppy with any hippy group who showed her friendship.

We urged her to return home, suggesting that the British Council might assist her with fares but she only laughed. "I like it here. I feel free and at peace with myself. I will never go back, never."

We had another encounter with an English hippy when we visited the little market town of Mapusa. In the bazaar we were approached by a young man who asked us for money. He did not belong to the dirty, dishevelled variety; in fact, he was clean and decently dressed, showing no sign of deprivation.

When Kerry spoke to him sharply, reproving him for 'letting the side down' the fellow unabashed, reacted angrily. "Why shouldn't I beg? Plenty of other people do. It is none of your business anyhow: I can do as I please in this country" and he rounded off his defence with a few choice expletives, as he made off to intercept some Indian tourist.

It was when we went on a picnic with our Belgian friends to Anjuna Beach, some miles north of Calangute, that we discovered where most of Goa's hippies live. We had gone to Anjuna by bus, along narrow roads through coconut groves and paddy fields, and little villages which looked prosperous and clean. In a hollow, under palm trees beyond the tiny beach, there was a cluster of bamboo huts thatched with banana leaves which, as we had learned from a passenger in the bus, was a hippy colony. Kerry and Albert went off to investigate and discovered that the word 'hippy' did not seem to fit all the occupants. A burly Brazilian in his late thirties was the self-styled leader of the colony where he had lived with his wife and two young children since his arrival in India two years before. Kerry and Albert found him and a Swiss boy playing chess with pieces which they had made with great ingenuity out of old tin cans.

"How does one get a hut?" asked Albert.

"I do the allocation," said the Brazilian. "There is one vacant which you can have if you want."

"Is there a charge?"

The man laughed. "No, they are all free."

Kerry asked him what he did with his time when he was not playing chess, and he was shown an expertly carved totem pole which he had made out of a piece of driftwood.

"We live a very quiet life," he explained. "You might call it a life of indolence, but at least it gives us the opportunity to avoid the pressures of modern society and to reflect on less material things."

"How do you manage to survive without working?"

"I brought with me enough money to enable my family to subsist simply but adequately for three to four years," was his reply.

Further along the shore there was another small colony with only one occupant, a drunken Scotsman, lamenting the departure of his companions who had left for Kathmandu. He had been unable to accompany them, he said, because he hadn't any money.

As we ate our lunch in the shade of the palm trees, several family groups of Australians living in motor homes above the beach came down to the shore to bathe in the nude. On this beautiful, remote beach the state of nakedness seemed natural and certainly did not offend our sensibilities.

Sometimes we would arrive on the Calangute Beach early in the morning to find it littered with silver fish. The sardine boats had come in during the night and disgorged their catch on the sand, and for days the women of the village would be busily engaged packing the sardines in the baskets between layers of brown salt, or turning them as they lay drying in the sun. During these operations we had to find another bathing spot as the sea and sand were full of dead fish. Strangely enough, in spite of the superfluity of fish on the beach, we hardly ever saw fresh fish for sale in the villages, although there was plenty of the tinned variety.

Most of the men of Calangute village earn their livelihood from the sea, and judging from the miserable conditions under which they live, it is far from being a lucrative business. This became more apparent to us after we had made several early-morning fishing expeditions with the fishermen we had met on the beach. Just as dawn was breaking the four of us would be on the shore helping to push the long, heavy boats into the sea. Then, followed by shoals of leaping porpoises, we moved over the clear, calm water until we were about half a mile from the shore. The nets were then dropped and the boats slowly returned to the beach where a large crowd of men was waiting to pull the catch in. It was usually a disappointing one with only a few large fish including some great eels, some squid, crabs, jelly fish with stinging tails, and sea urchins which the men ate on the spot with great relish. There was never enough fish to feed all the people who helped to pull the boats in, and the fishermen were clearly delighted with the few rupees we gave them for allowing us to accompany them. We now began to understand why so many Goanese leave their beautiful country to find jobs elsewhere.

One fisherman invited us to his house near the beach where he lived with his family and numerous relations. His shack was made of mud over a framework of bamboo, covered with a thatch made of plaited palm leaves as protection against the sun and monsoon rains. The women of the family were cooking outside on charcoal fires, while long-nosed piglets and skinny fowls scratched around in the sand. To show his hospitality, our friend cut some green mangoes from a tree and gave them to us to eat, covered with rough brown salt, and he also sent one of his children to fetch coconuts from a tall palm tree nearby. The little boy scrambled up the tree like a monkey and threw down some green coconuts full of delicious juice. Few of the fishermen's children attend school, not only because it costs money, but because they are needed to help with the nets and boats. We saw one youngster dipping his father's nets into a large steaming pot of seaweed and water and he explained that this concoction makes the nets strong and rot-resistant. The Goanese women are small in stature, and look attractive in their colourful cotton blouses and sarongs. They work hard and keep the area around their houses surprisingly neat and tidy, disposing of refuse in large pits which they dig in the sand.

In front of many of the village houses, whitewashed crosses raised on cement pedestals demonstrate that the inhabitants are members of the Christian community to which the majority of the population belonged in the Portuguese era. However, already there is a preponderance of Hindus in Goa, and they, too, have a symbol in front of their homes to denote their religious allegiance. We had noticed that a certain green plant in a pot had pride of place in many front gardens and Sheroo told us that this was 'tulasi' (or basil) which is venerated by followers of Vishnu. Early in the morning, the women of the house — for it is they who have this cult — say their prayers as they walk around this plant. Fortunately, in this happy little land, all the religious communities get on well, rejoicing together in their various festivals whether it be Christmas or Diwali (the Hindu Festival of Lights).

Several miles away at Vaga Beach, Albert and his family were blissfully happy, dividing their time between the sea and the sand in the company of other wanderers like themselves. Sometimes Titi and the children would walk along the shore to pay us a visit and to enjoy the luxury of a shower in the hotel. As there were neither water nor toilets at Vaga Beach, the facilities of the Tourist Resort were greatly appreciated.

On Véronique's birthday, we had a cardboard cake but the candles were real, and she had as much ice cream as she fancied. However, it was Patrick who really needed the ice cream, as, unobserved, he had stuffed a few green chillies into his mouth. "Too 'ot, too 'ot" he sobbed, as his dear Patapouffe (alias Kerry), tried to comfort him.

In the opposite direction from Vaga, one and a half hours' walk along the beach, lie the ruins of Fort Aquada, an ancient Portuguese fortress which long ago withstood the attacks of both the British and the Dutch. The hillside above the fort is now dominated by a new luxury hotel which we visited a couple of days after it was opened. In a few years, alas, the beautiful beach of Calangute will not doubt be overlooked by dozens of hotels like this, with cocktail bars, swimming pools, and natty straw umbrellas. Almost all the guests were North Americans, who must feel very much at home here, as the hotel is built in the same style as those we have seen in Miami and the Caribbean. As we sipped our lime sodas beside the pool, a waiter summoned us to the Conference Room to be entertained by a group of Goanese dancers, attired like court jesters with long staves in their hands. It was a rather pathetic exhibition, and the contrast between their misery and the hotel's opulence was so distasteful that we left within a few minutes to begin the long trek back to Calangute over the white beach still in its primeval state of beauty. Behind us, a firework display at the hotel lit up the ruins of the old fort, and as the moon rose, etching the edge of the water with silver, we saw dozens of white crabs, disturbed by our footsteps, scuttling back into the sea.

The placid and gentle Arabian Sea has another, less pleasant face, which we awoke to see one morning, as the wind scattered the blossoms of the hibiscus and bent the palm trees. There was a noise like the roaring of a gigantic waterfall as tumultuous waves raced each other towards the shore. We closed all our windows and wrapped in winter woollies we went to inspect the beach which was covered with flotsam and jetsam. The fishermen, who had hauled their boats high up on the shore, told us that the storm would last for several days, so we decided to explore the interior of Goa and the capital, Panaji, to which, hitherto, we had only given a cursory glance.

Palm fringed and dusty, the little road to Panaji winds its way through paddy fields, past salt pans and neatly painted houses with verandahs overflowing with flowers, and as our single-decker bus was in no particular hurry, we had plenty of time to inspect the fruit and vegetables in the village markets, and to admire the elegant outlines and dazzling white façades of the Christian churches dotted along our route. A splendid new bridge at Betim has replaced the ferry over the wide Mandovi river on the banks of which stands the sleepy little town of Panaji, the capital of Goa. One has the impression that the town has seen better days and that it was probably more lively and better maintained when the Portuguese were in control. There were few goods for sale in the dowdy little shops, and we had a very indifferent meal in the Tourist Hotel. However, when we had toiled up the steps to the whiter than white Church of the Immaculate Conception, we were compensated by a distant and more favourable view of the town; and as we waited for a tour coach to take us to Old Goa we noted the absence of beggars in the streets.

In Velha (Old) Goa time seems to have stood still since the middle of the eighteenth century when the Portuguese abandoned their old capital, which was beset with the plague, to build a new one at Panaji. It is difficult to believe that this town once rivalled Lisbon in splendour and that once it was said "He who has seen Old Goa had no need to see Lisbon". Like Fatehpur Sikri, it is now a ghost town, but whereas the Moguls left splendid palaces behind them, the main legacy of the Portuguese here as elsewhere in Goa, is a number of interesting churches and convents. Probably the biggest tourist attraction in Goa is the Bom Jesus Basilica, although its dull exterior belies the richness within. The basilica was built by the Jesuits, and although it was dedicated to the Infant Jesus, the Babe's image is dwarfed by a huge statue of Ignatius Loyala, the great Spanish saint. The brilliance of the gold leaf in the carvings above and around the altar is dazzling. However, it is not this baroque magnificence which the tourist come to see, but the silver casket lying to the right of the altar. This casket contains the earthly remains of the most famous man ever to set foot on the Malabar Coast — St Francis Xavier. In 1540 he came to preach in Goa, and, although he remained for only six or seven years, he was successful in converting many Indians, especially those of the lower classes, to the Christian faith. When St Francis died in 1550 on a mission to China, his body was brought back to repose in the magnificent silver casket, a gift of the Duke of Tuscany. Every ten years the casket is opened and the faithful are able to view the saint's body lying in a sealed, glass coffin. We missed the great event by only a few weeks, for the saint's body was on display in January 1975 amid scenes of religious fervour. In the years before 1952, when the body was not enclosed in a sealed coffin, two female fanatics actually bit off his big toes, one of which is preserved in a glass case in the crypt. After his death, the saint's right arm was severed on the request of Pope Paul V and sent as a holy relic to Rome. The amazing, and some think miraculous thing about St Francis' body, is that although it has shrunk, it has not decomposed, and the features are still recognisable. The great square outside the cathedral was once the site of religious trials and executions during the shameful period of the Inquisition, and some say that it was not because of the plague that the old capital was abandoned, but because it held too many memories of barbaric acts committed in the name of religion.

When Alfonso de Albuquerque captured Goa in 1510, he wrote to inform the King of Portugal that his soldiers had slain or roasted alive 6,000 Muslims and destroyed all their property. He attributed his victory to God and St Catherine, as the following passage in his letter reveals: "I am handing over the property and lands of the Mosque to the Church of St Catherine, on whose day, Our Lord gave us victory on account of her virtue and I am building this church in the large enclosure of the fort."

We visited this cathedral where St Catherine is enthroned above the altar, her bosom pierced by six swords. I wonder what her martyrdom really meant to the early Goanese converts, and was it in love or in fear that they bowed before her image?

Although the Portuguese had no great love for the Hindus, they treated them less harshly than they did the Muslims, probably because they needed their assistance to defeat the common enemy, for it was only thirty years before that the followers of Islam had overrun Goa. Nevertheless, the Hindus remained wary of the Portuguese invaders and erected their temples some distance from the capital. We visited a number of these shrines in the wooded country near Ponda, south of Panaji. All of these temples, dedicated to different Hindu deities, are built in the same style with a high ornate white tower overlooking the 'tank ' (pool) and the courtyard. Here crowds of children wait to coax visitors to buy their garlands of marigolds to lay at the feet of the gods. Here, too, the vendors of powdered chalk do good business, for devout Hindus purchase the stuff by the kilo to sprinkle on the shrines and to mark 'tikkas' on their brows. Mimi bought several little packets of red, green and yellow chalk to take back to Belgium as souvenirs. Unfortunately, the newspaper wrappings deteriorated by the time she reached Bombay, shedding the contents all over the inside of the van. There were plenty of coconuts and the fruit of the cashew which grows above the nuts. Kerry will not easily forget the cashews he purchased at the shrine of Shri Mangnesh, for he took a bite of an unripe nut and had his lips burned by the potent juice. Cashews grow in great abundance in Goa and one of their most intoxicating drinks — feni — is made with the fermented juice of the fruit.

On the steps of the temple we removed our shoes, as is the custom, and crossed the polished marble floor to the shrine of the deity whose symbol was adorned with flowers and liberal sprinklings of holy water and coloured chalk. I could not help wondering how long it took the attendants each evening to remove these decidedly anaesthetic and messy offerings. Mimi and Titi looked after us like the most dutiful of daughters, fetching our sandals as we emerged into the sunshine, and even offering to fasten the buckles, a service which Kerry was quick to discourage. "You musn't spoil us. How are we going to manage when you are not around?"

By now, we were very conscious that our idyllic interlude in Goa would soon be at an end, and the thoughts of our Belgian friends were already turning to their forthcoming journey round the Cape and to their homecoming. In the bazaar at Mapusa they purchased straw mats and wicker baskets, leather sandals and strings of beads made of nuts and shells, which were carefully packed along with the silks, embroidered shawls and cotton skirts and dresses they had bought in Kashmir and Delhi. Sheroo returned to Bombay by coach, an uncomfortable journey which took twenty hours. She had enjoyed herself in her quiet way, fitting in well with our very different lifestyle, and generously allowing Mimi and me to dress up in her beautiful sarees.

A day or two before we left Calangute, we had unexpected visitors, Perin's neighbours, Jal and Ruttee Ameria, who arrived at the hotel in a chauffeur-driven car. Jal had been asked to come to Goa to treat the chief minister's daughter and they were staying in a hotel in Panaji for three days. They brought us gifts from Perin, 'shrikand' my favourite sweet, made from yogurt, and sweetmeats for Kerry, besides the up-to-date news of our relatives and friends.

At dawn on the 18th March, we took final leave of our Belgian friends and headed south along the coast towards Mangalore. They were due to set sail from Bombay a few days later and we did not expect to hear from them again until we returned to Europe. However, a letter from Mimi, which reached us a month later in Kathmandu, told us the sad tale of their unexpected delay. When Albert called at the Lloyds Triestino office to make the final arrangements for their voyage, he learned to his dismay that the liner which was to carry them to Genoa was held up with engine trouble in Durban. The next passenger ship was not due for two months, and all airlines to Europe were fully booked until the end of April. Fortunately, our friend, Nellie, who works in Air India, was able to pull a few strings and obtain seats for them on a flight to Amsterdam on the 23rd April, one month later than they had expected to leave. In the meantime, Mimi and Titi returned to the Catholic ashram where they lived very frugally having spent most of their money, while Françoise and Albert paid a visit to Kerala with the children. Their Bedford and Volkswagen vans were dispatched by cargo boat to Genoa which they reached three months later with a few additional dents, and minus some of their most precious possessions. It was a disappointing and costly finale to their overland trip, but, by the time we met them again in Belgium, all these frustrations had long been forgotten.

We shall never forget the warmth of the welcome we received in Thuin on a cold December's day when the occupants of number 3 Rue St Roch came running out when they saw our begrimed and battered Transit pull into the village square. What tales we had to hear and tell over cream cakes and croissants: Albert and his family had found it much more difficult to settle down after their long trip than Mimi and Titi.

Albert had not returned to teaching and was looking around for a new career, and little Patrick was proving an unruly pupil at nursery school. It would seem that the difficulties which face the returned traveller are much greater than those he encounters on the long journey overland. We, ourselves, found it far from easy to adjust ourselves to the old routine, but younger people face much greater problems. Our French friends were unemployed for nine months, not because there were no jobs available, but because they had lost interest in their previous professions of teaching and accounting. Prosper is now working for a firm which makes oil rigs and Jackie has had a series of short-term jobs.

After this digression in time, let us return to Goa and to that March morning when we reluctantly took leave of that very pleasant land. In the cool of the early morning, people were hard at work in the paddy fields and banana plantations, and in the eucalyptus forests near the frontier, the air was sweetly scented. At the small seaside resort of Karwar, we were confronted with a broad stretch of river which we had to cross on the back of a diminutive ferry, not designed to transport unwieldy vehicles like ours. However, with goodwill and some manoeuvring on the part of the ferrymen, we eventually got on board and chugged across to the State of Mysore, which has acquired the new name of Karnataka.

The frontier officials — for each Indian state has its own guardians — were obviously surprised when we told them that we had brought no liquor with us from Goa. Mysore, unlike Goa, is 'dry', and as there is a good deal of smuggling from over the border, we were closely questioned.

"No feni?" they asked, looking astounded when we said that we couldn't stand the stuff, but they did not bother to inspect the van.

Almost at once we noticed a difference between the Kanadigas, as the inhabitants of this state are called, and the Goanese. Whereas the Goanese, with their live-and-let-live attitude, had never intruded on our privacy, the Kanadigas, like most other Indians, were inquisitive and interfering. Whenever we stopped the van to ask for information, we were immediately surrounded by a pushing, gaping crowd.

The countryside, however, was very similar to that of Goa, and as we travelled south, we caught tantalizing glimpses of miles of golden beaches to which there was no access except by narrow dirt tracks. Towards noon we came upon a stretch of road running close to the shore which was empty except for a few straw-thatched huts; so we quickly exchanged our sweat-drenched clothes for our bathing suits and threw ourselves into the waves. By the time we had emerged from the sea, a large crowd of naked children and poverty-stricken-looking women with jewels in their noses, had gathered to gaze on the strange intruders. Instead of lingering in the sunshine to dry our swimsuits, we set off again along the coast, through coconut groves and rice paddies bordered by smooth green rivers. In this part of the country the people are much darker than further north and wear very few clothes. Many of the women were 'topless', and most of the men wore diminutive sarongs. There were, however, no signs of poverty in the villages where the little mud houses were neatly tiled and well maintained. In Mangalore, which, apart from being the world's principal cashew nut port, is an uninteresting town, we parked in the compound of the largest hotel, the Moti Mahal. The manager kindly allowed us to plug into the electrical supply of his garden restaurant, which was just as well, for without our fan the heat would have been unbearable. By this time we had begun to realize the foolishness of proceeding further south when the long journey north over the Deccan was still ahead of us in ever soaring temperatures. So, with regret, we abandoned our plan to reach the southern tip of India, and leaving the coast road, we set off in an easterly direction to visit the famous Hindu temples of Belur and Halebid, en route for the princely city of Mysore.

The coconut and banana groves gave way to cocoa and coffee plantations, as the road climbed steeply over the mountains where sheep were cropping grass by the roadside. When we reached Belur, the sun was at its height and the temple steps were so hot that Kerry fetched his thickest woollen socks to protect our bare feet, to the obvious disapproval of the temple priests. However, it is worth having one's feet scorched just to see this extraordinary temple, covered from top to bottom with elaborate carvings. Although it was built 800 years ago, the stone has not weathered and one can distinguish every detail of the remarkable friezes which decorate the walls. The lowest layer depicts elephants; then come rows of mythical animals, full-breasted women, musicians and their instruments; and finally the whole pantheon of Hindu gods and goddesses. We rested in the cool, dark interior watching the play of sunlight on the carvings of the massive roof pillars then we set off to visit the equally-famous temple at Halebid which took eight years to construct and was never fully completed. In its setting, within a garden full of trees covered with bright blue and flame-coloured blossoms, this temple is even more impressive than its counterpart at Belur, and so fine and delicate is the craftsmanship that it is difficult to believe that the basic material is stone and not lace. Magnificent friezes of elephants, swift horses, mythical beasts and celestial beings cover the outside of the shrine, which is guarded by two huge stone bulls. By this time, having stood for hours in the open examining and photographing the carvings, we had become quite dehydrated, so we went in search of a cold drink.

But the Limcas and Fantas, the Indian equivalents of our soft drinks, had been standing in the sun much longer than we had, and as for ice, it is doubtful that it is known in that part of the world; so we drove on until we found a great avenue of teak trees and brewed ourselves a cup of tea in the shade.

I had always associated Mysore with bejewelled maharajahs and caparisoned elephants and had secretly hoped to see at least the latter, but both the elephants and the maharajahs have departed from the city and with them the pomp and grandeur which made Mysore one of the most outstanding of the old state capitals. At Independence, when most of the princely states were merged into larger units, Mysore was superseded by Bangalore and the maharajah became the first governor of the new state. Like Baroda, which suffered a similar fate, Mysore is still a splendid city with clean, wide streets, well kept parks and palatial buildings, but the great domed palace which was the hub of the town, stands empty and closed. We drove around trying to find a parking place in the compound of one of the large hotels, but we were told that we could only have permission if we booked a room. Finally, a small Indian hotel allowed us to leave the car in their tiny courtyard and to connect our electric cable. That evening our meal at the Kwality Restaurant was a disappointment with poor food and poorer service; what is more, we were deafened by blaring music from a loudspeaker which the management refused to tone down. Disgruntled, we returned to the caravan to find it reeking with the smell of curry and burning fat from the kitchen a few yards away, and as it was too hot to close the windows, we had to put up with unpleasant odours and clatter of dishes till the early hours of the morning.

Next day, the cook came to tempt us with rice and black rum pancakes for breakfast, but we settled for plain chappatis to eat with marmalade. Instead of delivering the milk in a bottle or can, they brought a water buffalo and milked it at our doorstep. At least we knew that the milk was fresh. While on the subject of breakfast, I must point out that it is purely a Western conception that breakfast should be a different kind of meal from lunch and dinner. In the morning, Indians usually eat the leftovers from the previous evening's meal, rice and curry or a vegetable stew, but somehow or other, I could never get used to the idea, and I often wonder how Indians visiting our country get used to our frugal morning fare. The Number One bus took us to Chamundi Hill which looks down on the maharajah's summer palace and the distant turrets and domes of the city. Our main reason for visiting this spot was to see Siva's colossal bull which stands on the hillside, carved from one great boulder. This sixteen-foot black Nandi, with its garlands and bells, is a very regal animal and a great tourist attraction. At Chamundi we met a young English couple who had travelled all the way to India by local transport. They had hoped to visit Ceylon, but unfortunately, since prices in India, as elsewhere, rose alarmingly in 1974 and 1975, they were having to cut short their trip and return home. The young man had had the added misfortune of falling ill with jaundice in Bombay, and still looked far from well. When we asked them what precautions they took when drinking water in India, we were surprised to learn that they took none, and we noted that they were drinking Lassi, a drink which is made from whey to which ordinary water is added.

North of Mysore, on an island in the Cauvery river, a battle was fought in 1799 between the troops of the British East Indian Company and the forces of the Muslim Tipu Sultan. Tipu was a colourful character like his father, Hyder Ali, who had defeated the British some years before. Although Tipu fought hard, he was overwhelmed and lost his life in the battle which gave the British suzerainty over this part of southern India. Tipu's fort lies in ruins, but his mosque is still standing and his luxurious summer palace with its gilded panels and coloured frescoes. Most imposing of all these remains is Tipu's mausoleum with its fluted black pillars which, unfortunately, we were unable to visit as we had forgotten to bring our woollen socks to protect our feet from the blistering heat. However, we did discover plenty of green coconuts nearby which provided us with a cool drink.

Most of the roads in Mysore State are good, and the highway to Bangalore is no exception. It passes through green valleys filled with mango and banana groves, then rises to bare uplands covered with huge white boulders and gigantic outcrops of rock, a primeval landscape which is, according to our guidebooks, one of the oldest parts of the world's crust. In Bangalore we experienced the same difficulty in finding a parking place as we had done in Mysore, but after we had interrupted our search to have a dip in the swimming pool of the luxury Asoka Hotel, we found that our problem was unexpectedly solved by a meeting with a family of Seven Day Adventists. Betty Knight and her three young children saw our motor home as they were passing the hotel and as they were planning to make the trip overland to England by car, they were giving our car a close examination when we returned from the pool. By the time we had shown them over our little abode, we had been invited to their home in a pleasant suburb on the outskirts of the town. In a garden full of flowering shrubs, which sheltered us from the glare of the sun, we spent two happy days in excellent company. Peter and Betty Knight had been in this part of the country with an American mission for fifteen years, and their main concern, in addition to preaching the gospel, was to involve their church members, most of whom were Indians, in social and health projects which would benefit the whole community.

For Europeans as well as for Indians, Bangalore is one of the most desirable places to live in India, since it has an ideal climate, neither too hot nor too humid. For instance, we did not require our fan during the night, and we did not feel the heat too oppressive in the middle of the day. Another reason for Bangalore's popularity is the presence of many major industries in the town. The headquarters of the aircraft and telephone industries are here, as well as textile, electronic, pharmaceutical and machine-tool factories. We went shopping with Betty Knight in the large covered fruit and vegetable market which had produce of much better quality than we had seen elsewhere in India; but the prices were much higher. The mango season was just beginning and we could not resist buying a few at 5p each, which Betty considered to be expensive; on the other hand, we had to pay 25p for half a pound of porridge oats. In the British Library, which is financed by the British Council, we found newspapers which were only two days old and were able to catch up on recent events at home. In the Botanical Gardens, the Lal Bagh, which is full of rare shrubs, lotus pools and fountains, a legacy of Tipu Sultan's era, we wandered in the shade of ancient trees. There were no beggars in sight, no slums to spoil the view; on the contrary, everywhere there was an air of prosperity and comfort, of order and decency.

Unfortunately, our good opinion of Bangalore was somewhat tarnished by a little incident which occurred while I was waiting in the car for Kerry who had gone to change money in a bank. We had parked in a side street near a gateway which turned out to be the entrance of a boys' school. It was lunch time and the boys came flooding out into the street. Seeing our strange vehicle they quickly surrounded it, pressing against the sides and bonnet and hanging on to the mirrors. I tried to ignore them as long as I could, thinking they might eventually go away. More and more youngsters arrived and some climbed up the ladder onto the roof. Others attempted to wrench the doors and windows open. I asked them to go away but they would not budge, so in desperation I got out and expostulated with them, calmly at first, then more fiercely. Of course, they were delighted that they had made me angry, and they laughed hilariously. I snatched some books from the boys nearest me and threw them over the wall, but this only made matters worse. One group of lads started to kick the side panels of the car and others threw stones. Only one passer-by came to my rescue, a little, inoffensive man in a Gandhi cap, who spoke to the boys in Hindi, asking them to go away. They jeered at him and one lad snatched his white cap and ran off with it. I had heard that it was easy to start a riot in India, and now I was in the midst of one. Fortunately, at this point, Kerry returned, and in a flash my tormentors vanished over the wall and down the street. However, we were not prepared to let the matter rest there, so we went into the school and asked to see the headmaster, but neither he nor his deputy were available and the master who had been left in charge did not consider that it was his responsibility to monitor the behaviour of his pupils outside the school buildings.

We had other things to worry us in Bangalore besides unruly children. Our tyres, which had given us cause for concern for some time, had deteriorated still further, and another puncture forced us to use our last spare tyre. We attributed some of our troubles to the excessive heat, and as the temperatures on the next part of our journey over the Deccan were bound to be high, we even considered the possibility of taking the train to Benares, 1,000 miles away. When we discovered that the train would take from ten to twelve days to reach its destination and that we and the car would have to travel separately, we abandoned this scheme and went in search of replacements for our tyres. We were dismayed to find out that tyres of the dimensions we required were not available in Bangalore, and we were advised to try our luck 700 miles away, at Jabalpur, where there was a Firestone factory.

The Knights saw us off before dawn, Betty with characteristic generosity giving us a jar of peanut butter which she had made. Soon we had reached the Nandi Hills where the more affluent residents of Bangalore have their summer villas. Ahead of us lay the barren uplands of the State of Andhra Pradesh, dotted with the same curious rock formations which we had seen on the way to Bangalore. Here nothing grew except scrub and cactus, and the only living things we saw were herds of antelopes which sprang across our path. At Kurnool we had a very welcome cold shower at the Dak Bungalow, and a cup of tea under a fan on the verandah. We gave one of the servants all our dirty cloths to wash, supplying him with soap powder, as we knew he would have none. He washed them in cold water in a large wooden tub and spread them on the lawn to dry, and in less than two hours he came back with a neat pile of spotlessly clean, neatly ironed clothes. Meanwhile, we took a bicycle rickshaw to the centre of the town to shop for our evening meal, and in the busy bazaar near the old fort we bought vegetables, melons and coconuts. The busiest stalls were those which sold fragrant, white flower blossoms for about 10p the kilo. We thought that they were intended for a religious festival until we discovered that Kurnool is on the route to one of the most important Hindu pilgrimage centres in India, the Shrine of Srisailam, which is visited by many thousands of pilgrims each year.

At the Dak Bungalow we met two civil engineers who were engaged in the construction of road bridges in the vicinity. Although their native language was Telegu, which is spoken in Andhra Pradesh, they also spoke English, so we passed the evening in their company until the arrival of mosquitoes drove us into the caravan.

The following day we reached Hyderabad, the capital of Andhra Pradesh, where our first concern was to find a refuge from the fiery sun. Fortunately, the Tourist Office gave us permission to park in their compound under a rough wooden shelter which gave us some protection from the heat. It was at the Tourist Office that we met a rather wild-looking American who told us how he had been robbed of all his money on the night train from Calcutta. Not being quite convinced of the truth of his tale, we hardened our hearts and did not part with any money in spite of his repeated requests. The van was now like a furnace, and not having any electricity we had no means of cooling it down, so we spent most of our time in Hyderabad viewing the inside rather than the outside of public buildings. Before Independence, Hyderabad was the largest and most important of India's princely states, and its ruler, the Nizam, was one of the wealthiest men in the world. During the British era, the rulers of Hyderabad considered themselves to be allies rather than subordinates, so in 1947, the Nizam, reluctant to lose his independence, refused to accept the terms offered and pressure had to be applied by India to force him to join the other states. Hyderabad, although it has lost some of its old glamour, is still a very handsome city, with wide streets and fine parks. Its most outstanding feature is the Char Minar Gateway which was built to commemorate the end of the Great Plague in 1591. We sought respite from the heat in the Salar Jung Museum, where, in spite of air-conditioning, the temperature was 90°F. Salar Jung, a hereditary first minister of Hyderabad, spent his life collecting unusual curiosities from all over the world. One of the most remarkable objects was a large clock from which a figure emerged every hour to strike a bell. The shady garden of the Zoological Park was our next place of refuge. We skulked from tree to tree, and drank great quantities of sugary, black tea. It was, we discovered, almost impossible to obtain a cup of plain tea (in cafes and restaurants) without the addition of either sugar or milk.

Next day, heading north through inhospitable country, we made our way to a tiny village which for more than a decade of this century was the nerve centre of India. Fifty miles south of Nagpur, in the very heart of

India, lies the little village of Sevagram, founded by Gandhi in 1936. The word 'Sevagram' means 'village of service', and it was Gandhi's intention to put into practice here his ideas for the regeneration of his country. In a very short time, this insignificant village had become a place of pilgrimage for the most influential people in India, including the viceroy, and many of the momentous decisions which affected the lives of 600 million people were made in Gandhi's small bungalow. A visit to Sevagram had been included in our itinerary for two reasons. First of all, we wanted to find out what had happened to Gandhi's many projects in agriculture, weaving, education and hygiene, and we also hoped to meet the man who has been named as Gandhi's successor, the venerable Vinoba Bhave, whose ashram is in the nearby village of Paunar.

When we reached the ashram at Sevagram we were made welcome by the secretary, Mr Pande, who installed us in the guest-house bungalow, where our bedroom, although dusty and bare, except for two iron double-tiered bunks enveloped in mosquito netting, was sheltered from the sun by the low verandah roof. The fact that the little washroom adjoining with its Asian toilet, its tap and bucket was obviously frequented by rats, did not dismay us in the least.

"Do be careful!" said Mr Pande. "There is a hornet's nest under the eaves at your doorway."

We did not suggest that it should be removed, as we realized that hornets and rats have as much right to live in an ashram as visitors like ourselves. As it transpired, the rats were even more aggressive than those we had encountered at Lonavla. During the first night they had devoured our soap and all the fruit which I had hung in a string bag on the metal post of my iron bed. In the morning the string bag was in shreds and only banana skins were left to tell the tale, so in the future we kept all of our possessions inside the caravan.

The whole ashram seemed to be pervaded by the unseen presence of Gandhi. You could almost imagine that it was he and not one of the old residents who was spinning on the verandah of one of the bungalows, or sunning his bony frame in the late afternoon sunshine. But his presence was felt most under the great tree where he always conducted evening prayers. As our hymns, accompanied by the music of the tablas, rose to heaven through the spreading branches, I recalled that this same tree had often looked down on the slight figure of the Mahatma in his white dhoti. Mr Pande told us that the growth of this banyan tree had been phenomenal, and that scientists had attributed its extraordinary vigour to vibrations. This theory is not so absurd as it may first appear for it is well known that sunspots can influence the growth of a tree, so it is conceivable that sounds of a particular pitch may have a similar effect. In Gandhi's time those who came to evening prayers sat on mats on the beaten earth which is now covered with rough gravel.

"We did this to discourage snakes," said Mr Pande, who went on to explain how an elderly resident was fatally bitten by a cobra on this spot some years before.

"Did you catch the cobra?" asked Kerry, who has a morbid fear of snakes.

"Yes, we caught it and let it loose in the jungle," replied Mr Pande. "There are still a few snakes here, and from time to time we engage a snake catcher to round them all up."

"Why don't you have a mongoose?" said Kerry.

"Snakes, too, have a right to live," was the reply.

"But not to kill, surely?" insisted Kerry.

Mr Pande did not answer, except to assure us that we would be safe, when at prayer on the gravel patch.

However, next morning as we prepared to make our way to prayers at 5 a.m., we thought of the snakes, and not daring to risk an encounter with a cobra, we waited until Mr Pande appeared with a lantern to guide us.

Morning prayers were held on the verandah of one of the bungalows, and we waited in silence as white-robed figures emerged from the darkness to join us. For about an hour we would sing hymns and repeat prayers from various religions including the Koran and the Bible, as Gandhi had always done. One of Gandhi's old associates, Shri Chimanlalji, explained to us that since Gandhi believed that God was Truth, he accepted the truth of all the world's great religions, and amongst the books which he always kept by his bedside were the Bible, the Koran and the Gita. Shri Chimanlalji, who was one of the most interesting men we met, has spent the last forty years at the ashram. Now a frail man of seventy-six, he lives on a diet of milk and oranges under the same Spartan conditions which prevailed when Gandhi was alive. We visited him several times in the wooden bungalow which he shares with several old-timers like himself, and he lent us some books, his only possessions, so that we should learn more about Gandhi's life and work.

It was in his little house, the Bapu Kuti, that we felt nearest to Gandhi, for here everything has been left exactly as it was at the time of his death. In his living room, where he used to receive the highest dignitaries of the land, stands his spinning wheel, reminding one of the importance which Gandhi placed on the spinning of cotton in order to make the villages independent of factory-made materials. In the ashram day book of 8th December, 1941, he wrote; "None of the residents . . . should waste a minute of his time . . . when there is no other work, let them spin or card cotton." To set an example to others, he used to spin for one hour each day. All his other worldly possessions are here, his spectacles and sandals, three wise monkeys, his books, a lantern and an inkpot. Three quotations are written on the whitewashed walls. One is from Ruskin, another from the Bible and the third reads — "When you are in the right you can afford to keep your temper. When you are in the wrong, you can't afford to lose it."

It is in this room that one is also aware of another shadowy presence, that of the mysterious Mira Behn. It was she who painted the palm trees on the walls and the sign of 'Om'.

"Who was Mira Behn?" we asked Mr Pande.

He told us that this was the name adopted by a Miss Slade, an Englishwoman, who came to Wardha, the nearby village, in 1935, a year before Gandhi decided to settle here. Dressed in a faded saree, her skin roughened and tanned by the sun, she was a well-known figure, as she travelled around the countryside on ponyback. It is possible that the Bapu Kuti was originally her house, and that she gave it to Gandhi when she went to share a house with Gandhi's wife, Kasturba.

I wanted to know more about Miss Slade. What had become of her? But no one was able to enlighten me.

Kerry and I had all our meals in the cookhouse where we had hoped to meet other residents. However, as Mr Pande explained to us very sadly, communal cooking and dining is no longer a feature of the ashram, as residents prefer to dine in their own quarters. Since Mr Pande was a married man, he had not been able to join the others at meals as one of Gandhi's rules was that all members of the ashram should be celibate. So, apart from a few visiting Hindu swamis who could not speak English, we dined alone in the kitchen. The food was infinitely better than the fare we had at the Sivananda ashram. For breakfast we had porridge of coarse, hand-ground wheat with milk; for lunch and for the evening meal we had vegetable stew, curds and fresh fruit, usually pawpaw. We had plates, but we noticed that the swamis ate from banana leaves and were not given curds. After the meal we had to wash up our dishes at the tap outside the kitchen, as there are no servants to do the chores. In the early days of the ashram, Harijans (people of the low caste) had done all the menial tasks, until Gandhi decided that everyone should lend a hand with the work. He, himself, set an example to the others by doing the most unpleasant jobs in the ashram, such as emptying the latrines. Judging by the kitchen, which was constructed to his design, Gandhi was a very practical man. It contains special features which he had hoped would be incorporated in the kitchens of the villages — an oven for baking bread, fly-proof cupboards and a chimney for carrying away the smoke.

From what we had read about the ashram we had expected it to be a hive of activity, as a result of the projects which Gandhi had started. We had looked forward, for instance, to seeing the boys' school where Gandhi's ideas in basic education had been put into practice. Gandhi had rejected the current system of education which he considered inappropriate for most children, as its content was too academic, and as he believed that children should learn by doing, in the ashram school each child had to learn a craft. Practical work together with the proficient use of the mother tongue formed the essentials of the system. Alas, the school closed several years ago, as it was unable to withstand the competition of the new Government High School which dispenses an academic education and much-prized certificates.

"What about the Rural Technical Education Centre?" we enquired. We had read about the workshops which had been set up to provide technical education for village children and where they had been taught to make and repair tools and agricultural implements. It seemed a very worthwhile and useful project and we were eager to see it. This centre, too, was closed. From the outset it had depended on the voluntary work of experts from Germany and England, and when this assistance came to an end, so did the whole project. We were shown the last experiment which the boys had undertaken with the help of a German engineer. They had produced methane gas from cow manure and used it to work the stoves in the hostel kitchen. It was the kind of experiment which would have gladdened Gandhi's heart, but which, unfortunately, was destined to be of little practical value, as an enormous supply of cow dung was required to produce a steady flow of gas. Since the ashram has now only a few cows, and since the hostel kitchen is no longer in use the experiment is of little use. Saddened by the premature end of all these imaginative schemes, we wondered if there was anything left at the ashram but a gallant, dwindling band of men, living as Gandhi had enjoined them to live.

However, we did discover that some of Gandhi's projects have met with success beyond the confines of the ashram. Spurred into action by Gandhi's propaganda in favour of spinning, the government has set up a Khadi (Homespun) Research Station in the village of Sevagram which has contributed to the current popularity of home-spun materials. When we met Dr Sushila Nayyar, who is in charge of the Sevagram Medical College, we heard of another successful project. Soon after Gandhi came to the village, he set up a small dispensary to serve the ashram and Sevagram. With Dr Nayyar in charge, it gradually developed into a health centre and after Gandhi's wife's death, it was renamed the Kasturba Hospital. It has now become a Rural Medical College, financed by the government and the State of Maharashtra, and it trains doctors specifically for work in Indian villages. The success of this highly commendable venture has, however, only been a partial one, as Dr Nayyar sadly explained to us. Since few rural communities can afford doctors, only one of the twenty-five doctors who had qualified several months before, had found a post.

The person who impressed us most at Sevagram was indubitably the secretary, Mr Pande. In spite of all the frustrations he must have suffered, and still suffers as he watches everything he has toiled for gradually deteriorate, he remains calmly confident that in the end Gandhi's ideals will prevail; and of all the remarkable people whom we met in India, it would be true to say that this man in faded and threadbare homespun was the most saintly. Mr Pande, now in his early fifties, had come to Sevagram in 1943 to take charge of the boys' hostel, and he vividly recalled for us his first meeting with Gandhi. "Bapu (Gandhi) came into the hostel early one morning, soon after the boys had got up. At one end of the dormitory they had left some of their clothes — little more than rags — rolled up in their mats. Bapu poked them out with his stick, rather disapprovingly, and told me to tidy things up a bit, so I said that I would dispose of these pieces of cloth."

"Never throw rags away," he replied. "That is a lesson which I learned from my grandmother who used to make wicks for lamps from shreds of torn cloth."

Speaking of another encounter which he had with Gandhi on one of his early-morning tours of inspection, Mr Pande said, "Bapu came and stood near the verandah where there was a tin drum full of water with a tap at which the boys used to wash their hands. After contemplating the drum for some time, he asked me what would happen if this water container was placed under that tree. The tree would get some moisture, I replied." "Exactly" said Bapu, as he walked away. Bapu was a very kindly man, but he was a great stickler for discipline. One day he reprimanded me for leaving the buttons on my shirt sleeves undone. You see, he expected us to set a very good example to the boys and the villagers."

Not far from Sevagram, near the small town of Paunar, is the Paramdhan ashram which is directed by one of Gandhi's most famous associates, Vinoba Bhave. A frail man of eighty-one, Bhave is one of the most venerated and influential figures in India, and only a few months ago when he was seriously ill, Mrs Gandhi abandoned all her state duties to hurry to his bedside. Over fifty years ago, Bhave joined Gandhi's first ashram at Sabarmati in Gujarat, and he remained one of the Mahatma's staunchest supporters. When Gandhi embarked on his civil disobedience campaign, it was Bhave who was the first to offer himself for arrest and he worked with Gandhi for a time at Sevagram before setting up his own ashram at Paunar. Bhave's name came to the notice of the world soon after Gandhi's death when he set out on foot across India on a mission which has been called the "Boodan" project — a crusade to obtain land for the landless. For over five years, his spare figure was to be seen striding along Indian highways and byways on his way to plead with landowners to part with some of their land, and owing to his efforts, millions of acres were handed over by the 'haves' to the 'have-nots'.

Bhave's ideas have made an impact on another sphere of Indian life which has been much neglected, namely that of women's education. He has always maintained that until women play a more active role in Indian affairs, the country will make little progress; so when he set up his ashram, it was for women only. Their work at the ashram has three main components; first of all there is the manual work which consists of animal husbandry, horticulture and agriculture; then there is the work on the printing press which produces a magazine and brochures; and finally there is the devotional side of prayers and meditation. In all these activities the main emphasis is placed on group work rather than on self-realization.

When we reached the ashram, eager to meet the great man, there was a disappointment in store for us. A few months before, Vinoba had taken a vow to remain silent for one year. Nevertheless, his secretary informed us that if we were prepared to wait, Vinoba might give us an audience. As we waited in the sunny courtyard, watching the women at work in the fields beyond, an attractive young lady approached us and offered to show us round the ashram. She was one of the thirty-three members of the ashram, a graduate in Philosophy, and we gathered from her conversation that most of the other women were also well educated. The ashram buildings are well maintained with flowerbeds in the compound, and there is a tiny temple surrounded by magnificent stone friezes which Vinoba had uncovered when he was digging the foundations of the ashram. One of these sculptures, the figure of a woman representing the River Ganges, is of exceptional beauty. Finally, we and two Indian visitors were ushered into the presence of the great Vinoba, and sat cross-legged on the floor in front of him, as he reclined on a mat on a raised platform. He was a tall, spare man in a white robe, his eyes hidden behind dark glasses and a green eyeshade. I had expected to see a saintly, kindly person, but Vinoba stared at us in an unblinking, unfriendly manner which made us feel rather uncomfortable. His secretary gave him a sheet of paper with information about his visitors and Vinoba perused this and peered at us again. Then he wrote down something which must have been the question — "How old are they?" for that was the question the secretary asked us. He also inquired if we wished to say something to Vinoba.

I said, "Have you a message for the women of the West?"

The answer came back in writing, "You will find my message in my books."

After another long silence we realized that the short interview was over, and we bowed our way out, emerging into the sunlight, feeling deflated and disappointed. Of course, we had expected too much, and the lack of dialogue had been frustrating. However, after reading his books we have come to realize that Vinoba makes no claims to be a saint, and his message is more a practical than a spiritual one. He is keenly aware of the defects in Indian society, the inequalities between rich and poor, between men and women, and he does what he can to put things right.

The morning before we left the ashram, Mr Pande invited us to breakfast with him and his large family. There were his three sons and one daughter, his wife's sister and her child, the blind musician, who played the tablas at prayers, and his wife. All of them shared the bungalow with Mr and Mrs Pande, although where they all slept was a mystery to us. We sat on the floor around a large board placed about seven inches above the ground. Our first course was a savoury one, made from wheat flour, oil, onions, lemons and coriander; then we had crisp, sugared flakes with slices of orange and pawpaw, washed down with fresh palm juice and tea. After breakfast we sat on the verandah steps talking to Mr and Mrs Pande while the others busied themselves removing stones and grit from their daily supply of rice. Mr Pande told us that it had been Gandhi's hope that the ashram should be at the heart of the community, initiating progress and improvements in living and working standards. Although these hopes had not been fulfilled, the ashram still endeavoured to improve the quality of life of the villagers. They were trying, for instance, to reduce drunkenness and alcoholism, which are on the increase, by persuading the women to vote only for those candidates who support prohibition. When we asked why the ashram could not exercise a more positive influence on the neighbourhood, we learned that its members have no power to initiate projects and schemes as they are governed by a trust, headed by a president who rarely visits Sevagram and is not closely concerned with the affairs of the ashram. It seems inevitable that as Gandhi's old associates die, Sevagram will become little more than a hallowed place of pilgrimage.

That evening, our last at the ashram, we were asked to take part in the service. Kerry recited a Persian prayer, and I sang the hymn "Dear Lord and Father of Mankind". As the last strains of the music faded into the spreading banyan tree, I looked round at the little band of worshippers, marvelling at their faith and wondering how long they would continue to worship together. When we said goodbye to Chimanlalji, he gave me a copy of Gandhi's favourite prayer, and as we were packing our belongings into thc caravan, an elderly lady, whom we had never met, brought us a dish of carrot savoury. These simple, kindly gestures were characteristic of the friendship we received during our five-day sojourn at the ashram.

Next morning, after the early service, we were on our way to Nagpur with Mr Pande as a passenger. As we passed his bungalow his wife was waiting for us by the roadside with two bunches of moruba blossoms. Thus we carried away with us some of the fragrance of Sevagram.

Nagpur, lying at the very centre of India, is reputed to be one of the warmest places in the land, and as we waited for a tyre to be welded, we gratefully accepted the invitation of a Parsee businessman to shelter from the sun in his office. He was a clever, articulate man who looked surprised when we told him that we had spent a few days at Sevagram.

"Now tell me honestly," he said. "Did you see any real evidence of constructive work being done there?"

We had to admit that we had not, at least not constructive in the material sense but we hastened to add that we had seen some useful work in progress at Vinoba's ashram.

"Vinoba wants to set himself up as a saint, but I think he is senile," said our new acquaintance. "And his associates, J.P. (Jayprakash Narayan), for instance, are Fascists."

"Don't you think that it is a good thing that women are becoming more emancipated?" I asked.

"Not in the least; men need jobs and families need mothers; besides, when girls get too much freedom there is the risk of immorality," he said angrily. Then we had the usual tirade about Indian inefficiency, graduates who can't spell, worthless certificates and so on. "When my children finish their education, I will make it my business to find people to sponsor them, with bribes if necessary. There is no other way."

Meeting this man so soon after parting from Mr Pande was a rather disillusioning experience, but his views were not untypical of many middle-class Indians.

Two hours later, our tyre was still not ready, and we were invited by a shopkeeper to have a glass of cold cane sugar and ginger in his office. He had a printing business and his motive for inviting us was to ask us to send him certain art books from England. In complete contrast to this man, however, the garage owner who had laboured for hours on our tyre, refused to accept payment for his work. Fortunately, we still had some packets of cigarettes which we dispensed on occasions like this.

Extensive orange groves in the vicinity of Nagpur reminded us that much of the town's prosperity depends on the fruit which we saw ripening on the trees. The road now ran through wooded, hilly country and was lined for almost a hundred miles with trees covered with brilliant red blossoms, from which flocks of blue birds rose as we passed by. We had to drive very cautiously round each bend as we never knew what obstruction lay ahead. There were black-faced monkeys feeding their young in the middle of the road, slow-moving bullock carts, brokendown trucks, and herds of water buffaloes. There was also the hazard caused by reckless drivers, most of them Sikhs hellbent on forcing everyone else off the road.

The Firestone factory at Jabalpur confirmed our suspicion that our tyres had been defective from the start, and alarmed us with the information that there were no tyres of the same specification available in India. However, we obtained a discount for our faulty tyres and purchased two new ones slightly smaller and with a narrower tread. It was while we were in Jabalpur that someone pointed out to us an old building which was set up over a hundred years ago as a reformatory for a very vicious pseudo-religious sect which terrorized the countryside. These villains dedicated their victims, whom they had robbed and strangled, to the Goddess Kali, and it took the British many years to stamp out their barbarous activities. It was at that time that the words 'thug' and 'thuggery' became incorporated in the English language, derived from the name, Thuggee, the bizarre religion of these people. North of Jabalpur a sudden rainstorm brought relief from the intense heat and laid the dust by the roadsides. As darkness fell and we were still many miles from our destination, the temple town of Khajuraho, a freak storm of wind and sand blotted out everything around us. As it was impossible to proceed, we made for the Government Rest House at Panna where we spent the night.

Next morning, on our way to Khajuraho, we saw a signpost with "Majhgowan Diamond Mines, 15 kilometres," so we turned off on a sandy track to investigate. The opencast mines lie in a grey, rocky hollow between the hills and a thousand people are employed on three seven-hour shifts, for a daily wage of three rupees (about 17p). The workers do get some extra benefits; however, namely, free accommodation, health services and schools. We watched great masses of rock being crushed in a series of machines, until all that was left at the end of a shift was seven piles of small stones. Peering through a high wire fence we watched three women, supervised by half a dozen soldiers, sift through the gravel looking for diamonds. At the end of the process we asked our guide what they had found.

"One stone belonging to the gem category, three off-colour stones and a few brown industrial diamonds," he told us.

I asked him if they ever found really large diamonds.

"We had one which was auctioned for 5,000 rupees (about £300)" he said, "but the majority are fairly small."

"How much do these women earn?" I asked, thinking that their back-breaking work in the full glare of the sun merited more than an average wage.

"The same as the others, three rupees per day."

Considering that in Jabalpur I had paid 2.75 rupees for a tin of sardines, 2.95 rupees for ¼lb butter, 1.70 rupees for four small eggs, this wage seemed pitifully inadequate.

The Tourist Bungalow at Khajuraho is situated in a garden and there we had electricity, a toilet and a shower. From our camping spot we could just see the top of the temples we had come to visit, outlined against the horizon like miniature mountains of stone. A thousand years ago this part of the world was ruled by the Chandella kings, members of a virile Rajput clan, whose symbol was a lion being attacked by a man, and it was they who raised the temples to the glory of their gods. Originally there were eighty-five temples, of which only twenty-two remain to remind us of past religious fervour, strange customs and beliefs. Our first glimpse of these remarkable temples was in the evening as the sun's last rays lit up the carvings on their façades, transforming the pink sandstone into a glowing red. On each temple a multitude of tiny spires thrust their way upwards towards the sky. There was something almost uncanny and surreal about the scene and its setting which reminded me of the strange, stone dwellings we had seen at Göreme.

Next day we engaged a knowledgeable guide and set off to examine the Western group of temples in detail. The stone used for the building was brought on the backs of elephants from a quarry near Panna, where the sections were cut and prepared, ready to be dovetailed into place, for these early builders worked to a plan. Like a series of outsize beehives, the temples stand on raised platforms, their walls covered with thousands of sculptured figures.

The main theme of these carvings is not so much gods and goddesses, although they are not lacking, but rather of 'woman' in all her aspects and activities. She is seen dancing and adorning herself, writing a letter, fondling her baby, scratching her back, taking a thorn from her foot and so on. There are other sculptures which seem to be rather out of place on a religious edifice, namely the erotic carvings of loving couples in very suggestive poses. Our guide explained to us that there was, and still is, a strong sexual element in Hindu religion, the Tantric doctrine, as it is called. According to this cult, woman is seen as the symbol of creation, and the senses are considered to have just as an important role to play in worship as the spirit. However, I heard another guide who was accompanying a party of Americans give quite a different explanation. He told them that these evocative sculptures were intended to encourage the faithful to procreate since the Chandellas needed a steady supply of warriors for their armies.

By the time we had completed our tour of the Eastern group of temples, which comprise three Hindu and three Jain shrines, we were suffering not only from 'temple indigestion' but from a mild attack of sunstroke. However, after we had relaxed in the garden of the Tourist Bungalow in the cool of the evening, our troubles were soon forgotten.

Since the temples of Khajuraho are one of the major tourist attractions of India, rivalled only by the Taj Mahal and the Caves of Ajanta and Ellora, the one luxury hotel in the village was full to overflowing. Even the modest Tourist Bungalow was inundated by visitors, and we met some of them when we dined there in the evening. There was an Australian couple working for the United Nations in India, and a Canadian doctor and his wife on a world tour. The Australians were despondent about India's problems, which they were convinced nothing short of a revolution could solve. The Canadians who had spent some time trekking in Nepal, warned us of the danger of contracting hepatitis in that country. "We always put iodine tablets in our drinking water," they said, "and we advise you to do the same."

We replied rather smugly that we always filtered and boiled our water.

"Remember," said the doctor "that really virulent viruses are not easily destroyed unless the water is boiled for a considerable time, and at high altitudes, this is often difficult."

As they gulped down large quantities of tepid, brown liquid, they extolled the virtues of iodine which, although not particularly palatable, is indubitably safe.

When our new friends heard that we intended to proceed to Benares the following day, they looked very surprised. "Don't you know," they said, "why so many tourists are here at this moment? Why we, for instance, are remaining here for a few days?"

We confessed our ignorance.

"We were advised in Benares, either to stay in our hotel for the next few days, or to leave the town until the Hindu Festival of Holi is over."

"What happens during Holi?" we asked.

Q

"People go mad and douse each other with coloured water. If you venture out in the streets you get your clothes completely ruined."

We recalled having seen on our way from Nagpur villagers constructing huge bonfires as we do for the 5th November. These preparations were for the Holi Festival which occurs in late March and which heralds the end of winter. The exact significance of the baptism with coloured water is not very clear, except that it affords an outlet for high spirits. Forewarned by our friends we decided to delay our departure for one more day so that we would arrive in Benares after the festival.

The next day bands of youths roamed the village spraying each other and all passers-by with coloured liquid, but they were kept away from the hotels by the police. We did not venture out of the compound and spent the time washing and polishing the car until it looked almost as good as new.

It was while we were thus engaged that the manager came to see us. "Would you like to meet the son of the former Maharajah of Chattapur?" he asked. "He is the Preservation Officer for Wild Animals in this district and this afternoon he is going on a panther hunt. Would you be interested?"

And so we were introduced to Balwant Singh, whom we had seen arrive in a jeep some time before. He had just heard that a panther had killed several cattle at farms thirty miles away and he was going to investigate. We piled into the back of the jeep together with three forest rangers and set off into the jungle, bumping our way over very rough tracks. A few years ago tigers and panthers were quite numerous in this area, but now only a few panthers remain and they are in danger of becoming extinct. We stopped at a remote farm to purchase a small black goat, then on we went again over dry riverbeds strewn with boulders until we came to the banks of a wide stream. It was only when the poor goat was tied to a tree, that I realized that it had been brought as a sacrifice to the panther. We retreated behind cover and listened to the pitiful bleating of the prospective victim.

An hour or two elapsed; several samba deer came to drink at the stream; a mongoose passed nearby and a green pigeon preened itself on the tree above us, but there was no sign of the panther, and the kid kept up its incessant cry of protest as the evening shadows deepened. In the end we gave up the vigil and returned to the jeep, taking the goat with us. As we did so, there was a sudden commotion in the forest which the men said was the alarm call of monkeys and signified that the panther was in the neighbourhood; so the goat was tied to another tree and left to its fate, while we made a hair-raising return journey through the jungle in the darkness.

In spite of our friends' warning that it was unwise for us to travel during the Holi Festival and that we were tempting providence with our gleaming white caravan, we set out the next day for Benares with two passengers, a Belgian couple whom we had met the previous day. The young man, an electronics engineer, had elected to do voluntary service in India instead of military service in Belgium, which has this very praiseworthy arrangement with certain underdeveloped countries. With his wife, a language teacher, he was working as one of a United Nations team at a pumping station near Calcutta. This scheme provides water for over two hundred farms, enabling them to produce two bumper crops every year instead of one mediocre harvest. They had spent the previous year with a Jesuit mission helping to construct houses for the homeless, but having come to the conclusion that the production of food was more important than the provision of shelter, they had transferred their efforts to the new power station. All the way to Satna, where the couple caught a train for Calcutta, the parched, cracked earth showed how great the need was for life-giving water. The harvest had been gathered in, and for the next three months until the arrival of the monsoon rain, nothing could be done with the soil.

When we reached the main road to Benares we noticed that the white shirts and trousers of the country people were stained pink and blue with coloured water and that even the sacred cows, the donkeys, the dogs and the camels were psychedelic having been liberally anointed with splashes of paint. It never occurred to us that we might suffer the same fate, since there were no sign of festivities and the villages looked as dead as the previous day's bonfires. However, near Mirzapur we passed a truck load of inebriated revellers who let fly at our car with their spray guns, and in a moment the outside of the van was stained with all the colours of the rainbow. Enraged by this assault, Kerry leapt out in front of the truck brandishing a walking stick and shouting all the invectives he knew in Hindi. I watched in horror expecting him to be drenched with paint at any moment, or struck down by spray guns and bicycle pumps. I shouted weakly, "Come back, come back, you are asking for trouble," but Kerry was not to be deterred. To my great surprise, nothing happened. The forty-or-so occupants of the truck just gazed at him, open-mouthed as if he were a strange figment of their imagination, and the driver, who seemed to be the only person still sober, said in a conciliatory tone, "Hogaya! Hogaya!" (which means 'it has happened'), a phrase used constantly when accidents or calamities occur. In fact, this word sums up the fatalistic philosophy of the Hindus who, rather than exert themselves to prevent a difficult situation, will calmly accept the consequences. And there was nothing else that we could do but to set to work with water on the offending dye. After an hour's labour our car was spotless again, but late that evening, when we arrived at Mirzapur, we discovered that one side of the van had been sprayed with a bright vermillion dye.

We were now in the State of Uttar Pradesh which, although smaller in size than Britain, has twenty million more inhabitants. It lies in a vast plain, watered by the Ganges, and it was over this plain that the first Aryans advanced into India, followed centuries later by the Muslim invaders. For thousands of years, however, throngs of peaceful travellers have been making their way along the valley of the Ganges to one of the oldest cities of the world, Benares, or Varanasi, as it is now called. From the dawn of history, Benares has been the religious capital of the Hindus and their main place of pilgrimage, and it is the lifelong aspiration of every devout Hindu to make the journey to Benares to bathe in the sacred waters of the Ganges, and to pay homage to Siva, the city's main deity. As we followed the pilgrims' road across the fertile plain, the golden wheat crop was being harvested, not by machines, but by rows of men and women, sitting on their haunches wielding small hand sickles. Combine harvesters would be of little use in this part of the world where crops are grown in very small plots surrounded by mud walls to retain the moisture. When the wheat is cut, it is carried away on the heads of the workers who trot along the road bearing enormous loads to the place where bullocks are treading out the grain.

We stopped at Ramnagar to view the huge, crumbling mass of the maharajah's eighteenth century palace, but there was nothing there to interest us, and soon we were on the long bridge which crosses the Ganges, looking down on the turgid water of the river. The last time we had seen the Ganges, it was flowing swiftly, pure and sparkling from the foothills of the Himalayas at Rishikesh. There its water was said to contain special medicinal qualities and to be excellent for drinking. Looking at the clear, green stream at Rishikesh, it was possible to believe that the water was health-giving, but at Benares this illusion could no longer be maintained. Bearing the motley debris of all the cities on her one thousand mile journey from the mountains, with withered garlands on her brow, Mother Ganga makes her way very slowly through Benares. From the bridge we could see a vulture attacking a white object, floating in the water, but we dared not look too closely. The pilgrims' progress into Benares is extremely slow, halted by trucks which block the narrow streets, by bicycle rickshaws weaving in and out, lean-ribbed sacred cows meditating in the centre of the road, long-nosed hogs routing in the rubbish heaps and pedestrians who seem oblivious of everything. Thus it was with relief that we reached the cantonment area with its open, green spaces and wide streets and parked in the pleasant garden of the

Government Tourist Bungalow. It was now halfway through the afternoon, but the heat of the day had not abated, and as there was no shade for our car, we took refuge on the verandah of one of the bungalows under a fan, where we enjoyed cool Limca and pots of tea.

It was almost dusk when we summoned up enough energy to explore the city and set off by bicycle rickshaw to the crowded and noisy bazaar area in the centre of the town. As we passed through the narrow winding streets, lined with temples and shrines, persistent vendors tried to coax us into buying their wares. Some had wooden flutes and fiddles, on which they gave untuneful demonstrations; others offered us an infinite variety of necklaces and rings or toys, wicker baskets, embroidered tunics and silken sarees. In small stalls by the roadside, savoury, spicy stews were bubbling on charcoal fires, and wheedling voices invited us to sit down on the rough wooden benches and partake of a meal, while uninvited, the sacred cows thrust their noses in the pots of food and were belaboured unceremoniously by the indignant cooks. We wandered through a maze of alleyways with stalls on each side which resembled large dark cupboards, crammed with merchandise — cloth, trinkets, copper pots, antiques, religious momentos and marigold petals. Small, grubby hands clutched our clothes and plaintive wails of "backshish", came from every direction. We hurried on, eager to escape from our pursuers and from these dark labyrinthine passageways, which spread like rabbit warrens throughout the bazaar area. On the main road we hailed a rickshaw and went jolting back to our base with the ringing of thousands of bicycle bells in our ears. The noise of bells was soon replaced by the buzzing of swarms of mosquitoes which rose in clouds from the showers and Asian toilets where they take refuge during the hours of darkness, and in spite of all our precautions, there were always one or two which slipped through our mosquito netting to bite us voraciously during the night.

Soon after sunrise, we returned to the centre of the town, to the Dashaswamedh Ghat (steps), for a cruise on the river, to watch the Hindus at their early-morning rituals. We rowed slowly past the main ghat watching the bathers descend the steps and enter the water. The men, wearing shorts or dhotis, immersed themselves shoulder deep in the river, whilst the women, fully clothed in sarees, stood waist high, washing themselves and their clothes decorously, pouring water over their heads and rinsing out their mouths. When their ablutions were completed, the bathers clasped their hands together and intoned their prayers to the rising sun, Mother Ganges and to Siva. This part of the ritual completed, some of the pilgrims sat for a time on the steps in the Yoga attitude of meditation, whilst others retreated behind large straw umbrellas to change into dry clothes and to receive the blessing of the priest who places tikka marks on the foreheads of the faithful.

High above the bathing ghats, which stretch for four miles, are the palaces of the former maharajahs of India who used to come to Benares every year for the opening festival. Although badly in need of a coat of paint, these buildings, with their carved balconies, turrets and arcades, remind us of the splendour of the past, splendours which are, alas, lacking in present-day Benares. A number of these ancient palaces are now the homes of wealthy citizens, but a number have been donated by the maharajahs as residences for pilgrims and widows. One of the most splendid houses on this stretch of the river belongs to the keeper of the sacred fire, who appears to have amassed a considerable fortune which is not surprising considering that all funeral pyres are required to be kindled by this sacred flame and the hereditary keeper charges one and a half rupees for every funeral. We were now approaching the main Burning Ghat where most of the funerals take place, and we were requested to refrain from taking photographs. It is the nearest male relative of the deceased who has the unenviable task of burning the corpse. We could see numerous processions bearing bamboo stretchers moving towards the ghat which was partly hidden by the black, acrid smoke from the funeral pyres. It is a daily occurrence in the streets of India to see a small group of men bearing a stretcher on which a corpse lies, enveloped in a white shroud, except for the face which is usually uncovered. There is no pomp and circumstance surrounding these funerals, nor do the relatives lament or shed tears as they bear their dead to the river, for they firmly believe that the soul of the departed has gone to inhabit another body, and has thus an opportunity of enjoying a happier life than hitherto. Our guide confirmed the information which we were given at Rishikesh that victims of infectious diseases, such as smallpox are not burned but weighed down with stones and dropped in the centre of the Ganges. We were also informed that the bodies of children and those who have died as a result of a snakebite, are not placed on funeral pyres, but are left to float down the river.

After cruising up and down the river, past temples half-submerged by flood water, and the washing ghats where hundreds of dhobis were busy thrashing their clothes, we returned to the main ghat to visit the Vishwanath (Golden) Temple. The original Golden Temple was destroyed by Shah Jahan's Hindu-hater son, Aurangzeb, who built a mosque in its place. The present temple was erected in the eighteenth century just behind the mosque, and was dedicated to Siva. Part of the pilgrim's morning ritual, after he has washed himself in the Ganges, is to carry water from the river to the temple and offer it to the deity. We followed the throngs of pilgrims, each with his little copper pot filled with sacred water, through the narrow streets, lined with votive shrines which lead to the temple. At every corner sit the flower-sellers, in front of their mounds of marigold petals and heaps of fragrant garlands which the pilgrims purchase as offerings to Siva. As non-Hindus are not allowed to enter the Golden Temple, we climbed a staircase nearby to catch a glimpse of what was happening inside. Siva's shrine takes the form of his sacred symbol, the 'lingam', the male organ of generation, which represents the force behind creation. We watched the pilgrims around the shrine scattering petals and pouring their libations on the lingam, while the priests in attendance gave them their blessings.

The second most holy temple in Benares is dedicated to Durga, one of Siva's consorts, and is commonly called the Monkey Temple, because of the hordes of monkeys which haunt the area. We were not allowed to enter this temple, so we viewed the proceedings from a balcony from which we could see the faithful in the inner sanctuary placing garlands on warlike Durga mounted on a lion. Our guide, who had provided himself with a stout stick, enjoined us to look after our possessions, otherwise the monkeys would appropriate them. In spite of his warning, a young American in our group lost the guidebook he was studying which was snatched from his grasp by a diminutive monkey. We looked on helplessly as the monkey climbed an inaccessible pillar and proceeded to tear the book to shreds.

When we visited the Hindu University of Benares, we were very impressed by the fine modern buildings of this, the largest residential university in India. Set amongst trees and parkland, its extensive and well-planned campus, with separate buildings for each faculty, caters for fourteen thousand students. Our reason for visiting the university was to meet the Dean of the Medical Faculty, Dr Udapa, to whom we had an introduction. We had realized when we were at Sevagram that it was more than six months since we had had our cholera injections, and we were advised by Dr Nayyar to contact the Medical Faculty at Benares. There, Dr Udapa, who had done some of his training at Hammersmith Hospital, in spite of being a very busy administrator and surgeon, gave up his time to explain to us the work of the University Medical School and of the Ayurvedic Unit which deals with native healing methods. Ayurvedic remedies play a very important part in an average Indian's life and are included in the medical students' curriculum. Dr Udapa arranged for us to have our cholera injections the following day at the University Health Centre which was equipped to the highest modern standards. The only difficulty we encountered was when we tried to get our health cards stamped, for we spent many hours searching for the official whose responsibility it was to do this. Finally when we did discover his office, the man in charge was out of town and the stamp was safely locked up in his room; thus we had to wait until we reached Patna before we had our cholera injections certified officially.

Remembering the advice of our friends in Bombay that we should purchase silk when we visited Benares, we shopped around to see what we could find. First of all we visited a factory where priceless silk brocade was being woven on huge, crudely built handlooms. To our surprise, the operators were boys of between eight and ten years of age, whose nimble fingers manipulated the gossamer-like threads and intricate designs with incredible skill. We would have loved to have purchased a length of this magnificent material, but it was quite beyond our means, so we returned to the bazaar area where the silk shops with their colourful displays were plentiful. There, the shopkeepers sit cross-legged on raised wooden platforms, with their wares spread out around them, while their customers seated on benches opposite them, closely scrutinize every yard of fabric. In one of these shops, a young girl accompanied by her parents and friends was buying sarees for her wedding. Delicate silks in all the colours of the rainbow, some covered with sequins, others embroidered or plain with borders of gold or silver thread, were unfolded for inspection. The lucky bride had a choice of fifty or more garments, costing from £40 each, which she did not need to try on as the saree fits every shape and size and does not need to be altered with changing girth. She was probably a Hindu because the saree she chose for her wedding dress was red, which is considered to be a propitious colour. White, of course, would never be chosen, as it is the colour of mourning. Our purchase was a much less colourful one of a length of plain tussore silk, costing about £5 per metre, which I had made into a dress in Kashmir.

About eight miles from the holy city of the Hindus, lie the ruins of another sacred city which we had been eager to visit ever since our interest in Buddhism had been aroused. It was in the Deer Park at Sarnath that Buddha preached his first sermon to five friends who became his disciples and accompanied him all over Northern India to spread the new doctrine. The story of Buddha is told in pictures on the walls of a temple built near the ruins of Sarnath. The scenes tell how Buddha, who was born about 566BC of a princely family, became more and more dissatisfied with life as he grew to manhood. One night he left his wife and young child to live the life of a yogi hoping to find the path to salvation through meditation. After meditating for forty-nine days, Buddha became enlightened, that is to say he understood the cause of suffering in this world, which was the problem he had tried to solve. He discovered that suffering is due to human desires and only when these are eliminated can the state of nirvana be reached. His first sermon in which he expounded his revelations is called the Turning of the Wheel of Law, and is the foundation of the Buddhist faith. He maintained that salvation can only be reached by the Eight Fold Path which leads to a balanced, moderate life. This mode of life, which has been described as the 'Middle Way', consists in the right — views, resolves, speech, conduct, livelihood and effort, and in recollection and meditation. Two hundred years later, the Emperor Asoka was converted to Buddhism and during his reign the religion spread rapidly throughout India. Asoka had been a great warrior until he was filled with remorse after one of his victories when he realized the extent of the destruction his campaigns had caused. Attracted by the Buddhist philosophy of non-violence he became a convert, and under his patronage Buddhism flourished. It has been said that what Emperor Constantine did for Christianity, Asoka did for Buddhism. On the site at Sarnath, amongst the ruins of ancient monasteries, we saw the remains of the stupa which was set up by Asoka and which was said to have contained the relics of Buddha in a marble casket.

From its zenith in the fourth century AD, when fifteen hundred monks are said to have been in residence, the fortunes of Sarnath and Buddhism gradually declined, and in 1836 when the site was discovered by the British, it was completely overgrown and its stones and bricks had been used to build the town of Benares. The ruins were excavated by Sir Alexander Cunningham and an archaeological museum was erected at the site, which contains a unique collection of Buddhist sculptures, and one of the most interesting we saw during the whole of our tour. One fascinating exhibit is a pillar in highly polished stone topped by the heads of four lions. This is one of the pillars which the Emperor Asoka raised in several parts of India to display his edicts and to affirm his religious belief. This carved pillar has become the national symbol of India and can be seen on the coins of the realm, on currency notes and on government buildings. On the base of the capital are inscribed the symbols of Buddha — an elephant (representing his mother's dream of an elephant before his birth); a running horse (signifying his renunciation of worldly desires); a lamb (showing that he came from a regal family); a wheel (referring to his sermon on the Wheel of the Law). There is a remarkable resemblance between the capitals of the Asokan pillars and those we saw at Persepolis, a similarity, which is, however, not surprising when one considers that by the time of Asoka, regular contacts had been established with the Greek and Persian empires. Soon after the reign of Asoka the personal worship of Buddha became prevalent, whereas hitherto he had been represented only by various symbols, and it is certain that he himself would have rejected any suggestion that he should be regarded as a saint or deity. The Sarnath Museum contains some of the earliest statues of Buddha, and he is seen standing in Grecian poses beneath a stone umbrella, the ancient sign of a ruler, or seated in the more familiar devotional attitudes.

On leaving Benares, we had planned to go direct to Patna, but after visiting Sarnath we elected to proceed to Bodh Gaya, the place of Buddha's enlightenment. This journey took us along the Grand Trunk Road which leads eventually to Calcutta, and although, according to our guidebooks, this is supposed to be one of the smoothest runs in India, we had one of the roughest rides of our trip. On a hundred mile stretch, the road was being widened and resurfaced at one and the same time, leaving only a narrow tarmac strip of serviceable road, and even that was pitted and uneven in places. In order to overtake trucks and carts we had to cross over onto the unpaved way or rough stones lying several inches lower than the tarmac roadway. We had covered about thirty miles, and I was driving very cautiously when I swerved to avoid an oncoming truck and one wheel hit the side of a pothole with considerable force. There was a tremendous clatter above our heads as the six-foot front window came crashing down onto the road, followed by all our bedding, spare clothes and our new electric fan which we kept, wrapped in blankets, on the single bed. Fortunately, I was able to stop the car before it ploughed into our belongings, but that scarcely lessened the magnitude of the disaster. How could we proceed with the top storey of our house open to all weathers and to all kinds of predators? On closer inspection, however, we discovered that the plastic window, although badly scratched, was still in one piece. On the other hand, the fan was so twisted that it appeared to be a write-off. Undeterred by the accident and with only a mild reproof, Kerry set to work with plastic padding, and two hours later we continued on our way, proceeding with even greater care lest another jolt should dislodge the damaged window.

Sheltered by a low range of hills, amongst woods on the banks of a river, Bodh (or Buddh) — Gaya, which is to the Buddhists what Bethlehem is to Christians and Mecca to the Muslims, has the perfect setting for a place of pilgrimage. In the middle of the village rises the high tower of the great Mahabodhi Temple, shaped like a pyramid with small turrets at each corner and covered with carvings. It is a masterpiece of architecture which has been the model for many Buddhist temples in India, Burma and Nepal. A long flight of steps leads to the entrance, and we were thankful that this was carpeted, otherwise the burning stone would have scorched our bare feet. Inside the temple is a huge, gilded image of Buddha facing east. This is supposed to be the spot where Buddha received enlightenment as he sat with his back to the Bodhi Tree. The courtyard of the temple is dotted with votive stupas of every shape and size, erected by fervent disciples over a period of a thousand years. There are also a great many images of Buddha in various postures, the significance of which our guide explained to us. Buddha in a devotional attitude has his hands in his lap; when preaching he raises his right hand with his thumb and first finger touching; when he blesses, his right arm is raised, and when he bears witness, one finger of his right hand is pointing downwards.

Near the northern wall of the temple is a small roofless shrine where Buddha used to meditate, and it is said that when he was in a state of deep meditation, blue, yellow, red, white and orange rays emanated from his body. That is why the Buddhist flags of India and Ceylon use these colours. Beyond the Jewelled Cloister where Buddha used to walk up and down, on the western side of the temple, is the sacred Peepal or Bodhi Tree; the tree of enlightenment and wisdom. Although this is not the original tree, for that was cut down many centuries ago by anti-Buddhist fanatics, it must be one of the most ancient trees in the world. When Asoka's daughter was sent on a mission to Ceylon to promote the cause of Buddhism, she took with her a branch of the parent tree. This was planted with great ceremony in the sacred city of Anuradhapura from whence, centuries later, saplings which had sprung from the original branch were returned to the temple at Bodh Gaya. To the south and west of the temple is a remarkable stone screen with carvings of mythical beasts and scenes from the life of Buddha which is said to date from the time of Asoka and must be amongst the most ancient remains in India. Beyond this screen lies the tranquil lotus pond where the monks used to bathe.

The presence in and around the temple of throngs of purple and saffron robed Tibetan and Chinese monks, indicated that the Mahabodhi Temple is revered by Buddhists from all over Asia. One husky monk was engaged in what we took to be a series of strenuous physical exercises during which he raised and lowered himself on a specially constructed, sliding, wooden board, but our guide explained that he was carrying out a vow to make a million obeisances to the image of Buddha. Bodh Gaya has Tibetan, Burmese, Chinese and Thai monasteries, which have been built during this century, and in the Tibetan library in the temple we saw monks consulting ancient manuscripts. In Central and South-East Asia, Buddhism is still a flourishing religion, whereas in India, from being a formidable rival of Hinduism, its popularity has waned and its adherents now number less than one per cent of the population.

Proceeding on our way to Patna, beneath a searing sun, we tarried at

Gaya, eight miles north of Bodh Gaya, only long enough to visit the Vishnupada Temple which is a place of pilgrimage for devout Hindus. It is here that pilgrims come from all over India to offer funeral cakes (pindas) to the departed souls of their parents. This ritual is intended to free the dead from earthly ties and to ensure for them everlasting peace. Vishnupada Temple is of no great antiquity, as it was built in the eighteenth century, but, in its inner sanctum, it has the footprints, said to be of Vishnu, sunk in a pavement. The vast remains of Nalanda, north of Gaya, deserved more than the rather cursory glance we gave them, for between the fourth and the eighth centuries AD, ten thousand Buddhist monks and students, from places as distant as China and South-East Asia, lived in this great monastery, the foremost educational centre in the north. To be a "Fellow of Nalanda", was the aim of every Buddhist scholar of this period, and this title carried great prestige throughout the Orient. As the monastery was well endowed, it was able to provide free educational facilities and lodgings for most of its students. By the thirteenth century, Nalanda was in ruins, destroyed by Muslim invaders, who killed all the monks and burned the famous library, leaving only the remains of the Great Stupa and several votive shrines. After the destruction of Nalanda, Buddhist scholars took refuge in the monasteries of South-East Asia, and Buddhist education in India came to an end.

With hindsight, it would have been wiser for us to proceed due north from Nalanda to Birauni and Vaisali on our way to Nepal, but at the time the route via Patna seemed to have more advantages. Since Patna was the last large town we would visit before leaving India, we could stock up there with provisions and have our gas cylinders filled. So we set off on a winding, narrow road through a flat countryside where the cracked earth was waiting for the monsoon rain, as were the peasants who sat idly in groups under the date palms. The villages looked very poverty-stricken, and whenever we stopped, beggars pressed forward with outstretched hands, reminding us that we were in Bihar, one of the poorest states in India.

Although Patna has a very ancient history, dating from at least 500BC, little remains of its proud heritage, and it is an undistinguished, modern town, sprawling along the banks of the Ganges. We made haste to find shelter from the sun, for although it was only the beginning of April the heat was intense. Two months later, in the cool heights of Kashmir, we learned that sixty people had died from heatstroke in this part of Bihar when the temperature rose to over 120°F. With the permission of the district magistrate, we obtained a room at the Circuit House, on condition that we vacated it if it was required by government officials. We had a meal in the large lounge-cum-dining room, where nothing seemed to have changed since 1947 when the British departed. The sofas and easy chairs with their faded and threadbare English chintz looked forlorn and unused, and the cumbersome wireless set, dating from the thirties, had long since ceased to function. We sat at the high table, the only diners, as Indians prefer to eat in their own rooms, but the cook, who told us with pride that he had been trained by the British, served us an excellent four-course meal, with old-time courtesy. Then in the cool of our shuttered room, after a cold shower, we slept blissfully under mosquito netting.

One of our first priorities was to have our gas cylinders filled as they were almost empty, but here we were unsuccessful. The nearest filling station was at Birauni, eighty miles away, and too far off our route. However, we did manage to find a handyman who undertook to make our fan "as good as new" — and he did, at the very reasonable cost of the equivalent of £1.50. We had read in the newspapers that there was a teachers' strike in Bihar, and, since we had an introduction to a senior official in the Education Department, we made contact with her for information about the strikers' grievances. Mrs Sinha was typical of the considerable number of older women who hold very responsible positions in India. Extremely competent and hardworking, she faced the enormous task of administrating primary and secondary education in Bihar with admirable equanimity. With a literacy rate of less than thirty per cent, Bihar has fifty thousand primary schools, and in the secondary section there are large numbers of private and denominational schools which will be incorporated in the State system when funds become available. The teachers on strike taught in private schools where the pay is even lower than that of their primary school counterparts who receive a mere pittance. Although teachers' centres are being set up to improve standards and methods, we learned that practical and craft subjects do not form a part of secondary school curriculum, for Gandhi's progressive ideas have not yet reached the State of Bihar.

On our way back to the Circuit House by bicycle rickshaw we saw in the distance a strange monument which looked like a gigantic haystack. This, we discovered, was Golghar, a ninety foot high granary, built after the terrible famine of 1770, on the instigation of Warren Hastings, Governor General of Bengal. It is an impressive building with its whispering gallery affording a wonderful view of the town, but as a granary it had one very serious disadvantage — the grain was poured in through a hole in the top, but the doors at the bottom opened inwards, making it almost impossible to extricate the contents when the granary was full.

When we returned to the Circuit House, we were rather discomfited to find that VIPs had arrived and our room was required. While we were searching for a suitable parking place for the night, we enquired of a garage proprietor when we filled up with petrol, and to our surprise he invited us very warmly to park in his garden. At first, we were reluctant to accept his offer, as we had found that invitations like these are sometimes a prelude to a variety of requests such as "Will you sponsor me in England?" "Will you help my son to find a place at a university?" or "Have you any whisky, brandy, tape-recorders, etc. for sale?" If one has accepted hospitality or assistance from strangers, one cannot be so churlish as to refuse to be of service in return. Thus we tended to be suspicious of benevolent offers and to be cautious in accepting them. However, our new friend was so charming and so insistent, and as we were desperate, we agreed to his suggestion. As it happened, we would have been very sorry to miss the pleasant experience we had of spending an evening in a Hindu home.

The Patels lived in a large villa on the outskirts of the town, and we parked our vehicle beneath the trees in their garden compound and prepared to spend the night there. However, our kind hosts had other plans for us. Mrs Patel came out to greet us with the unassuming graciousness which so many Indian women possess and invited us for a meal. She had prepared food to suit our Western palates — a not too spicy mutton curry, pilau rice, dhal, fried potatoes, beans and ladies' fingers (a green vegetable), and for dessert we had rice pudding with nuts and cardamoms. While our husbands discussed Indian politics and international affairs, we wives, talked about household matters, exchanged recipes and went round the house on a tour of inspection. Swaran (Mrs Patel) showed me the lovely bedspread she was embroidering, and the silk sarees she had bought for her teenage daughter who was at college in Delhi. It is the custom for Indian mothers to purchase sarees and jewellery in preparation for their daughter's wedding day, just as many mothers in the West keep a stock of bed linen and household goods to present to their daughters when they wed. When Swaran showed me into a room with a large double mattress under a tent-like mosquito net, I realised that she intended that we should sleep indoors and not in our van. What is more, I could see that we were being specially honoured by being given her 'puja' (prayer) room, with her favourite Hindu deities, Ganesh, Krishna and Parvati in a lighted niche in one corner. Next to this room was a bathroom suite with hot and cold showers — for us the height of luxury.

As the four of us talked together until late in the evening, I could not help reflecting how much we had in common, although our backgrounds and way of life were so different. For a start we had the English language, which our hosts like so many upper and middle-class Indians spoke fluently. We found, too, that our views on most of the subjects we discussed either coincided or were complementary, and that by conversing together we all gained a deeper understanding and respect for the other's point of view. This was the feeling of 'oneness' which we had already experienced in the Parsee circle of Bombay, amongst the swamis at Rishikesh, and with Gandhi's co-workers at Sevagram. It was personal contacts, such as we made during this short stay with the Patel family which gave us invaluable insight into the lives of large groups of people.

Before we set off next morning to catch the first ferry boat across the Ganges, I made a frantic search through my possessions to find a little gift for our gracious hostess. All the trinkets, pens, lipsticks, bottles of scent, packets of cigarettes, etc., which we had brought with us as presents for friends and helpers, had already been donated, and the only thing, I had left was a small bottle of frozen Cologne water, which I gave to Swaran as a parting gift. Then, after we had waved goodbye and were moving out of the compound, she came running after us with something loosely wrapped in paper, which we assumed to be fruit or sweets for our journey. It wasn't until we reached the ferry that I opened up the parcel to find a beautifully embossed jewel box in burnished copper, which will always be one of my most cherished possessions.

Kerry and Elizabeth in Goa

Chapter Ten

ON TOP OF THE WORLD

Two and a half hours after it left Patna, the ferry boat deposited us on the other side of the Ganges. We enjoyed our leisurely morning cruise on the river, watching the dhobis hard at work, knee-deep in water, with mounds of dirty washing piled on stones around them. As they whacked and pounded the clothes upon the rocks, I recalled Rudyard Kipling's apt remark about his washerman, of whom he complained, "He breaks the stones with my shirts". The riverside villages were awakening and groups of women could be seen making their way towards the water with shining pots upon their heads. At the river's edge, men were busy with their morning ablutions; their clean white dhotis spread out on the bank beside them, while those who had completed their toilet were on their knees intoning their prayers. We were reminded of the fact that none of the villages we passed had any sanitary arrangements, when we saw scores of people squatting amongst the reeds by the water's edge to relieve themselves. The truck drivers and other passengers on the ferry boat had obviously never seen a vehicle like ours before, and they spent their time with their noses pressed against our windows, examining our van and us very closely, as we sat at the rear window, enjoying a hearty breakfast of porridge, toast and marmalade, trying to ignore our onlookers. In contrast to our plain white car, the trucks which surrounded us were very gaudily decorated. Truck drivers in India take an inordinate pride in their vehicles which they adorn with coloured glass, flags, tinsel trappings and a variety of painted motifs. In addition to exotic women, one of their favourite subjects is a fierce, sabre-toothed tiger, which leaps upon one from the rear of many a truck.

After we left the ferry boat, we had to travel about fifty miles on a very rough road, and we again regretted our decision to take the "short-cut" across the Ganges. Our route took us through banana groves and over a fertile plain where golden wheat was being harvested. The villages in this area with their straw-covered mud houses were extremely poor and all the inhabitants looked undernourished, but there was one commodity, namely toddy, which appeared to be produced in abundance as was evident from the unmistakable odour in the air and the pots dangling from the tops of the palm trees. We stopped for the night at Raxaul, a depressing, little border town, which did not possess either a decent restaurant or a clean hotel. After a good deal of argument we were allowed to park for the night in the pleasant garden of the Inspection Bungalow, and as no meals were available there, we dined on tough chicken at the Tourist Bungalow Restaurant, which was full of hippies bound for Kathmandu.

By this time, we were more than eager to exchange the heat of the Indian plain for the cooler mountain air of Nepal, and we were also very excited at the thought that we were at last within reach of that fascinating country. It is only during the last twenty years that Nepal has been accessible to tourists. Before that time, not only were the roads impassible, but strangers were not welcome in the land. Nowadays, Nepal with its many attractions, which include an abundance of hashish as well as its spectacular scenery, has more visitors than anywhere else in Asia, and overland travellers, especially those from New Zealand and Australia, usually spend more time in Kathmandu than in Delhi. We had only one objective in travelling to Nepal, and that was to see the mighty Himalayas, of which we had already caught one breathtaking and tantalizing glimpse from Mussoorie, in northern India. That panorama was, however, too distant to be entirely satisfying; we wanted to see these snow-capped giants at close range and to wander amongst the rare flowers in the foothills.

On the 24th February, six weeks before our visit, amidst great pomp and ceremony, a new king was crowned in Nepal. Twenty-nine year old Birendra, who was educated at Eton and Harvard, has ruled Nepal since the sudden death of his father in 1972, but his coronation was delayed for three years because the stars were not in his favour. Before the ceremony, custom decreed that Birendra must have a bath in milk, yoghurt and butter, a rub-down with mud from various parts of the kingdom, followed by a ritual anointment with curds and honey. After a final soak in holy water from the River Ganges, Birendra was ready for his crowning moment, and a procession of more than twenty elephants, which had trekked over the mountains from the southern plains, carried the royal couple and their retinue to the coronation. Eyewitnesses, whom we had met in Goa, had described to us the colourful pageantry of the crowning in Kathmandu, which had been spruced up for the occasion by the World Health Organisation. Hundreds of stray dogs had been disposed of, and hippies had been barred from entering the country for several months before the coronation. We expected, therefore, to see Nepal's capital under the very best conditions, before the gilt had worn off, and although we had been informed that April is not a good month to visit Nepal, as the mountains are often obscured by a thick haze, we were undeterred and hoped for the best.

Our plans to make a quick getaway from Raxaul in the morning, were foiled by the only official on duty at the Indian frontier who decided to have a long chat with us, keeping us waiting for more than an hour while he allowed other travellers to proceed. Fearing that brusqueness on our part might lead to a lengthy examination of our van, we exercised great patience, but in the end we had to remonstrate half in jest, half in anger, before he let us go. There were few formalities at the Nepalese border, and soon we were speeding away from the dried-up plain towards a range of high, green mountains where a glorious breeze gave us new vigour. Up over the pine-covered slopes we climbed, our pace slackening as we encountered innumerable hairpin bends, dislodged boulders and potholes. Rickety bridges shook as we crossed over, but how they must have shuddered under the weight of those lumbering royal elephants! The road between Raxaul and Kathmandu is one hundred and nineteen miles long and has the grandiose title of Tribhuban Raj Path. King Tribhuban, grandfather of the present king, is greatly revered in Nepal and his statue graces one of the main squares in its capital. Although the highway did not match its regal name, the scenery it revealed compensated for all its deficiencies.

As we made our way to the top of the highest pass (9,200 feet), the mountain sides were covered with giant rhododendron trees and great clusters of white orchids hung from the rocks overhead. The land in this area is terraced from the bottom of the valleys right up to the rim of the horizon, and from the top, these terraces look like cascades of lava. Vivid splashes of green in the valleys showed where young wheat was growing and above, on the brown dry ledges, the peasants were busy hacking the ground in preparation for sowing. These stocky, little people with their broad faces and cheeks like russet apples, look quite different from Indians and appear to be more cheerful. They greeted us with smiles and called out 'Nameste!' as we passed them toiling up the slopes, bent double under enormous baskets resembling Hebridean creels, which they carry on their backs and support by bands of cloth across their foreheads. The men wear jaunty, little multicoloured caps shaped like a fez, long cotton tunics and jodhpurs fitting closely above the ankle. The women's dress can scarcely be termed elegant, and it certainly does not do justice to these comely people. It consists of a blouse and long skirt, in different colours, joined together at the waist by a broad, nondescript piece of cloth which serves as a receptacle for vegetables and even babies, and gives the wearer a bulbous appearance. The villages with their narrow, brick houses, looked less squalid than those of their Indian counterparts. According to our guidebook, we should have had a good view of Mount Everest (or Mount Sagaramatha as it is called in Nepal), and other great Himalayan peaks at Daman, the highest point on the highway. We found the view tower and the motel, but both were closed and in a dilapidated state and thick clouds hid the distant view.

At last the mountains levelled out and a vast, green valley opened up in front of us, cradling in its midst, the pagoda-roofed city of Kathmandu. We found a camping site on the outskirts of the town which was tolerably clean and had a large compound fringed with rose bushes and dahlias. There were a number of other campers, including two parties of Germans, a Scottish couple in a Volkswagen, and an English couple with two children on their way to New Zealand. Thanks to the camaraderie which exists everywhere amongst overlanders, we were soon on friendly terms with all of them, and obtained the information we needed about Kathmandu. In fact, before we were comfortably installed in a shady part in the compound, we knew where to find the best restaurant, the finest yak cheese, and a better rate of exchange for our money than the official one — 27 rupees to the pound, instead of 25.15. If we had wanted to know where to get the best price for our car, that information would have been readily available, as all of these travellers were in the process of selling their vehicles. The Scots couple had been offered a satisfactory price for their Volkswagen, but there was some difficulty over their 'carnet' which had not been stamped at the Nepalese border. This necessitated another journey to the frontier before the sale could be completed. The English couple, who were emigrating, had left England towing a caravan, which had begun to disintegrate by the time they reached Iran. However, they had managed to sell it in Tehran, and were now in the process of negotiating a handsome deal for their Land Rover. There were, however, certain conditions attached to this sale. Our English friend, Peter, had to agree to drive the car back to Pakistan and to hand it over there to its new owner, while his family proceeded to Calcutta to wait for him. In the course of our one month's stay in Nepal, we heard of many such arrangements, some of them extremely dubious, as they entailed the addition of secret compartments to vehicles before they left Nepal for the West.

Kathmandu, like many cities in the East, has two distinct parts; the old town with its narrow streets and huggermugger of temples and bazaars, and the new town with spacious boulevards, large hotels and palatial buildings. The centre and showpiece of the old part of the city is Durbar Square, with its pagoda-shaped temples and palaces. The pagoda style of architecture, which is found in Ceylon and Indonesia, as well as in Nepal, is derived from the Buddhist stupa, which as time went by, was sheltered by a series of wooden umbrellas, replaced at a later date by tiers of pyramidical roofs. One of the best examples of ancient Nepalese architecture is the Kasthamandap Temple (from which the word, 'Kathmandu' is said to be derived), which stands on the edge of the square. Even more splendid are the three-storied Taleju Temple, and the Basantpur Durbar, a nine-storied pagoda palace, decorated with intricate carvings and mouldings. The Living Goddess resides in a temple near the square and we caught a glimpse of her one day, as she gazed forlornly from a balcony window. She looked about nine or ten years of age and the bright paint on her cheeks contrasted with the sadness in her eyes. From babyhood until puberty, when she is replaced by a younger child, she lives apart, appearing only briefly at religious festivals, her life dedicated to the service of the gods.

From Durbar Square, narrow streets lead off in all directions, lined with ancient houses, which, judging from their finely carved wooden façades and balconies, must once have been very handsome, but are now falling into decay. Many of the upper storeys are no longer in use, and the wooden beams which support the jutting roofs are rotting away. Likewise, in streets and courtyards, innumerable stupas are crumbling down and sprouting trees and grass. The sad remains of these religious symbols are evidence of the decline of Buddhism during the last three or four hundred years. Before that time most of the Nepalese were Buddhists and there were very few Hindus. Now the position has been reversed, and even the Buddhists who remain have adopted many Hindu practices and worship the same deities. The two religious communities live together very amicably and celebrate the same festivals. However, in spite of the constant ringing of temple bells, we saw little evidence of real religious fervour in Nepal.

In the tiny shops which open on to the streets like outsize cupboards, we found a great variety of vegetables of reasonable quality — cauliflowers, white radishes, green beans, ladies' fingers, spring onions and tiny tomatoes. Fruit, apart from pawpaws, was much more expensive and poorer in quality than in India; oranges were diminutive and bananas in black skins looked unappetising. There were plenty of tinned goods, including dried milk, Nescafé, Ovaltine and butter, but all were expensive, as were eggs and processed cheese. However, we did discover one good dairy and a bakery where we bought delicious fresh rolls and bread. In the meat shops, the scraggy carcasses of sheep and goats were covered with flies, which the shopkeepers languidly fanned away from time to time. The stagnant and malodorous water in the open gutters, which provided an ideal breeding ground for mosquitoes and other insects, was also used by the shopkeepers to douse their fruit and vegetables to keep them fresh. Goats, hens and children rummaged in the piles of garbage in the narrow backstreets and in the ruins of ancient Buddhist shrines. All the work which is usually done in the West by delivery vans and trucks, is carried out by porters who bear tremendous loads upon their backs or balanced on poles across their shoulders. They push their way along the streets with their baskets full of cow dung, bricks and stones, bales of straw, lumps of brown molasses and other merchandise, as passive and as uncomplaining as the beasts of burden we had seen elsewhere in the East. The shops near Durbar Square with their variety of knick-knacks and curios, cater for the tourist trade. There are antique shops with ornamental daggers, brass symbols, miniature prayer wheels, bells and statuettes, etc. There is a good deal of trash and many of the articles are crudely executed. But we did find some well-made, multi-coloured string bags, stout wickerwork baskets and serviceable circular mats made from rope, to take home as presents.

Although the restrictions imposed at the time of the coronation prevented hippies from flocking to Kathmandu, there were, nevertheless, a great many bizarre-looking Western youngsters loafing around Durbar Square. Some of them, dressed like Buddhist monks, had their hair tied up in a top-knot, while others tried to outshine their female companions with their display of beads, earrings and bangles. One of their favourite haunts was the little street of Jhochhen Tole, off Durbar Square, which is known to the Westerners as Freak Street. Here you find the moneychangers, the hash sellers and cheap restaurants with strange titles, such as 'The Old Hungry Eye', 'Don't Pass Me By', and 'Jimmy's Wagon', which are reached through narrow openings leading from the street, where, when your eyes become accustomed to the darkness within and to the haze of tobacco smoke, you can see weird and fearful masks and daggers on the walls. However, although the food smelt very appetising, the incessant din of stereos and the pervading smell of hash, dissuaded us from dining in any of these places. The very young, who can only spare a few rupees for lodgings, take their pick from the sleazy hotels in Freak Street — the Monumental Lodge, the Century Lodge, the Happy Home, and so on.

One day, when we were exploring this area, we followed two bearded, saffron-robed Westerners through a low wooden door, and found ourselves in a dingy courtyard. As we were about to retrace our steps, we were surprised to be greeted by someone on a balcony above us. Looking up we recognised a Swiss boy and his English girlfriend whom we had met on Calangute Beach in Goa. Although we hardly knew them, they seemed pleased to see us, so we sat down together on a wooden staircase and exchanged news. They were paying seven rupees (about 20p) for their room, but the hash was costing much more than in the previous year, they said. As we were eager to find out about the secret 'dope joints' which attract so many hippies to the town, we did a little prompting and they agreed to take us to their favourite haunt one evening.

It was with some trepidation that we went to our rendezvous a few days later. Kerry was wearing his most tattered jeans and I wore a long, faded skirt and an ancient embroidered blouse. In spite of our 'with-it' clothes we were painfully aware that no disguise could hide the fact that we were in the wrong age group for this sort of expedition, and we hoped that the lights in the dope parlour would be dim. In this we were not disappointed. Halfway down Freak Street we entered a shop full of bric-à-brac. Franz exchanged a few words with the man behind the counter, who eyed the two of us very suspiciously, but nodded his assent when Kerry slipped a few rupees into his hand. He pulled aside a curtain which revealed a steep staircase descending into total darkness from which rose the warm, sweet smell of hash. When our eyes became accustomed to the darkness, we saw that the tiny points of light around us were the lighted tips of cigarettes. Several groups of people were sitting huddled together on cushions on the floor. Franz piloted us to a mat in a corner, then he and Jane abandoned us to join a group of friends. There was hardly a sound in the room, only an occasional whisper, and we did not dare to break the silence. We sat there for some time wondering what we should do next and reproaching ourselves for having come to such a place, when a couple of Nepalese pushers approached us and tried very persuasively to sell their wares. At that point we thought the time had come to take our departure, and it was with a great sense of relief that we took our leave of the twilight world of the weed smokers.

About a week later, we met Franz again. He was sitting on the steps of the Telegu Temple staring blankly into the distance. He did not seem to recognise us, and he did not look up when we asked where Jane was. "Gone away," he said and we did not pursue the matter.

When you reach Kanti Path which traverses the whole length of the city from north to south, you are in the New Town. Here, in the wide, straight streets lined with modern buildings, you might well be in a Western city, except for the presence of scores of bicycle rickshaws and the Gurkhas encamped in Ratna Park. At the southern end of Kanti Path is a fine new sports stadium, and at the other end stands the royal palace surrounded by a high wire fence. Foreign embassies, hotels, airline offices, travel agencies are in this area as well as the Central Immigration Office, where tourists who wish to remain in the country longer than fifteen days must procure extensions to their visas. It is here, too, that trekkers must apply for special permits if they wish to go on expeditions beyond the Kathmandu Valley. Near the Immigration Office is the imposing Singha Durbar, an imposing palace of eight hundred rooms, which now houses the Central Secretariat, but which was once the official residence of the Ranas. They were the powerful landowners who dominated the country for hundreds of years, often usurping the authority of the kings. One great, landed family claimed the hereditary right to be prime ministers of the country and made itself heartily disliked by both the peasants and the royal family, but it was not until 1951 that the tyrannical regime of the Ranas was overthrown by a popular revolution which had the full support of the king.

In and around Kathmandu, the most pleasant way to travel is by bicycle rickshaws. Shaded from the sun by a canopy, one moves at a leisurely pace through the streets, enjoying the sights without any effort. One day, however, our bicycle ride almost ended in disaster. Returning from the Immigration Office, we hired a bicycle rickshaw to take us back to camp. Our driver did not know the way to Tachal, and as he did not speak any English we had some difficulty in giving him directions, which in any case, he refused to follow. What is more, we had grave misgivings about the road-worthiness of the bicycle which was rusty and battered. He pedalled furiously down the narrow alley which leads from Durbar Square and swung round the corner onto the steep descent to the bridge over the river. We shouted at him to slow down, but as we hurtled towards the bridge we realized that the brakes were not functioning. He clung on to the handlebars with a look of desperation on his face, and leaning at an angle of forty-five degrees, we shot past the stalls on the corner, where pedestrians and animals alerted by our yells, scattered before us. It seemed as if nothing could save us from being dashed against the wall at the bottom of the slope and pitched headlong onto the riverbed. But such was the strength of the man, that we actually reached the bridge in one piece, sick with fright and badly shaken, vowing never to hire a rickshaw again without first ensuring that the brakes were in working order.

Back in the camp, our Scottish friends were preparing to leave, having completed the sale of their car, tent and cooking utensils. We fell heir to the remains of their provisions — a tin of fine sugar, unobtainable in the East, tea bags, an unknown luxury in these parts, and a folding, plastic water carrier which was to prove very useful later on our pony trekking expeditions. The family with the Land Rover was busy transferring all its worldly possessions to a large packing case, and books, tools, Afghan coats, etc., littered the ground around them. We had grown quite attached to the two little girls and especially to Susan, aged six, who used to come to our van with her reading book, as she was anxious not to fall behind with her school work. It is always a sad moment when the travelling companions with whom one has shared the joys and frustrations of camping, depart, leaving an empty space.

Soon, however, there were new arrivals in the camp and the site was covered with the tents of climbing parties returning from treks to Everest. Four Germans, two Swiss lads and an English couple had made the three-hundred mile trip to the Khumbu region, which takes about thirty-two days to complete. In spite of the fact that one of the Germans had suffered from an attack of mountain sickness and one of the English lads had a bad bout of diarrhoea, all were enthusiastic about their journey. Only the Swiss boys, who were experienced climbers, had reached the Khumbu glacier (17,000 feet), in the moraines of which the Everest base camp is situated. The others turned back at Thyangboche, which is fifteen miles from Everest, where there is a spectacular view of the world's highest mountain. There too, is a famous Buddhist monastery with a guest house attached, where the trekkers are allowed to spend the night. Apart from a supply of tinned food, which they had taken with them from Kathmandu, the trekkers lived on lentils, barley, potatoes, eggs and yak milk which they bought from the villagers and at the various bazaars on their route. It is in this bleak area, carpeted with alpine scrub and twisted juniper, that the sturdy Sherpas live and their largest village, Namche Bazaar, has become the point of departure of many climbing expeditions, especially since the construction of an airstrip nearby. The Sherpa hero, Tensing, of the first successful Everest climb, was born at Thami, and a little further north, at Kundi, Sir Edmund Hillary has established a small hospital.

After listening to the experiences of these trekkers, we decided to realize our secret ambition to explore one of these remote valleys, and after spending hours poring over the maps in the trekking agencies, we selected our route for a week's expedition. The trek we planned was to the Malemuchi Khola Valley, about thirty-two miles north-west of Kathmandu. As the trail via Helambu seemed fairly straightforward, we decided that we did not need the services of a guide, but would require a porter to carry our tent, cooking utensils and provisions. Equipment was no problem, as we had brought with us a light tent, sleeping bags and climbing boots. Porters can be hired quite reasonably for twenty-five to a day, and they find their own food. The Annapurna Trekking ndertook to find us a porter and we began to stock up with ns for our mountain expedition.

Two days before our trek was due to start, we discovered, hidden away in one of the backstreets, a delightful little Tibetan restaurant which served unusual and appetising food. A notice on the wall informing us that the drinking water was safe as it had been "boiled before refrigeration", persuaded me to drink a large quantity with my meal. Kerry, being suspicious of the truth of this declaration, did not drink a drop, and he warned me throughout the evening of the dire consequences of my foolishness. He was right, as usual.

The next day I felt far from well and my legs and ankles began to swell alarmingly. On the advice of the camp manager we went to the little Mission Hospital on the outskirts of the town, and as I waited my turn in the queue, I learned from other Westerners that two wards of the hospital were filled with foreigners suffering from hepatitis. Recalling that this infection is usually due to drinking polluted water, I began to fear the worst. Fortunately, however, my symptoms did not seem to be those associated with hepatitis, and the Nepalese doctor assured me that his prescription of belladonna would soon put matters right.

The next morning I felt much worse as my limbs seemed to have stiffened up, and we moved into a small guest house, in order to have a few extra home comforts. As it turned out, I would have been much more comfortable in the caravan, as a severe water shortage prevented the toilets from functioning, and water for washing was in short supply. Most of the guests were climbers and the noise of their heavy boots reverberated on the wooden staircase and through the thin wooden partitions which separated the rooms. What made the bedroom even more depressing, was the thick layer of dust on the floors and windows, and the dirty, discoloured walls. Kerry went in search of a doctor and was fortunate in finding one who had been trained in the West and spoke English fluently. He diagnosed my symptoms correctly, although, in true medical fashion, he did not disclose what I was suffering from. However, the pills he prescribed had the desired effect and by the end of a week, I was feeling much better and we moved back again into the caravan; but naturally, I did not feel fit enough to set out on a long trek, so the expedition we had planned so joyfully and carefully, never took place.

One day, when I was recovering from my indisposition, Kerry went in search of a carpenter to mend our wooden box, which, in spite of the repairs carried out at Agra, had begun to disintegrate. He was directed to a newly-built house in front of which a small crowd had congregated. The owner explained that he and his friend, the local priest, and everyone who had worked on the house, had gathered to celebrate its completion. "Come and join us," he said to Kerry. "We are just about to start the ceremony." Whereupon, a scraggy goat, bleating loudly, was dragged in front of the house and dispatched with a deft blow of an axe. A great shout went up as the blood from the severed arteries spurted all over the walls, for this was the sign that the house was now anointed and the happiness of its future inmates assured. Prayers were said and mantras (chants) sung, as the priest put red tikka marks on the foreheads of all the participants and decked them with ribbons. Meanwhile a great fire had been lit and a feast was being prepared with barbecued goat as the main dish. Kerry was warmly invited to join in the festivities, but somehow his appetite failed him, and he slipped away to wash the sacrificial blood from his brow.

Sometimes in the early morning, before the sun rose too high in the sky, we would explore the narrow paths which run alongside the paddy fields. One path led us across the valley, past tiny wooden houses half-hidden by hollyhocks, towards the Monkey Temple which stands on the top of a hill overlooking Kathmandu. Observed from afar by the eyes of Buddha, which are painted on the base of the temple, we would clamber up the long flight of steps, accompanied by a whole tribe of large, grey monkeys. The Monkey Temple is one of the oldest and most venerated shrines in Nepal, and crowds of pilgrims come every day to prostrate themselves before the Buddha, and to offer gifts of flowers and money. As in India, the flower favoured in worship is the marigold, but other blossoms, provided they are yellow, are also used. A mysterious woman used to come every morning at daybreak and strip the yellow flowers from a shrub next to our caravan; then when her basket was brimful of golden petals, she slipped away stealthily into the paddy field.

About a fortnight after our arrival in Kathmandu, we were joined by our niece Yasu, from Bombay on a fortnight's holiday. She did the exhausting forty-hour journey to Patna by train, and flew on to Nepal. We arranged for her to stay in a small guest house, but she had all her meals with us in the caravan. Lively and energetic, Yasu was as keen as we were to explore Kathmandu, but for different reasons. For her, the main attractions of the town were not the quaint pagoda temples, palaces and the tiny backstreets, but the bazaars and the shops. Before she arrived we had had little success on our shopping expeditions, and although we had spent considerable time searching for typical Nepalese goods, all we had to show for our efforts were a couple of Gurkha daggers set with semi-precious stones, a few Tibetan cushion covers and a multicoloured woollen shoulder bag. We had also thrown away about £5 on what turned out to be very clever imitations of turquoise stones. There is no dearth of goods to attract tourists, for Kathmandu, like Kabul, abounds in shops and stalls full of knick-knacks of every description; but unless the shopper is discerning, he lands up with a load of decorative junk. We soon found out, however, that we had not discovered a fraction of the goods which are available for the persistent and tireless shopper, which our niece turned out to be. Furnished with a long list of requests from friends and relatives in Bombay, she made straight for the New Road area of Kathmandu. There the shops, which from the outside look very drab and unexciting, are veritable treasure troves of goods imported from all over the world. There were silks and jewellery from China, pens, nylon and made-up garments from Hong Kong, perfumes from France, handbags from Italy, electrical gadgets from Germany and Britain, and watches from Switzerland. As most of these goods are not obtainable in India, or are extremely expensive, Indian visitors come in droves to Nepal to purchase these luxury goods. We helped Yasu to buy some lovely sarees in voile and nylon, yards and yards of fine shirting material, stretch tops in a variety of sizes, cosmetics, pens and watches. As the prices were fixed, and, on the whole, reasonable, there was no haggling, no protracted bargaining such as we had become used to in the Middle East and India.

On the 14th April, there was a public holiday to celebrate the Nepalese New Year's Day — Nova Barsha. The people of Nepal adore festivals, and there can be few countries which have as many special occasions on their calendars. In addition to the festivals connected with their various deities, they celebrate the birthdays of their kings (past and present), the advent of winter and the completion of the rice planting. Each one of these occasions is an opportunity for a holiday, for hanging out flags and for dressing up in one's gayest clothes, and such is the degree of religious tolerance in Nepal, that no matter whether the festival is Hindu or Buddhist in origin, it is celebrated communally. At Nova Barsha, thousands of people congregate at Bhaktapur or Bhadgaon (as it is often called), which lies about eight miles north of Kathmandu. There the special feature of the festival is a procession in which two immense chariots, carrying the effigies of Hindu deities, are drawn through the streets.

We joined the throng of revellers surging through the Zion Gate at Bhaktapur in the wake of the festival chariots. We were amazed at the magnificence of the Durbar Square which surpasses that of its counterpart at Kathmandu. In the middle of the square, perched on a tall stone column, under a diminutive umbrella, sits the golden effigy of one of the Malla kings who reigned in the sixteenth and seventeenth centuries. It was the Malla kings who raised the beautiful palaces and temples of Bhaktapur and Patan (a nearby town), which have been mercifully spared from the ravages of time, and ugly new developments. Opposite this column, gleaming in the sun, stands the Golden Gate, said to be the most beautiful example of its kind in the whole of the Orient. Carved in the solid gold of the gate, is the figure of the Goddess Kali, riding on her steed, Garuda, which is half-man, half-bird. Another of the marvels in the square is the sixteenth century palace of the Malla kings, with its fifty-five windows leaning out at an angle from a carved balcony. Nearby is the Temple of the Barking Bell, so-called because at the sound of its great bronze bell, all the dogs within range, are said to howl in agony.

We followed the chariots and the crowds through Durbar Square and along the street which leads to the market place. This square is dominated by a remarkable five-storied pagoda temple, said to be the tallest of its kind in Nepal. The five terraces upon which the temple is built are adorned with quaint stone figures which are graded in strength from the bottom to the top. At the foot of the steps two strong men stand on guard, and at the top are the Tiger and Lion Goddesses. In the square below, a large herd of goats was awaiting sale, but no one was interested in such mundane purchases. The street stalls, on the other hand, were doing a roaring trade in sticky sweets and buns, savoury titbits cooked in oil and portions of tandoori chicken. As the chariots rumbled on down the narrow streets, we lagged behind to admire the intricate woodcarving, the decorative brickwork and the finely chiselled balconies and doorways of the ancient houses which are in a much better condition than those of Kathmandu. We wandered off into a side street in search of a monastery which is renowned for its exquisitely carved windows, fashioned in the shape of peacocks. But we never found it, nor did we ever catch up with the procession and the chariots. A few days later however, in the late afternoon, we came across another procession in the backstreets of Kathmandu. This time the occasion was the Festival of the White Goddess, when for three days her great chariot, decked with foliage and flowers is dragged through the streets. It is during this festival that goats and buffaloes are sacrificed in the town's squares in honour of the Goddess Durga. We pushed our way to the head of the crowds to catch a glimpse of the White Goddess, but the very moment we reached the chariot, there was an electricity failure and all the streetlights went out. By the time power was restored, the high chariot had been abandoned and the White Goddess had disappeared.

Every day we strained our eyes in the direction of the Himalayas, hoping to catch a glimpse of their snowy crests on the skyline, but the heat haze which hid them from view, only thickened as the days went by. The prospect of leaving Nepal without seeing its crowning glory was quite unthinkable, so we decided to investigate the possibility of viewing the Himalayas from the air. When we discovered that the Royal Nepalese Airlines has a daily flight over the mountains, lasting just over an hour and costing about £12, we were overjoyed, and ignored the warnings of some of our fellow campers who had already taken the flight and had seen very little because of low-lying clouds. The day before our trip, however, we were shaken by the tragic news of the death in an air crash near Everest of Lady Hillary and her daughter, who were returning from the hospital at Kundi. We reflected that it was a strange turn of fate that the mountain which had witnessed Sir Edmund Hillary's greatest triumph, should also witness his greatest tragedy. Undeterred by this event, however, the following morning before 7 a.m., we were at the airport ready for what was to be the most unforgettable flight of a lifetime.

As we rose from the valley, the haze seemed impenetrable and endless, then suddenly there was a great pool of blue sky, and rising above the swirling grey clouds were the shining, stark peaks of the world's highest mountains. Although we had our cameras at the ready, the spectacle was so overwhelming that for the first few moments we were quite incapable of focusing either our eyes or our lenses on the scene before us. At a height of 20,000 feet we cruised alongside the massive wall of mountains trying to identify the individual peaks from the pictures supplied by the airline. An air hostess pointed out the cleft in the range where the road winds upwards to Lhasa, in what was once Tibet and now is China. One by one, the gigantic mountains of the Himalayas came into view — the sharp cone of Numbur, the massive shoulder of Melingtse and the pyramidical shape of Chugimago. Far below and out of sight in the mist, lay the Namche Bazaar where the trail to Everest begins. Now we were waiting breathlessly for the moment when we would see the top of the world.

The passengers on the right-hand side of the aircraft were growing impatient as their chance of getting a good view would come only when the aircraft turned for home. "Can you see it?" they shouted.

"Not yet, not yet," we answered, our excitement mounting as Nuptse came into view. Then, towering above its companions with the sun's rays lighting up its dark summit was Everest, the monarch of them all. The aircraft seemed almost to stand still as we came abreast and gazed up to the world's highest point, 29,028 feet above sea level. By its side, Llotse, only 1,500 feet lower, merited scarcely a passing glance. As the aircraft veered round and started on its homeward journey, all our cameras were tilted at impossible angles to catch the last glimpse of the receding giant. There was still one more thrill in store for us when our turn came to be escorted to the cockpit, where for a few brief moments, we had a bird's-eye view of the whole Himalayan chain and a closer look at some of its great profiles. When we returned to the airport each of us was presented with an impressive scroll bearing a picture of Everest and these words:–

This is to certify that,
Mount Everest (Sagarmatha)
had the privilege of greeting today
ELIZABETH AND RUSI KERR-WALLER

It is a pleasant momento to put in a frame or to show to one's friends, but no one who has been on the flight to Everest will require a souvenir like this as a reminder of this thrilling and unique experience.

Twenty years ago, when the Chinese occupied Tibet, thousands of refugees, who had made the perilous journey over the Himalayas, flooded into India and Nepal. The Indian and Nepalese governments set up camps which were expected to be temporary, but which have become the permanent homes of the Tibetans. The first camp which we visited, situated near the town of Patan, was typical of the many settlements we were to see in other parts of Nepal and in India. The approach to the refugee village is heralded by a veritable forest of prayer poles covered with tiny, coloured flags. These little fluttering flags are to be found wherever there are followers of Buddha, and Tibet was a country where Buddhism was not just a religion, it was a way of life. Even in the refugee camps the Tibetans have not changed their mode of living, and they adhere to their old customs and wear their national costumes. The women's apparel, a dark wrap-over tunic worn over a brightly-coloured dress, is particularly becoming, and is worn with style by those well-built and good-looking ladies. Their modest houses of wood and brick are scrupulously clean and tidy, as one would expect from people who have the reputation of being both hard-working and independent.

When we got out of the car, crowds of rosy-cheeked children came rushing towards us, not to beg, as would be the case in India, but to gaze wide-eyed at our pale faces and strange attire. They must have found us amusing, as they started to laugh heartily, screwing up their little, almond-shaped eyes. We would have loved to have been able to talk to those lively and merry youngsters and to their mothers who smiled at us from their doorways, but alas, we could not communicate with them. The children were obviously eager to show us something and we followed them along the village street to a large modern building which turned out to be a factory employing a large number of Tibetan men and women. This factory, which was in fact merely a large shed, had been set up by the Nepalese to enable the Tibetans to be self-supporting by exercising their traditional craft of weaving. Most of the work we saw was done by women, who sat on the floor in groups, weaving rugs, cushions and cloth on crude-looking wooden looms. We could not resist buying some of this handiwork with its bold and original designs, although prices were much higher than we had anticipated. Outside in the compound were groups of young men who appeared to have nothing to do but to loaf around in the sunshine. To our surprise we discovered that a few of them could speak English really well, and it was obvious that they had received a good education in the school attached to the settlement. They were, however, disgruntled and full of grievances because there were no jobs available for them in Nepal. The conversations we had with these young Tibetans aroused our interest in their plight, and whenever we came across their camps in Nepal and in India, we made a point of visiting them. In a large settlement about a hundred miles west of Kathmandu, we found the Tibetan villagers making rugs and other handicrafts in their own homes, but the work they produced was of a very poor quality. They also had a great variety of antique objects which they said they had brought with them from Llasa; small brass bells and prayer wheels, heavy bracelets and necklaces, all rather crudely executed, for which they asked exorbitant prices. Some months later, we found similar settlements in Kashmir and the same discontent amongst the young as we had seen in Nepal.

Discontent with their lot in life is, however, not the prerogative of only the young Tibetans, as we discovered when we became friendly with a young Nepalese couple whom we met in a café a few days after we arrived in Kathmandu. Sati, the wife, was a student at Kathmandu University, where she was studying English. Her husband, Narayan, who had graduated in law four years before, was unemployed. It was through them that we became acquainted with the background of present-day Nepalese politics, and with the frustration experienced by many of the young intelligentsia. Narayan's father had been a member of the ill-fated first and only democratically elected government of Nepal, which was dismissed by the present king's father in 1960, a year after it came into office. According to our friends, the king had only given permission for elections to be held in the expectation that a right-wing government would come into power, but it was a left-wing government, and the king, feeling his position threatened, found an excuse to disband it. He alleged that the leading members of the government were subordinating national interests to socialist dogma, and that they were not capable of maintaining public order. A number of ministers including Narayan's father, and Prime Minister B. P. Koirala, were imprisoned without trial for more than five years. Most of them are now in voluntary exile in India. After the Dissolution of Parliament, political parties were banned in Nepal, and in 1961 King Mahendra introduced a party-less system, based on the village "panchayats" (councils), which send representatives to the Lower and Upper Houses of Parliament. The new king, Birendra, in spite of his Western education, has the reputation of being even more autocratic than his father, and our friends and other young Nepalese whom we met, claimed that parliament is the king's puppet. Anyone who dares to criticize him is clapped in jail, and people with left-wing views are denied employment. This was the case of Narayan, who was suffering because of his father's political convictions, but fortunately for him, his family had some property in the country and he is able to exist on the rents from the land. His father, mother, and two younger brothers have been living in exile in India for the last ten years.

On several occasions, we were invited to visit Sati and Narayan in the large, rambling house which they shared with elderly relatives. It was an old house, badly in need of repair, with heavy antique furniture decorated with Nepalese lions carved in wood, but the small room in which we were entertained had modern furniture and a large rug with the word 'Welcome' woven into it. We enjoyed these evenings immensely, not only because the conversation, which usually turned to politics was interesting and informative, but because Sati was such an excellent cook. After the unfortunate consequences of eating out in town, we had been having all our meals in the van and were tired of unending vegetable stews and curried eggs. In Narayan's house, the meal was a feast, to be savoured to the accompaniment of taped Nepalese music, as we sat on cushions around a low table. Sati usually prepared a dozen or so tasty dishes — portions of chicken or meat in sauce, spicy black beans, small peas, spinach, puffed rice, nuts and curds, with sweet pastry rolls for dessert, followed by tea and more tea. Apart from the puffed rice, which is eaten uncooked, we enjoyed all the food which was to our taste, being not too highly spiced.

On the eve of our departure from Kathmandu, we made arrangements to visit Narayan's parents in India and to take with us letters and gifts for his family. We were also given a letter of introduction to the ex-prime minister who is a great family friend and now lives in Delhi. At that time we had no intention of revisiting the capital, but, as I explained in chapter five, unforeseen circumstances forced us to return to Delhi in May when we contacted Mr Koirala. When he heard that we were friends of Sati and Narayan, he readily agreed to give us an interview, and our meeting with him was one of the most interesting of the whole of our tour.

As we sat in his little bungalow, shuttered against the burning heat of May, this modest, unassuming man in his mid-fifties told us, without a trace of bitterness, the story of the failure of Nepal's first attempt at democracy and of the clandestine struggle which is still in progress to re-establish democratic processes. When we asked him if there was any substance in the late king's assertion that his government had not been capable of maintaining public order, he told us that the king and his associates had employed agitators to foment trouble in various parts of the country. He also maintained that the Nepalese people, if they were given the opportunity in free elections, would again return a left-wing government to power. The possibility of this happening, however, appears to be rather remote as the king's position is stronger than ever, and Koirala and other dissidents, who have joined him in India, have little power at their disposal. The Indian Government has given them asylum but does not wish to be seen to take sides in a struggle against the king, for it is well aware that if it did so, China who is waiting in the wings and whose influence in Nepal is already considerable, would certainly step up its involvement. All that Koirala can do, therefore, is to support the guerilla groups which are operating across the Nepalese frontier, and to produce political leaflets which are smuggled into Nepal and distributed by his supporters there. However, as most of Nepal's twelve million inhabitants are poverty-stricken peasants whose main aim is not to revolt but merely to survive, the road to democracy will be a long uphill struggle.

Now let us return to Kathmandu which we were preparing to leave to spend a week in Pokhara with our niece before she returned to India. Everyone at the camping site had spoken enthusiastically about the magnificent scenery at Pokhara, which lies about a hundred miles west of Kathmandu at the base of the great Annapurna range. In bright sunshine we set off through the mountains on the new asphalt road which has been built by Chinese engineers. In the valleys, the air resounded with the clear call of the cuckoo, which I had always assumed to be a bird of the West. Golden eagles soared above us and flurries of multicoloured butterflies rose from the roadside as we passed by. There was water in abundance in the wide rivers and rice paddies. In the little villages, the houses with their many tiered thatched roofs, were better maintained than their counterparts in India. As we drew near to Pokhara, we were halted at five or six checkpoints manned by soldiers and the ensuing delay frayed our patience and tempers. It was now raining and thick clouds swirled around the base of the mountains, obscuring the beautiful view we had been promised. Finding a hotel room for Yasu, who was, unfortunately, very travel-sick, was more difficult than we had expected; the guest houses near the lake, where most of the young trekkers live, being cheap but shabby and lacking in amenities. The hotels near the town and airport were expensive — about £7 per night for a single room without food. Then we discovered that the Hotel Crystal had a little annexe in the garden with reasonably-priced single rooms, near which we could park our van and have a supply of electricity for a few hours each day. However, we did not realize how really fortunate we were until the bird chorus wakened us at dawn next morning, and drawing the curtains aside, we were completely overcome by the unexpected sight in front of us. Pure white against the deep blue of the sky, glittering in the first rays of the rising sun and soaring high above the other snowy crests of the Annapurna range, was Machapuchhre, the incredible Fish Tail Peak. Although it was about twenty miles distant, it seemed to lie just on the edge of the hotel garden, and until the clouds obscured it around noon every day, we could not keep our eyes away from it.

In Pokhara itself, which is a long, straggling village, there is nothing to see and very few goods for sale. However, we managed to buy some potatoes, onions, eggs and pawpaws and Yasu purchased some colourful, woven shopping bags and cushion covers. At the northern end of the village, the trail to the mountains begins, winding along the grey River Seti. Here the mule trains, heavily laden with grain and blankets from Pokhara's markets, set off towards the Himalayan villages, with their sturdy drivers trudging behind them, heavily booted and coated in anticipation of the freezing temperatures above. We met two middle-aged Englishmen returning from a seven-day bird-watching excursion in the mountains. They had hired four porters to carry their tents and provisions up to 12,000 feet, at the cost of fifteen dollars a day — (nowadays, everything is reckoned in dollars). One of these climbers confessed to feeling relieved to be back at the comfortable level of 2,400 feet, as he had felt very giddy on the heights. But he stressed that it had all been very worthwhile, especially to see the rare and colourful water birds in the mountain streams.

During the next few days, we met quite a number of trekkers, most of them in their twenties, who had accomplished the difficult treks to Jomosom and Muktinah on foot, with or without porters. All were ecstatic about the scenery and the friendliness of the villagers in whose houses they had found shelter for the night. One or two did complain, however, about the fleas which they had collected in their sleeping bags, although they considered them to be no more than minor discomforts.

In the course of our modest treks around Pokhara, we visited a Tibetan Refugee Centre and a number of Gurung villages. The faces of the Gurungs were familiar to us, as most of the Gurkha soldiers in our regiments are Gurungs. We met several retired Gurkha soldiers who had served abroad in the British and Indian armies. They spoke excellent English and were extremely proud of their British connections and of their army medals, and everyone of them commented sadly on the news that soon there will be no more Gurkha regiments serving with our army, since these are being disbanded. It was men like these, with experience of life in other countries, who helped to bring the left-wing government into power in 1960.

On the roads leading to the villages, women of all ages were to be seen struggling along with enormous baskets of firewood on their backs. Every now and then, they would pause to adjust the leaves or straw which served as a buffer between themselves and their burdens. As there were no means of transport, aged persons and invalids were carried to their destinations in cane chairs fixed to porters' backs or slung on poles across their shoulders. Mule drivers used to stop to offer us trinkets and aconites at exorbitant prices, but we had the greatest of difficulty in making the farmers part with their tiny eggs at the cost of 5p each.

Two miles south of Pokhara is the beautiful Phewa Tal Lake which reflects the Fish Tail Peak in its clear waters. Here we hired a canoe and bathed in the lake from a little island with a temple. Nearby, overlooking the lake, is the only camping site in the area, which, unfortunately, has neither water nor toilets, and is far from secure, as it is not enclosed.

Most of our excursions had to take place in the mornings, since by noon, great thunder clouds had begun to gather over the mountains spilling out torrential rain by the evening. We would be basking amongst the roses in the hotel garden when the sky would suddenly darken and we would be drenched before we could reach the shelter of the van. Great flashes and rumblings would come from the mountains and hailstones as large as pebbles would scud across the lawns and pathways, and on more than one occasion we were marooned in a great pool of water, longing for gumboots to carry us across to the welcoming warmth of the hotel foyer.

As there was no meat available in the village and we were rather tired of our vegetable diet, we had several evening meals in the hotel, where we thoroughly enjoyed the luxury of being served a good four-course meal at a very reasonable cost. Most of the hotel guests came by air from Kathmandu and stayed for only a few days. We met a Dutchman from Borneo who had taken part as a geologist in an expedition to

Annapurna thirty years before. At that time there were no hotels and his party had to camp on the airstrip. Now there are four or five hotels near the little airport. A German, working on a United Nation's project in Nepal and India, talked to us of his difficulties and frustration. It was his job to advise and assist the Indians and the Nepalese on the bottling and canning of fruit and vegetables, and he was very critical about the lack of proper administration and efficiency. His difficulties were not confined to their process of canning which was not hygienic enough to comply with Western standards, but he had also great problems in arranging for the collection and marketing of the produce. We became very friendly with the manager of the hotel who wore a white suit and had all his hair shaved off, as his father had died recently, and this is the custom during the period of mourning.

After a week in this idyllic spot, we set off to the Indian frontier with the mighty mass of Annapurna still visible on the horizon after a hundred miles. The surface of the highway was so bad and the gradients so steep, that we covered only twenty miles in the first two hours. Our road snaked along the sides of countless valleys, through straggling villages, perched precariously above steep escarpments. Here and there, the metal surface of the road had fallen away and we had to scrape past on the landward side, scarcely daring to glance at the sheer drop below. For Yasu, the journey was agonizing as she was sick for most of the way, and we were all heartily glad to see the land flatten out in front of us towards evening and we sped over the plain to the Indian border.

There was, however, one very important factor which we had tended to forget in the cool heights of Nepal, but which impinged itself upon us as we journeyed southward across the plain — the tropical heat of India, which rose to greet us. It was now the end of April, and at 8 p.m. when we reached Gorakkpur, there was no welcoming evening breeze. Before we looked for a hotel, however, we went in search of Narayan's parents' house on the outskirts of the town. Unfortunately, no one was at home, but the soldier who stood guard at the house (the Indian Government protects political refugees), agreed to take charge of the gifts we had brought. We were glad to get rid of the large container filled with puffed rice which Sati had sent to her in-laws, as it was too big to fit into our larder and had been an encumbrance. Besides, we had had the niggling and no doubt unworthy suspicion, that the tin might contain something other than rice, which a search by the Nepalese customs officials might reveal to our great embarrassment. We found a small hotel in the main street and turned on all the fans in the bedroom in an effort to keep cool. They were, however, quite ineffective as they only churned the hot air round and round. The rubber mattress reminded me of the hot sand on Calungute Beach, and there were no cooling drinks to assuage our thirst. It was impossible to sleep.

For the next ten days, until we reached Simla, we were engaged in an unrelenting struggle with the heat. And yet, in spite of this battle, and all the discomforts which accompanied it, we were happy to be back in India.

When we travelled on to Lucknow and from thence to Delhi we were on the road at 4 a.m., an hour before sunrise. For that hour we had the road to ourselves. Then, as the sun shot up over the horizon, peasants came streaming out of the villages to work in the fields, and women came to draw water at the wells or to wash their clothes in the ditches. Suddenly, there was a mass of people in front of us, walking, riding bicycles, driving bullock carts, or squatting by the roadside. With one hand on the hooter we proceeded at a snail's pace along the Grand Trunk Road. It was so different from the green and tranquil Nepalese countryside. We were now aware of the absence of private cars which had cluttered up the streets in Nepal. On the other hand, there were the ubiquitous trucks which constantly drove us off the tarmac strip into the dust. The stalls by the roadside had a wonderful display of fruit and vegetables; the mangoes looked especially delicious, but it was too hot to stop and shop; we had to reach our destination before fiery noon.

The Tourist Bungalow at Lucknow, with its shuttered windows and tiled floors, was a welcome haven from the heat. The water in the shower was cool, and the fans kept the heat at bay. The fact that there were enormous cockroaches in the hand basin, and processions of ants across the floor and up the walls is hardly worth a mention when all else was so satisfactory. During the few days we spent there, we became quite attached to Lucknow which is a pleasant town with wide streets and gardens and minarets and cupolas rising above the trees. It is a far cry from the time of the Indian Mutiny of 1867, when the British garrison at Lucknow was under siege. Only the ruins of the 'Residency', lying in a peaceful garden remind us of the eighty-seven days during which the three thousand troops and their dependants refused to surrender to the insurgents. Relief came with General Campbell, but only one thousand survived the ordeal. All that is long forgotten. In fact, the people of Lucknow are very welcoming to strangers and to the British in particular, as we discovered on a number of occasions.

Life here seemed less hurried and more gracious than in the other Indian cities which we visited. There was less poverty and squalor, and fewer beggars. In the Chowk (or bazaar), which is one of the most interesting parts of the old town, with its eighteenth century buildings, we purchased embroidered tablemats and handkerchiefs, and a hubble-bubble pipe. There was a great variety of attractive goods for sale, including gold and silver brocades, pottery and silverware. Riding on a bicycle rickshaw, shaded from the sun, we toured the city, visiting the Great Imambara, an imposing palace with a vaulted hall, and the tombs of former rulers by the river. We sampled the Mogul cuisine of some of Lucknow's luxury hotels. Mughlai food is usually highly spiced, but we were always able to obtain mildly flavoured biriani pullau (meat and nuts cooked with spiced rice) and kagori kebab (long tender pieces of spiced meat), all served with cooling, savoury yogurt. Then there were delicious sweetmeats and mangoes for dessert.

Yasu's holiday had now come to an end and she decided to make the thirty-six hour return journey to Bombay by train. As a first-class ticket in an air-conditioned train costs almost as much as travel by air and was beyond her means, she had brought with her a bedroll to travel overnight second-class. As we had no experience of travelling by train, our visit to Lucknow railway station to see her off was a revelation and a shock. When we went through the main entrance, I had the impression that there must have been a riot, as hundreds of dead bodies littered the approach to the trains. Then it became apparent that these inert ragged figures were alive, but weary and exhausted by the heat and by lack of food. They did not appear to be waiting for trains: they had nowhere else to go. We picked our way over bodies, stumbling over bundles of bedding, drinking pots and baskets. As we had heard that second-class rail travel was very cheap, we had at one time contemplated touring India by train, but it is an idea which we are not likely to entertain again, unless we elect to travel by one of the very comfortable air-conditioned express trains. As the engine was not yet attached and the fans were not functioning, the inside of the Bombay train was like an oven. On each side of the compartment, three wooden shelves, devoid of any kind of padding, served as berths. As there were no doors on these compartments, there was neither privacy nor security, but the small, grimy, barred windows, although they obscured the view, would mercifully also exclude the sun's rays. Undaunted by the prospect of travelling under these conditions for over 1,000 miles, Yasu unrolled her sleeping bag, filled up her Thermos with cold Limca and waved bravely as the train carried her away into the night.

Annapurna — Nepal

Kathmandu — Nepal

Chapter Eleven

NORTH WITH THE NOMADS

A fortnight after leaving Lucknow, we were heading north, away from the heat and dust of Delhi, towards the cool, green foothills of the Himalayas. With the permit for our car safely in our possession and with two new spare tyres, we hadn't a care in the world as we sped towards Simla along a fast, smooth highway. This two-hundred mile journey, which is little more than a morning's drive, used to take the families of British Tommies at least twenty-four hours by train thirty years ago. My daily help, whose husband was a sergeant in the British Army before 1947, had often described these journeys to me. The dispatch of hundreds of women, children and government personnel to the hills for the summer months, was, as one would expect, planned like a military exercise. At daybreak, leaving their quarters scrubbed clean as per regulation, mothers and children waited with their bedrolls, (one each, and tied in a certain manner), and a few belongings (a specified number) for army lorries to transport them to the station. Then throughout the long summer's day, the train chugged its way over the plain whilst its occupants sweated and the children sobbed with weariness. All these trials, however, were soon forgotten as they felt the cool mountain breezes and watched the town of Simla rise out of the morning mist.

We thought of these uncomfortable journeys as we travelled north with all mod cons. In the fertile and prosperous part of the country north of Delhi, we passed a number of small restaurants with intriguing names — The Whistling Teal, The Golden Oreole and The Red Robin. As we had left Delhi, before breakfast we stopped at The Red Robin to have a snack, but neither this nor any of the other restaurants opened until the afternoon, so we took out our chairs and tables and breakfasted in the compound, surrounded by a group of inquisitive onlookers. Bypassing Ambala, we made for the new town of Chandigarth which has been taking shape since partition divided the Punjab between Pakistan and India. Lying in the plain south of Simla, Chandigarth replaces the old capital of the Punjab, Lahore, which now belongs to Pakistan. In its layout and style it reminded us of Islamabad, Pakistan's new capital city, with its rows of cube-shaped houses separated by great stretches of undeveloped land. We went in search of bread and fruit and were directed to a large complex with plenty of shops, but none were selling food, so we had to travel some distance to another shopping area to find what we wanted. This uneven distribution of shops must be most inconvenient for the inhabitants of Chandigarth which is not well served with public transport. The public buildings were shabbier and less imaginative than those we had seen in Pakistan's capital, apart from Le Corbusier's stuccoed High Court building which looks like the shell of a giant tortoise.

Beyond Chandigarth, the road spirals steeply upwards into pine-clad mountains towards Simla which is perched precariously on the crests of several small hills. As the roads leading into the town are very narrow and motor vehicles are not permitted in the centre, we pulled into a small car park on the outskirts to ask the way to the Government Rest House. Near a rather battered Ford Transit van, a young fair-haired Western woman was washing babies' nappies in a plastic pail, while her bearded, long-haired husband tinkered with the car engine. Inside the van a chubby, blond child was asleep, curled up beside a large black cat. These three individuals and the cat were, although we did not know at the time, to be our constant companions in Kashmir for several weeks. Our first meeting, however, was a brief encounter from which we learned little except that they, like ourselves, were on their way to Kashmir and that the Rest House we were seeking was at the top of a hill on the other side of the town.

From our vantage point at the Rest House we could see the whole of Simla spread out below us with its houses hugging the mountain side and its streets connected by a series of long staircases. Although it is probably less trim than it was in its heyday when the British viceroy and his officials spent the summer months in the palatial residences now crumbling on the hillsides, Simla has retained much of its dignity and style. Looked at from a distance, with its church spires towering above the clusters of houses, it still has the semblance of an English country town. However, if one takes a closer look at the bazaar area with its motley crowd and makeshift stalls, there is no mistaking that one is in the Orient.

It was while we were surveying the landscape, that we suddenly remembered that we were running short of money so, in spite of the fact that we were extremely tired after the long drive and early start, we set off to find a bank in the centre of the town. We cantered downhill to The

Mall, which is one of the best laid out streets we saw in India, only to find that, as in England, the banks closed before 4 p.m. Since no vehicles are allowed in this part of the town and there was no means of transport, we were faced with the long, steep climb back to the Rest House. We were dead beat and, to add to our discomfort, it was a very warm evening. How did the former British residents cope with this situation, we wondered? Our problem was solved by the sudden appearance of six diminutive coolies with two rickshaws balanced on their shoulders. After a little bargaining we fixed the price, 20 rupees each (just over £1 per head), and we were borne aloft through the narrow streets of Simla and along the hill paths. Far from enjoying the ride, we felt acutely embarrassed at being transported by other human beings. We could now imagine what it must have been like in the days of the British Raj when hundreds of undersized porters toiled uphill and down bearing the weight of portly ladies and gentlemen. No doubt these passengers saw nothing incongruous in the situation, and as for the coolies, porterage used to be considered an honourable occupation. Our porters, however, had little sense of honour, for when we reached our destination they demanded double the fee they had agreed on, and argued loud and long in a vain attempt to make us comply with their request. Fortunately, Kerry was always able to handle these confrontations in a masterly and decisive fashion.

Next morning, after one of the best night's sleep we had had for weeks, we set off through the cool pine woods in the direction of Mandi. Beyond Simla the road wanders north through the lower Himalayas, rarely descending below 5,000 feet, with frequent sharp bends and steep gradients which restricted our speed to ten miles an hour. Spring time and the cuckoo had arrived in the high valleys, and the hillsides were covered with pink and white wild roses and fragrant bride's blossom. At one turn of the road we were hailed from above by an English voice and looking up we saw the couple with the baby whom we had met at Simla, encamped by a mountain stream with their washing spread out on the bushes. We shouted and waved back, but did not stop as we were in a hurry to reach Mandi. By the time we had descended to the plain where Mandi lies in a sleepy hollow at the head of the Kulu Valley, it was one o'clock on a Saturday afternoon and the banks were closed until Monday. All we had left to pay for food and petrol for the next two days was a hundred rupees (£5.50). The State Bank, the only bank which can be relied upon to change traveller's cheques in India, was still open when we called, but the official on duty informed us that the account had been made up and the bank manager had gone to lunch. As we did not relish the thought of being stranded over the weekend in Mandi where it was oppressively hot, we went in search of a money exchange. But Mandi has no such service and does not even boast of a sizeable hotel where foreign currency might be exchanged. Back at the bank we begged the manager to change some of our German marks into rupees, but he was unable to do this after business hours. However, when he had locked up the bank and we were about to depart, disconsolate, he had a surprise in store for us. He took out his own pocketbook and handed Kerry two hundred rupees, saying, "I know I can trust you to repay me when you are able to change your money." He refused the German marks we offered him and he would not even consent to noting the numbers of our passports. It was an amazing and unexpected act of faith on the part of a complete stranger.

That evening we parked in the compound of a fine new State-run Tourist Bungalow near the village of Jogindernagar in a prosperous farming area where a number of research institutions dealing with horticulture, agriculture and animal husbandry are situated. In the restaurant of the Tourist Bungalow we met an Indian doctor who had practised for many years in Bristol and the local chemist who invited us to his home after dinner for coffee. Our host was a very intelligent man and, judging from his bookshelves, which were filled with books on Philosophy, English Poetry, German Literature, Gardening and Architecture, his interests were wide. He had designed his own house and was self-taught in both English and German and strangely enough we found we had much more in common with him than with the doctor who had been in England.

The latter who seemed pre-occupied all evening and made no attempt at conversation, suddenly roused himself after midnight with the startling request to me, "Would you be kind enough to sew up my trousers which I have split?"

Had it not been for his friend's hospitality, I would have suggested that, as a doctor, he should have been capable of stitching up a seam. However, without making a comment, I acted as seamstress.

Early next morning, there was a knock at the caravan door and a scruffy-looking Frenchman explained that his wife had been taken ill in the hotel and he needed some medicine urgently. Unfortunately, he had run short of money and required ten rupees. I was sure that he was a scrounger but Kerry reminded me of the generous Indian we had met the previous day. "We must give him the benefit of the doubt," he said. Then, having second thoughts he added, "Or at least half the benefit," and he handed him five rupees, explaining that we, too, were short of cash.

On making enquiries later, we discovered that there were no French visitors in the hotel, and when we described our caller to our chemist friend, he said he was one of a group of hippies who lived in the vicinity, without any visible means of support. "Be very careful" he warned, "with your money and belongings in Dharmsala, for there you will find as many hippies as Indians."

We had been looking forward eagerly to our visit to Dharmsala, which is the home of the Dalai Lama, the former spiritual head of Tibet, who fled from his country after the Chinese invasion in 1959, and it was one of our cherished ambitions to have an interview with this exalted personage. We followed a winding road, flanked on the right by towering, snow-covered peaks to beyond Kangra where there is a steep ascent into the mountains, and the luxuriant vegetation of the valley gives way to pine covered slopes. Overshadowed and sheltered by the great rock wall of Dhaula Dhar, Dharmsala perches on a narrow ledge on the mountain side with streets only a few feet wider than our caravan. As we had found in the other hill towns, there was nowhere to park and not sufficient space anywhere to turn our vehicle. The metal road petered out at the end of the village and a rutted cart track took us higher up the mountain side, finishing up in the garden of a large old-fashioned house. It was an ideal parking place, quiet and spacious with a magnificent view over the valley below. But, would the owner allow us to stay here? It was almost too much to hope for. A slim, middle-aged man, in a tussore silk tunic over white trousers answered our knock and listened to our request. Then he shook his head. "As a government official I cannot allow people to park at my residence. But do come in and tell me about your travels, and perhaps I can suggest where you could find a parking spot."

We were ushered into a sparsely furnished room, the walls of which were covered with large pictures of the Dalai Lama, and a number of photographs featuring our host at the side of the illustrious man. Our new friend, Mr Sherma, was, in fact, the Liaison Officer between the Indian Government and the Dalai Lama, having previously served as an embassy official in Kenya, Brussels and Egypt. For two hours we talked with this interesting man while his pretty daughters served us with cups of tea and home-made sweetmeats. The main topic of our conversation was the Dalai Lama whom our host greatly admired, and since he accompanied him on all his journeys, he knew him intimately. The Dalai Lama was only twenty-four when he escaped from the Chinese who had overrun his country and came to India, where he and thousands of fellow Tibetans were given refuge. "The Dalai Lama does not claim to perform miracles," said Mr Sherma, "but he has a very powerful presence, great wisdom and an exceptional knowledge of world affairs."

"Do you think he would grant us an interview?" we asked hopefully.

But we were out of luck, as the Dalai Lama was not going to give any interviews for the next few weeks. It was a bitter disappointment, mitigated somewhat by our host's sudden and unexpected acquiescence to our request to park in his lovely garden.

From our perch on the mountain side, we looked down over the Dalai Lama's palace and the new Buddhist temple which the Indian Government has built for the Tibetans facing the vast fertile plain of the Punjab. Behind us towered the snow-covered summits of the lower Himalayas where golden eagles nest. We watched these beautiful birds poised in the air above us, flexing their wings to the air currents. Unfamiliar butterflies, black with spots of colour, hovered around us in the garden; strange birds and the familiar cuckoo called at dawn and dusk, and when night fell the lamas in the monastery below began to chant their prayers. Their singing, together with the wind in the pine trees, lulled us to sleep.

Almost all the inhabitants of Upper Dharmsala are Tibetans and their lifestyle is imprinted on the village. Fresh-cheeked women in aprons, with their dresses tucked up to their knees, trampled out their washing in wooden tubs, and in the street near the temple the great brass prayer wheels were kept turning ceaselessly as passers-by prayed with a flick of the hand. The stalls in the street were covered with the same knick-knacks we had seen in Nepal; silver bangles and ornaments, miniature prayer wheels, wooden articles, bags and brass work. As our chemist friend had predicted, we met plenty of Western hippies, many of whom were squatting in the former residence of the Dalai Lama. Although their slovenly attire contrasted with the neat style of the Tibetans, they appeared to be well-behaved youngsters who appreciated the peaceful, relaxed atmosphere of this unspoilt village. Lamas with shaven heads, dressed in red cloaks were streaming into the new temple near the Dalai Lama's palace, and it was in the temple precincts that we caught sight of three familiar figures — the couple with the baby whom we had met at Simla. The fair-haired, blue-eyed child, crawling over the grass in the temple garden was the centre of attraction, and a crowd of Tibetan villagers and young lamas stood gazing at him in wonderment. His name, we discovered, was Tory, short for Torialli, an Afghan name, for he had been born in Afghanistan, where his English father and American mother had been working for the last three years. They were such a lively entertaining trio that we took to them at once and it was with the hope that we might meet again in Kashmir that we mentioned that we planned to camp at Pahalgam in The Liddar Valley.

In the meantime, we had become more closely acquainted with the Sherma family, and especially with the two eldest daughters who, like their father, were very well educated and spoke perfect English. At our first meeting Mr Sherma had confided to us that the problem of finding suitable husbands for his daughters in this isolated spot was exercising his mind, and it was obvious that the girls were glad to have the opportunity of meeting people from the West. In the evening when they watered the flower garden we used to discuss all manner of subjects. They told us about a nomadic tribe called Gaddis, who inhabit the surrounding region, tending their sheep on the heights in summer and descending to the plains in the winter. They believed that these people, who have fairer skins than other Indians, are descendants of the soldiers who deserted from Alexander the Great's army after they reached the Indus. We do not know whether there is any truth in this story, but these Gaddis are certainly clothed in a unique way, their long woollen cloaks closely resembling a toga.

A few days later, when we took leave of our kind hosts, we gave them our home address never dreaming that we would meet again quite soon. Less than a year after our return to England, Mr Sherma, having found suitable partners for his daughters, was posted to the Indian High Commission in London and we have become very close friends with him and his wife.

When we descended to the plains to continue our journey to Kashmir, we found the heat almost suffocating and our thirst unquenchable. Fortunately, however, we had a continuous supply of cold drinks as we were able to keep our refrigerator in operation by filling it daily with lumps of ice.

At Jammu, which is Kashmir's winter capital, we found a room with shower attached in the Tourist Reception Centre at a very reasonable cost, before setting off in search of our mail which we had had forwarded poste restante. This was the first time we had used a post office as a forwarding address as we had always been able to collect mail, either from an embassy or from an American Express office. This had proved very satisfactory. Unfortunately, as there is neither an embassy nor an American Express office in Kashmir, we had to make other arrangements for our correspondence. From our experience we would not recommend the use of poste restante in a provincial town in India. When we finally located the office in Jammu we were informed that there were no letters for us, but we insisted that another search should be made, and when that was unsuccessful we asked how the mail was filed. To our surprise, all the letters, etc., were arranged under Christian names, mine under E and Kerry's under R (Rusi being his Christian name). After examining all the letters, we collected half a dozen, and returned joyfully to pore over the first news we had received from home since we left Kathmandu a month before. Unfortunately, the news was far from cheerful being a sorry tale of rising prices and a steady fall in the value of the pound.

That night we spent at Jammu, was the most uncomfortable one of the whole of our journey, for the heat was so intense that the bedroom fan was quite ineffective and the water in the cold shower was positively steaming. We dragged our mattresses onto the little balcony, hoping to find a cooling evening breeze, but the hot, fetid air, trapped within the central compound rose up and enveloped us.

The next day there was a long delay before we proceeded on our way towards the mountains, since our front springs required some attention and we had difficulty in finding a garage which would do the job at once. It was well past noon when we followed the road which the Mogul Emperor Akbar first took in 1587, fleeing like us from the dust and heat of the plain. It was this route, too, which top-ranking British officials used to take in ever-increasing numbers during the last fifty years of British rule in India, making their way to their houseboats at Srinagar or their villas at Gulmarg. Akbar's retinue must have toiled on foot over these high passes carrying their royal passengers in dandies (sedan chairs), or riding on the backs of mules or ponies. The hazards of these early journeys became apparent to us as we climbed the zigzagging two-hundred mile mountain road which even today is often blocked by landslides, snow and floods. Nowadays most foreign tourists fly into Srinagar from Delhi or Amritsar on a flight which takes under three hours, but there are still many travellers who come by rail to Pathankot or Jammu and complete the journey to Srinagar by bus or taxi. As only affluent Indians can afford a car, there are few private vehicles on this road, except in the holiday season in May to July. However, the absence of motorcars is more than made up for by the streams of trucks and army lorries, buses and taxis which ply on this road to Srinagar. This is the only motorable road to Kashmir, but if one looks at the map there is a much shorter road to Srinagar for travellers coming by road from Europe, via Muzaffarabad in Pakistan. Alas, partition and disputes over the ownership of Kashmir have blocked this western access, forcing travellers to make a seven-hundred mile detour to reach their destination. The old Kashmir of British days has been divided into Azad (green) Kashmir, which is governed from Islamabad, and the State of Jammu and Kashmir which owes allegiance to Delhi.

Following the winding course of the River Jhelum, we rose out of the plain, catching tantalizing glimpses of snow-covered peaks in the distance and feeling the welcome freshness of mountain breezes. A chain of Dak Bungalows and Indian-style hotels cater for weary travellers on this tortuous road to the north. We spent the night at the Tourist Bungalow at Kud in a room without bedding, water or electricity, but which was pleasantly cool and cost a mere 60p.

As dawn lit up the mountain tops, we were on the road which switchbacks up and down with good stretches of tarmac alternating with patches full of potholes. We began to catch up with large groups of nomads on their annual trek from the plains to their summer pastures in the Valley of Kashmir. Handsome, sturdy people with bright, flashing eyes and strong Semitic features, they strode along beside their ponies or behind their herds of goats and cattle. They travelled in family groups with babies dangling in cloth bags on their backs; colourful folk with their red cloaks and pony trappings weathered to gold and orange by the sun and rain, and their quaint leather shoes with up-turned metal toecaps. The women wore jaunty, little embroidered hats with a flap at the back, and around their necks and arms and hanging from ears and nose was a shining, tinkling collection of gold and silver jewellery — all their worldly wealth. They took it in turn to carry on their heads the household's copper pots, strung together in bags made of rope. Once or twice a day the ponies were set free to scamper up the mountain sides to forage with the goats and cattle for the sparse grass on the stony slopes and to quench their thirst by a waterfall.

After many days of travelling as they toiled up towards the 9,000 foot Banihal Pass, their pace slackened; children and older women lagged behind, lean-ribbed animals strayed from the roadside and lame calves and kids had to be carried, slung round their owners' necks. In the wake of the nomads, behind a queue of buses and taxis with roof racks piled high with bulky bedrolls, hampers and cases, we crawled at a snail's pace towards the new tunnel near the crown of the pass. The word, 'Banihal', means blizzard, so it is not surprising that the entrance to the tunnel is frequently blocked in the winter by snowdrifts some twenty feet deep. The nomads, however, following age-old tracks where the gradients are almost perpendicular, scrambled straight over the top of the pass. At last we too reached the summit and caught our first glimpse of the 'Happy Valley', lying beneath us like the Promised Land. This vast luxuriant valley, fringed with snow-covered peaks, was one of the most stupendous sights of our journey. The contrast of the bare, dark mountains on the southern side of the pass with the lush exuberance of the vale, covered with the greenery of spring, had a magical effect upon us, and from that moment until we left four months later, Kashmir held us in thrall.

In springtime there is water everywhere in the Vale of Kashmir. In the middle of the valley the foaming Jhelum makes a headlong dash towards the scorching plains. In more placid streams, edged with white laburnum and wild roses, willows dip their green tips, and by the roadside tiny brooks course merrily along and meander off into the paddy fields.

At Khanabal we left the main road to follow the winding course of the Liddar to Pahalgam, lying at a height of 7,000 feet in one of Kashmir's most beautiful valleys. It was on our way to Pahalgam that we saw, repeated at frequent intervals, a notice stating that 'Spinners are Sinners'. We were puzzled at first, presuming that it had some religious significance, until we realized that its intention was to dissuade anglers from using spinning tackle. Incidentally, Indians have what amounts to a mania for notices and captions. Their buses are plastered with 'God is love', 'Trust in God' and 'Good luck', which do little to inspire confidence in the driver. All the way from Jammu we had been distracted, usually at hairpin bends, by signs such as; 'Be on the alert, accidents avert', 'Take your time and not your life', 'Be gentle on my curves', 'It is neither a race nor a rally', 'Go slow and enjoy Kashmir Valley', 'Death is a five letter word' and, 'We love our children, don't you?'. On our way back to Jammu in September, after weeks of rain had caused havoc on the road, blocking it with landslides in a number of places, we were brought to a halt by a notice which stated, 'I am Miss Nasku my slip is showing'. The fact that all these notices are in English, presupposes an extensive and intimate knowledge of our language, not only on the part of educated Indians and tourists, but by the humble 'truckie' who plies the route between Jammu and Srinagar.

It took us five hours to find a suitable parking spot at Pahalgam. We could easily have parked on the outskirts of the village on the banks of one of the rushing streams, but there we would have had neither drinking water, electricity, nor security. Most of the hotel compounds were small and cramped, with just enough room for their clients' cars; and the State-owned bungalows were fully booked and had no access for vehicles. In the end, we returned to the Plaza, the first hotel we had visited, which has a large unfenced compound. The manager had been reluctant to allow us to park there, but Kerry managed to persuade him to give us permission; so by nightfall we were happily installed outside the hotel, at the foot of a grassy slope covered with pine trees. One of the hotel servants filled up our tanks with water from the garden hose and brought us two buckets of warm water to wash away the dust of the journey, before the sound of the Liddar river lulled us into a blissful sleep.

The full beauty of our parking spot was not revealed to us until next morning at daybreak when we pulled aside our curtains and looked up at the snow-clad mountains towering above us, at the cherry trees in blossom on the hillsides, and the swards of blue and white irises in the marshy ground by the river. We were not the only ones to consider the site eminently suitable, for on the crumbling stone wall behind the caravan sat a pair of tawny-crested hoopoes surveying the possibilities for nesting. They settled in a crevice between the stones and by July they had raised a brood of three, within six feet of our abode. These beautiful birds with their brightly-striped wings, were a daily source of joy to us and we took almost as many photographs of them as we did of the majestic peaks around us. What delighted us too was the infinite variety of new sounds to which our ears became gradually attuned. There was the continuous roar of the Liddar river as it came thundering down the valley from the snowy reaches of the Himalayas; the unusual calls of birds; the clatter of horses' hooves; the sharp cries of the cattlemen and goatherds who whistle through their teeth to attract their animals; the steady pounding of clothes in the hotel wash house, and the monotonous chanting of Muslims in the mosque on Fridays.

The Tourist Office arranged for us to have a supply of electricity (albeit somewhat intermittent), at the cost of about £1 per month. Without this facility, life would have been much more difficult for us, as our gas cylinders were now empty. It took six weeks and several visits to Srinagar to have our canisters refilled, for not only was there a great shortage of cooking gas in Kashmir, but there were no connections for our type of cylinders. In the end, Kerry had to design a special connector and have it made in a workshop before our containers could be filled. After the first few weeks, during which we had to rely solely on the spasmodic supply of electricity, we were able to hire a large gas cylinder from the Tourist Office. We certainly required every available source of heat, since the weather, which had greeted us so warmly on our arrival, decided almost at once to demonstrate how fierce and inclement it could be. A sudden chill filled the air, louring clouds obscured the view as the rain whiplashed the valley, flooding the area around the caravan and transforming the river into a foaming torrent. To keep warm we piled on all our woollen clothes and heated hot-water bottles at bedtime. Then the rain found its way through our damaged roof and soaked all our cushions and bedding. Kerry ventured into the quagmire outside and fixed a tarpaulin over our roof, but as there was no means of drying our clothes, we decided to spend a night or two in the hotel until the storm abated.

The Plaza, a large, old-fashioned hotel with high rooms and open verandahs, ideal for summer weather, was not constructed to withstand cold or to keep guests warm during a wintry spell. The Indian tourists, ill-equipped for chilly weather, retreated to their hotel bedrooms, where they sat wrapped in blankets, waiting for the sun to shine.

The hardy Kashmiris, on the other hand, barefooted in the mud, seemed to be impervious to the cold. They have however, a very useful little gadget called a 'Kangri', which helps them to withstand the worst of the weather. It is a small wicker basket with a container filled with burning charcoal which they carry under their voluminous cloaks. This device is not without its drawbacks, however, as it leaves unsightly scars and burns on the wearer's chest and stomach. Not having a kangri, we used our equivalent, the hot-water bottle, as our hotel bedroom was exceedingly draughty with a gale blowing through the chinks around the window frame. As the supply of electricity was disrupted, we were unable to cook any food and had to have our meals in the hotel where we had the dining room to ourselves. The other guests dined in their bedrooms, for that is where most Indian tourists prefer to take their meals.

When the rain stopped, Kerry removed the wooden box from the roof of the caravan and filled up the cracks with a bituminous substance, while I spread our wet clothes on the bushes to dry in the sun. Soon the rain was pouring down again, but fortunately not into the van as Kerry had managed to stem the flow. However, it was now apparent that we would have to put a new roof on our vehicle in the very near future. Late that evening there was a knock on the caravan door, and there, drenched with the rain and looking utterly miserable were our friends, Carol and Terry Hart with the baby, who had been washed out of their camping place in Srinagar. By the time they had had a meal and warmed themselves at our electric fire, their spirits had begun to rise, and Tory was crowing with joy as he scrambled about on the floor. Carol's main concern was the laundering of the baby's nappies, more than thirty of which were piled up at the back of their van. Obligingly, the hotel dhobi agreed to do their washing and to dry their wet clothes in the cookhouse. So by midnight the Harts were happily encamped nearby in the hotel compound, and for the next few weeks, they were our neighbours and constant companions.

The weather now put on its most dazzling smile, with the sun shining out of a cloudless sky from dawn to dusk. Every day we set out on foot to shop in Pahalgam, half a mile away, or to explore the green valleys around us. Viewed from a distance, the little village of Pahalgam, which is situated at a height of 7,500 feet, resembles an Alpine village. At close quarters, however, it is a typical Indian hill resort, with one long, straggling, unpaved street lined with small hotels, knick-knack shops and rickety street stalls. The main tourist season starts in the middle of May when affluent Bombay-wallas take their holidays; so a few days after our arrival, the hotels were packed with visitors and the valley resounded with Marathi and Gujarati voices. In the village street, ladies in bright sarees, sparkling with tinsel or fringed with silver or gold borders, paraded with their escorts who, in their multicoloured shirts and waistcoats, looked almost as colourful as their companions. They would stroll along the village street, stopping at the samosa stalls to nibble titbits in pastry or sizzling jellabis, oozing syrup. They crowded into the Art Emporiums (little shops use these inflated titles), to purchase embroidered stoles and sarees in fine Kashmiri wool, patterned rugs, gilded papier-mâché trays and bowls, and quaint bric-à-brac in carved wood. Indeed there was no need for them to stir from their hotels to purchase these articles, for on the terraces and verandahs, legions of vendors with packs on their backs were lurking ready to display their wares if as much as a glance was thrown in their direction. As for us, in our faded cotton jeans, we shopped from stall to stall, bargaining for vegetables and fruit. Mangoes and cherries were now in season but they were quite expensive and we only purchased them as a special treat, our main diet consisting of vegetables, supplemented with eggs and samosas. Occasionally Carol and I joined forces to produce a meal, and as she had a pressure cooker and a petrol stove, these meals were more elaborate. Tough pieces of mutton were rendered down into tasty curries which we served with fresh peas, kohlrabi or artichokes. With our tarpaulin stretched above us to afford shade, we cooked and dined outside, savouring the glorious view almost as much as our meal.

In a meadow between us and the village there appeared, almost overnight, a whole host of tents, transforming the valley into what appeared to be a large army encampment. It is here that Indian tourists of modest means come to spend their summer vacations, and we watched with interest as relays of porters scurried to and from the camping agencies in the village with charpoys (beds), chairs, cupboards, chipped enamel jugs and basins. There was no piped water, so the campers drank from the river regardless of health risks; nor were there any public toilets, although a few of the larger tents had commodes; but all the tents had electricity for a few hours each day. There was feverish activity, too, on the fringe of the village where the State-owned Tourist Bungalows are situated. Porters, bent double under bulky holdalls, bedding and picnic baskets, were to be seen trotting along the paths and rough tracks on the hillside with their clients panting behind them, their eyes fixed on their swaying luggage and their porter's little beehive of a hat.

On foot or on ponyback, we roamed the countryside, visiting the little villages and following the course of the rivers to wild and beautiful valleys. Although somewhat squalid and poverty-stricken, the Kashmiri villages, perched on the mountains or on the banks of a stream, have a charm of their own. The ground floor of the lopsided, wooden houses accommodates cattle, sheep and poultry, and the family lives on the first floor under a wide eaved attic where firewood is stored for the winter. The village street, furrowed by frequent rain, is scarcely more than a muddy ditch through which the inhabitants squelch with their sturdy bare feet. They are colourful people, especially the women, with their brightly-coloured tunics, bloomers and headscarves. Early each morning they set out in groups for the mountains to gather brushwood for fuel, and before noon they stagger back bearing great loads upon their shoulders.

Meanwhile the older women and children sit on the ground outside in the sunshine, plaiting and delicing their hair and chasing predators away from their grain which is spread out to dry on large mats. Whenever we arrived in these villages, we would be greeted from afar with cries of 'backshish', and crowds of ragged, smiling children would come running towards us. It was obvious that this kind of begging was considered quite legitimate by their elders who looked on indulgently and hopefully, expecting us to be generous towards them. The fact that very few men were to be seen in these villages was due to the exigencies of the tourist season when all able-bodied fellows are engaged as porters, hotel employees or pony attendants. Pony riding and trekking is one of the chief occupations of holiday-makers in Kashmir and by mid-May the valleys resounded to the clatter of ponies' hooves. Indian ladies ride demurely with their sarees tucked up between their knees while the coolies keep a tight hold of the bridles. Their husbands, a little more daring, break into a trot now and then, closely followed by their light-footed attendants, while their teenage sons and daughters, in Western-style jeans, come charging down the mountain side, lashing their steeds and whooping like the wild hordes of Ghengis Khan.

There was another holiday occupation which was more popular with Indian ladies, although it was much more costly. The photographic studios of Pahalgam (there must be about a dozen) display large colour photographs of beautiful women in Kashmiri dress, sitting by a stream with mountains in the background, or reclining on a grassy sward, clutching a posy of flowers with an admiring male in attendance. At first we were puzzled by these pictures as we could not understand how the native women could afford to be photographed, or how they came to possess such elaborate dresses and jewellery. The mystery was solved, however, when we realized that we were looking at the holiday souvenirs of Indian ladies dressed in Kashmiri clothes. From our vantage point in the compound of the Plaza Hotel we watched the photographers arrive with their props — bundles of brightly-coloured traditional garments, showy silver jewellery, baskets of artificial flowers, clay pitchers and so on. The ladies posed on the banks of the river, silhouetted against the snow-capped peaks. It was a lengthy operation, during which the clouds often covered the sun and the rain poured down on the unfortunate models, shivering on the icy stones.

We had not forgotten the unpleasant experience of being doused with rainwater, indeed the ominous bulge in our ceiling was difficult to overlook. One day Kerry prised away some of the timber, and gallons of water poured into the pails which we had wisely set out in readiness. It was evident that something had to be done at once before the heavens opened yet again. As there were no materials available in the vicinity, we set out early one morning by bus to Srinagar sixty miles away. The bus, which was due to leave at 5.30 a.m., did not in fact leave until one hour later, so we took refuge from the cold in a shack where tea was being brewed over a charcoal fire, and a group of men were sharing a hubble-bubble pipe. The tea which we sampled is the tea most Kashmiris drink, pale pink in colour, very sweet, but not unpalatable.

When we did arrive at Srinagar, after a long and very cramped ride, we had no time to explore the town, so busy were we haggling over the price of a sheet of aluminium to cover our roof and a metal box to replace the wooden one. After a good deal of searching, we purchased the metal for about £25 and found someone prepared to make a box to our specification. The aluminium was hoisted on top of the bus which was already piled high with bundles and boxes. It was now raining heavily, and by the time we reached the bottom of the Liddar Valley it had reached torrential proportions. In the paddies, the newly-planted rice was covered with water, and the mountain streams, brimful and milk-white, came thundering down over the rocks.

Heedless of the downpour, groups of Kashmiris were trudging up the valley, their wet cloaks hanging limply around them, and the goatherds were sitting below the trees passively watching their flocks. Before the bus had come to a halt in Pahalgam, a host of wiry porters had climbed inside to stake their claim as carriers. Three or four attached themselves to us, but when they saw our large sheet of metal they shied away. No one was willing to carry it to the Plaza, and we were drenched to the skin before we were able to cajole one brave little man into being our porter. Handing me his kangri (heater) he hoisted the metal sheet upon his head and jogged off, swaying dangerously over the wooden bridges, one of which had lost its side rails and half of its wooden planks. We were so relieved to reach home safely that we gave him much more than he asked for. All our discomfort and weariness were forgotten when we heard Carol's voice calling, "Your meal is ready, we are bringing it over to the caravan."

Kerry spent most of the following week on the roof of the van, bending and hammering the metal into shape, and fixing it with nails, as pop rivets were unknown in Kashmir. Then, with the help of a local handyman, he renewed the ceiling timbers which had begun to rot as a result of the accumulation of rainwater. Meanwhile Terry was busy replacing the sliding doors in his van and installing an alarm device. This gadget turned out to be a source of annoyance to all of us as Carol used to let if off inadvertently during the night, rudely jolting us out of our sleep. It was only Terry's skill as a mechanical engineer which enabled him and his family to travel safely to and from the East in a van so well past its prime and so heavily laden as his Ford Transit. During their sojourn abroad they had collected so many possessions — rugs and brass work from Afghanistan, bric-à-brac from Nepal, clothes from India, etc., that there was only sleeping room inside for Tory and the cat. Carol and Terry slept in a little, home-made plastic tent fixed onto the roof, and they cooked outside in all weathers. It was an extremely rigorous existence and we admired their cheerful toughness, especially that of the baby, a large, bonny child who was just as resilient as his parents. He spent the day crawling round the compound, surrounded by an admiring circle of herd boys, unscathed by his daily intake of dust and animal manure. His greatest joy was to sit propped up in the driving seat turning the wheel of the car ecstatically, until this practice had to be abandoned when he discovered how to open the door and bounced out on his head. In spite of the limited space and lack of facilities — there was no running water, no toilets — Carol was an exemplary mother, cooking three-course meals and continually washing clothes. Whenever she had a spare moment, she took out her typewriter and caught up with her correspondence, keeping an eye on her energetic, wandering son. She found a willing helper in Kerry who is very fond of young children and enjoyed the role of an indulgent godparent. Every evening we joined forces for a game of Scrabble while Tory played happily on our caravan floor, and sometimes when he was safely asleep, we had a meal together in the Plaza Hotel.

By this time, we were on friendly terms with Ranjit, the young Sikh manager of the hotel, who was a frequent visitor to our caravan. He had just returned from two years in Germany and after tasting the pleasures of the permissive West, he found his present circumstances very restrictive. His parents wanted him to settle down and were doing their best to find a wife for him, but he had turned down all the girls they had chosen. He confided to us that what he really wanted was a Western girl, who had to be not only 'beautiful and elegant', but also 'docile and submissive', a combination of qualities, which we felt he was unlikely to discover, although we did not disillusion him. With his brilliant turbans and Western-cut suits, he was a bit of a dandy, but this bold front concealed his naivety and lack of confidence. He was, however, a popular and well-known figure in the village and through him we became acquainted with the life of the local community. He took us to a concert given by international students at the Country Club of which he was a member and to a campfire singsong in which hundreds of young Sikhs participated.

One evening, about midnight, he woke us up and invited us to join him and some friends in a moonlight picnic in the mountains. We dressed hurriedly and squeezed into his Ambassador car which already had half a dozen occupants and as many baskets and tiffin tins. We set off along the rough road that leads up through the pine woods to a wide meadow, which was bathed in the light of the full moon, a spectacular setting for a picnic with the towering peaks of the Himalayan foothills standing guard above us. Ranjit had provided all kinds of appetising dishes made in the hotel kitchen; roast mutton, chicken, river trout, rice, cauliflower, chapatis and chilled melon, washed down by an abundant supply of beer. Then to the strains of Western music played on a tape-recorder, we danced until we were exhausted and sang ourselves hoarse. It was only when the moon grew pale, that we piled back into the car for the homeward journey.

It was now the beginning of June and almost all the snow had disappeared from the mountain tops, leaving only the last vestiges glistening in the gullies which run like veins through the pine-covered slopes. The woodlands were carpeted with violets, mallow and strawberry flowers, and by the roadside and river banks, pink vetch and red and white roses grew in profusion.

Having explored the area around us, we now ventured further afoot, following the mountain streams to the top of remote valleys, where we sat with our feet in the cool water observing the birds and listening to the cuckoo whose call was growing fainter day by day. Often during these excursions we would come upon a nomad encampment in an upland meadow, with buffaloes and goats munching the lush green grass, and women drying their grain in the sun. Sometimes these nomads build themselves houses of hardened mud, roofed with turf on which their chickens perch and feed, and make clearances in the forest where they plant and harvest grain. Usually, however, they purchase their food in the village, and whenever we went to obtain our ration of flour, rice and sugar, there was always a large number of nomads in the queue. They carry their water and grain in dried goatskins which are put to a variety of uses. Near Mandi, for instance, we saw people crossing a river, lying face downwards on inflated goatskins and paddling with their hands.

The tourist season was now at its height and all the hotels and boarding houses were overflowing with holiday-makers from Delhi and the Punjab. Ladies in brightly-coloured silk bloomers, tunics and tinsel-fringed scarves had replaced the ladies in sarees, and their escorts in eye-catching turbans were even more decorative than the visitors from Bombay. Little boys with their hair tied up in top-knots secured by mobcaps, and girls with long dark pigtails played upon the lawns. Day and night, taxis and cars arrived in the compound packed with people looking for accommodation, but by now the hotel was full and they were sent elsewhere. In the compound we were now hemmed in by taxis and private cars. Most of the vehicles were driven by chauffeurs who slept in the cars and washed in the river as there were no facilities for servants in the hotel and their masters and mistresses paid scant attention to their needs. We felt very sorry for one elderly 'gunga' who spent many hours each day sitting forlornly on a heap of gravel in the car park and spent the night on the floor of one of the verandahs.

From dawn till dusk there was great activity in and around the hotel. Early in the morning a couple of nomads used to arrive with buffalo milk in copper pots upon their heads. They were a colourful pair, the woman in red bloomers with an enormous jewel in her nose, the man in a tunic and a bright lungi (skirt). Then the dhobi could be heard whacking the sheets against his wooden tub, and soon the compound fence was covered with laundry and an assortment of clothes. Once we saw a buzzard lift a shirt from the fence and carry it away, the sleeves flapping in a helpless fashion. We helped the dhobi to retrieve it from the branch of a pine tree. As is often the case in hotels in the East, the cookhouse was situated some distance away from the main building, and from our window we could see the white-coated waiters scurrying to and fro in all weathers, carrying laden trays. We could also see men sawing wood outside the kitchen where the cooking was done on a wooden stove. One of these woodmen, a wiry, middle-aged Kashmiri, attached himself to us and took it upon himself to be our servant. He brought us hot water, emptied our commode and assisted Kerry whenever required. He was called Akbar, and he certainly was the greatest.

One evening he came to our door, carrying something wrapped up in a newspaper and casting furtive glances behind him. "May I come into the caravan?" he said. Safely inside with the door closed, he handed the parcel to Kerry. "It is a present, sahib, and it didn't come from the hotel."

Kerry unwrapped the paper to find a large brown river trout.

"My brother caught it in the Liddar," added Akbar.

We assumed that it was poached, for it was unlikely that his brother had a fishing permit, but we did not ask any questions, so delighted were we with the gift and with the prospect of a change from our rather monotonous diet.

Our opportunity to repay Akbar for his kindness, which went far beyond the service for which we tipped him daily, came one day when we went to shop in Srinagar. We asked Akbar, who could not afford bus journeys, if we could bring him something. He needed a new pair of shoes and he specified the sum he was prepared to pay. We purchased a really splendid pair and gave them to him as a present.

Scarcely believing his good fortune he almost wept with joy as he ran off shouting with childlike glee, "Just look at my new shoes!"

We had another good friend in the hotel, Verendra, one of the waiters, a very intelligent young man with a good command of English and a keen interest in Western philosophical and religious books. Early every morning he went to the local ashram to practise Yoga, as it was his ambition to become a swami. He was also well versed in ayurvedic (nature) remedies and he received instructions from a famous 'medicine man' who spent the summer months in the Liddar Valley. I gave Verendra an opportunity to practise the art of healing when I slipped on the hotel steps and sprained my ankle. He bathed my foot in hot mustard oil and massaged it gently before applying a poultice of herbs which was left on overnight. The treatment was effective, for the following day the swelling had disappeared and I could walk without pain.

Now that the tourist season was in full swing, our camping spot in the compound had one great disadvantage. Since our vehicle was unusual, it attracted everyone's attention and every day dozens of hotel visitors would knock at our door. "Mr Ranjit says you will not mind showing us your caravan." At first we did not object, in fact we were rather flattered by so much interest, but when queues began to gather to view our little home our irritation grew. I resented the constant interruption of my day and the accumulation of dust and dirt on our carpet. Sometimes the callers did not wait to be invited in, assuming that they could enter unannounced. Since privacy is a concept which most Indians find difficult to understand, they were genuinely puzzled and hurt when we explained angrily that this was our home and we did not like these intrusions. The final straw came when a group of tourists, intent on seeing the inside of our vehicle, woke us up around midnight. Enough was enough, we were not running a peepshow, so after that no one was allowed entry, although that did not deter the more brazen holiday-makers from coming right up to our windows and pressing their noses against the glass to see what was going on inside.

It was this lack of privacy, coupled with the lack of toilet and washing facilities, which made the Harts decide to look for another camping place further away from the village, and at Dar Camp on a plateau overlooking the valley they found the ideal spot. At this site there were furnished tents, running water and a small restaurant. All the people in the camp were Westerners, Danish, Canadian and English, most of whom were missionaries on leave from other parts of India. Although Dar Camp was suitable for our friends, it was of little advantage to us, as we would have lost our precious supply of electricity and easy access to shops. Carol and Terry promised to return every afternoon, which they did, carrying Tory in a knapsack, and when they went shopping they left him with us.

By this time we had made friends with some of the villagers, especially with two helpful young men from the Tourist Office who often called in at our caravan for a chat. It was from our conversation with them that we learned of the strong feeling of resentment which many Kashmiris feel against India. Our two friends, who, like eighty per cent of the population of the Vale of Kashmir, were Muslims, complained bitterly of the discrimination practised by the Indian Government in favour of Hindus. They alleged that Muslims have difficulty in obtaining good posts and promotion in government service, and that little has been done to develop new industries in Kashmir. Many Kashmiris believe that they would obtain better treatment from Pakistan, and should there be a tug-of-war for their country between the two powers they would join forces against India. Subsequent discussions with Kashmiris confirmed that these separatist sentiments were widespread, and that many Muslims would like to join Pakistan.

To understand the political situation in Kashmir, one has to delve into history. Although it was one of the regions especially favoured by the Great Moguls, its very remoteness kept it isolated from the rest of the country. In the middle of the last century the British handed it over to the Hindu Rajah of Jammu, and in 1947 it was one of the few states which remained with its future undecided. The Hindu ruler, whose position as head of a predominately Muslim state was a difficult one, played for time, then acceded to India in a panic when insurgents from Pakistan crossed into Kashmir. Nehru promised the people a plebiscite to decide their own future, a pledge which for a variety of reasons he failed to keep, and Kashmiris are not likely to forget this breach of faith.

At the beginning of June, the former Maharajah of Kashmir, Dr Karan Singh, Minister of Health in the Indian Government, came to a meeting at the ashram in Pahalgam to which Kerry received an invitation. It was a few days after the British Medical Association, in an effort to ensure that the qualifications of foreign doctors should be of a certain standard, had introduced more stringent acceptance tests. This measure had caused an uproar in Indian medical circles where it was claimed that discrimination was being practised against Indian doctors in the UK. Dr Singh discussed this issue with Kerry, asserting that the National Health Service in Britain would collapse if he withdrew the passports of all the Indian doctors in Britain. Being a very reasonable man, however, he agreed that Britain had the right to regulate and maintain medical standards, but he regretted that his government had not been informed of the new measures before they were introduced.

The little ashram on the hill, was a place of some significance, as the chief swami was well known throughout India and in the West. A large party of Belgians, who stayed at the Plaza for two weeks, had come to study at the ashram, and Ranjit invited us to meet them.

I shared a table with one young Belgian who explained to me why he believed so firmly in reincarnation. "I know that I have lived before," he said, "and I know also that I lived in India, because when I was a very small child I drew an elephant without ever having seen one."

One interesting Indian whom we met at the ashram was Judge Khanna, the Chief Justice of Delhi, and since he and his wife wanted to see our caravan we invited them to tea. The main topic of conversation in India at that time was the dispute between Mrs Gandhi and the courts over alleged electoral malpractices, so we talked of the implications of the case, although the judge was careful to remain impartial. He explained to us that as he expected to be chosen as the next Chief Justice of India, in which capacity it would be his task to deal with Mrs Gandhi's appeal, he could not pass judgement in advance. We formed a high opinion of his shrewdness and integrity, and we were sorry to learn some time later that Mrs Gandhi had not appointed him to the supreme post in the judiciary.

Most of the people with whom we came in contact in Pahalgam, however, were not the rich and famous, but the humble inhabitants of the region. Herdsmen and nomads would knock on the door, or intercept us in our walks with requests for medicine, or to be exact for 'pills', and 'penicillin'; they knew these words. We assumed that these remedies were required as an insurance against future maladies, but unfortunately, we were unable to help them as we had only sufficient medicaments for our own needs. Kerry's help and knowhow were always in demand. The dhobi brought his transistor set to be mended; the carpenter used to borrow his electric drill, and Ranjit expected him to repair his garden sunshades. One daily visitor who tried our patience sorely was a little shoeblack who frequented the hotel compound, and bawled "Shoes-ss clean: Shoes-ss clean", every time we emerged from the caravan. He was so insistent and so importunate that after several weeks Kerry lost his temper with him and emptied the contents of his box into the nearby bushes, an action which he immediately regretted when the little fellow began to snivel. Kerry, who is very soft-hearted, helped him to reassemble his belongings and allowed him to polish his tattered sandals for a princely tip, but the lad was much more circumspect after this incident, and approached us with caution.

The vendors, who lay in wait for the tourist on the threshold of the hotel, never ceased to tempt us with their wares, and needed no encouragement to spread them out for our inspection. They brought semi-precious stones, intricately carved wooden trays and dishes, woollen rugs and cushions and embroidered shawls. One hardy pedlar, who had trudged with his pack on his back all the way from Rajasthan, tried to sell us musk, which is extracted from the abdominal gland of certain species of deer. He brushed this over my hand to prove its authenticity, and it must have been the real thing, as the scent lingered for days. As the summer progressed, the number of travelling salesmen increased and so did our purchases of luxuries like walnuts, which we bought by the sackful, and honey which the nomads sold to us in bottles.

Kerry had to make two journeys to Srinagar before he could collect his new metal box which did not fit the roofrack and had to be hammered into place. This splendid box of which Kerry was so proud, was destined never to reach England, and its demise was one of the most frightening experiences of our journey. Returning to Tehran one dark October night, we drove down an underpass to reach the centre of the city. Had it been daylight we would have seen that the bridge was too low for our vehicle, but there was no illumination, and after a sickening crunch we found ourselves wedged in the archway, unable to move in either direction. Kerry climbed on the roof to survey the wreckage by torchlight, and he found that the box had taken the brunt of the shock. To dislodge it from the masonry he had to take the air out of the tyres and discard the twisted metal and the damaged contents — leaking tins of oil, shoes, the ill-fated oil stove, etc. This operation took more than two hours during which the flow of traffic moving past us never ceased and no one came to our assistance. It was a nightmare which ended only after Kerry had backed the van slowly up the slope against the constant flow of vehicles and pumped the air into the tyres once more.

Each time we returned from Srinagar, laden with provisions, weary and dishevelled, we had to face long bargaining sessions with the porters before we could make our way home. When we came back with our gas cylinders and a roll of lino, which we had purchased to replace our dirty carpet, the porters insisted that three men were required to carry our possessions. We would probably have argued all evening if an elderly coolie had not suddenly hoisted the lino on his shoulder and made off across the fields with a cylinder in each hand. Whereas Kerry enjoyed those protracted arguments and maintained a firm stand, I lost patience almost at once and would have given in to their exorbitant demands. Porters, pony hirers and shikara (boat) owners, were the worst offenders and were quick to exploit foreign visitors. It would be wrong, however, to give the impression that most Kashmiris are rogues, ready to fleece the stranger, because the majority of tradesmen and shopkeepers we encountered, were honest and reasonable.

View of Leh — Kashmir

U

Fatula Pass, 13,479 feet — Kashmir

With the Medicine Man, Jen and Verendra — Kashmir

Chapter Twelve

JEN'S ARRIVAL

Things began to happen after the middle of June. On the 16th June, we celebrated Tory's first birthday and the first tottering steps which he obligingly took to mark the occasion. It was a happy event, summed up by Tory in a typically American fashion "Wow! Wow!" which were the only words he was able to utter in spite of our attempts to teach him to say "Mama", "Papa", "Yes", and "No". But there was a hint of sadness in the air, because the Hart family was leaving the next day for Srinagar, and there was no certainty that they would be returning to Pahalgam.

A week later, a telegram informed us that they were on their way to Ladakh, 275 miles north-west of Srinagar, a part of Kashmir which had just been opened up to tourists for the first time.

On the 27th June, ten days after Judge Khanna's visit to us, a state of emergency was declared in India, and a number of Mrs Gandhi's political opponents were put in jail. We heard the news from the postmaster when we went to collect our mail. He showed us telegrams addressed to government officials and to the police, cancelling all leave. We were perturbed by this unexpected development although we had been aware of the relentless campaign carried on against the Prime Minister and Congress by J. P. Narayan and others in open-air rallies and in the columns of the newspapers. We concluded that it was not wholly unreasonable for Congress to take action to keep its credibility, but we never dreamt that the state of emergency would last for eighteen months and result in the overthrow of Mrs Gandhi. In the months which followed the crisis we noticed an improvement in public morale and discipline. There was also a steady fall in prices and the cost of meals in restaurants was reduced by about a third.

We had no time to brood over either the vicissitudes of government or the departure of our friends, for we were now in the midst of preparations for the arrival from England of our twenty-four year old niece, Jennifer, and her friend, Diana, who were coming to spend their summer holidays with us. When Ranjit heard about their visit, he was almost as pleased as we were, and we teased him about his preference for Western girls, but this was not the reason for his interest. He wanted Jennifer to bring with her as many lipsticks and bottles of scent (articles which are very expensive in India) as she could carry as presents for a prospective bride. As we could neither accommodate the girls in the caravan, nor afford rooms for them in the hotel, we decided to hire a tent from one of the camping agencies.

A day or two before their arrival, coolies struggled over the meadows carrying wooden floorboards, poles and canvas which they assembled in the compound. It was a splendid edifice, more like a marquee than a tent, twice as spacious as our dwelling, and its bold red and yellow lining made it look like the home of some gypsy queen. In addition to the beds and cupboards there was a separate compartment which served as a washroom, and nearby was a tiny tent with a commode. As Kerry was fixing up electric light, I noticed storage pockets sewn on to the sides of the tent and remarked on their usefulness. A few days later I was much less enthusiastic about these holdalls.

As Jen and Di were to be with us for almost two months, we had given some thought to suitable diversions for them. Ranjit suggested that we should hire ponies and make the six-day trek to the sacred Cave of Amarnath, high in the mountains thirty miles north of Pahalgam. The pilgrimage to Amarnath which takes place at the end of July, is the most important annual event in Kashmir, and Ranjit, who had made the journey several times, described it to us in detail. Three days before the full moon, a great host of pilgrims assemble in Pahalgam; saffron-robed swamis and ash-covered sadhus mingling with men, women and children in colourful regional costumes. Singing hymns and blowing on conch shells, they set off up the valley, halting for the night at Chandanwari, where they pitch their tents and cook over wood fires. From there the ascent is very steep to the shores of Sheeshnag Lake and to the top of the 14,000 foot Mahagunus Pass. A day later, they struggle up the narrow defile which leads to the holy cave where the object of their worship, the phallic symbol of Siva, glistens in greenish-white ice.

On the 3rd July, our visitors arrived, having flown direct to Delhi and from thence to Srinagar, exhausted by the heat and by the sudden change from the West to the Orient. They confessed later that their first glimpse of the streets of Srinagar had been something of a 'cultural shock', as they had been horrified by the squalid backstreets and the sight of so many poor people; but with the resilience of youth, they quickly adjusted themselves to their new surroundings. We were delighted to have the youngsters' company and to see everything around us through new eyes. The girls, who loved to experiment with food, brought changes in our rather restricted diet. After we had consumed all the lovely titbits they had brought with them from England — cheese, biscuits, fudge, cake, etc., we were introduced to a variety of dishes served with yoghurt, stuffed aubergines, spinach with fried cheese, apricot and plum crumbles, and spicy chutneys, which Jennifer concocted. Yoghurt was their favourite food, especially the Indian version which is thick and creamy. Their first attempt to make cream cheese, however, was a great disappointment. Jen had hung the yoghurt, wrapped in cheesecloth, under the eaves of the tent, where she thought it would be protected from flies and dust. In the morning only the shreds of material remained, the contents having been consumed by some predator, probably a stray dog. Thereafter the curds were left to drip from the tap in our shower cabinet, and we had a constant supply of cream cheese, sometimes flavoured with onion or garlic, sometimes sweetened and used as a dessert.

We had to remind the girls constantly of the dangers of eating unwashed fruit and vegetables, a warning which Di resented, and on more than one occasion Kerry caught her surreptitiously chewing discarded apple peelings. Our continual nagging, "Don't drink the water, it hasn't been boiled." "Peel the tomatoes." "Leave the cherries in the sterotabs," etc., was rather inhibiting for the girls who probably thought we were being over-fussy. However, after one bad experience which I will describe later, they understood the significance of our warnings. We also urged them to be very careful with their possessions, and to leave their valuables in the caravan, but even we did not realize how vulnerable they were in the tent. Amongst the goods they had brought with them were two bottles of whisky which they had hoped to exchange at a profit with Ranjit, and which they kept in the side pockets of the tent.

A couple of days after their arrival, they awoke to find that a thief had cut through the canvas and extracted their precious bottles, and what was even more alarming, their wristwatches, which were lying at their bedside, had been stolen. We reported the theft at once to the local police and asked them to make an official statement so that the girls could make a claim on their insurance policies. For some reason or other the police were most reluctant to do this and it took six visits to the police station to obtain the necessary document.

From the moment he saw her, our friend Ranjit decided that auburn-haired Jennifer was his ideal girl, and he appointed himself as her escort. He drove her around the countryside, entertained her at the Country

Club and brought her roses from the hotel garden. At first Jennifer enjoyed Ranjit's attention, which fortunately Diana did not resent as she had taken an instant dislike to him, but after a few days Jennifer began to make excuses when he called to take her out. However, he was still determined to accompany us on a trek to Amarnath. The girls, who had in the meantime met other trekkers in the village, decided that a trip to the Kolhoi Glacier sounded much more exciting than a pilgrimage to the Holy Cave. It was while we were making arrangements for this expedition that we began to doubt the wisdom of including Ranjit in our party, since he was constantly changing his mind and our plans, which was a bad omen for the success of our trek.

We had given up hope of seeing the Harts again, as they had written from Srinagar informing us that they were returning to Europe and would probably not have time to come to Pahalgam. Great was our delight, therefore, when late one evening, the familiar blue Transit took up its old position behind our caravan, and Carol, Terry and Tory climbed out. They stayed with us for two days, during which we heard every detail of their exciting visit to Ladakh where they had attended the great annual festival at the ancient monastery of Hemis. "You must make the journey to Leh," they said. "It is fantastic — out of this world," and when they assured us that our car would stand up to the rather 'rough' road conditions, we started thinking about a visit to this little known part of India.

The evening before our friends left, we gave a party for nine, which included the young Australian and a young German who were accompanying the Harts back to Europe. Carol made the pre-dinner snacks of prawn and onion dip. Then we sat down to a bumper meal of mutton curry, stuffed aubergines, pilau rice, apricot crumble, plum jelly and coffee.

In the early hours of next morning our friends set off to reach Amritsar by the evening, and we wondered as we waved goodbye whether we would ever meet again.

In the months which followed, postcards and letters from Carol charted their progress towards the West. They now live on a farm in New York State where Terry grows Christmas trees and Carol bakes bread for a living, and as for our godson Tory, he has probably no recollection of us or of the time he spent in Kashmir.

A few hours after the Hart's departure, a little posse, with two riding ponies and a packhorse, set out for the Kolhoi Glacier, twenty-six miles north of Pahalgam, accompanied by Ahmed, Akbar's brother, who was to act as guide and general factotum. After leaving the Liddar Valley, the route climbs upward through thick pine forests with majestic peaks rising higher and higher on the horizon. At Aru, Ranjit purchased three skinny fowls for about £1.50, which we considered an exorbitant price to pay for bone and gristle. We were already annoyed with him because he had not brought his share of provisions. We followed the path, precipitous in places, which skirts the foaming river through a narrow leafy gorge. From time to time Ahmed's voice could be heard calling "Keep to the right, Mr John (Jen)." "Hold tight, Mr Di," and to me, "Hold him back, Mem Sahib," as we plunged down a slippery slope. We, ladies, unaccustomed to a long spell on horseback, had begun to feel uncomfortable by the time we reached Lidarwat and saw the familiar, low roof of a Dak Bungalow in the distance. Although somewhat dilapidated, its two rooms and large verandahs afforded welcome shelter to trekkers, and it actually had a flushing toilet. Ahmed made tea for us in the chawkidar's (caretaker's) hut, and as we sat outside in the evening sunshine, gazing up at the soaring peaks which ringed the upland meadow, we felt that this was bliss indeed.

That evening we gathered round the wood fire which Ahmed had made, as Ranjit was intent on barbecuing two of our chickens. We were joined by two English climbers and an American couple who had rented a room from the chawkidar, and with whom Ranjit struck up a friendship. Unfortunately, his barbecued chickens were not a success as the firewood was too damp to glow, so the meat was only half-cooked, and to our annoyance, in a fit of generosity Ranjit gave away almost one whole chicken to his new friends. When the sun disappeared behind the mountains, a sudden chill, followed by a wet mist, descended upon us and we retreated to the dormitory; but in spite of the cold, the girls slept on the verandah, awaking in the morning to find their sleeping bags covered with hoarfrost.

Next morning, in a pale pink dawn, we were on our way to the glacier, without Ranjit, who had decided to rest. Jen rode on the packhorse, a most uncomfortable mount, as its back was wide and knobbly. We made our way upwards through pine and birch forests, over boulders and streams, fording raging, icy torrents, in which Ahmed stood waist-deep hanging on to our bridles, urging the ponies forward. Soon we had left the forests behind and crossed a series of upland meadows carpeted with wild flowers. There were anemones, blue and white primulas, tufts of blue irises and white petunias growing in great profusion. Above us, in crevices between the rocks were bushes of pink rhododendron. As we approached the glacier, the valley narrowed and became more desolate, with only a few alpine plants surviving amongst the boulders. At this inhospitable spot, on the snow line, we came across a Gujar encampment where we had tea brewed over a smoky fire while Ahmed had a few puffs of a hubble-bubble. The Gujars, who are nomads and live in tents, are smiling, friendly people whose only English is "What time is it?" repeated over and over again, regardless of the answer. Leaving our ponies with the Gujars, we proceeded on foot along the muddy edge of the glacier towards the huge, white mass of Kolhoi which stands like a sentinel at the head of the valley. On each side, great waterfalls come thundering down to join the main stream hidden beneath a series of snow bridges. We struggled over the icy boulders to the source of the Liddar which gushes from the spout of a waterfall at an altitude of 11,200 feet. As we turned for home, a glacial wind filled the valley, the sky darkened, and within a few moments, rain was lashing down from a slate-coloured heaven. In spite of our raincoats and hoods, we were drenched to the skin, and to make matters worse, I was so saddle-sore that I abandoned my horse to Ahmed who returned to the hut with the girls, while Kerry and I plodded back on foot.

Next morning the rain was still pouring down and the clouds hid the mountains from view. Ranjit who had found a new companion, a pretty French girl, announced that he was returning to Pahalgam with her, so we parted, pretending that we were still friends. For most of the day we sat by the chowkidar's fire which we shared with Gujar herdsmen, sheltering from the storm. We had eaten up most of our provisions, and after having tried, unsuccessfully, to make pancakes with oatmeal and dried milk, we happily agreed to the chowkidar's suggestion that we should have curried goat, rice and cabbage for supper. This was going to be a real treat and for hours we thought of little else.

About eight o'clock, Ahmed came in with our meal which smelt delicious. We had taken one or two mouthfuls and pronounced it 'first class' when a peremptory voice from the doorway called out, "Stop at once".

Looking up, we saw one of the English students with a serious expression on his face. "What's the matter?" we asked.

"Promise me that you won't tell the chowkidar" he said.

So we promised.

He went on, "Yesterday when we were at Lake Tarsar, a Gujar tried to persuade us to buy a goat, but our guide said it was ailing, so we refused." He paused, meaningfully, but still the truth did not dawn upon us. "This morning, the same Gujar sold the goat, which had expired in the meantime, to the chowkidar and —"

"And we are eating it," we chorused. Stunned and sickened we pushed our plates away.

Jen said, "Perhaps the goat died from a horrible disease."

"But it has been cooked," ventured Di, "perhaps we could —."

But we had all lost our appetite, and the meat, rice and cabbage was consigned to the fire, extinguishing it completely, and for the first time in our lives we went supperless to bed.

The rain was still pouring down relentlessly when we set out for Pahalgam next morning; Di and I on horseback, and the other three on foot. On the downhill slopes the horses skidded in the mud while we held on grimly for fear of being catapulted over their heads. Ahmed was the hero of the hour, guiding his animals away from the steepest slopes by strange calls and prodding the stolid packhorse which obstinately lagged behind. From time to time he stopped for a puff on a hubble-bubble with some of his friends, and each time he did so he brought us a kangri to keep us warm. Five hours later we were back at the Plaza soaked but exhilarated, laughing almost hysterically as we emptied the water out of our boots.

After our Kolhoi expedition, we saw very little of Ranjit, and when we did, he was polite but distant. We were sorry to lose his friendship because he had been most helpful and we had enjoyed his company. Our time in Pahalgam was, in any case, drawing to a close; in fact, we had planned to leave the valley on our return from the trek, but this proved impossible because of the floods, which closed the road to Srinagar for several days. It was at this time that we made the acquaintance of the medicine man whom we visited in the company of his disciple, Verendra. Di had had a rash on her foot which her doctor had not been able to cure and Verendra assured her that his master would have a suitable remedy for this ailment and for my arthritic finger joints. Jennifer had neither aches nor pains but she had a diminutive white spot on one cheek, scarcely discernible amongst her freckles, which she wanted rid of. We rode to the hamlet four miles away where the old man lived in a small, mud house. With his flowing white locks and beard and white robe, the medicine man reminded me of a biblical patriarch. Verendra said he was a hundred years old, but he looked vigorous and strong. As directed by Verendra who kissed his master's feet, we took off our shoes and sat on the piece of sacking which covered the dirty floor. In the corner of the hut was a smoky wood fire, around which a number of sadhus (wandering monks) were gathered waiting to be fed from the iron pot which hung above the fire. Verendra explained that his master never turned anyone from his door and always shared his food with strangers like these.

On the floor around us were small jars and bottles filled with potions and powders, and heaped up behind us were wicker baskets filled with dried leaves and herbs. The mud wall near the straw mat, which served as his bed, was covered with tattered pictures of Hindu saints, and in one small niche there stood a faded plaster model of his particular guru. After the sadhus had been fed, we were given a small tin platter with a portion of the food which tasted like very sweet semolina. Then Verendra explained our symptoms to the old man in Hindi, as he did not understand English. He checked our pulses and peered intently into our faces, muttering quietly under his breath. I was given small brown pills and a little packet containing 'ashes of copper'. Jen and Di's ailments required ingredients which he did not have and which Verendra had to fetch from the village chemist the following day. I said that the medicine man did not understand English, which was true, except that there was one word which he understood only too well, namely 'Scotch', as the empty whisky bottles lying outside the hut testified. The payment of his services was by a half bottle of whisky, not any whisky, however; it had to be 'Black Knight'. Unfortunately, we had purchased another brand, and our doctor's face fell when we presented it. This mistake was remedied on the following visit when Jen collected a white liquid for her blemish, and Di an evil smelling black ointment. As for our cures, my pills made no appreciable change in my condition and I did not venture to take the ashes of copper. After several applications of her lotion, Jen noticed that the skin around her spot was growing lighter, and we began to suspect that the liquid was some kind of bleach and that the medicine man, misunderstanding her complaint, had supplied her with something to get rid of her freckles, which Indians consider unsightly; but in Di's case the foul black ointment worked wonders, and by the time she returned to England her foot was completely healed.

When he heard that we were leaving Pahalgam, Bushir, our friend the carpenter, invited us to his home for tea. As he lived with his mother in a modest two-roomed bungalow next to the dhobis wash house and did odd jobs about the compound, we had assumed that he was a hotel employee. It was, therefore, with some surprise that we learned that he was, in fact, the owner of the Plaza, which had been built by his grandfather in the twenties. The original hotel, where Nehru and his daughter, Indira, had often spent their holidays, was burned down a number of years ago and was rebuilt by his father. Bushir and his mother, a charming, spirited Muslim lady, seemed to live quite happily without any of the facilities of which the hotel boasted, such as running water, a bath and a toilet. As they had no chairs, we sat on Bushir's bed and his mother brought us tea and almonds and Bushir talked of his hunting trips to the mountains in search of snow leopards and brown bears.

When the tent had been dismantled and all our provisions stowed away in the van, we said our goodbyes with a real sense of loss. Akbar, in tears, hugged Kerry and begged him to return one day. Ahmed, standing by his ponies looked rather wistful, but was cheered by the gift of my climbing boots as a reward for his faithful stewardship. Verendra gave us his address and a book about his guru, but Ranjit did not appear, although we caught a glimpse of him at a window. Most of the tents had disappeared from the valley, for although it was only the middle of July, the holiday season was over, and, apart from the Amarnath pilgrims, there would be few visitors to Pahalgam. Bushir accompanied us to Srinagar, bringing with him a sackful of live fowls which danced a jig over the caravan floor all the way to the town. It was during this journey that Bushir explained to us how houseboats came to Kashmir. Foreigners, and this includes all Indians who are not Kashmiris, are not allowed to own land in Kashmir. Before 1947, the rule prevented Britishers from owning property, until they discovered that there was nothing to stop them from owning a home, built on the water, not on the land. There are now thousands of these dwellings, many of them used exclusively to accommodate tourists.

As we had promised the girls a week in a houseboat, we hired a shikara (a gondola-like punt), to explore the possibilities of Dal Lake where most of the boats are moored, and where one can live in carpeted comfort on a luxury boat, or under Spartan conditions on a bark well past its prime. The names of these boats gave some indication of the kind of tourists their owners wished to attract. There was the *Neil Armstrong, Washington, Texas Variety,* vying for custom with *Sans Souci, Beausite, Paris, Buckingham Palace, HMS Pinafore* and *Queen Elizabeth*. If the boat was in a dilapidated condition, with few amenities, the price of a room could be as little as two rupees per person; on the other hand, on some of the luxury boats, accommodation and meals cost as much as a four-star hotel. We were looking for something in the middle price range, in a quiet spot, and we discovered our ideal houseboat in lovely Nagin Lake, isolated amongst the reeds on a tiny floating island of flowering shrubs. Appropriately, our boat was called *Golden Flower*, and it was roomy and well appointed with a sitting room, dining room, two bedrooms with showers and toilet attached, and a verandah looking over the lake. Moored alongside was the kitchen boat where the owner and staff lived, and for one memorable week we lived and dined in style for the modest sum of £3 each, excluding lunch. Our van was parked on the shore of the lake at a spot which could be seen from the verandah, but to ensure that it was not tampered with, we found a chowkidar to stand guard 'day and night'. He may indeed have done so, for the car came to no harm, and we were only too glad to recompense the fellow handsomely for his long vigil.

About a mile away across the lake, three bathing boats were moored and the next day we set off by shikara for a swim. Kerry needed some persuading because he was convinced that the lake, which looked crystal clear, was polluted. This the girls contested, since they had asked the owner of the boat what happened to the effluent and he told them that the sewage from his tank was regularly pumped into a special boat. We were somewhat reassured by this information although we had not seen a vessel equipped for this particular operation on the lake. For several hours we swam around the bathing boats and sunbathed on the upper deck where Di and Jen were soon surrounded by a little group of admiring males.

Di, with her thick dark hair tied into a top-knot, was sitting in the sunshine when a young Indian approached her. "Are you sick?" he asked.

Rather surprised, Di replied, "Of course not, what makes you think I am?"

"Because your hair is tied up on the top of your head," was the answer.

It took us a moment to figure out this non sequitur, then we laughed so heartily that the poor fellow was quite discomfited. What he had intended to say was "Are you a Sikh?" but the omission of the indefinite article, which Indians tend to make, changed 'Sikh' into 'Sick'.

Perhaps it had nothing to do with the bathe, perhaps it was something we ate or drank, but the fact is that we really were sick the following day, and Kerry's doubts about the purity of the water were confirmed when the girls discovered that the sewage from our boat flowed directly into the lake.

Fortunately, as we had the appropriate remedies, we had all recovered sufficiently by the evening to enjoy a four-course meal, which as always, was cooked to perfection and served with the niceties of a luxury hotel. If the mosquitoes were not too active, we used to sit on the verandah after dinner, watching the changing colours of the lake as the sun set behind the mountains and the shikaras gliding past our pallisade of reeds, leaving scarcely a ripple behind them. When the sun's rim had disappeared and the golden light had drained away from the sky, the boats were etched in black against a pale lemon horizon.

In contrast to the evening glow, the morning light shone with metallic brightness, transforming the dewdrops on the lotus blooms around us into translucent crystal. Flashes of blue amongst the bulrushes betrayed the presence of tiny, pink-breasted kingfishers which nest in the reeds. We spent many happy hours exploring the lake, clearing the way with our paddles through tangles of floating weeds and water lilies, and we made some very interesting discoveries. We found, for instance, that most of the vegetables, fruit and flowers, which are sold to the houseboats on the lakes, are grown, not on land, but on the water. There are extensive water gardens where tomatoes, melons, cucumbers, marrows, gladioli, etc., grow in profusion on floating strips of matted rushes. What is even more remarkable is that these garden plots can be moved from place to place, and it is not unusual to see a vegetable garden being towed across the lake, behind a shikara.

The shikara is not the easiest of boats to steer, unless one crouches on the prow as Kashmiris do, so we used to hire an oarsman to take us on long excursions. Travelling the length of Dal Lake we visited the Shalimar Gardens which were designed more than three hundred years ago by the Great Moguls. Landscape gardening incorporating lotus ponds is a very ancient art in India, but it was from Central Asia and Persia that the idea came of introducing cascades and fountains into gardens and palaces. Akbar, whose ancestors came from Samarkand, was the first to plan pleasure gardens in Kashmir, and his descendants completed and perfected his work. Shalimar, with its marble pavilions and terraces, surpasses its namesake in Lahore because of its magnificent setting on a hillside, shaded by great plane trees (chenars), the Mogul's favourite tree. Unfortunately, the water channels and fountains were empty, and we could only imagine what the gardens must have looked like when cascades ran merrily through the flowers, reflecting the lamps in the black marble pavilion.

Our favourite excursions were shopping expeditions to the town of Srinagar which lies at the head of Dal Lake. For this trip we used to hire a shikara with a straw-plaited canopy, padded seats and colourful cushions on which we reclined like the Persian grandees of old. Out of the calm, green waters of the lake, we glided into narrow, murky waterways, past ancient, high-storeyed wooden houses with carved panels and balconies, still splendid in spite of their disrepair, past boat yards, papier-mâché factories into the heart of the old town. Here the river banks are lined with Noah's Ark-like boats which are the homes of many thousands of Kashmiris, and as we passed alongside we caught glimpses of their daily life. At one window, hands emerging from gold braided sleeves would be wringing clothes; at another a woman would be cleaning vegetables in the turbid water. Gaily-dressed ladies sat in the sunshine plaiting their long, dark tresses or embroidering cloth, or polishing their copper pots. As we slid past we were conscious of being intruders in the intimate world of houseboat dwellers, who frequently showed their resentment by turning their backs on our cameras. In Srinagar, the girls went on a shopping spree to buy cloth for dresses and jeans, which they took to a tailor to have made up. Di had brought with her one dress, a smart French model gown, which the tailor copied in various lengths. At the shoemakers they had sandals made to measure and purchased shoulder bags and purses to take home as gifts.

On one of our visits to Srinagar we went to the Government Tourist Centre to obtain information about the Province of Ladakh of which the Harts had given us such a glowing account, but the officials tried to dissuade us from making the journey. "The road is very bad," they said. "We would not advise you to take your caravan; you can go by bus in two days."

Few of the Kashmiris we met had even been as far as Leh in Ladakh, except the houseboat proprietor, who had trekked there ten years ago when the journey took sixteen days. But undaunted, we began to make preparations for what turned out to be the most exciting journey of our lives.

Before we set out, Kerry had the Transit overhauled and serviced, but although he supervised the four mechanics deputed to do the work, he was not at all satisfied with the car's performance after the service. The garage made a further check and the car took the Shankaracharaya Hill without any difficulty, so he assumed that everything was in order.

The first lap of the journey took us to Sonamarg, across an open green valley, then up through the narrow gorge, gouged out by the turbulent River Sindh to an upland meadow of golden flowers. I drove on this section of the road and remarked that the car was not pulling very well, but it was not until we had left Sonamarg far behind us that it became apparent that the engine was labouring. When we approached the first pass, the Zoji La, which rises to the height of 12,000 feet, we were delayed for two and a half hours by a landslide which had blocked the road. When we were given the all-clear by the army, which patrols this area, we began the ascent on the pass, on a rough, unpaved road which spiralled into the dizzy heights above us. We struggled upwards round countless hairpin bends with our pace reduced to a crawl, as the engine began to feel the strain. Halfway up the pass, the car came to a stop and refused to be coaxed into climbing any higher. Di and Jen, who had been sitting at the back of the car, looking down at the fearsome chasms below, joined me in urging Kerry to turn back while daylight lasted, but he kept on tinkering with the engine, hoping to find the mechanical fault. It was then that a 'deus ex machina' in the shape of a high-ranking army officer, drove up in a Land Rover and Kerry explained our dilemma to him. We were in luck, for the officer was both helpful and understanding, and as it happened he had at his disposal the only device which could solve our problem — a giant bulldozer used by the army to clear the roads. This was fetched by one of his men and soon we were chugging our way to the top of the pass behind the massive vehicle. It was the strangest ride we ever had, or are likely to have in our lives. Up we went with the temperature dropping dramatically, as we ploughed through ice and snow, for even in the height of summer, the snow never melts on the summit of the Zoji La.

Once we reached the top we were able to proceed under our own power, but as darkness was beginning to fall, we were glad to accept an invitation to spend the night in an army maintenance camp, lying in a windswept hollow in the Drass Valley. To us, these scattered tin huts represented security and protection from the bitter weather, and the welcome we received from the road engineers and their assistants was a very heartening experience. Nothing was too much trouble for them, and some of the mechanics worked for hours in the darkness and intense cold trying to discover why our engine was losing power. Meanwhile the girls and I sat on the bunk beds in the cookhouse-cum-bothy, where a meal was being prepared for us on an oil stove. The little Keralan cook, dressed in a bright cotton lungi (skirt), sat on the mud floor frying chapattis. When he had made several dozens of these, he cooked a large potful of black beans, then rice, and finally a large omelette. By this time most of the food was stone-cold, but it did not really matter, because we were all ravenously hungry. As the temperature was well below freezing, we were shivering with cold in spite of our warmest clothes, and we could well believe the engineer's claim that Drass was the second coldest inhabited place in the world. However, in spite of the cold, we all slept well; Di in the spare bed and Jen on the floor. Next morning I was preparing breakfast when someone knocked at the door to inform us that our food was ready in the bothy, but our appetites failed us when we discovered that we had to eat up the remains of the previous evening's meal — half-frozen rice and beans and rock-hard chapattis. Kerry, who had risen early to work on the engine, cheered us by announcing that he had found the cause of the trouble — the carburettor jets were incorrectly adjusted and the butterfly arm had been placed upside down, so we took leave of our kind hosts and proceeded on our way to Leh.

The Drass Valley must be one of the most bleak and inhospitable places on the face of this earth, with glaciers covering the mountain sides and a slate-coloured river flowing under broken snow bridges. Although there were no trees and little vegetation, we saw large nomad encampments surrounded by flocks of goats and herds of ponies. At Drass we stopped for a snack at the Dak Bungalow, which to our surprise, had a flushing toilet — but no water. The sun was now shining and it was pleasantly warm as we followed the course of the River Drass through the mountains and over a barren plateau, in the midst of which we came across a grassy meadow full of flowers. We stopped the car, and in a few minutes we had collected twenty-three varieties of wild flowers, including edelweiss.

In Kargil, which is a miserable little town with a few down-at-heel hotels used by bus passengers on their way to Leh, we had hoped to find bread and eggs, but all the stalls had to offer were potatoes, onions and cabbages. Kargil did, however, boast of a petrol pump; the only one we discovered on the 275-mile journey. We spent that night at an army post, not realizing that it was a camp with trucks and lorries rumbling in and out at all hours. None of us slept well, least of all Jennifer, who had made her bed on the roof of the van, where she was constantly disturbed by flashing headlights and by the catcalls of the soldiers. It was only after 4 a.m. when a great convoy of army trucks preceded by the bus from Srinagar, lumbered off in the direction of Leh, that we got some rest.

Beyond Kargil, where mulberry and apricot trees grow in abundance, and willows and poplars line the water's edge, the road winds up and down through barren mountains. For mile after mile there was not a soul to be seen; then, in a green hollow, we would come across a quaint little village with mud houses, topped with fluttering flags. These were the homes of the Ladakhi who are quite unlike the other inhabitants of Kashmir. With their broad features, almond-shaped eyes and russet complexions, they resemble the people of Nepal, and like many of the Nepalese they, too, are Buddhists. What intrigued us most, however, was their extraordinary clothes. The men wore long, dark coats over baggy trousers, and their pigtails hung down from flowerpot-shaped felt hats from which a chunk had been cut away in front. Their stately womenfolk were resplendent in long, full-skirted gowns, lined with purple and adorned with bright sashes. They, too, wore the same strange hats. At first we thought that the individuals we encountered were specially attired for a festival or carnival, but we soon realized that this unusual costume was their ordinary garb. Their villages, too, were unlike those we had seen elsewhere and reminded us of pictures we had seen of Lhasa in Tibet where houses and monasteries are built high up on spurs of the mountains. Behind the plough they use the long-haired zho, which is a hybrid of the yak and the cow, and also serves as a beast of burden. Beyond Mulbek, where we stopped to photograph a large rock carving of Buddha, the road climbs steeply towards a horizon of dark, serrated peaks, and the 12,200 feet summit of the Pass of Namika La.

The highest pass was still to come, rugged and windswept Fatula which dominates the landscape at a height of 13,500 feet. The view we had from the top, across a vast array of spiky granite peaks, all over three miles high, was one of the most spectacular of our journey. The descent from Fatula is a hair-raising ride past the mysterious Lamayaru Monastery, perched high on a rock, round innumerable hairpin bends until one reaches the bridge over the Indus at Khalsi. Here the road improved and flattened out and we sped over a plain, dotted with crumbling stupas and 'mani' walls towards a ring of snow-capped mountains. We were already familiar with the stupa having seen it in its original shape of a cylindrical dome at the Karla Caves. In the course of many centuries, the dome has become a spire, and it is in this form that the stupa is seen all over Ladakh. The earliest stupas were said to contain relics of Buddha, but later, when they proliferated, they came to be regarded as a Buddhist symbol equivalent to the cross in Christianity. The long, low structures, called 'manis', which are a feature of central Ladakh, were built to provide shelter for the spirits of the departed, and the flat stones which cover them are engraved with prayers and the names of the dead.

Leh, the capital of Ladakh, lies at an altitude of 11,500 feet on a plateau, almost completely surrounded by high mountains, to the north of which lies the land which was once Tibet and is now China. It is to safeguard this frontier against possible aggression that a large contingent of the Indian Army is stationed in and around Leh. It is a compact, picturesque little town with its houses huddled together around an ancient, eight-storey palace and sheltered by a high mountain ridge, on which can be seen the outlines of old fortifications and a beflagged 'chorten' (monastery). We found a parking place in the tiny compound of the Ibex Hotel, recommended to us by the Tourist Office, and we booked a room there for the girls for ten days. We also managed to arrange to have a supply of electricity for a few hours each day. It was too good to be true. Unfortunately, the manager who spoke very little English had assumed that the girls were going to have all their meals in the hotel, and he became most unpleasant when he realized that they were having their meals in the caravan. For the rest of our stay we were subjected to petty incidents of harassment, such as the constant disconnecting of our electric cable and the pushing up of our caravan step at night in an effort to drive us away. However, as we had discovered that there was nowhere else in the town that we could park our caravan, we decided to ignore these irritations and to make the most of our sojourn in the strange land of Ladakh.

We certainly found plenty to interest us in and around Leh, but it was its colourful inhabitants who fascinated us most. The womenfolk were especially friendly and they smiled as we passed by, greeting us with 'dulay', (the equivalent of 'God bless'). In their prune or brown coats and quaint cutaway hats, they were stunning when viewed from the front, but viewed from the back they were even more bewitching. Across their shoulders most of them wore either a thick sheepskin rug or a brightly-coloured triangular silk shawl over which their black beribboned pigtails dangled like outsize tassels. On high days and holidays, these ladies exchanged their flowerpot hats for flat headdresses ornamented with turquoise stones, after the fashion of our pearly queens. Sitting on the ground in the little market place with their shining vegetables heaped around them, they looked as if they were taking part in a grand opera, with the old palace and high mountains forming part of the scenario. Fortunately, they seemed to enjoy being photographed and it never occurred to them to hold out their hands for 'backshish'. Before June 1975, Ladakh was a restricted area, so we were amongst the first tourists these people had ever seen. We must have looked just as strange to them as they to us, and what we interpreted as smiles may well have been giggles of surprise, but unfortunately, since none of them spoke English, we were unable to communicate.

Since meat and eggs were scarce, we lived on a vegetarian diet as there were plenty of carrots, potatoes, cucumbers, marrows, tomatoes and cauliflower at reasonable prices, and although imported fruit was expensive, locally-grown apricots and apples were ridiculously cheap. There was no bread available, but we had 'puris' as a substitute although Kerry was not at all happy about the hygiene of the little shop which produced them. The hotel, however, was spotlessly clean in spite of a chronic shortage of water, which kept relays of women toiling back and forth to a stream to fill petrol cans with water which they discharged into a tank on the roof. Di and Jen kept us supplied with cream cheese which they left to drip overnight on the taps of their wash-hand basin. The girls, who spent hours wandering up and down the streets, met a number of young Westerners who had made the journey from Srinagar by bus or were trekking in the vicinity. Most of them were students from Europe or America, and two were Scottish friends of Jen who had just returned from a climbing expedition.

One evening, the girls who were very keen to sample Ladakhi food, arranged for fifteen of us to have a meal in a small restaurant. Kerry whose first reaction was, "Not on your life", needed a great deal of persuading but finally he consented for fear of being branded a 'fuddy-duddy'. There are very few restaurants in Leh, and this particular one, like the others was a poky little hole, with an earth floor and unscrubbed wooden tables. All the cooking was done on an oil stove in a corner where there were neither washing facilities nor any outlet for the smoke and fumes. There were only two dishes on the menu; masala dosai — a kind of spicy pancake served with a meat sauce; and an omelette. Twelve of us had the masala dosai, which was delicious, but we suffered the effects for several days with bouts of sickness and diarrhoea. Di, who before the outing had said, "Remember, Uncle Kerry, Jen and I have between us fifty years' experience, which is almost equal to yours," now humbly admitted that he had been right, and promised to be more careful in future. She would have been even more contrite and alarmed if she had known that one of the Swiss boys we met was to die three weeks later in the hospital at Leh, from food poisoning.

We made friends with an Indian from Srinagar, an agricultural adviser who spoke English fluently, and he invited us to tea with his family. His little house was dark and dismal with brown paper pasted over the windows and plastic sheeting fixed to the ceilings to keep out the cold during the long winter. He told us that government officials, who are sent to Leh from other parts of India, serve from one to two years only because of the inhospitable climate and the high altitude, for Ladakh is one of the loftiest inhabited areas of the world with no part of it below 8,000 feet and most of it lying between 11,000 and 15,000 feet above sea level. Most of the Ladakhi are small farmers but their main problem is the lack of water, as the average rainfall is three inches per year, so it is not surprising that it has one of the lowest population densities in the world — two or three persons per square mile. Their main crop is huskless barley from which they make a heady liquor called 'Chang', which has disastrous effects on these gentle people.

One day we visited a Tibetan Refugee Camp on the outskirts of Leh. In comparison to the camps we had seen in Nepal and Dharmsala, it was a miserable place, consisting of a number of huts set on a barren plateau without the basic amenity of piped water. There were over five hundred people on the site, including three hundred children, who crowded round us excitedly, smiling broadly as all Tibetan children do. We talked to their teacher, a young Tibetan who had been educated in India, and he showed us the two large sheds where the children received instruction. He told us that they had neither slates, nor paper, no pens and very few books. "Please tell the people of England" he said, "that we need those things, also winter clothes and blankets." We were greatly impressed with this young man who could have found a less arduous post elsewhere in India, but had chosen to dedicate his life to these children.

We made the acquaintance of two other teachers, natives of Ladakh, who had trained at the University of Kashmir. As graduates they received £40 a month (non-graduates — £35) which was apparently a satisfactory wage. They told us that it is obligatory for all children to attend school from the age of six, and that there were rarely more than twenty children in a class. We plied them with questions about Buddhism, in which our interest was still very keen, but although their lives were surrounded by the trappings of this religion — stupas, manis, prayer wheels and prayer flags, they knew very little about it, and cared less. Undeterred, we set off to visit all the gompas (monasteries) which are one of the great attractions of Ladakh. Most of these gompas are situated high on the mountain sides where they can only be reached by foot, and at an altitude of over twelve thousand feet, walking is a very strenuous exercise. There are twelve gompas in Ladakh and about 5,000 monks, or lamas, as they are called. It is still the practice for one child of each family to be sent to a monastery to become a lama. This is done not so much on religious grounds but from economic necessity as there is insufficient food and few opportunities for employment. At Spitok Monastery, which stands on the crest of a small hill overlooking the Indus, we found the lamas redecorating the main shrine room, sticking brightly-coloured cloth to the ceiling. Demons, painted on the ancient rafters, reminded us of much older beliefs than Buddhism, which still coexist in isolated districts. We were shown small chambers containing statuettes of Buddha wearing gold headdresses, studded with precious stones, and enormous masked statues of the goddess Kali. These masks are removed once a year on the occasion of their annual festival. The most interesting monastery of all was Hemis Gompa, lying in a fold in the hills, about twenty-five miles east of Leh. It was the mela (festival) of Hemis that Carol and Terry had attended at the end of June.

Crossing the Indus, we followed a rough track which petered out some distance away from Hemis, which stands in a dell by a rushing stream. Clustered around the central courtyard, which is a feature of all gompas, are the main rooms and cells containing enormous prayer wheels. In one of the larger rooms was a gilded statue of Buddha seated in front of a stupa. There were also remarkable tankhas (paintings on cloth) but we were not able to see the largest tankha in existence which is only on show to the public once in every eleven years. As we watched the lamas perambulating in the courtyard, we looked on their faces for signs of spirituality, but were disappointed to note that the older men looked somewhat gross, and the younger ones, mere boys, called out to us in a rude, ill-mannered way. From what we saw, therefore, in these monasteries, and elsewhere in Nepal and India, we came to the conclusion that all that remains of Buddhism in these countries is a decorative shell, and even this is crumbling away.

In the hills near Hemis, we found to our delight, a water spout; and regardless of a crowd of curious onlookers, we washed our clothes and the caravan and in preparation for our return trip to Srinagar, we filled up our tanks with clear, if rather gritty, water. Our next problem was to find sufficient petrol for the journey, and for this we had to go to the airstrip at Leh where we were allowed to purchase just enough to take us to Kargil. The airstrip is used mainly by the army, and during the long winter it is the only link between Leh and the rest of India. Kerry also managed to find someone to weld two defective tyres (punctured on the inward journey), which were now our only spares. With stretches of bad road ahead of us and the Zoji La Pass, we realized that we would have to drive with the utmost care to avoid further damage to our tyres.

Our journey to Srinagar, although it was less eventful than the outward trip, was not without its moments of excitement. As we followed the course of the Indus which carves its way through a narrow gorge, we were surprised to see a rubber boat with a three-man crew careering over the rapids. It was, we discovered, an Indo-German expedition to the upper reaches of the Indus. We caught up with them fifty miles further on and talked to the Indian member of the crew, an army captain. Their worst moment, he told us, was when they foundered on the rocks eighty miles north of Leh and had to be rescued by the army.

Near Khalsi, we found a shady spot by a rushing stream which looked so invitingly cool and remote from human habitation that we decided to spend the night there. After ten days of washing in bowlfuls of water it was real bliss to immerse ourselves in a rocky pool, hidden with foliage from prying eyes. Leaving Di to do her laundry and Kerry to wrestle with the new oil stove we had bought in Leh, after running out of Calor gas, Jen and I walked to a hamlet a mile away. There was nothing for sale except apricots, so we bought two kilos for about 15p and hurried back to make jam. Kerry was still struggling with the new stove which obstinately refused to function. We were making a wood fire when a young Belgian whom we had met at Leh, seeing our car on the road came to investigate. He had an extra stove which he kindly lent us, and we finished potting up delicious apricot jam at midnight. As for our new stove, it never worked in spite of Kerry's efforts, and it was one of the articles which came to grief when our metal box was crushed in the underpass in Tehran.

We had all been looking forward to a good night's rest, for our sleep at Leh had been badly disturbed by the barking of dogs and the high-pitched hum of an electricity generating plant near the hotel. We fell asleep at once, and Jen and Di took their sleeping bags and settled down on the stones on the river bank. Suddenly we were awakened by a loud knocking on the door, and there were the girls, white-faced and scared. As they lay awake they had become aware of movements in the bushes around and footsteps which were gradually coming closer, so they had fled in panic. Jen took up her usual position on the floor while Di climbed onto the spare bed, and we all slept soundly in spite of a torrent which roared down to join the stream below.

Near the top of the Fatula Pass, we parked the car and set off on foot to visit the Lamayuru village, which, dominated by its monastery, must be the nearest thing on earth to Shangri-la. It lies in a hidden valley with its houses plastered against the rock face of the mountains, and its inhabitants with their long brown robes and hand-sewn sheepskin leggings, look as if they have been cut off from the rest of the world for hundreds of years. The monastery, however, was a disappointment for it had few real treasures, and the lamas pestered us to buy so-called ancient medallions and trinkets which were probably worthless. We were held up on the Fatula Pass for over an hour by an army convoy of more than one hundred heavily-laden trucks proceeding towards Leh. There are two such convoys every day, one in each direction, to maintain supplies for the many thousands of soldiers who man the Indian frontier with China.

About ten miles from Kargil, as darkness began to fall, we were looking for a parking spot for the night, when we saw a few tents by the riverside and went to investigate. It was a small army depot, used as a halt for convoys with tents to accommodate officers and other VIPs. The soldier on duty immediately offered us the hospitality and security of the camp, and the girls were given a splendid tent, complete with matting, mosquito nettings and a lamp.

By the next evening, we had reached the Dak Bungalow at Sonamarg, having stopped at Gumri to take sweets and apricots to our friends, the engineers. Then, with the last bend of the dreaded Zoji La Pass behind us, we felt a feeling of elation and satisfaction at having safely returned from an unknown land.

Back in Srinagar, we found a very pleasant room with a shower for the girls in the Tourist Reception Centre while we parked next door near a police post. It was a swampy site, frequented by rapacious cows and stray dogs, and had no amenities apart from the water tap we shared with the police force. However, it had the advantages of being in the shade of large chestnut trees and was reasonably secure. It was also the main meeting place for overlanders, being the only camp site in the valley. As we had done in Goa and Nepal, we enjoyed the best of both worlds, living in the open and sharing the girls' shower and toilet facilities.

On the day we returned to Srinagar, we found all the shops and many of the restaurants closed, as it was a public holiday to celebrate the anniversary of Mohammed's birthday. Crowds of excited Muslims were making their way to the mosque at Hazratbal, on the western shore of Dal Lake, the repository of a sacred hair of the prophet. Thousands of his faithful followers make this pilgrimage every year to view this holy relic which is only exhibited on special occasions. Not long ago there was almost a riot when it was discovered that the hair had disappeared from its casket, and order was only restored when the mosque authorities announced that they had recovered the missing treasure. How they discovered it, is open to conjecture. Later in the month the Hindus displayed their religious fervour by gathering in their hundreds for the Yatri (Pilgrimage) to Amarnath. Most of these sadhus, nutbrown and fleshless, were wearing no more than a loincloth as they set off on the long trek to Pahalgam and Siva's sacred cave.

Besides these diversions, we found plenty to interest us in the busy streets and waterways of Srinagar. There is probably nowhere in India that you can find such a variety of goods for sale as Kashmir, and nowhere are the salesmen more diligent. They have, too, a real talent for choosing an eye-catching name for their shops, which in itself attracts customers. There is Honest Injun — the tailors, Cheerful Chippendale — furniture makers, Suffering Moses and Subhara the Worst — dealers in arts and crafts. When the girls went back to collect their dresses from the tailor, they were told that they would have to pay more as 'the price of stitching had gone up'. They made such a fuss that the tailor, realizing he had met his match, agreed to the original price. But he still had a trick or two up his sleeve. Keeping the dresses on display in his shop window, he made the girls wait for several days on the pretext that 'there was still some finishing to be done'. However, when Jen finally managed to wrest her navy-blue denim dress from the shop front, she had to admit that for £3 it was a real bargain. We were less impressed with the shaggy sheepskin coat she purchased for £22, which was enormous and must have come from an outsize sheep. In the middle of the back was a ridiculous little black tuft where the tail had been, which I considered to be a flaw, but which Jen thought added a touch of class.

On a sudden whim, Di had bought a length of plum-coloured velvet in Leh at a very reasonable cost, and in one day the tailor made her a smart, décolleté evening gown. It was, however, not quite her style, as she looks more at home in jeans, and I doubt whether she will ever wear it.

Following the girls' example, Kerry and I visited the tailor and had several suits, coats, blouses, etc., made to measure at half the cost we would have paid at home. In Kerry's case, however, it was false economy because on his return home when he had regained the two and a half stones he had lost during our journey, none of the clothes fitted him.

At the camp site, we met a number of the friends we had made at Leh. There were Mike and Lore from Switzerland who were waiting for a new gearbox for their Land Rover which had come to grief on the Zoji La. We also met three French students who had set out on foot along the four hundred km route from Leh to Manali over the 18,000 foot Khardong Pass. They had had to turn back after three days when their provisions ran out and there was nowhere to buy more. Hughie and Sally, a young Australian couple who had spent several weeks under canvas at Leh, rediscovered us when they were searching for a houseboat at the cheap end of Dal Lake. They found one which cost only 4 rupees (about 25p) per night — without meals, of course, and they stayed there until late September.

After a spell of lovely, sunny weather, a wild wind whipped up the waters of Dal Lake and tropical rain poured down from leaden skies. We awoke to find ourselves marooned in a sea of mud into which we were slowly sinking, so we had to abandon the camp site and move onto the hard surface of the main road. We were preparing for breakfast, when there was a loud crash in our bathroom compartment and we found that the window had been shattered by a large stone. Kerry grabbed a walking stick and leapt into the street, just in time to prevent a weird-looking individual from hurling a second missile through the front window. The man made off down the street with Kerry in hot pursuit. When he caught up with him he belaboured him with a stick before dragging him off to the police post. There, the culprit, either because he was half-witted, or because he wanted to give the impression that he was out of his mind, began to divest himself of his clothing.

"We know this fellow," said the police, "he is not responsible for his actions, we can do nothing with him."

"At least you could lock him up," shouted Kerry, "to keep him from damaging other people's property. And who's going to pay for my window?"

But the policemen only shrugged their shoulders.

To add insult to injury, when we returned to the caravan, we found our porridge burnt to a cinder.

One of the most pleasant features of Kashmir, are the flowering upland meadows (margs) which lie in the folds of the hills, and of which we had visited the most famous, Sonamarg (golden meadow) on our journey to Leh. Yusmarg, twenty-five miles south of Srinagar, lying at the foot of the Pir Pantsal range, in a valley carpeted with flowers, looked its best when we saw it after the summer rain. We had driven over small hills covered with apple orchards to the little town of Chari Sharif, a place of pilgrimage for Muslims and Hindus, for it is here that the patron saint of Kashmir is buried. Beyond Chari Sharif, giant pines and firs rise above the valley where, following the course of a meandering stream, we reached the village of Yusmarg; that is if you can call a few huts and a Dak Bungalow a village. A group of men with ponies tried to interest us in a trek over the mountains to see the turbulent Doodganga river — 'As white as milk', they said; but we chose to picnic in a wild meadow by the river. Fortunately for us and for posterity, conservationists are at work in Kashmir, endeavouring to preserve the precious heritage of flowers which the omnivorous goats and sheep are nibbling away. In Yusmarg, large stretches of land have been fenced in and Mother Nature given a free hand to produce of her best which she has done, and there can be few places in the world with as many wild flowers and grasses as Kashmir.

The excursion to Yusmarg, was the last one we made with the girls, who a few days later, left by air to visit Delhi and Agra before returning home. The evening before they left, they invited us to dinner at the Broadway Hotel, which shares with the Oberon, the reputation of being the best hotel in Srinagar. As it was a special occasion, the girls and I dressed up in sarees and Kerry donned his white guru suit. We had dined at the Broadway on several occasions and had had first-class meals and service, but this time we encountered an unexpected problem. Jen suggested that we should have a drink at the bar before going into the dining room; so we had a gin and tonic each. As usual the meal was excellent — hors d'oeuvres followed by gushtabas and kofta balls in curried sauce, raita and all the extras, but Jen, who had been examining the menu between courses had fallen silent.

"What's the matter, Jen?" asked Kerry.

She laughed nervously and pointed to the wine table. Gin was classed as a Western drink; Indian drinks were cheap and our visit to the bar was going to cost us £8, which was almost as much as our meal, and much more than the girls had budgeted for. Our fears were confirmed when the waiter brought the bill, but such was the reasonableness of the management when we remonstrated at the excessive charge, that our drinks bill was halved, much to our surprise and to the girls' relief.

Next day, with presents and new clothes, including Di's fancy evening gown, stuffed unceremoniously into their rucksacks, the girls left for Delhi. Jen had to wear her sheepskin coat, as it was the easiest way to carry it, and it was to prove an almost intolerable burden in the sweltering monsoon heat of the capital, but a godsend in Moscow where they had an unexpected two-day stay at Aeroflot's expense.

After their departure, we settled down to a month of quiet enjoyment of Srinagar and the countryside around it. As the camp site was still flooded, we moved to the pleasant, shady garden of the Hotel Shaheen which lies at the foot of Shankaracharya Hill. The hotel had been a private house, belonging to an English lady who had taken a great pride in her garden, which was laid out in lawns and rose beds. We had sole possession of a grassy patch which had probably been the drying green, next to the gardener's quarters, where we had use of the shower and toilet. As the hotel specialized in adventure tours, we were not surprised to see a group of Japanese climbers brewing up next morning on one of the adjoining lawns, with their camping gear strewn around them, and during the weeks which followed there was a succession of similar parties from all over the world. There was only one disadvantage; close by was a Hindu temple frequented by pilgrims, and at times its bells and loudspeakers were deafening. But this was only a minor irritation, for nothing, not even the incessant rain, could diminish our joy in being in Kashmir. In the wake of the rainclouds, the sunsets were glorious, and we used to park by the side of Dal Lake and gaze in wonderment until the gold had drained from the sky behind the squat mass of Akbar's fort and the houseboats were aglow with lights.

We used to spend hours wandering through the markets of Srinagar, searching for gifts of embroidered cloth, and articles in gilded papier-mâché and walnut wood. We were sorely tempted to buy an exquisitely carved dining-room table with chairs to match, but the cost of transporting them back to England was beyond our means. However, we did purchase a handsome cocktail cabinet in carved walnut for £65, which Kerry dismantled and stored on our spare bed in the caravan. Kerry had to replace the broken toilet window and fix the shelves in the wardrobe and larder, and the door locks, all of which were loose. When these odd jobs were finished to his satisfaction, he took out a temporary membership of the Srinagar Golf Club, hired a set of clubs, and spent many happy hours improving his game. Sometimes I joined him and with the help of the club's chief coach, who charged a very small fee for his services, we made some progress. Our little caddy, a boy of about ten years of age, was engaged in the lucrative trade of re-cycling the golf balls he had failed to find on the fairway. It was only when he sold us our own 'lost' balls that we discovered his little game, but we paid up realizing that he was probably the only breadwinner in the family.

We waited for a good spell of weather before we set out to explore the countryside to the north and west of Srinagar. Then, in bright, warm sunshine, we followed the flat, poplar-lined road which runs northward through the paddy fields towards Lake Manasbal, lying in a hollow in the hills. What makes this tiny lake so attractive, are the masses of pink lotus blooms which rise above the dark green surface, and the gaily-coloured shikaras which glide over its calm water. We found a secluded spot for our picnic amongst the reeds and hoped to be undisturbed, but, as always in India, just as we had settled down to our meal, inquisitive eyes appeared behind the greenery.

Thirty-five miles west of Srinagar, lying at a height of 8,500 feet, is another of Kashmir's beauty spots, Gulmarg (meadow of flowers) which is being developed as a skiing centre. One can travel by bus as far as Tangmarg, and complete the last four miles on foot or on the back of a pony. By car or taxi, however, it is an easy journey on a reasonably good road which climbs steeply up to the undulating Valley of Gulmarg. We parked on a small hill overlooking the golf course, said to be one of the finest in the world, and much loved by British officials in pre-Independence days. Gulmarg was one of their favourite hill stations, as the bungalows and villas they built for themselves bear witness, as does the little Church of St Mary, standing forlornly on a hillock.

In order to catch a glimpse of Nanga Parbat, one of the highest mountains in the world, we hired a stout mountain pony (for me) which bounded up the slopes and had no objection to Kerry pulling himself up by the tail on the steepest inclines. When we reached Khilanmarg, which lies four kilometres above Gulmarg, the view over the Vale of Kashmir amply rewarded our efforts. Dominating the northern skyline, over eighty miles away, was the great mass of Nanga Parbat, and in the foreground, glistening in the sun, were the waters of Wular Lake, the largest expanse of freshwater in India. To the west lay Azad Kashmir which belongs to Pakistan, and our guide told us about the armed guerrillas who had penetrated as far as Gulmarg in 1947 and burned down some of the villas. A few minutes later, as we were drinking tea in a little shack, which called itself a 'restaurant', we noticed that Nanga Parbat had disappeared from view in whorls of white cloud and that the shining lake had lost its sparkle. We set off downhill at a trot, but were drenched with rain before we could reach the caravan.

For the next two days it rained nonstop, with a chill in the wind which heralded the coming of autumn. We were quite snug in our caravan, but two Swiss couples who had joined us in our parking spot the previous evening, and had to do their cooking under an awning slung between their cars, were wet and miserable. They left early the next morning and by the late evening we were on our way back to the Hotel Shaheen.

By this time we were on friendly terms with the hotel manager, a retired police inspector, with whom we frequently discussed the current problems of Kashmir. In these conversations there was one name, which kept cropping up; that of Sheikh Abdullah, the chief minister, often referred to as the 'Lion of Kashmir'. Unlike our friends, the tourist officers at Pahalgam and many other Kashmiris we had met, who regarded Abdullah as a traitor because he joined the Indian Congress Party, the manager had an unbounded admiration for the sheikh. It had been his painful duty in 1958, to arrest the sheikh, whose campaign for freedom and justice for Kashmir had resulted in riots. He held his prisoner in the Dak Bungalow at Anantnag and he felt really hurt when the tasty breakfast he prepared for him was rejected on the grounds that it might be 'doctored'. The more we heard about Sheikh Abdullah, the keener we were to meet him, and we were encouraged by the manager to think that this was possible, as the sheikh did occasionally grant interviews.

To our delight, our request to meet him was granted, and a few days after our return from Gulmarg, we were ushered into the great man's presence. We immediately felt at ease with this tall, handsome man in his late sixties, and for almost an hour we discussed a whole range of subjects relating to Kashmir.

As a young man, Sheikh Abdullah had led the struggle for constitutional government against the Maharajah of Kashmir, but he had never favoured the idea of founding a separate nation for Muslims, as he believed that religion alone cannot form the basis of a country's unity. He had warned Jinnah (the main protagonist for a separate Muslim state) that it would be only a matter of time before East Pakistan (Bangladesh) would break away from West Pakistan, and this came to pass. Although he had agreed to the accession of Kashmir to India to prevent infiltration from Pakistan, he never ceased to affirm the right of the people of Kashmir to decide the future of the state by their own freewill. Nehru had promised to give the people the right, a promise he did not fulfil, sensing, no doubt, that the majority of Kashmiris would choose to join Pakistan. However, Nehru did release Sheikh Abdullah from prison to pay an official visit to Pakistan to try to come to some agreement; but in spite of the fact that Kashmir and Pakistan share the ties of language, ethnic origins and Islamic brotherhood, the sheikh did not find any basis of permanent agreement.

In fact, he confessed to us that educated Kashmiris have, ideologically, more in common with India than with Pakistan.

"What are the chances of becoming independent, as Switzerland is in Europe?" asked Kerry.

"Independence would bring its own difficulties. The great powers have agreed to leave Switzerland alone, but Pakistan, India and China, to whom Kashmir is of strategic importance, have made no such agreement, and are not likely to do so. In the meantime, because of its uncertain future, neither the Indian Government, nor private enterprise, is likely to assist Kashmir to any great extent in establishing new industries."

We were very impressed by Sheikh Abdullah's impartial appraisal of the current situation in Kashmir and by his candour and sincerity. It was evident, too, that although he had spent more than seven years in prison at the instigation of Indian politicians, he harboured no rancour against them. After the interview, as we were on the point of leaving, the sheikh's daughter, Soraya, came into the room and was introduced to us. She was on her way to the Women's College where she lectures, and when she heard of our interest in education she invited us to visit the school on the following day. The students were aged between fifteen and eighteen and many of them intended to take up teaching as a career. They were bright, lively young ladies, who spoke to us very confidently in English about their studies, which included Mathematics, Science, English, Current Affairs, Music and Painting. As Muslims have always preferred to keep their teenage daughters within the confines of the home, it is only fairly recently that Kashmiri girls have had the same opportunity as their brothers to continue their studies at secondary and university levels.

Our interview with Sheikh Abdullah, was the last significant event of our sojourn in Kashmir; which, as we were only too aware, was now drawing to a close. With ten thousand miles between us and home, we had planned to leave before the end of September in order to reach Europe before snow made the roads impassable in Turkey and Austria. Signs of the approach of autumn were evident all around us. It was too chilly to dine outside in the evening at Adhoo's Restaurant, and the chairs had been moved from the patio into the dining room. The great chestnut trees near Dal Lake, were tinged with gold; the road sweepers were brushing up the first of the fallen leaves; and in the herbaceous borders the dahlias, zinnias and marigolds were shrivelled and dusty. The fruit season was now at its height and the street stalls were heaped with all the varieties of apples and pears which they grow in this country. We began to stock up for our long trek homewards with packets of porridge oats, gram flour, dried milk, cooking oil, tins of fruit and juice, rice, lentils and walnuts. Kerry worked for days on the car, checking every detail, and he was hopeful that the three tyres we had ordered by air from Delhi, at great expense, would take us at least as far as Iran. In this he was to be disappointed because, by the time we reached Lahore, we had so many punctures that we had to purchase two more tyres and our problems were by no means at an end. On a chilly wet morning in November, as we were making our way from Yugoslavia to Hungary, one of the Indian tyres in the front of our vehicle burst and threw us into a ditch. If our car had been less sturdy, and had we struck a wall instead of soft mud, we would certainly not be alive to tell the tale. As it was, we escaped with a broken front axle, torn side panels and all our tyres in shreds. It took two weeks to repair the damage, and, abandoning our plans to visit Budapest, we crawled home over Austria's snowbound roads in subzero temperatures which froze our engine oil.

When we left Kashmir at the end of September, we were mercifully unaware of our future difficulties, and were only conscious of a sense of personal loss in parting from a land where we had been blissfully happy. Heavy rain and floods delayed our departure for five days, but this time we were grateful to the rain for giving us a last minute respite to watch the sunsets over the lake. As we passed through the Vale of Kashmir, the farmers were harvesting rice crops from the paddy fields, and the deep purple crocuses in the saffron beds at Pampore were beginning to flower. South of the Banibal tunnel the road was strewn with dislodged boulders and parts of the surface had subsided into the gorges. It was here that we caught up with groups of nomads returning from the upland meadows to their quarters in the Punjab, and in spite of the rain which had followed them all the way from their summer pastures, they looked fit and vigorous and their goats were less scraggy than those we had seen five months before.

Early next morning, we joined a queue of four hundred trucks, held up by a great landslide of mud and stones which had obliterated the road, and throughout the day army bulldozers worked to clear away the rubble. The sun was setting when we edged our way over the bed of stones which had been laid in the mud. Before we reached Jammu we stopped the car to have a last look at the mountains, darkly etched against the skyline.

We recalled the words said to have been spoken by the Mogul Emperor, Jehangir, on his deathbed:

> "Adam was turned out of paradise for eating a grain of wheat.
> Since I have been living on barley water.
> O God, permit me to reach Kashmir once more."

EPILOGUE

The Mogul Emperor, Jehangir, was not able to return to Kashmir and, alas, neither were we. Most of the reasons for this were beyond our control, as I shall explain later.

For nearly a year after our return, our motor home stood forlornly in the front garden blocking out the light from the dining-room windows. We were reluctant to dispose of it as it reminded us of our great adventure.

By 1978, we realized that another extensive journey to the Orient was virtually impossible. The unrest we had sensed in Iran resulted in a general uprising which toppled the shah and started an Islamic revolution. This was followed by a civil war in Afghanistan and the ineffectual intervention of the Russians. Today that country is still a war zone. For twenty years there have been few, if any, overlanders traversing Iran and Afghanistan as they did in the early seventies. Only recently, in the summer of 1999, have a few tour operators begun to advertise trips to 'Persia', highlighting the delights of Isfahan, Shiraz and Tehran.

Further afield in the far north of India, what we predicted has come to pass. The beautiful valleys of Kashmir no longer resound with the happy cries of holiday-makers and pony trekkers, but with the roar of gunfire from the mountain tops. In the Drass Valley near Kargil, the Indian Army is facing Pakistan infiltrators who are aided and abetted by the local inhabitants.

While these events were unfolding, Kerry and I were busily getting on with our lives. During our travels I had made copious notes in my diary and within two years I had completed the twelve chapters of this book. However, as I was unsuccessful in finding a publisher straightaway, I lost patience and decided to use my energy in other directions.

For seven years I was a voluntary worker for the Citizens' Advice Bureau and later I became a member of the Community Health Council. At the same time I pursued my interest in education as a school governor, a position I still retain.

Kerry, meanwhile had launched himself anew into local and national politics, and in fund-raising for a local charity. Soon, however, he had a new interest — pottery, when he joined an adult education class. In no time the garden shed and attic were full of pots and moulds of every shape and colour. It was his enthusiasm and the satisfaction he derived from being creative, which prompted me to have a 'go' at painting.

Travelling to foreign parts remained one of our major pastimes. Every year in early spring we set out for warmer climates with rucksacks on our backs. We explored most of South America, including the Amazon Jungle and the Galapagos Islands. We visited the ancient temples of the Aztecs in Mexico, the Mayan ruins in Guatemala and the Incas' strongholds in Peru. We toured the North and South Islands of New Zealand in a hired motor home, returning to England via French Caledonia, Tahiti and the United States.

On several occasions we visited our relatives in India, staying with my sister-in-law Perin and Yasu and husband, Homi. On one of our trips we spent several days exploring the remarkable Buddhist cave-temples of Ajanta and Alora, two hundred miles north of Bombay. These must truly be one of the wonders of the world.

We revisited Goa, where we had been so happy. Sadly we found that within a few short years, Goa had transformed itself into a global holiday resort. The small hotel where we had parked our motor home had become a sleazy café, and blaring music disturbed the once peaceful beach of Calangute. In spite of these changes, however, Goa still has great charm.

During these years, we kept in touch with many of the friends we had met on our journey to India. Michèle and Titi paid us a visit. Françoise and Albert came with the children on a cycling tour. Carol and Terry Hart with Tory and his baby brother turned up unexpectedly from time to time on holiday leave from Mali where they now resided.

Thus the years sped pleasantly. We were enjoying a seemingly endless Indian summer. However, an incident which occurred in August, 1988, jolted me into the realisation that this period of happiness was about to come to an end. We were travelling on the Trans-Siberian railway from Irkutsk to Outer Mongolia on the long, dreary stretch across the Gobi Desert. Someone suggested a game of bridge and Kerry agreed to play. He had always excelled at this game, but as I looked on, alarm bells began to ring in my head. It was evident that he had completely forgotten how to play. Something was sadly amiss.

In the years which followed, there was a gradual decline in his faculties. He died in May, 1996, two months after our golden wedding. In spite of the fact that I had had a long time to come to terms with my eventual loss, many months passed before I felt any joy in being alive.

One day, I decided to convert the attic, which was chock-full of the debris of fifty years, into an art studio. My friend, Phil Lanigan and two of her sons, came to assist me, bringing a large removal van. The remains of Kerry's lifetime hobbies lay where he had discarded them — marquetry veneers, photographic equipment, camping gear, terracotta pots, etc. I decided to dispose of everything except the photographs and projectors. I felt immensely sad, as if a tidal wave was about to sweep my past away.

As they lugged the boxes downstairs, I saw a bundle of papers which I recognised as the typescript copy of the book I had written more than twenty years before. This I retrieved and that evening I sat down and began to reread the account of our journey. I became quite absorbed in it, reliving the excitement of the adventure, recalling forgotten episodes, seeing Kerry as he was before his long illness — resourceful and unflappable. This is the way I wanted to remember him. There and then I decided to go ahead and publish my book in his memory.

When I wrote to Michèle about my project, she wished me luck and supplied up-to-date information about our erstwhile travelling companions. One of the items of news was very upsetting. Patrick, that loveable little lad, had died in a road accident. It appears that he fell asleep at the steering wheel, returning from his first week at work. Françoise and Albert were overcome with grief. Their only consolation is that they now have a little grandson, the child of Véronique. Titi, now a teacher, has a six-year-old daughter. Michèle, herself, has two bonny children, a boy and a girl. Unfortunately I have not heard from Carol Hart since she wrote to me two years ago that her marriage with Terry was over. My niece, Jen, is happily married with a family of three charming boys.

Looking beyond the pleasant memories recorded on film and photographs and in this book, I often reflect on what I learned from our journey to the Orient. There is no doubt that I came back with changed perspectives, and I believe, a much wiser person. I had become aware of the enormous problems which beset most of the countries we visited and was humbled by the generosity of poverty-stricken people.

Before my visit to the East, I had believed that the architectural achievements of the West were unrivalled. Then I discovered the delicate beauty of the mosques in Persia, the splendour of the Mogul edifices and the sheer magnificence of the rock temples in India.

On a smaller scale, but just as amazing, was native craftsmanship. From Istanbul to Kashmir, in cramped and dingy workshops, I saw the production of veritable *objets d'art*. Nor was there any lack of technical skill. Should your Land Rover or Volkswagen require a new gearbox or clutch, at the back of beyond, you can find an artisan to fashion one for you in his makeshift garage.

My stay in India changed my attitude towards animals. Although I had laughed at the Jains' efforts to save insects and was annoyed with Manchi for wanting to save the life of the intruder rat, these incidents forced me to think more about other living creatures. I am now very uneasy about the way we treat farm animals. It may be for that reason, without conscious effort, my diet is becoming more and more vegetarian.

The reader may ask an obvious question. "Were you successful in your search for Zoroaster?" I must admit to a certain amount of failure as I did not uncover any exact details of his life and death, but I did discover his message which is contained in Zoroastrian hymns — The Gathas. He asserted that there is only one God — Ahura-Mazda, the God of Light, who will ultimately prevail over Ahriman, the God of Darkness and Death. He advised his followers to live by good thoughts, good words and good deeds. Thus at least six hundred years before Christ, an Eastern prophet was expounding ideas similar to his. For me this discovery justified the search.

However, I think it must be obvious that the search for Zoroaster was much more than the pursuit of an individual. It was, above all, a journey of exploration into the unknown; it was a probing into truth about people, customs and religion. So, in conclusion, I would urge everyone, especially those over the age of retirement, who can and wish to travel as we did — 'Go in search of Zoroaster!'